AF757547

Alliance Capitalism and Corporate Management

NEW HORIZONS IN INTERNATIONAL BUSINESS

Series Editor: Peter J. Buckley
Centre for International Business,
University of Leeds (CIBUL), UK

The New Horizons in International Business series has established itself as the world's leading forum for the presentation of new ideas in international business research. It offers pre-eminent contributions in the areas of multinational enterprise – including foreign direct investment, business strategy and corporate alliances, global competitive strategies, and entrepreneurship. In short, this series constitutes essential reading for academics, business strategists and policy makers alike.

Titles in the series include:

Corporate Governance and Globalization
Long Range Planning Issues
Edited by Stephen S. Cohen and Gavin Boyd

The European Union and Globalisation
Towards Global Democratic Governance
Brigid Gavin

Globalization and the Small Open Economy
Edited by Daniel Van Den Bulcke and Alain Verbeke

Entrepreneurship and the Internationalisation of Asian Firms
An Institutional Perspective
Henry Wai-chung Yeung

The World Trade Organization in the New Global Economy
Trade and Investment Issues in the Millennium Round
Edited by Alan M. Rugman and Gavin Boyd

Japanese Subsidiaries in the New Global Economy
Edited by Paul W. Beamish, Andrew Delios and Shige Makino

Globalizing Europe
Deepening Integration, Alliance Capitalism and Structural Statecraft
Edited by Thomas L. Brewer, Paul A. Brenton and Gavin Boyd

China and its Regions
Economic Growth and Reform in Chinese Provinces
Edited by Mary-Françoise Renard

Emerging Issues in International Business Research
Edited by Masaoki Kotabe and Preet S. Aulakh

Network Knowledge in International Business
Edited by Sarianna M. Lundan

Learning in the Internationalisation Process of Firms
Edited by Anders Blomstermo and D. Deo Sharma

Alliance Capitalism and Corporate Management
Entrepreneurial Cooperation in Knowledge Based Economies
Edited by John H. Dunning and Gavin Boyd

Alliance Capitalism and Corporate Management

Entrepreneurial Cooperation in Knowledge Based Economies

Edited by

John H. Dunning

Emeritus Esmee Fairbairn Professor of International Investment and Business Studies, University of Reading, UK and Emeritus State of New Jersey Professor of International Business, Rutgers University, USA

and

Gavin Boyd

Honorary Professor, Political Science Department, Rutgers University, Newark, New Jersey, USA, and Adjunct Professor, Management Faculty, Saint Mary's University, Halifax, Canada

NEW HORIZONS IN INTERNATIONAL BUSINESS

Edward Elgar

Cheltenham, UK • Northampton, MA, USA

© John H. Dunning, Gavin Boyd 2003

All rights reserved. No part of this publication may be reproduced, stored in a retrieval system or transmitted in any form or by any means, electronic, mechanical or photocopying, recording, or otherwise without the prior permission of the publisher.

Published by
Edward Elgar Publishing Limited
Glensanda House
Montpellier Parade
Cheltenham
Glos GL50 1UA
UK

Edward Elgar Publishing, Inc.
136 West Street
Suite 202
Northampton
Massachusetts 01060
USA

A catalogue record for this book is available from the British Library

Library of Congress Cataloguing in Publication Data

Alliance capitalism and corporate management : entrepreneurial cooperation in knowledge based economies / edited by John H. Dunning and Gavin Boyd.
p. cm. – (New horizons in international business)
Includes index.
1. Strategic alliances (Business) 2. International business enterprises–Management. 3. Investments, Foreign. 4. Competition. 5. Knowledge management. I. Dunning, John H. II. Boyd, Gavin. III. Series.

HD69.S8 A434 2003
338.8′7–dc21 2002029831

ISBN 1 84064 839 2

Printed and bound in Great Britain by MPG Books Ltd, Bodmin, Cornwall

Contents

Figures

Tables

Contributors

Claude E. Barfield is a Resident Scholar and Director of Trade, Science and Technology Policies at the American Enterprise Institute, Washington DC, USA

Gavin Boyd is an Honorary Professor in Political Science at Rutgers University, Newark, New Jersey, USA, and an Adjunct Professor in Management at Saint Mary's University, Halifax, Canada

Paul A. Brenton is a Senior Research Fellow at the Centre for European Policy Studies, Brussels, Belgium

John H. Dunning is Emeritus Esmee Fairbairn Professor of International Investment and Business Studies, University of Reading, Berkshire, UK and Emeritus State of New Jersey Professor of International Business, Rutgers University, Newark, New Jersey, USA

John Hagedoorn is Professor of Business and Economics, University of Maastricht, The Netherlands

Neil Hood is Professor of Marketing, University of Strathclyde, UK

Sarianna M. Lundan is a Professor in the Department of Management Sciences, University of Maastricht, The Netherlands

Terutomo Ozawa is Professor of Economics at Colorado State University, Fort Collins, Colorado, USA

Pierluigi Morelli is at Centro Europa Ricerche, Rome, Italy

Pier Carlo Padoan is Executive Director, International Monetary Fund, Washington DC, USA

Nigel Pain is at the National Bureau of Economic and Social Research, London, UK

Lisa Rodano is at Centro Europa Ricerche, Rome, Italy

Nadine Roijakkers is at the Department of Business and Economics, University of Maastricht, The Netherlands

Alan M. Rugman is L. Leslie Waters Chair in International Business, Kelley School of Business, Indiana University Bloomington, Indiana, USA

Cordula Thum is a Research Associate at the American Enterprise Institute, Washington DC, USA

Desirée van Welsum is at the National Bureau of Economic and Social Research, London, UK

Stephen Young is Professor of Marketing, University of Strathclyde, UK

Foreword

This volume has been planned as a tribute to the work of John H. Dunning. A distinguished British scholar with visiting appointments across the world, his studies of inter-corporate cooperation have become increasingly significant for international management research and for policy makers concerned with structural issues in the corporate-state domain.

Quests for competitive advantage motivating firms and the efforts of governments to enhance structural competitiveness draw much attention in current literature, but happenings in the real world of business cycles, trade conflicts, exchange rate volatility and policy failures as well as market failures raise urgent questions about the potential for more active inter-corporate cooperation. Hard competition between firms and between governments can be destructive, all the more so when there is rivalry in large-scale high risk speculative ventures. Re-orientations of corporate strategies, based on these understandings of *cooperative* as well as competitive advantages, can be seen to offer possibilities for higher, more even, and more stable growth and for more productive corporate inputs into national policies.

Efficiency and social justice perspectives on the balance between competition and cooperation between firms have been obliged to recognize problems of entrepreneurial coordination in interdependent knowledge-based economies. The promotion of recovery in the USA from the underlying recessionary trends in the economy which were accentuated by the September 11th tragedies had become an urgent task while this book was in preparation. The dimensions of this task were dramatized by the collapse of Enron, the US energy firm, which became the largest bankruptcy in US history. Efficiencies which might have been possible under pressures of accountability and transparency in a cooperative network of inter-corporate relations did not develop. The fortunes of thousands of workers and investors have been severely affected but the repercussions are more severe. They have created what many commentators have referred to as the unacceptable face of capitalism which strikes at the very heart and expectations of corporate America.

John Dunning's work has provided a research orientation that can open up possibilities for highly constructive knowledge intensive approaches to international management tasks. It has been an honour to have John as the lead speaker at Saint Mary's University's annual international political economy conference and as the lead editor of this resulting volume. His contributions to our discussions included a public lecture on the Moral Responsibilities of International Business and this combined efficiency and social justice perspectives in a way which gave greater significance to his introductory chapter on relational assets. An important message of this chapter is that the development of relational assets through cooperation is conducive to higher overall productivity with stability. This is a message for business schools and economic policy institutes. An immediate consequence, for Saint Mary's University, is that it has helped to prepare the way for a conference on the Structural Foundations of International Finance in which the logic of developing relational assets through cooperation will be further explored.

I wish to thank all the participants in our conference for their insightful and enthusiastic contributions to what, I hope, will be a continuing debate among academics, corporate and government policymakers on Alliance Capitalism.

J. Colin Dodds, PhD
President, Saint Mary's University and Professor of Finance,
Frank H. Sobey, Faculty of Commerce

Preface

The operations of multinational firms, spreading production and marketing activities across many countries, are studied mainly as competitive processes in international political economy literature. The strategies of these firms are studied as rationally managed rivalries for world market shares, leading to gains and losses that have cumulative effects. The main trend is seen to be toward the development of an oligopolistic global economy, in which the more successful enterprises are able to further increase their market strengths while bargaining more effectively with governments and with labour unions on issues affecting growth, employment and taxation. International competition policy cooperation between major governments is recognized to be difficult; it has developed between the European Union and the USA, but with strains, in a context of bargaining strengths that are tending to change to the disadvantage of the Europeans.

The oligopolistic trend is a problem of market failure, and demands investigation in conjunction with other internationalized market failures, including those in financial sectors that affect the evolution of structural interdependencies between real economies. While those interdependencies are shaped by the transnational production and marketing operations of multinational enterprises, the funding of all this activity favours the winners, but there are considerable diversions of investment into potentially destabilizing high risk speculation, as has been evident in the Enron case. This has had severe effects on the US economy.

Questions about international public goods tend to be obscured in perspectives focusing on the complex effects of global intercorporate rivalries. When attention is given to cross border public goods issues, however, the productive significance of intercorporate cooperation becomes evident. Firms are seen to have cooperative as well as competitive advantages, and functional balances between competition and cooperation can be considered attainable, with overall efficiencies according with concepts of social justice. Elementary contrasts between instrumental and relational cooperation have to be recognized, and the significance of relational assets, increasing with the latter, has to be appreciated. With the sharing of such assets, managements can become oriented more and more toward innovative complementary forms of entrepreneurship. The efficiency effects, with positive implications for overall welfare, and for the development of dynamic balanced structural interdependencies between countries, can inspire efforts to promote alliance capitalism, that is because its collegial spirit can promise greater multiplications of productive innovations, with harmony, than those possible in an intensely competitive and less coordinated economy.

The potential efficiencies of coordinated entrepreneurial innovations, developing relationally through concerted applications of advanced technology, can be seen to open the way for further analytical development of the logic of internalization, on the basis of which functional benefits are achieved by firms through in-house operations. Collegial entrepreneurship, in line with Aristotelian concepts of civic friendship, can be regarded as a higher application of internalization logic, complementing that at the corporate level, and according with the systemic developmental imperatives of the vast pattern of international corporate activities.

Major trade conflicts, problems of excess capacity in steel and automobiles, and the widely noted costs of globalization have made alliance capitalism a concept of great significance for policymakers and corporate managements. It can indicate ways of working toward the development of a new international structural architecture, served by more efficient and more stable financial markets. This is one of the major themes which has engaged the attention of contributors to this volume.

Preparation of the volume was aided by stimulating discussions at a conference on Alliance Capitalism sponsored by Saint Mary's University, Halifax, in November 2001. We wish to express our thanks to the university for arranging this event, and we are especially grateful to the President, Colin Dodds, for having hosted some very pleasant social occasions.

John H. Dunning
Gavin Boyd

1. Relational assets, networks and international business activity

John H. Dunning

Most paradigms and theories of the determinants of international business activities – and particularly those designed to explain the extent, pattern and composition of multinational enterprise (MNE) systems – are essentially asset based.

Three kinds of income generating assets are usually considered:

1. Those specific and unique to particular firms, notably MNEs or potential MNEs: these may be located in the home country of the MNEs, or in the countries which are host to their affiliates.
2. Those which are external to MNEs, but are accessed and then deployed by them: these assets may also be located in the home country of the MNEs or in foreign countries.
3. Those which relate to the ways in which these two kinds of assets are created, harnessed and co-ordinated by the management of MNEs – be that of the parent companies or their foreign affiliates.

As set out in Table 1.1, over the years the nature, relative significance and governance of these different types of assets have changed. Until the industrial revolution, and today in some developing countries, the critical wealth-creating assets were (and are) land and property owned by households, and the way in which these assets were (are) husbanded. For much of the 19th and 20th centuries, they were the physical and financial assets owned by firms, but supplemented by those of other institutions, and accessed primarily through the market. Today, the critical assets consist of a kaleidoscope of intangible assets, especially knowledge and information embodied in human capital, both owned and accessed – from a variety of sources – and by firms.[1] Though physical and financial assets remain important, they are increasingly playing a supportive rather than a primary role in the wealth creation process.

The last decade has seen an explosion of the literature of the nature and significance of knowledge capital and its competitive enhancing qualities

Table 1.1 The changing characteristics of income generating assets

	1. Specific to ownership	2. Accessed by firms	3. Organized by firms
(a) Pre-Industrial Revolution	● Land, property	● Labour, materials	● Internal to households ● Elementary markets
	[Mainly domestically created, sourced and utilized]		
(b) 19th & 20th century	● Machines, buildings ● Financial assets ● Property rights	● Labour, intermediate products	● Largely hierarchical, within firms ● Growth of joint ventures ● More sophisticated markets
	[Mainly domestically, but increasingly foreign sourced]		
(c) 21st century	● Property rights ● Intellectual assets ● 'Connectivity' advantages (including R-assets)	● Leasing of property ● Intermediate products ● Knowledge and information ● Collective (social) assets	● Heterarchical within firms ● Coalitions between firms ● Networks ● Markets
	[Accelerated movement towards the global or regional creation, accessing and utilization of assets]		

for both firms and countries; and of the appropriate organizational modalities for its creation, sustenance, exploitation and diffusion. Indeed, one might be led to believe that the intellectual component of human capital was now the 'be all and end all' of a firm's or nation's competitive prowess.

This, in our opinion, would be misguided. Certainly when one widens the unit of analysis from that of the firm to the country, a good deal of evidence is emerging on the critical role of *social* capital (later to be defined) as a prerequisite for, and facilitator of, the productive creation and deployment of both tangible and intangible assets. Yet, in the business literature, only scant attention has been paid to (what we shall term) relational assets (R-assets) – as they affect the success or failure of intra- or extra-firm associations; the latter encompassing linkages both between private and public organizations, and between organizations and persons. This domain has largely been occupied by sociologists and, latterly, by organizational scholars. Economists and business strategists have tended to approach the subject of R-assets hesitantly and obliquely, by their analysis of market failures and hierarchical modes of governance; and by analysing the critical conditions for successful inter-firm alliances, in terms of such concepts as trust, reciprocity and forbearance. In recent years however, three important articles have appeared – one by Holm, Eriksson and Johanson (1996), one by Dyer and Singh (1998), and one by Kale, Singh and Perlmutter (2000) – which explicitly deal with the role of R-assets as a competitive enhancing advantage of firms. And it is the purpose of this chapter to offer some exploratory observations on the nature, significance, and governance of R-assets: and, in particular, to examine their relevance in explaining the recent growth, structure and form of MNE *related* activity. We use the adjective 'related' advisedly, for we shall concern ourselves with not just MNE *owned* activity, i.e. activity financed by foreign direct investment (fdi), but with the totality of activities under the *effective control* of MNEs. Such activity is based not only on resources and capabilities which MNEs actually *own*, but also those which they can *access* by one means or another, and then internalise for their own use.

THE CHARACTERISTICS OF FIRM SPECIFIC R-ASSETS

A Definition

First a working definition. We shall define firm specific R-assets as:

> The stock of a firm's willingness and capability to access, shape and engage in economically beneficial relationships; and to sustain and upgrade these relationships.

Such relationships, though always conducted by and between individuals, may take place both within the confines of a particular firm, or between that firm and other organizations and individuals.

The relationships between R-assets and other kinds of corporate assets – be they owned or accessed by firms – are set out in Figure 1.1. As can be seen, they run alongside human embodied intellectual capital, but are more empathetic and emotionally based. (This may be why economists are uneasy in dealing with them!) They are different from other assets in a number of ways, but their essential uniqueness lies in the fact they can only be *productively employed if they are used jointly with the R-assets of another economic actor*. The sociologist, Amitai Etzioni, believes that, to be successful, partnerships, be they between persons, corporations or govern-

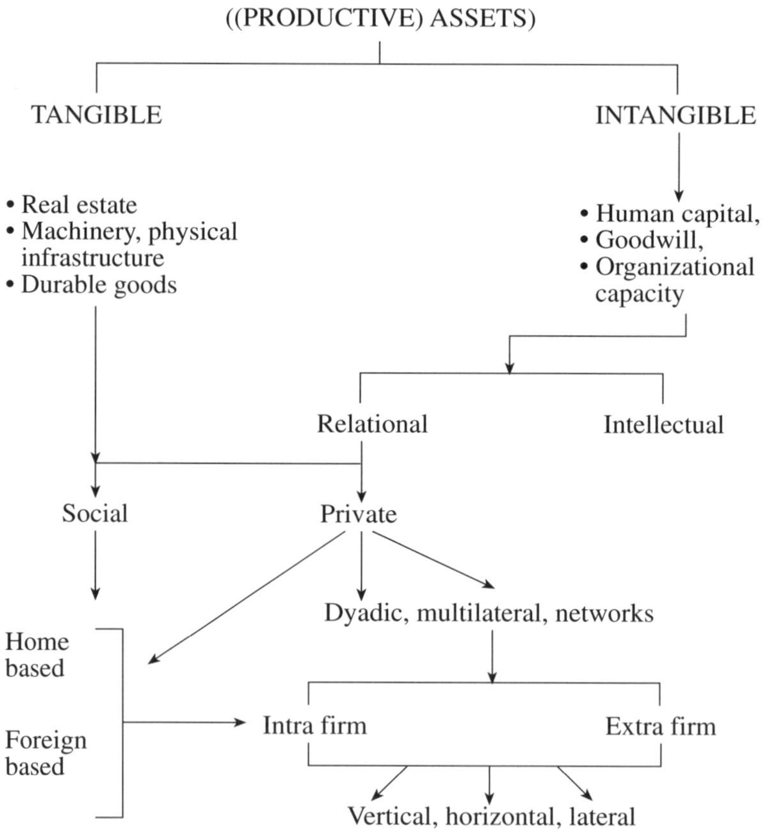

Figure 1.1 The pyramid of corporate assets

ments need to share a set of core values and objectives (Etzioni 1996). R-assets are essentially facilitating assets. When properly deployed, they enhance – one way or another – virtually all functional activities of the possessing firm. These include R&D, production, sourcing, financial management marketing, as well as the exchange specific activities of firms.

R-assets are then entirely human intensive; although such assets may be embedded in, and articulated by individuals or organizations. In their usage, R-assets can give rise to a plethora of relationships, ranging from the simple, shallow and one-off, to the complex dense and ongoing.

Table 1.2 Some unique characteristics of R-assets

- A bundle of attributes/values
- Multifaceted in origin: internally generated, externally accessed
- Shallow and simple ⇔ deep and complex
- Dyadic ⇔ network relationships
- Like other assets, R-assets need to be unique and imperfectly imitable if they are to confer a sustainable competitive advantage
- Vary according to function and activity: they range from routine to highly idiosyncratic relationships
- Likely to be strongly contextual: (reflecting cultures and ideologies which may be both country and firm specific)
- Unlike most other assets R-assets are only of value when combined with those of other firms: the concept of shared core values
- Unlike other assets they do not deplete when used
- Difficult to measure as their values are not independent of other assets with which they are combined
- Value of R-assets is likely to be cumulative and path dependent
- Cannot be owned; only controlled or influenced in their development
- Are only partially mobile across national boundaries

Some other characteristics of R-assets are set out in Table 1.2. Note, for example, they may be used in the pursuance of dyadic, multilateral or network relationships. As with other resources and capabilities, R-assets need to be scarce, unique and imperfectly imitable, if they are to confer a sustainable competitive advantage on the firm(s) deploying them. Unlike some other, for example tangible, assets, R-assets may be of negative value (i.e. a liability) to the firm; on the other hand, they do not deplete when used. They cannot be *owned*; only accessed and then controlled or influenced in the way in which they are deployed and combined with other assets. They are likely to be tacit and idiosyncratic; and more context specific, yet more pervasive, than most other assets. In particular, their content and effectiveness is likely to vary according to the culture, values and ideologies of each of the countries in which they are employed, and those of the firms creating or utilizing them. Lastly, although the focus of our current interest is on the R-assets of corporations, the concept of social R-assets (or social capital) is gaining increasing attention by researchers. We shall give this latter concept more attention a little later in our presentation.

The Ingredients of R-assets

What then are the ingredients – as opposed to the characteristics – of R-assets? How fungible are they? R-assets are a composite or mixture – a salad bowl – of a complex set of values, attitudes and virtues, the relevance of which is likely to be highly context specific. Unlike that of tangible assets, or even knowledge capital, the value of R-assets rests in the structure of the relations between and among the economic actors involved.

As set out in Table 1.3, the list of ingredients of (productive) R-assets is an extremely lengthy one. Moreover the content and configuration of these ingredients critically rests on the *raison d'être* for, and the goals of the respective partners in the relationship; and of their particular characteristics. Thus such values as enthusiasm, entrepreneurship, and a spirit of curiosity, risk taking, and a keenness to learn, are especially important for innovating activities. Those such as diligence, team orientation, flexibility, reliability and quality enhancement are more important for production and sub-contracting related relationships; while trust, integrity and reciprocity are the key components of successful adversarial (zero-sum game) exchange relationships.

The Governance of R-assets

Relationships between economic actors stretch along a continuum ranging from arm's length markets to those embedded in hierarchies. In between, there is a labyrinth of non-equity bilateral and pluralistic associations – including networks. The literature is replete with explanations as to why one relationship mode is preferred to another; though most are couched in terms of the comparative transaction costs (TC) of a discrete exchange of intermediate products, rather than on the wider benefits of cooperation in non-exchange functions to the participating firms. Moreover, most explanations tend to assume there *are* alternative modes of undertaking a particular activity or task; when this may not always be the case.

While, since its inception, the TC literature has always explicitly considered a number of relational specific costs and benefits – both in respect of fdi and alliances – it is less forthcoming in explaining the appropriate

Table 1.3 Selected ingredients of R-assets: what do they consist of?

Virtue/values	Activities/functions
Trust	All activities
Loyalty	Innovation, production, subcontracting
Reciprocity	Innovation, production, subcontracting
Dependability	All
Willingness to learn	Innovation
Forbearance	Subcontracting, exchange
Adaptability	Innovation, production, subcontracting
Work ethic	Production
Spirit of community	All except exchange
Commitment	Innovation, production, subcontracting
Radius of virtues	All
Part of society with fund of social capital	All
Ideologies and beliefs	Innovation, production, marketing
Empathy	To some extent, in all
Curiosity	Innovation
Honesty	All, but especially in exchange and/or where there is information asymmetry, and opportunities for opportunism
Integrity	All, but especially subcontracting and production
(Avoidance of) Negative virtues/values	
Opportunism	Subcontracting, exchange
Moral hazard	All
Corruption	Production, exchange
Free riding	All
Volatility	Subcontracting, marketing, exchange
Instability	Exchange

Notes:
- R-assets consist of a bundle of values and virtues which need to be nurtured. The optimum bundle will vary according to the type of relationship being concluded, and the R-assets of the partner organization, and are likely to be country and firm specific.
- We consider five main functions viz: innovation, subcontracting, production, marketing and exchange.

vehicle for identifying the contribution of R-assets to the innovatory or even the productive activities of firms – or indeed, of the contribution of being part of a network of firms to the up-grading of firm-specific R-assets. Because they are often project based and intended to promote time-limited and very specific objectives, many contemporary cross-border strategic alliances cannot be regarded as substitutes to an fdi; nor may a purely market solution be viable.

Nevertheless, some generalizations are possible, which I think can be usefully taken up by TC scholars. In the case of shallow and simple economic relationships, and where the value of R-assets is likely to be insignificant, relative to that of other resources and capabilities which are neither tacit nor proprietary, then the market route or a straightforward contractual agreement may be the most cost effective mode of usage. At the opposite extreme, in the case of thick, complex and highly idiosyncratic relationships, the success of which is vital to the competitive advantage of the firm, then, depending on the *relative costs* and benefits, and the extent to which control over the non R-assets can be exercised without ownership, the activity, or the products being traded, will either be internalized, or an alliance, with or without an equity interest, will be concluded. Since, however, by their nature, R-assets are tacit and function or project specific, and they are being increasingly directed to learning-related activities, it follows that the alliance route is likely to be the one more generally favoured.

Form of R-assets

As we have just indicated, any relationship or association forged by a firm (or individuals within the firm) may either be among its constituent units of decision taking (over which through ownership, it has *de jure* control) or between itself (or parts of itself) and an external economic actor or actors. These actors may be other private firms, a group or network of firms, nongovernmental organizations, public corporations or international agencies.

The choice between an intra- or inter-firm creation, protection and use of R-assets (the make or buy decision), is one critical decision a firm has to make. Another concerns the kind of associations to which R-assets are applied. Here the extant literature on linkages, spillovers and integration is useful. Figure 1.2 identifies the main kinds of relationships. These may be between individuals, teams, special interest groups, or corporations. They may be intra- or extra-firm. We shall focus on extra-firm (and especially *inter*-firm) relationships. These, in turn, may be grouped according to the nature of the relationship. (Is it, for example, between a firm and its supplier or customer, or is it an alliance between a firm and one of its competitors? Or is it by the type of activity, process, function or markets served?)

To be successful, each and every association – whatever its kind – requires a bundle of R-assets to be possessed by each of the economic actors involved. But how much, and what kind, and the appropriate governance form of these assets, is likely to be highly context specific. The more intensive, pervasive and complex relationships (and hence the need

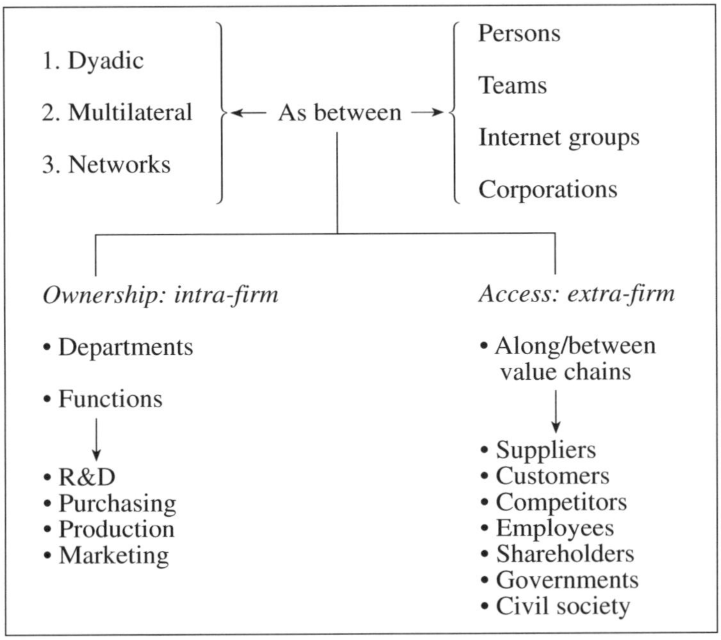

Figure 1.2 Types of R-assets

for more or better quality R-assets) are likely to arise in coalitions between firms with different value systems, competences and experiences, and which engage in innovatory and learning activities. The less demanding relationships (and hence the need for fewer R-assets) involve the exchange of fairly standardized products among firms from similar economic, ideological and cultural backgrounds. *It is the contention of this chapter that the RA intensive activities of firms have been increasing relative to other activities in recent years; and that an increasing proportion of the former have been taking the form of cross-border extra-firm associations intended to access new knowledge-related and learning capabilities.*

Where do networks fit into this analysis? Consider again Figure 1.2. Unlike firms, most networks do not create wealth for themselves. Their value is demonstrated as and when the participants in the network internalize and efficiently utilize the benefits they offer. Frequently the gains of networks take the form of augmented R-assets. If nothing else, networks help foster intra-network and inter-firm relational capital. From the work of Putman (1993), Porter (1998), and Enright (2000) – to cite just three contemporary exponents of the benefits of the spatial clustering of related activities – we are seeing a great deal of evidence that such networks not only offer the constituent firms knowledge and information-related externalities, but also strengthen many of the ingredients of R-assets – notably a sense of empathy, bond building, adaptability, open communication, and the promotion of shared core values and learning capabilities.

How Does One Value R-assets?

How are R-assets measured? How does one quantify their output – or indeed their constituent inputs. The answer is with very great difficulty! To a certain extent, similar problems beset scholars trying to put a monetary value on other forms of intangible assets – and of knowledge capital in particular. But they arise in acute form in the case of R-assets for two reasons. The first is there is no market, either for the inputs or the output of R-assets, separately from that of the other assets in which they are embedded. The second is that the main ingredients of R-assets (as set out in Table 1.3) are not themselves directly measurable, let alone marketable.

Table 1.4 summarizes some of the attempts by scholars to measure the R-assets of firms and of countries (or societies). By and large, the proxies for social R-assets, and/or their output, can more readily be obtained and are more meaningful than those of corporate R-assets. Such indices as the extent of civil litigation, crime – particularly violent crime – drugs, terrorism, truancy, divorce rates, bribery, tax evasion and corruption, all testify to a degree of social dysfunction, and a breakdown of inter-personal rela-

Table 1.4 Some measures of R-assets (or liabilities!)

At a firm level (Corporate R-assets)	At a country level (Social R-assets)
• Number of repeated inter-firm ties • Number, frequency and density of inter-firm linkages • Types of alliances • Survey material on significance of R-assets • Codes of conduct • Absence of industrial unrest: low labour turnover • Social responsibility • Transparency and openness	• [No one measure – but package of same] • Number/quality of community groups (NGOs) • (Negative) Extent of crime/corruption • (Negative) Breakdown of personal relations/divorce • (Negative) Civil litigation • Radius of trust • Prison population • Surveys on quality of social capital/justice systems • Extent and depth of tax evasion

tionships; just as others such as membership or participation in churches, clubs, charitable institutions, voluntary associations and so on, point to the robustness of social bonding and the moral health of the community. Some measures, such as the size of the police force, the number of social or behavioural counsellors, and property rights protection may also be regarded as positive indices in so far as their presence and action are designed to protect or improve the existing stock of social relational capital.

The suggested proxies for the RAs of firms are generally much less satisfactory. There are a few exceptions. One is firm level data on labour turnover, industrial disputes, strikes, etc. but, even here, economic or regulatory, rather than social, reasons may be the main explanation for such incidences, or changes in same.[2] Other proxies include the extent of social responsibility – or its absence – in the form of corporate corruption, lack of safety standards, and unacceptable business practices. Recent research on inter-firm coalitions has suggested measures such as the number of past alliances concluded between any two firms, the number of cliques to which a firm belongs, the type of alliance, and the level of mutual trust and commitment that arises out of the close interaction between the partners to the coalition. While some of these data make use of secondary and relatively objective measures, more recent work, especially by Dyer and Chu (2000), Holm, Eriksson and Johanson (1996), Kale, Singh and Perlmutter (2000) and Ariño, de la Torre and Ring (2001) has relied on the perception of corporate executives as obtained by survey or case study data. We feel bound to aver, that, notwithstanding all the problems and deficiencies of these data, we believe, for at least the next stage for advancing our understanding about the significance of R-assets for corporate success, the field or case study is likely to offer the most productive way of proceeding.

Already, as documented by Daniel Coleman in his book *Working with Emotional Intelligence* (Coleman 1999) there is a good deal of casual evidence that successful corporations are identifying their possession of (different kinds of) R-assets as the critical distinguishing feature between themselves and their less successful competitors. Similarly, in an analysis of the distinctive qualities of star performers among 286 US and other firms by Lyle Spencer Jr, it was found that an overwhelming proportion – 80 per cent – that set apart these performers from their average counterparts – depended on the emotional intelligence of their senior executive and professional staff rather than on their cognitive ability (Coleman 1999, p. 379).

R-assets and Social Capital

What now of the relationship [sic] between R-assets and social capital. The term 'social capital' has a variety of meanings (a recently published book edited by Partha Dasgupta and Ismail Serageldin (2000) for the World Bank catalogues these in some detail). For our purposes, we may start by taking a very broad interpretation of the term to include 'that part of a country's stock of tangible and intangible assets which is socially owned or controlled'. Under this umbrella, social capital includes much of the physical, legal and commercial infrastructure critical to the competitiveness of firms. A definition more directly related to R-assets is 'the accumulated societal fund of economic relationships, which are embodied or reposited in both individuals, organizations, and networks of organizations, engaging in economic activity'.

Francis Fukuyama puts it a little differently. He perceives social capital as 'a country's stock of informal values or norms shared among members of a group that permits cooperation between them' (Fukuyama 1999, p. 16). The value of this stock is likely to be more than the sum of its constituent parts, as a collection of connected R-assets is likely to generate its own externalities. The balance of social capital – taking the broader definition – is then made up of an infrastructure (including tangible assets and institutional structures which 'house' social R-assets (or the absence of same), such as prisons, courts of justice, religious and educational establishments; and also of societal rules, procedures, customs and routines.

Like corporate R-assets, social relational capital is not a single entity, but a variety of different entities. It is identified by its function; and inheres in the macro-structure of relations between actors and among actors. The extent and content of a community's social relational capital both affects the capacity of particular firms to generate and deploy their own R-assets and, as we shall see later, it can be a major influence on the kind and purpose of relationships, their form and their location – both between and across national borders.

THE CHANGING SIGNIFICANCE OF R-ASSETS

Why is more attention now being given to R-assets? The implication is that the extent, form and depth of economic relations between individuals and organizations has increased over the last 30 years or so. (Stretching back much further in time – and well before to the industrial revolution, R-assets, particularly in primitive (e.g. tribal) societies (and some still exist in the least developed countries) were a critical component of the wealth creating processes.) We believe this in fact has occurred, and that it has been the direct result of five inter-linked developments that have taken place in the world economy. These are first, a series of dramatic, and for the most part, systemic technological advances – particularly in all forms of informatics including e-commerce; second the widespread liberalization of markets – both domestic and cross-border; third the growing significance of most service sectors, which tend to be more R-asset intensive than their primary or secondary sector counterparts; fourth, the emergence of several important new players on the world economic stage, e.g. China and Russia; and fifth, the emergence and maturation of the global economy, which is essentially both a facilitator and an outcome of the first four factors.

Exactly how have these changes increased both the significance of firm specific R-assets and particularly (as we shall tackle in the next section) their role in determining the extent, pattern and form of the cross-border activity of firms? Space permits me to highlight just seven of these.

1. The cutting edges of economic activity have become more idiosyncratic and innovation driven. This has increased the extent, depth and complexity of intra- and inter-corporate economic relationships.
2. The scope and depth of *cross-border* economic relationships has noticeably increased, and in doing so, has embraced a new and wider range of values, ideologies and social customs. In successfully dealing with such associations, a fund of R-assets, which acknowledges these country or region specific differences, and promotes the well-being of each of the participants is critical.
3. Societal, and to some extent business, goals have changed. Rather than concentrating on efficiency related issues, increasingly the focus is directed to transforming societies and upgrading the role of cultural values and experiences and the quality of life, e.g. with respect to leisure and the environment (Stiglitz 1998; Rifkin 2000). These changes are spawning many new coalitions, both among firms and between firms and other organizations, including governments and non-governmental organizations (NGOs).
4. Competitive pressures following market liberalization have led to shedding or more disinternalization of activities of firms; and, with this, an increased reliance on external suppliers for intermediate products.
5. At the same time, the interdependence between the technologies required at different stages of the value chain, or indeed to produce any particular product, is increasing. This means that intra-firm transactions are not being replaced by arm's length transactions but by inter-firm coalitions.
6. The rate of technological obsolescence is accelerating, and this places a premium on speeding up the learning process and the innovation process. In order to achieve their objectives, and as R&D is becoming increasingly expensive, firms are being forced to engage in the kind of

strategic innovatory alliances which demand considerable R-assets on the part of the constituent partners if they are to be successful.

7. Partly as a result of the above factors, firms have reconfigured their organizational profiles, and are increasingly substituting or augmenting their hierarchical (pyramidal) command structures by more heterarchical structures. These latter structures encourage more co-operative and deeper horizontal, and vertical inter-personal relationships; and, in the case of MNEs, allow foreign subsidiaries greater responsibility and autonomy in their decision taking. As a result, these affiliates are forming more and closer relationships with their local suppliers, customers and competitors, and also with their own workforce.

R-ASSETS AND THEORIES AND PARADIGMS OF MNE ACTIVITY

What then are the implications of the growing importance of both corporate relational assets and social relational capital for our theorizing about the cross-border activities of firms and, in particular, fdi and the formation of non-equity alliances. The following paragraphs tackle this question from the lens of the eclectic paradigm;[3] and also from that of a selection (and it is only a selection) of the contextually specific theories it embraces.

The 0 Specific Competitive Advantages of Firms

Let us first consider the ownership (0) specific, i.e. the sustainable and unique competitive advantages of firms. These are usually considered under two headings. The first set of advantages (0a) embrace the specific assets or proprietary rights which are under the jurisdiction of the firm, whether this is by dint of ownership, or by controlling the use of resources and capabilities which it accesses, from the market, from other firms, or from the community at large. To reiterate an earlier point; firms do not own human capital or the assets of other firms, but, by a variety of means, they are able to exercise governance over their use. Though intangible, these assets usually enable the tangible assets owned or accessed by the firm to be created or deployed more effectively.

The second type of advantage (0t), is that which is derived from the efficient coordination of the first kind of assets. *Inter alia*, this includes the capability of the firm to optimize its locational portfolio of these assets, and to choose the optimum modality of governance. It is this kind of capability which is made up of an amalgam of intellectual and R-assets owned or accessed by corporations. Such a capability may be exercised at various strata within and between firms, according to the purpose of the association, and the nature of the assets, including the R-assets of the other actors participating in the activity. Such capabilities include those arising from being part of a network of related firms, and from the cumulative experience of past relationships. MNEs in particular, may be expected to augment their RAs as a result of their value adding activities in different economic regimes and cultures. *Inter alia* this has been shown to be the case in a recent research project on the internationalization of professional service firms recently completed at Rutgers University.[4]

It is the accumulated stock of R-assets, the learning and experiences attached to them, and how these are combined with externally accessed resources and capabilities, which, we are suggesting, should be more explicitly acknowledged by the two main contextual theories seeking to explain the content and character of the 0 specific advantages of firms *viz* the industrial organization and resource based theories. Neither theory explicitly incorporates RAs into their thinking, though, as I have already mentioned, recent efforts by Dyer and Singh (1998), Kale, Singh and Perlmutter (2000) and Chang, Singh and Lee (2000) on the protection and building of relational capital attempt to do just this.

R-assets may be internally or externally generated. Indeed, the willingness and ability of firms to gain new R-assets from both dyadic and network relationships is itself becoming an important core competence. Since the pioneering work of Johansson and Mattson (1988) and Walter Powell (1990) a decade or more ago, various attempts have been made to explore how, and in what conditions, networks may enhance the intellectual and relational capabilities of their participants.[5] A recent paper by Tai Jy Chen (2000), for example, has identified the benefits to Taiwanese electronics firms from their membership of domestic and foreign networks. These include access to more efficient production and innovatory activities, and the opening up of new cultural horizons as a direct result of relational subcontracting. Work by Michael Enright (2000) on clusters of both foreign and domestic firms in the Hong Kong financial district mirrors and extends earlier work by Ray Vernon (1960) and Dunning and Morgan (1971), which focused on the building of trust, group loyalty, and openness, among a dense concentration of financial and other office activities in the New York metropolitan region, and in the 'Square Mile' of the City of London.

For reasons already stated, technological advances and globalization are underlying both the rationale for, and the benefits flowing from, dyadic alliances and network relationships. We have further suggested that, as these relationships deepen and become more complex, so the choice of partner(s) and the networks in which they participate is influenced not only by the knowledge capital offered, but also by the ability and willingness of the partners to be empathetic towards each other. While is 'takes two to tango' (as the expression goes), the likelihood of forming and sustaining such an association does very much depend on the number and quality of R-assets each organization is able to bring to any cooperative or exchange venture.

Three related propositions which arise from this analysis are then:

1. *R-assets are becoming a more important component of the resources and competences of firms engaging in cross-border activity.*
2. *MNEs are likely to possess a greater stock of R-assets relative to non MNEs (*inter alia *because of the greater, more complex number, and wider geography of linkages with which the former are associated).*
3. *MNEs are increasingly likely to protect or augment their core competences as a direct result of their access to, and deployment of foreign located, R-assets.*

A final point about corporate R-assets is that they are likely to be context specific. Thus research has suggested Japanese, relative to US and European MNEs, in the 1980s possessed the kind of R-assets most likely to promote efficient production and subcontracting arrangements in the auto and consumer electronics sectors (Dunning 1994); while US MNEs in the 1990s recorded a comparative advantage in the kind of R-assets which helped encourage team entrepreneurship and R&D type alliances. The virtues of openness, loyalty, leveraging diversity, curiosity, reliability, empathy, prudency, bond building, and commercial integrity also vary considerably between national and/or corporate cultures. Some firms such as the Quaker originated UK firms of the 19th century also paid especial attention to building R-assets – particularly of an intra-firm character. Corporate culture can, and does, often play a pivotal role in promoting R-assets (or inhibiting their promotion).

To what extent are R-assets – which reflect the ideologies and values of a particular country – transferable across national borders? For, unlike most other types of assets, e.g. a particular kind of technology, R-assets are not viewed as the same product by different institutions or people. Again, the experience of Japanese investors in the European and US auto industries in the 1980s and 1990s suggests that this is so. On the other hand, the literature is full of examples of the lack of sensitivity by many MNEs in seeking to impose (rather than adapt) their own R-assets to those valued by their foreign associates or customers. The question of blending R-assets from different cultures and social mores, is likely to be one of the most taxing challenges open to MNEs over the next decade or more; and it is the firms that are successful in creating, sustaining and sympathetically melding such capabilities into their own organizational culture which are likely to be the future winners in the global marketplace.

The Location Advantages of Countries

The 'where' to locate decision of MNEs or potential MNEs has been extensively surveyed in the literature (Dunning 1998; Rugman and Verbeke 2001; Siebert 2000). Scholarly research has revealed that the critical variables are likely to be both time and context specific; and are especially sensitive to the *raison d'être* for MNE activity. For example, is it natural resource or market seeking? Is it intended to be (existing) asset exploiting or asset augmenting? Is it directed to mainstream manufacturing or to services – and, if the latter – to what kind of services? Is it part of a multi-domestic strategy or a globally integrated strategy by MNEs?

One thing seems certain. In most developed countries, at least, over the last three decades or so, the most important location-bound attractions of countries have shifted from the availability, cost and quality of natural factor endowments (including unskilled labour) to that of created assets, notably intellectual capital, innovatory systems, and the institutional and communications infrastructure. As global competitive pressures and the increasing mobility of knowledge and information have brought about at least some convergence in such attractions, so attention (both by firms and governments) is being focused on 'soft' locational variables, of which social capital – and more particularly social R-assets – is perhaps the most decisive. Such 'quality of life' variables, including the minimization of crime, pollution, corruption, congestion and unacceptable social behaviour are now taking pride of place as investment determinants. And while I would not wish to press this point too far, research by Herbert Giersch (1996) and others (Britten and Hamlin 1995) is emphasizing the increasing role played by economic morality as a location specific competitive enhancing asset.

Turning now to developing and transition economies, while there is no doubt that the availability and quality of natural resources and low (real) labour costs remain important locational attractions (notably in the less developed and resource rich countries), there is increasing evidence – particularly from erstwhile communist countries like Russia and Cambodia – that deficiencies both in institutional infrastructure and social relational capital are among the greatest obstacles to inward fdi. Business surveys on the attractiveness of both developing and developed countries to potential investors (such as those reported by the Economist Intelligence Unit, the World Competitiveness Forum and the European Round Table of Industrialists) are consistently putting the quality of social capital, and the R-assets of organizations with which they have (or wish to have) associations, at, or near, the top of their locational preferences. It may be further inferred that MNEs who can optimize their global portfolio of location specific R-assets – while, at the same time, judiciously adapting their own and their affiliates' R-assets to local requirements, are likely to be among the winners in an increasingly integrated, yet multi-cultural, world.

From this brief analysis we would offer two further propositions:

1. *Location specific R-assets are becoming a more important influence on the location choices of MNEs, both between and within countries.*
2. *The locational portfolio of assets by MNEs, chosen on the above criteria, and the interaction between their own R-assets and those of the institutions and individuals of the countries in which they operate, is becoming a more significant determinant of their global competitiveness.*

The Organization of R-assets

As we have already observed, a good deal of both internalization and network theory, initially designed to explain the organizational mode (or modes) of IB activity, can be used to explain that specifically relating to the creation and use of R-assets. This is because each approach focuses on the motives for, and the content of, human relationships, both at an individual and an organizational level. Indeed in their attempts to identify the reasons for market failure, TC scholars have pinpointed not only knowledge related deficiencies of arm's length exchanges – e.g. information symmetry and bounded rationality – but also relational deficiencies, notably those arising from a lack of trust, between the participants, opportunism and moral hazard. Much, too, of the literature on alliances – both domestic and cross-border – explicitly acknowledges the importance of many of the ingredients of R-assets (as set out earlier) as being critical to their success.

However, what is relatively new in the last decade or so and is increasingly engaging the attention of scholars researching into networks and alliances, is first, the emphasis now being given to the character and contents of intra- and inter-firm relationships as assets in their own right; and second, to the ways in which their creation, access and use are organized.

Let us elaborate on these last two points by offering just three examples.

First, the flattening of decision trees and the movement towards heterarchical organizational structures has (a) reduced the role of the 'command' route of generating intra firm R-assets, and replaced it by a visionary, strategic guidance and decision sharing route and (b) fostered a new appreciation that the management of subsidiaries are often more cognisant of the needs and strategies of indigenous suppliers, customers and governments, and are better able to relate to them, than are their counterparts in head offices. Both these developments have led to a re-examination of the governance and geographical locus of intra-firm activities (ranging from R&D through to marketing), and have done so precisely because of the recognition of the importance of R-assets as a created competitive advantage.

Second, the choice between cross-border intra-firm and alliance relational activities is being fundamentally affected by the reduced role of *ownership* (via fdi), and the increasing importance of *access* in obtaining and controlling the use of competitive enhancing resources and capabilities. We have already alluded to the fragmentation and disinternalization of the value chain of many firms – which is occurring despite, or in conjunction with, the mergers and acquisition boom of the mid- to late 1990s (UNCTAD 2000). There are many reasons for favouring a more market oriented route of subcontracting – which has been aided and abetted by e-commerce (Dunning and Wymbs 2001). But knowing *where* and *how* to harness resources and capabilities you do not own (or wish to own), and how best to coordinate these with your own core competences, requires a series of inter-institutional relationships, which, to be successful, needs a fund not only of intellectual capital, but of R-assets as well.

We will not labour this point further, save to mention that since R-assets are often directed to achieving very specific objectives – and that these objectives are frequently geared to optimally transforming the activities of firms rather than increasing their efficiency – the received internalization theory needs revisiting.

Third, it is here, too, where we believe the network approach comes into its own. As is generally acknowledged, firms participate in networks because of the externalities they are perceived to confer. In as much as these benefits require to be internalized by the participating firms if they are to be realised, there is no conflict between the network approach and internalisation theory. But internalisation in this case is based not on the *ownership* of assets, but on control over those which are externally *accessed*. Moreover, since the intra-network connections are usually non-contractual and frequently idiosyncratic and value laden, the willingness and ability of firms to gain from any exchange of knowledge, ideas or contacts, is likely to be strongly dependent on the R-assets they possess, and how these interact with those of other participants in the network.

These thoughts can be reiterated in the form of three related propositions.

1. *Access to resources and rights rather than ownership of resources and rights is likely to increase the value of R-assets of firms used in conjunction with those of other organizations. Thus one might expect cross-border M&As and cooperative non-equity ventures to play a more important role in the future portfolio of MNE activity.*
2. *Because of learning* et al *and relational enhancing benefits generated by networks, it may be predicted that the participation by MNEs and/or their affiliates in cross-border networks will increase, relative to purely dyadic associations with foreign firms.*

3. *The contribution of the R-assets of the foreign affiliates relative to those of the MNEs of which they are part is likely to increase. Partly this is the result of flatter intra-MNE organizational structures; and partly of the closer and deeper linkages between the affiliates and indigenous firms. Such linkages are themselves fostered by the improved relational space generated by networks.*

Reconfiguring the Paradigm

Putting these thoughts together, what are the implications of explicitly incorporating R-assets into the theories and paradigms of MNE activity? At this exploratory stage of thinking we would offer just four further general propositions.

1. *The ability to create and sustain firm-specific R-assets, and to efficiently co-ordinate these across national boundaries, both within their own organizations and between their and other organizations, and networks of organizations, will increasingly influence the extent and pattern of MNE activity.*
2. *The presence or absence of networks of related activities is likely to be a more important determinant of the geography of MNE activity in the next decade or more.*
3. *The increasing significance of cross-border R-assets as generating and sustaining the competitive advantages of firms is likely to lead to an increase in MNE-related activity, relative to that which otherwise would have occurred.*
4. *Though FDI seems likely to continue to be the main modality of the territorial expansion of firms, the rising importance and need to tap into extra-firm R-assets is likely to lead to a higher proportion of the global sales of MNEs being accounted for, or sold to, foreign organizations with whom they have a non-equity economic linkage; and over whose resources and capabilities they have some continuing control or influence.*

CONCLUSIONS

In conclusion, in this chapter we have sought to do three things:

1. First, and foremost, we have attempted to give a sense of the importance of a hidden group of assets available to corporations, which are not often explicitly identified – much less rigorously analysed – in the literature. These are assets that we have called R-assets, which all firms have the power to access, internally create, sustain and productively utilize.
2. Second, we have suggested that R-assets have become, and are becoming, a more important part of the portfolio of competitive enhancing assets of MNEs; and have explained why the characteristics of the 21st century innovation-driven global economy are demanding more attention be paid to them.

3. Third, we have identified some of the ways in which extant IB theories and paradigms may need to be modified to better incorporate both firm and country specific R-assets. In particular, we have suggested that the growth of networks has provided additional insights into (i) the way which industrial, and other, clusters might augment the competitive advantages (and especially the R-assets) of the participating firms; (ii) the content and value of their locational portfolios, and (iii) the ways in which they may best relate their own R-assets to those of other firms, and to the contours and space of the networks, to advance their own efficiency and learning capabilities.

This contribution has been a very exploratory one. We would be the first to accept that it has raised more questions than it has answered. In fully acknowledging all the difficulties inherent in measuring R-assets it has sometimes tried 'to square the circle'. Neither (to the disappointment of some readers, no doubt) has it offered a single explanatory statistical equation! But while I would be the first to point out these lacunae in the work of one of my PhD students, I would like to think that age and experience offer me some privileges, including the luxury of getting away with a less than rigorous analysis while still making a useful contribution to a relatively unexplored area of research.

NOTES

An earlier version of this chapter was first presented at a Conference on Cooperative Strategies and Alliances, organized by Farok Contractor and Peter Lorange in Lausanne in June 2001.

1. One writer (MacPherson 1973) regards 'the right not to be excluded' from the access to the productive resources of society as one of the key emerging competitive advantages of firms.
2. As, for example, in the case of the dramatic reduction in strikes in the UK in the 1980s.
3. As set out most recently in Dunning (2000 and 2001).
4. In this survey, access to R-assets was ranked the 7th most important of some 26 competitive advantages, identified by professional service firms. They were also ranked the 6th most likely to be derived from the foreign operations. Among the most multinational and largest of these firms, this advantage was ranked 1st or 2nd. Network related benefits – particularly with clients, customers and suppliers, were generally ranked between 3rd and 5th in order of significance (Dunning and McKaig-Berliner 2001).
5. See especially the writings of Gulati (1998 and 1999), Holm, Eriksson and Johanson (1996), Uzzi (1997) and Chen and Chen (1998).

REFERENCES

Adler, P.S. and Kwon S.-W. (1999), *Social Capital, the Good, the Bad and the Ugly*. Paper presented to the Academy of Management meeting in 1999. Los Angeles: University of Southern California, Mimeo.

Ariño, A. De la Torre, J. and Ring, P.S. (2001), 'Relational quality: managing trust in corporate alliances', *California Management Review* (forthcoming).

Brittan, S. and Hamlin, A. (eds) (1995), *Market Capitalism and Moral Values*. Cheltenham: Edward Elgar.

Chang, S., Singh, H. and Lee, K. (2000), 'Complementarity, status, similarity and social capital as drivers of alliance formation', *Strategic Management Journal*, **21**, 1–22.

Chen, Homin, and Chen, Tain-jy (1998), 'Network linkages and location choice in foreign direct investment', *Journal of International Business Studies*, **29**, 445–69.

Chen, T.J. (2000), *Network Resources for Internationalization: The Case of Taiwan's Electronics Firms*.Taipai: National Taiwan University.

Coleman, D. (1999), *Working with Emotional Intelligence*. New York: Bantam Books.

Dasgupta, P. and Serageldin, I. (2000), *Social Capital: A Multifaceted Perspective*. Washington, DC: The World Bank.

Dunning, J.H. (1994), 'The Strategy of Japanese and US Manufacturing Investment in Europe', in Mason, M. and Encarnation, D. (eds) *Does Ownership Matter?* Oxford: The Clarendon Press, pp. 59–86.

Dunning, J.H. (1998), 'Location and the multinational enterprise: a neglected factor?', *Journal of International Business Studies*, **29**, 67–83.

Dunning, J.H. (2000), 'The eclectic paradigm as an envelope for economic and business theories of MNE activity', *International Business Review*, **9**(1), 163–90.

Dunning, J.H. (2001), 'The eclectic (OLI) paradigm of international production: past, present and future', *International Journal of the Economics of Business*, **8**(2), 173–90.

Dunning, J.H. and Wymbs, C. (2001), 'The challenge of electronic commerce for IB theory', *International Journal of the Economics of Business*, **8**(2), 273–302.

Dunning, J.H. and McKaig-Berliner, A. (2001), 'The geographical sources of competitiveness of professional business firms', *Transnational Corporations*, **10** (forthcoming).

Dunning, J.H. and Morgan, E.V. (1971), *An Economic Study of the City of London*. London: Allen and Unwin.

Dyer, J.H. and Chu, W. (2000), 'The determinants of trust in supplier–automaker relationships in the US, Japan and Korea', *Journal of International Business Studies*, **31**(2), 259–85.

Dyer, J.H. and Singh, H. (1998), 'The relational view, cooperative strategy and the sources of interorganizational competitive advantage', *Academy of Management Review*, **23**(4), 660–79.

Enright, M.J. (2000), 'Globalization, Regionalization and the Knowledge Based Economy in Hong Kong', in Dunning, J.H. (ed.) *Regions, Globalization, and the Knowledge Based Economy*. Oxford: Oxford University Press, pp. 131–69.

Etzioni, A. (1996), *The New Golden Rule*. New York: Basic Books.

Fukuyama, F. (1999), *The Great Disruption*. New York: The Free Press.

Giersch, H. (1996), 'Economic Morality as a Competitive Asset', in Hamlin, A., Giersch, H. and Norton, A. (eds) *Markets, Morality and the Community. Melbourne, Australia: Centre for Independent Studies*, Occasional Paper, No. 65.

Gulati, R. (1998), 'Alliances and networks', *Strategic Management Journal,* **19**, 293–317.

Gulati, R. (1999), 'Network location and learning: the influence of network resources and firm capabilities on alliance formation', *Strategic Management Journal*, **20**, 397–420.

Holm, D.B., Eriksson, K. and Johanson, J. (1996), 'Business networks and cooperation in international business relationships', *Journal of International Business Studies*, **27**(5), 1033–53.

Johansson, J. and Mattson, L.G. (1988), 'Internationalization in Industrial Systems – A Network Approach', in Hood, N. and Vahlne, J.-E. (eds) *Strategies in Global Competition*. London: Croom Helm, pp. 287–314.

Kale, P., Singh, H. and Perlmutter, H. (2000) 'Learning and protection of proprietary assets in strategic alliances: building relational capital', *Strategic Management Journal*, **21**, 217–37.

McPherson, C. (1973), *Democratic Theory: Essays in Retrieval*. Oxford: Clarendon Press.

Porter, M. (1998), *On Competition*. Boston: Harvard Business School Press.

Powell, W. (1990), 'Neither Markets Nor Hierarchy: Network Forms of Organization', in Cumming, L.L. and Straw, B.M. (eds) *Research in Organizational Behavior*, vol. 12, Greenwich, CT: JAI Press, pp. 295–336.

Putman, R.D. (1993), *Making Democracy Work: Civic Traditions in Modern Italy*. Princeton: Princeton University Press.

Rifkin, J. (2000), *The Age of Access*. London: Penguin Books.

Rugman, A. and Verbeke, A. (2001), 'Location and the Multinational Enterprise', in Rugman, A. and Brewer, T. (eds) *Handbook of International Business*. Oxford: Oxford University Press.

Siebert, H. (2000), *The Paradigm of Locational Competition*. Kiel: Institut für Weltwirtschaft, Discussion Paper No. 367, August.

Stiglitz, J. (1998), *Towards a New Paradigm of Development*. Geneva: UNCTAD, The Prebisch Lecture for 1998.

UNCTAD (United Nations Commission on Trade and Development) (2000), *World Investment Report* 2000.

Uzzi, B. (1997), 'Social structure and competition in inter-firm networks: the paradox of embeddedness', *Administrative Science Quarterly*, **42**, 35–67.

Vernon, R. (1960), *Metropolis 1985*. Cambridge, MA: Harvard University Press.

2. Alliance capitalism and macroeconomic policies

Gavin Boyd

The relational assets discussed in the previous chapter are acquired by firms in different forms of alliance capitalism – in patterns of intercorporate cooperation that have varying dimensions, intensities, and durations. These draw attention as applications of internalization logic that enable alliances, networks, and industry groups to coordinate the productive activities of individual enterprises in ways that result in synergistic complementarities. Technology advances tend to increase the utility of these types of collaboration, causing them to expand. Configurations of orderly growth that are thus constituted became highly significant for the management of macroeconomic policies. The growth and employment effects can ease the tasks of monetary policy: there can be price stability, high employment, and exchange rate stability on a sound basis because of the scale of spontaneous order. Meanwhile adequate financing can be provided for the funding of infrastructure development, the provision of administrative and security services, and the distribution of welfare benefits. Moreover there can be functional balance between production in the domestic economy and that which develops as firms extend their operations across national borders. Harmonious internal production specializations can blend with harmonious international specializations, with balanced overall gains.

Policy level and corporate views about the efficiencies and welfare effects of different forms of intercorporate cooperation, however, are influenced by understandings of competition as a force driving performance. Economic growth is seen to depend primarily on rivalries between firms for market shares, competition between workers for employment, and pressures exerted by governments against each other in quests for enhanced structural competitiveness, and in leverage over issues of market access. The efficiencies can be expected to be greater if the competition is hard, unrestrained by common interests.[1] The competition between workers for employment can be given such importance that a level of unemployment is considered necessary to ensure productivity gains and to limit inflation.

Understandings of the efficiencies resulting from competition and those possible with cooperation are influenced by beliefs, morals, cultures, and basic policy orientations. Strong individualism, a source of entrepreneurial dynamism, can be evident in pervasive emphasis on the value of intense competition between firms. In a communitarian political economy there is usually stress on corporate collaboration as a public good. Relevant contrasts that are commonly recognized are those between the USA, achieving high but unstable performance through competitive dynamism, and Germany, achieving moderate but more stable growth with extensive collaboration that restrains competition. Japan, until severely affected by financial sector failures during the 1990s, had achieved a highly functional blend of intercorporate competition and cooperation, in a system of comprehensive alliance capitalism.

Differing national patterns of corporate operations are active in deepening integration, as structural linkages between countries expand and become more complex with increases in transnational production and trade. In the global pattern the USA is more prominent than Germany, but has been challenged by the dynamism of the Japanese combination of competition and cooperation. The gradually integrating global economy is being shaped much more by international competition than by collaboration between transnational enterprises, and this competition is driving concentration trends. Hence there are increasingly serious challenges for less competitive enterprises, and for countries less structurally competitive than others. The overall configuration has changed in recent years because of Japan's acute economic difficulties, and accordingly research for policymakers and managements has to focus on the dynamics of structural and policy linkages between the USA and the European Union.

The primary concern, in studies of the effects of different balances between competition and cooperation, is that these have consequences for real economies. Those consequences, however, are conditioned by, and can be severely disrupted by, activities in financial sectors. These have become internationalized with very high volume speculative operations. The management of monetary and fiscal policies by governments in industrialized states has become all the more difficult because of the ways in which large scale rent seeking by global financial enterprises affects exchange rates, the funding of productive activity, overall investment flows, structural competitiveness, corporate competitiveness, price stability, and employment.[2] For macroeconomic policymakers, and for corporate managements advising governments, patterns of competition and cooperation between firms, at home and externally, have growth effects and potentials, in terms of the evolution of real economies, that can be all the more significant because of associated vulnerabilities to, or degrees of protection against, disruptive stresses imparted by the speculation in world financial markets.[3]

The American recession which became severe during 2001, and which had adverse effects in Europe and Japan, has necessitated close examination of the ways in which macroeconomic policy capabilities can be weakened or enhanced by the growth, employment, and stabilizing effects of forms of intercorporate cooperation and competition. One major problem has been that rather pervasive hard competition has adversely affected business confidence. Another has been that corporate incentives to produce abroad, for higher profitability and with wide risk spreading, have been increased. A further problem has been that diversions of investment into international speculative operations have continued, in effect limiting the funding of productive ventures for recovery at home.

CORPORATE COOPERATION AND COMPETITION

Differing forms and balances of competitive and cooperative activity are evident in national patterns of corporate behaviour, and these extend into international operations as deepening integration continues. The contrasts reflect causal factors studied in institutional economics. Basic value orientations, distinguished primarily as communitarian or individualistic, and high or low principled, are given expression in systems of corporate governance and intercorporate governance, and in conventions regulating market functions.[4] The national patterns of corporate behaviour have overall growth and employment effects which reveal the consequences of differences in corporate–government relations, and in macromanagement performance by governments, as well as the intrusions of foreign patterns of corporate competition and cooperation.

The basic value orientations in national cultures tend to be expressed in relational or instrumental cooperation between firms, and in soft or hard intercorporate competition. The culture of Japanese capitalism is active in mainly relational intercorporate cooperation, mixed with soft competition. The sharpest contrast is with American capitalism, distinguished by forms of instrumental cooperation and hard competition. In Europe, German capitalism has affinities with that in Japan; Germany is the core state of the European Union, and its system is being subjected to pressures for adaptation to competitive challenges in the Union. Japan is experiencing different pressures because of severe deficiencies in its financial sector, which have raised questions about efficiencies in its system of cooperative capitalism. American capitalism is under serious strain because of its recession, and a critical determinant of its prospects is its potential for developing a broadly integrated approach to the promotion of recovery.[5]

In the major industrialized states the emergence of new technologies tends to increase production interdependencies between firms: technology based forms of cooperation thus increase, with mixes of goodwill and opportunism, trust and mistrust. Much managerial interest thus focuses on opportunities for complementary entrepreneurial specializations.[6] Rivalries for world market shares between principal competitors, however, result in continuing concentration trends.[7] The incentives for technology based cooperation between major contenders for market shares decrease as these rivals merge with or acquire each other, and the dominant positions acquired tend to motivate more active exploitation of those market strengths. Relational assets can then become less significant. Meanwhile, as dominant market positions are consolidated, pressures to concentrate on core competencies can be seen to be less compelling: diversification opportunities can become more significant, as ways to acquire supplementary forms of market power.

The various balances between competitive and cooperative corporate activity, as they link what have been entirely national economic structures, contribute to a vast pattern of internationalized market efficiencies and failures. For each government, distinctive features of the pattern, affecting relative gains from involvement in the deepening integration, constitute challenges that demand macroeconomic policy responses, notably for the financing of adjustment through fiscal stimulus or restraint; monetary loosening or tightening; and microeconomic measures, particularly for enhanced structural competitiveness, internal market protection, or external market opening leverage. Functional and political exchange links between macroeconomic and microeconomic policy areas become more significant in deepening integration. Elements of economic sovereignty are lost as transnational enterprises increasingly shape economic structures in each country and the interdependencies between them, but in various ways a policy mix can restrict and even reverse this process. What can be achieved depends on the balance between competition and cooperation in national corporate activity, and on degrees of cooperation that may develop between national firms and the administration.

In deepening integration, national firms tend to evolve more and more into transnational enterprises, building international production systems to secure larger global market shares.[8] National attachments and loyalties weaken, and previous balances between competition and cooperation in the home economy generally alter, while the external environment induces stronger focus on quests for international competitive advantage. If policy orientations are substantially liberal, the losses of economic sovereignty are largely accepted, with hopes that favourable business environments will attract high value added activity by the transnational enterprises. Such expectations may be relatively well founded if there are high levels of intercorporate cooperation in the home economy, and if these contribute to effective international involvement by its outward oriented firms. But, if levels of intercorporate cooperation at home are low, maintenance of the liberal policy orientation will entail vulnerabilities, resulting principally from the development of foreign production by home based transnational enterprises on a scale much greater than home production for export, and from foreign sourcing at high volume for the home economy by national firms. The vulnerabilities can be all the more serious if the financial sector's funding of the real economy is dominated by large scale speculation that attracts foreign capital, thus increasing the cost advantages of international production for home based transnational enterprises, while drawing imports in excess of domestic output.[9]

For the USA the vulnerabilities are serious, because, while its established policy orientation is liberal, its intercorporate pattern is intensely competitive, and is distinguished by distant and distrustful attitudes to the national administration. The strongly speculative orientation of the financial sector adds to the vulnerabilities, by in effect giving impetus to foreign production and aggravating the import drawing effects of domestic demand, while causing sequences of booms and declines.[10]

A policy orientation toward very active measures for enhanced structural competitiveness can be effective if there are high levels of intercorporate cooperation and corporate–government collaboration. The solidarity based political economy that can result will tend to be advantaged, in deepening integration, by functional balance between domestic and foreign production, and substantial funding of productive activity in the real economy, and by a capacity to control and adjust to foreign structural penetration. These advantages are very significant in a context in which deepening integration results from hard competition between transnational enterprises for world market shares, without an effective system of global collective management that could implement, in particular, an international competition policy.[11] In the absence of such a system the potential benefits of a solidarity based political economy tend to increase while the ungoverned processes of globalization continue.

For refined assessment of the efficiencies and welfare aspects of a balance between competition and cooperation tilted in favour of the latter, it must be stressed that the most desirable results will depend on the degrees to which the cooperation is relational, integrative, and oriented toward the common good, while ensuring that competition is restrained, and remains soft. The goodwill and trust of such a solidarity system can make possible an orderly development of efficiencies superior to those that could be driven by hard competition, because of the negative effects of opportunism, distrust, limited information sharing, and weaker commitments to the development of enduring entrepreneurial complementarities. This conclusion can be reinforced if the effects of intensely competitive orientations in the financial sector are considered, in conjunction with those in the real economy. In a financial sector, hard competition, it must be stressed, tends to be expressed in very high volume speculation, diverting considerable volumes of investment away from productive use, contributing to the growth of a consumer culture, and, it must be reiterated, causing asset appreciations to become acutely unstable.[12]

MONETARY POLICY

Deepening integration increases monetary policy responsibilities regarding price and exchange rate stability, and the financing of growth, while making these responsibilities more difficult to meet, especially because of the disruptive effects of import penetration, outward and inward direct investment, and changes in the volume and direction of portfolio flows, as well as shifts in exchange rates. All these problems are well recognized, generally with observations that the associated declines of economic sovereignty set requirements for wide ranging international economic cooperation, for which there is insufficient political will. What is usually not acknowledged is the significance, for monetary policy management, of the balance between competitive and cooperative activity by firms in the pattern of domestic and foreign operations, which has overall consequences for growth and employment.[13] In this balance the scale of speculation in the financial sector tends to became an increasingly important factor affecting investment movements, the funding of productive activity, price and exchange rate changes, and overall stability.

If there is extensive integrative relational cooperation between national firms, as their domestic operations extend further into the international economy, their collaboration can ensure orderly absorption of incoming direct investment, limit disruptions of the domestic market by imports, contribute to price stability, and sustain domestic and foreign investor confidence. Prospects for exchange rate stability can be favourable, for these reasons and because government borrowing can be limited, due to the overall growth effects of the intercorporate cooperation, and to the influence of aggregated corporate views and preferences on the maintenance of fiscal discipline.[14]

Yet corporate cooperation that has been, or appears to have been, relational, can give way to oligopolistic collusion, forcing prices upwards. Vigorous hard competition may thus be considered necessary for price stability. Over time, however, such competition activates concentration trends, and tacit collusion between firms with very large market strengths tends to drive up prices, while the tacit collusion evades competition policy enforcement. Whatever the intensity of competition and the scale of oligopolistic collusion, meanwhile, investment inflows, if at high volume, can exert upward pressure on prices, and on the exchange rate. These price increases, as affecting basic consumer items, may be moderated by low cost imports, but this can happen in a setting in which the overall inflation effects of the high volume investment inflows can be quite potent. Monetary tightening to moderate those effects may be of limited utility, especially in a context in which monetary policy is also challenged by substantial speculation driven stock and property appreciations that add to the attraction of investment inflows.[15]

In the absence of extensive relational intercorporate cooperation, monetary policy has to cope with the growth, employment, price, and exchange rate effects of operations by firms largely unconcerned with public goods issues and open to opportunities to exploit economic processes which monetary measures may be intended to activate. In line with objectives to facilitate growth and full employment, with low inflation and exchange rate stability close to purchasing power parities, monetary tightening to slow inflation will contribute to currency appreciation, slowing export expansion and increasing corporate incentives to produce abroad rather than at home for export; but investment inflows, especially if attracted by asset appreciations induced through speculation, may more than offset the effects of the credit tightening. In a post boom economic decline, moreover, monetary loosening to spur growth that has contracted because of falls in investor confidence can cause financial institutions to exploit the availability of lower cost bank lending in order to fund foreign operations offering higher returns. Investor confidence in the home economy can thus remain low, because of awareness of this funding problem, and of the increased corporate emphasis on foreign production. Meanwhile capital flight that continues to be attracted from lower growth foreign areas may, in varying degrees, feed into the international speculative operations by financial enterprises sensitive to the uncertainties in the home economy.[16]

The logic of developing technology based forms of corporate cooperation tends to develop naturally if cultural and institutional factors are already orienting managements toward all forms of relational collaboration, as has been evident in Japan. In a strongly individualistic culture, however, with a well established liberal policy orientation, the logic of technology based corporate cooperation, although growing stronger as frontier innovations increase, does not tend to activate relational intercorporate collaboration on a scale that would be responsive to public goods imperatives and monetary policy objectives.

US monetary policy thus has to contend with continuing losses of economic sovereignty, because of the expansion of independent operations by its firms as they became more deeply involved in the world economy.[17] This has to be reiterated, but not in a way that would exclude hope for solidarity building innovations by policymakers and corporate managements that would enhance the domestic effectiveness of monetary measures, while, more fundamentally, facilitating spontaneous orderly growth that would lighten monetary policy tasks.

The pattern of trends and issues affecting governance in the American political economy presents challenges for the European Union, and in particular for Germany, as its central member, with a solidarity based political economy that can respond to the objectives of monetary management by the European Central Bank, in which it has strong influence. Pervasive relational intercorporate cooperation in Germany, expressed politically in constructive inputs into economic policymaking, to a very significant extent ensures that the securities industry remains a modest sector of the economy, that there is relatively little speculation to drive asset appreciation, that foreign production, on a moderate scale, does not contribute to deindustrialization, and that inflation is kept low. The overall stability, however, has to be maintained while coping with high unemployment in the Eastern part of the country, formerly under Communist mismanagement.[18] Technological progress, moreover, tends to be slower than in the USA because of the conservative influence of banks as major funding institutions, and the gradualism favoured by labour unions, as beneficiaries of stakeholder forms of corporate governance.[19]

The European Central Bank's management of monetary policy lacks the support of a large system of relational intercorporate cooperation elsewhere in the Union: Austria, Belgium and Holland have small affinitive systems of capitalism, but France, Italy and Spain have less integrated systems. Hence there are strains, especially because the conflict ridden French political economy generates pressures for fiscal expansion while preventing forms of coordination conducive to growth. France, although it is Germany's main partner in the politics of the Union, limits support for the macroeconomic prudence which Germany endeavours to maintain in the European Monetary Union. Other low growth states in the Union can understandably align with France.[20]

The German relational intercorporate system may lose some cohesion as its firms extend operations in the Union and in the rest of the world, while it accepts direct investment from other Union members and from the USA. The large US corporate presence in Europe is a formidable competitive challenge, and is expanding, with strong entrepreneurial dynamism, into the less integrated and less developed Union states, in rivalry with German firms. The very active US corporate involvement appears to contribute to the orientation of many European investors toward the placement of funds in the USA. Altogether, European monetary policy management may well become less functional because of less integrated German participation, and because regional growth and employment objectives may be more difficult to achieve, due to continued capital flight to the USA and to changes in regionally based output caused by increasing service of the Union market by the international production systems of US enterprises.[21]

Japan, in a comparative perspective, presents contrasts which can further illuminate the significance of forms of intercorporate cooperation for monetary policies. The Japanese experience has shown how large scale ventures in international production can cause cleavages in a relational intercorporate system. Increasing capacities for internal financing made highly successful Japanese outward oriented manufacturing firms less dependent on bank funding during the 1980s, and the banks then engaged in risky property speculation. A collapse of investor confidence in the early 1990s precipitated a severe recession, and monetary loosening to facilitate domestically based recovery had little effect. Administrative control of the financial system weakened, as the economic bureaucracy lost much of its power, in the course of political changes which reduced the status and effectiveness of the Liberal Democratic Party, the main political organization identified with corporate interests. Restructuring of the banking system, burdened with bad loans, became very difficult, and increased monetary loosening failed to achieve significant results. A perverse consequence of the loosening was that it encouraged increases in investment flows to the USA.[22]

The Japanese experience has been contrasted mainly with that of the USA because the United States does not have a relational pattern of cooperation between firms; because the speculative boom in the USA, unlike that in Japan, attracted high volume investment from the rest of the world, while the openness of the US economy caused the boom effects on demand to draw in large imports that to some extent kept inflation low, thus providing a politically significant excuse for delayed monetary tightening; and because very large scale speculative international operations by the US financial sector have continued to draw investment from the rest of the world. Yet the profitability of this international speculation has also drawn investment from domestic sources in the USA, taking advantage of low interest rates that have been intended to stimulate a US recovery from its post boom recession.

Monetary policy is very much an elite process, in the USA, Japan, and Europe, but as shown in the European and in previous Japanese cases its functional significance can reflect responsiveness to representations of interests and views from relatively integrated patterns of corporate cooperation, and can be sustained by the productive effects of such patterns. In the USA, fragmented interest representation and lack of consensus within the predominantly competitive pattern of intercorporate relations in effect allow idiosyncratic factors to assume greater importance in the management of monetary policy. An important consequence was the delay in monetary tightening which allowed speculation led asset appreciation to reach dangerous levels before the 2001 recession.[23]

FISCAL POLICY

As a highly politicized process, fiscal policy management tends to be more directly responsive to advice and assertions of interests by an integrated pattern of intercorporate cooperation, like that in Germany, but the politically fragmenting effects of intense competition in a corporate pattern tend to necessitate large scale trading of political favours, in very numerous unique contexts. In the USA this happens through continuous political campaigning that reflects institutional weaknesses in the main political parties. Strong pressures are thus generated for fiscal expansion.[24]

Levels of development in political institutions have vital significance for the shaping of views and preferences in fiscal policymaking, determining, overall, the ways in which the common good is served. A pattern of relational corporate cooperation, working constructively with institutionally well developed political parties, can contribute to holistically functional fiscal decision making, while activating orderly economic growth and orienting entrepreneurial energies toward full support for such growth, so that the funding of industry is not reduced by speculation in the financial sector. The principal contrast is a system in which the level of institutional development is too low to transform aggressively competitive political demands for distributional or regulatory measures into sound fiscal policies, and in which this dysfunctional pluralism expresses the dynamics of a corporate pattern that is much more competitive than cooperative.[25]

Comparative studies of fiscal policies give much attention to the persistence of large budget deficits in many industrialized states that have led to burdensome accumulations of public debt, and to high taxation levels that have retarded growth, caused capital flight, and adversely affected exchange rates, while provoking shifts of popular support to political parties competing as distributional coalitions, thus further discouraging productive investment at home. Quantitative comparative studies of the deficits have tended to obscure contrasts in political dynamics, but these have reflected the functional consequences of different balances between competition and cooperation in patterns of corporate activity.[26]

Government failures in fiscal management have more visible international effects than those associated with deficiencies in monetary policies: the internationalization of problems resulting from fiscal mismanagement has wider consequences, although these tend to be mixed with those caused by defective monetary policies. Internationalized market failure problems are commonly associated with the fiscal and monetary shortcomings. In this large context, problems of advanced political development within major industrialized states are evident, and are related to the patterns of intercorporate relations.

The recent history of major fiscal policy deficiencies that have been associated with monetary policy failures and that have had extensive effects in the international economy began with the large budget deficits and monetary contraction in the USA during the first half of the 1980s. The absence of a strong system of relational intercorporate cooperation made it possible for this contradictory mix of macroeconomic policies to be given expression through idiosyncratic choices in a context of irresponsible political trading, and in effect allowed continuity until the middle of the decade, when warnings of a foreign exchange crisis necessitated interventions to cause dollar depreciation.[27] The large budget deficits, however, continued, and were accompanied by high volume trade deficits. Dollar overvaluation had been responsible for substantial declines in exports, and had motivated increased corporate emphasis on foreign production for external markets, while strong internal demand, due to the expansionary fiscal policy, drew in large imports. The budget deficits were financed to a considerable extent by borrowing abroad, which was made easier than it might otherwise have been by Japanese investment in US government debt.[28] This appeared to be a source of restraint on US market opening leverage against Japan, the principal trading partner with which US commerce was in deficit.

This contradictory policy mix would not have been possible in Germany: its pattern of relational intercorporate ties, aggregating interests in line with functional concepts of the common good, in a political economy at a higher level of institutional development, would have been a potent force for rational macroeconomic management. When dollar depreciation was officially encouraged after the mid-1980s, the emphasis of US corporate strategies on foreign production continued, reflecting a low probability that corporate collaboration would develop to strengthen production at home for export; that is, in recognition that the trade deficits were threatening to become unsustainable. US outward direct investment, with large scale merger and acquisitions activity, contributed to concentration trends in the world economy, with sectoral dislocations at home that caused insecurity and unemployment, and this internationalization of market failure problems roused public anxieties about the costs of globalization. The distributional appeal of the Democratic Party was thus increased. Corporate interest in expanding foreign production was thus further encouraged, and responded also to opportunities presented by the formation of the Single Market in Europe and by a weakening of competition by Japanese firms, as their home economy's recession began.[29]

The structural problems of the USA during the 1990s, however, were obscured by a speculative boom as investor optimism pushed up stock and property prices to very high levels, causing expectations that productivity raised by investments in new technology would sustain the asset appreciations. Fiscal policy in this setting contributed to the optimism through projections, based on the wealth effects of the boom, that encouraged hopes of budget surpluses. Monetary tightening that might have moderated the speculation tended to be avoided, it must be stressed, despite indications that stocks were dangerously overvalued, and this accorded with the interests of Democratic Party contenders for office, although these also benefited from popular concerns about the costs of globalization.[30]

The US recession which became very serious in 2001 necessitated fiscal expansion. Tax cuts and increased public spending were intended to reflate the economy, but their effects on the structural problems that had developed had to be assessed with reference to indications that corporate interest in foreign production had understandably increased, and that the funding of industry at home was being limited by the financial sector's attraction toward the higher profitability of international speculative operations and of distressed lending at home. It was also necessary to note that, in general, large firms in the US economy were better placed to cope with the recession than small and medium sized enterprises, because of superior resources and greater significance for lending agencies: a trend to be expected, then, was further concentration. Moreover, it seemed probable that competitive pressures during the recession would alter forms of corporate cooperation based on complementary specializations: major partners, managing such collaboration instrumentally, could well be more strongly motivated to acquire cooperating enterprises, so as to reduce risks and increase profits while the prospects for recovery remained uncertain.[31]

The US record of macroeconomic management contributed to the development of European political will to achieve greater economic integration and establish a monetary union with rules to limit budget deficits. Germany was the main source of initiatives for these objectives, and they acquired an additional rationale as measures that would reduce Union vulnerabilities to adverse trends in the USA and to US pressures for accommodating shifts in European macroeconomic policies.

A widely recognized consequence of the import drawing effects of the US budget deficits was that these had motivated US pressures for fiscal expansion in Europe, which had been resisted, especially by Germany, already burdened by the costs of national reunification. In the German perspective, aversion to inflation was linked with a well established understanding that economic growth depended on broadly coordinated productive activity, and that this could not be aided by fiscal expansion in excess of the funding of necessary infrastructure development and administrative services, and in opposition to the preferences of managements in the national pattern of intercorporate cooperation. German policy level understanding was that the fragmented fiscal policy process in the USA, due to strong pluralism, was responsible for an expansionary orientation which would remain active even if trading partners made accommodating fiscal changes.[32]

Restraints on deficit financing by Union governments, under the Growth and Stability Pact of the European Monetary Union, have to be made effective through formal compliance, because, as noted regarding the dynamics of monetary policy, the German pattern of corporate cooperation and the smaller ones which have affinities with it do not constitute a sufficiently pervasive source of preferences aligned with the common interest. Outside that pattern there are pressures for fiscal expansion, based on expectations of growth, despite awareness that continued deficits and the accumulations of government debt have been hindering growth and obligating heavy taxation, while limiting the availability of financing for industry. Numerous references to the problems of maintaining fiscal discipline in the Union appear in assessments of the European Central Bank's performance, but their warnings about the dangers of expansionary pressures in member governments can be relativized in the dynamics of fragmented and conflicted fiscal decision making.[33]

The future of fiscal management under the agreed provisions of the European Monetary Union depends to a considerable extent on the evolution of the German intercorporate system and the effectiveness of political institutions that have been oriented toward consensual policymaking. A widening of the ideological gap between the two major political parties, the Christian Democrats and the Socialists, has been signalled by the latter's willingness to hold office with the support of radical environmentalists in the Green Party. The wider cleavage could cause strains in the pattern of intercorporate relations, while giving some impetus to more independent pursuits of opportunities in the rest of Europe and in the USA by German firms that have limited confidence in the Union's prospects and those of their own country. Strains in the national system of alliance capitalism, meanwhile, could restrict its capacity to expand through new alliances and partnerships in the rest of the Union. At the same time, German efforts to ensure the maintenance of fiscal discipline by less industrialized and highly indebted member states could cause problems in the Monetary Union.[34] Fiscal expansion by such states would not be expected to overcome their economic difficulties, and German reluctance to support Union level financing of their industrial development would probably be more evident if there were increased strains in the German pattern of entrepreneurial collaboration.

Japan's fiscal policy has long been affected by a division between domestically oriented corporate and political groups and those focused on export development, with foreign production. The division has been made more serious by the Liberal Democratic Party's internal conflicts, and, more recently, by strains resulting from the financial crisis which began in the 1990s. This crisis has raised extremely difficult issues regarding the use of government funds to rescue very heavily debt burdened banks, and the potential for increasing large budget deficits to finance recovery through domestically based growth. The outward oriented firms have in effect made the intercorporate cleavage quite significant by building international production systems on a much larger scale, and more profitably, than German enterprises, while causing considerable deindustrialization in the home economy.[35] The recession in that economy, however, has weakened the Japanese competitive challenge to the USA, while the US recession has caused difficulties for the transnational enterprises presenting that challenge.

Dangerous irrational speculation in Japan's financial sector has had some similarities with that which prolonged the USA's speculative boom in the 1990s. In Japan the relational pattern of intercorporate cooperation, weakened by the divergence of interests between domestically oriented and outward oriented firms, did not activate a drive for effective policy level responses, and political leadership of the kind made possible in the German system was lacking. In the USA, intensely competitive intercorporate relations prevented the emergence of a consensus to dampen the unsustainable speculation and, as in Japan, this ended with a collapse of investor confidence. US financial enterprises, however, were much better placed than their Japanese rivals to exploit opportunities in world financial markets.

MACROECONOMIC POLICIES AND INTERNATIONAL FINANCE

The significance of patterns of corporate competitive and cooperative activity for monetary and fiscal policies can be changed with the diverse effects of investment flows, and these can present challenges for macroeconomic management. Incoming direct investment, contributing to increased growth and employment, can increase revenue for infrastructure financing and basic administrative services, but with some opposite effects through the displacement of national firms. Outward direct investment may entail some deindustrialization, and dangers of this may obligate higher spending for infrastructure development and the provision of a more attractive business environment, with reduction of taxation, at the cost of increased deficit financing. Portfolio flows, acutely sensitive to rent seeking opportunities, moving in response to national and foreign prospects for asset appreciation or decline, can present more difficult challenges, and can require faster adaptations.

Altogether, the shifting costs and benefits of deepening integration, with its internationalization of market efficiencies and failures, and of government efficiencies and failures, set requirements for high degrees of integration in industrialized states, to ensure effective adaptation. The commonly recognized imperatives, however, are to enhance structural competitiveness, with applications of internalization logic in industry groups and in relational forms of corporate cooperation on a wider scale. Yet with the growth of complex interdependencies in deepening integration, there are also manifest obligations to engage in comprehensive cooperation with foreign governments *and firms* for effective management of those interdependencies, as is argued in the final chapter of this volume.

The requirements for integrative cooperation in national political economies become more demanding as complex structural interdependencies increase, and as financial sector linkages expand. Forms of alliance capitalism become increasingly significant in this context for the management of monetary and fiscal policies, and for spontaneous coordinated corporate responsiveness, through entrepreneurial activities and through inputs into decision making at the macroeconomic level. Deepening integration in the world economy has to be matched by the formation of highly integrated national political economies that reverse the losses of economic sovereignty to transnational enterprises building international production systems, and to international financial institutions that independently channel funds across borders. Market forces, in deepening integration, do not activate adaptations at the policy and corporate levels that overcome problems of market failure and government failure.

The challenges for national political economies to achieve greater internal integration, for management of the structural linkages in globalization, are individual in the sense that, in the absence of integrative cooperation by other major structurally linked partners, a country must strive to build a system of domestic collaboration that will cope with the competitive activities of foreign firms and governments that may not be motivated to cooperate. This has to be said in a context in which there is little basis for optimism about prospects for full international competition policy cooperation, and in which judgemental differences and subjective preferences in attempts at such cooperation lead rather to bargained outcomes, as in relations between the European Union and the USA.[36]

Technology advances do increase production interdependencies between firms, adding to their incentives to develop relational assets, and to seek security as well as synergies in entrepreneurial complementarities. The intense competition for global market shares, however, results in very strong concentration trends, which understandably appear to have been increasing during the US recession. Processes of technology based collaboration between enterprises thus tend to be replaced by mergers and acquisitions, instead of continuing in line with the benefits of agreed specializations: in particular, partners under stress tend to be viewed as targets for acquisition strategies. Understanding this, however, should not hinder awareness that the development of complementary specializations, on a relational basis, accords with public goods imperatives for internal integration in national political economies.

Relational intercorporate cooperation, inspired by country attachments and loyalties, is conducive to the internal integration needed in an industrialized state that is becoming more and more closely linked with other national economies through trade, direct investment, and financial flows. Imperatives for internal integration, it must be reiterated, become stronger as the vulnerabilities of structural interdependence become larger and more complex, and are exploited in virtually unregulated processes of international competition, which tend to become more severe as concentration trends continue. In the evolution of structural interdependencies, however, there are also imperatives for governments and firms to strive for the development of relational cooperation: an international public good to be provided for the global community, is what the Germans might call an international social market economy of harmonious entrepreneurial specializations, constituted by solidarity based national political economies.

Forms of alliance capitalism can thus be seen to have much significance for the implementation of microeconomic policies. These have the potential to guide and support the building of complementary production specializations, with relational synergies, in internally integrated political economies, with capacities for comprehensively productive interaction in structural interdependencies with other states. What may be achieved, through high principled and concerted efforts by policymakers and corporate managements, could sustain very constructive management of the macroeconomic policy interdependencies that have had to respond to the problems of globalization without adequate structural policy capabilities.

FUNDAMENTALS

Economic openness facilitates deepening integration, allowing firms to build international production systems for the service of numerous markets, with mainly very competitive specializations, while engaging in trade that is increasingly related to the international production. In this vast process, less competitive enterprises are displaced, and international market strengths become more oligarchical. The competition drives corporate efforts to maximize locational advantages, including those provided by the efficiencies or failures of host governments, acting often as rivals in investment bidding. Internationalized financial markets provide, in effect, priority funding for the more successful enterprises, but in these markets portfolio investment is drawn to areas of speculative asset appreciation.

Comparative studies of national political economies, responding to research on the costs and benefits of deepening integration – the emergence of what is tending to become a global business system – have to focus on macromanagement tasks in the uncertainties and strains of largely ungoverned international commerce. The spread of gains from this commerce is uneven, within and between countries, and is not simply a consequence of production efficiencies. The fortunes of firms producing high quality products and avoiding anti-competitive practices can be drastically affected by the predatory pricing and crude advertising of larger, less efficient rivals, as well as by the collapse of a speculative boom, or by the willingness of competitors to secure cost advantages through investment in countries under repressive regimes that tolerate the exploitation of labour. Further, a highly efficient firm avoiding anti-competitive practices may find that its operations have been severely affected by adverse shifts in exchange rates caused by speculative market manipulations. General awareness of all these problems often occasions observations that there are winners and losers in globalization.[37]

If market processes are internalized within alliances, networks, and industry groups through long term commitments, with obligations to respond in concert to external shocks, the participating firms can function with greater security, and greater capacities for adaptation to challenges in the international economy. The logic of internalization can then be given broad expression by combining industry groups, networks, and alliances in larger and more comprehensive associations. Openness to international trade and investment can then be more discriminating, and there can be substantial capacities for spontaneous coordinated structural adjustment to strains in external commerce.

Imperatives for internalization increase as trade and investment links with other states expand. With the growth of relational ties in a national political economy, however, large firms can be inclined to engage in excessive diversification, resulting in under-specialization. The expansion of trade and investment links externally can be a check on this excessive diversification, but it may persist in the relative security provided by the scale of internalization. Interlocking interests may well prevent restraint on the excessive diversification, unless there is technocratic guidance, in the public interest, to reverse trends toward under-specialization, and to allow scope for the emergence of new firms with innovative specializations.[38]

Associated with excessive diversification there can be a growth of oligopoly power. The main restraint on the exercising of this power in a relationally integrated political economy has to be a combination of spontaneous pressures for fair internal commerce and public spirited competition policy enforcement. In deepening integration, however, oligopoly power at home is not only challenged by, but can also become linked with international oligopoly power. The managements of transnational enterprises with such power, moreover, may well be unwilling to be drawn into relational bonds with national firms in the numerous host countries where they are operating. National firms moving into international production, meanwhile, may see relational ties at home as hindrances to their foreign operations, although in many respects these ties may augment capabilities for such operations.

For monetary and fiscal policy decision makers motivated by commitments to the domestic and international common good, the potential advantages of substantial relational intercorporate bonds for growth, employment, stability, and security against disruptive penetration will become more significant, on present indications. International concentration trends are continuing, and are especially prominent in the cross border expansions of other forms of market failure, including the employment losses associated with multinational changes in the exploitation of location advantages: orderly development of domestic and external sectoral and intrasectoral interdependencies is hindered. Vulnerabilities to shocks resulting from competitive production activities, moreover, are all the more serious because of vulnerabilities to shocks caused by high volume speculation in financial markets. With the latter vulnerabilities, it must be reiterated, there is investment diversion into very profitable and virtually tax free rent seeking that limits the funding of productive activity.

The dominant macroeconomic policy concern, in Europe and the USA, has to be the probability that the costs of deepening integration – the overall effects of the changing balance of internationalized market efficiencies and failures – will fail to evoke sufficient spontaneous corporate cooperation in line with the clear structural imperatives for building more integrated national political economies, and for reform in international financial markets to correct their misallocations of investment. In the absence of substantially constructive corporate responses, which may appear to be less and less likely as deepening integration goes further, fiscal and monetary policy tasks must be expected to become more difficult. Meanwhile, microeconomic policy problems may well become intractable.

The rationale for government and corporate initiatives to promote the development of more integrated national political economies, through relational cooperation oriented toward the multiplication of complementary production specializations, thus deserves great emphasis. In prospect would be the development of more harmonious structural interdependencies, principally through the effects in macromanagement interactions between governments. These, with inputs from the integrated patterns of mainly domestic economic activity, could be expected to aid forms of integrative policy coordination through deliberative exchanges that would have some affinities with the open method of policy harmonization that has developed within the European Union.[39] At the basis of this collegial rationale would be the processes of entrepreneurial discovery facilitated by technocratic sponsorship of corporate conferences devoted to the exploration of potential corporate complementarities indicated by ongoing advances in frontier technology.

The expanding configuration of internationalized market failures is the basic challenge confronting policymakers and managements. The increasing dimensions of cross border oligopoly power are prominent in this challenge; associated with it are the externalities of employment losses and sectoral disruptions resulting from shifts in location choices; also associated with it are informational failures, incidental to the concentration trends. Further, there are the ominous failures in world financial markets, due especially to the exploitation of volatility, with risks and costs for real economies.

NOTES

1. For a doctrine of hard competition to guide economic policy see Ralph E. Gomory and William J. Baumol *Global Trade and Conflicting National Interests*, Cambridge, MIT Press, 2000.
2. See *International Capital Markets: Developments, Prospects, and Key Policy Issues*, Washington DC, International Monetary Fund, August 2001, and Wendy Dobson and Gary Clyde Hufbauer *World Capital Markets*, Washington DC, Institute for International Economics, 2001.
3. See Peter A. Hall and David Soskice (eds) *Varieties of Capitalism: Institutional Foundations of Comparative Advantage*, Oxford, Oxford University Press, 2001.
4. See Stephen S. Cohen and Gavin Boyd (eds) *Corporate Governance and Globalization*, Cheltenham, Edward Elgar, 2000.
5. See Hall and Soskice, cited, and Mark Casson *Entrepreneurship and Business Culture*, Cheltenham, Edward Elgar, 1995, chs 7 and 8.

6. See Nicolai Foss and Volker Mahnke (eds) *Competence, Governance, and Entrepreneurship*, Oxford, Oxford University Press, 2000, part C, and Sheila C. Dow and Peter E. Earl (eds) *Contingency, Complexity and the Theory of the Firm*, Cheltenham, Edward Elgar, 1999.
7. See surveys in *World Investment Report 1999* and *World Investment Report 2000* Geneva, United Nations Commission on Trade and Development.
8. *Ibid.*
9. See projections for the USA in *International Capital Markets*, cited.
10. Unwarranted investor optimism has been a factor in the 2001 decline: see Barry Riley 'The Troubles with Technical Trends', *Financial Times*, 5 October 2001.
11. On the difficulties of developing international competition policy cooperation see *The World Economy*, 21, 8, November 1998 – symposium on competition policy.
12. See references to asset repricing in *International Capital Markets*, cited.
13. On the macroeconomic significance of coordinated production systems see Hall and Soskice, cited.
14. See discussions in Torben Iversen, Jonas Pontusson and David Soskice (eds) *Unions, Employers, and Central Banks*, Cambridge, Cambridge University Press, 2000.
15. The availability of credit for speculation is a critical factor. See symposium on financial instability in *Oxford Review of Economic Policy*, 15, 3, Autumn 1999.
16. *Ibid.*
17. This observation refers to the building of international production systems by US manufacturing firms and the global operations of US financial enterprises. On the former see *World Investment Report 2000*, cited.
18. See references to Germany in *Unions, Employers, and Central Banks*, cited, and symposium on labour markets in *Oxford Review of Economic Policy* 16, 1, Winter 2000.
19. See references to German industries in David C. Mowery and Richard R. Nelson (eds) *Sources of Industrial Leadership*, Cambridge, Cambridge University Press, 1999.
20. See references to French labour market problems in symposium on labour markets, cited, and Andrew Hughes Hallet, Peter Mooslechner and Martin Schuerz (eds) *Challenges for Economic Policy Coordination within the European Monetary Union*, Dordrecht, Kluwer Academic Publishers, 2001.
21. On the US corporate presence in Europe see references in Thomas L. Brewer and Gavin Boyd (eds) *Globalizing America*, Cheltenham, Edward Elgar, 2000.
22. For a review of Japan's problems see Magnus Blomstrom, Byron Gangnes and Sumner La Croix (eds) *Japan's New Economy*, Oxford, Oxford University Press, 2001.
23. See comments in *71st Annual Report*, Bank of International Settlements, Basel, 11 June 2001.
24. See Norman J. Ornstein and Thomas E. Mann (eds) *The Permanent Campaign and its Future*, Washington DC, American Enterprise Institute and Brookings Institution, 2000.
25. This observation builds on the contrasts noted in Hall and Soskice, cited.
26. See reviews of fiscal policies in James M. Poterba and Jurgen von Hagen (eds) *Fiscal Institutions and Fiscal Performance*, Chicago, University of Chicago Press, 1999.
27. See review of US monetary policy in C. Randall Henning *Currencies and Politics in the United States, Germany, and Japan*, Washington DC, Institute for International Economics, 1994, ch 6.
28. On the outflows of investment from Japan see F. Gerard Adams and Byron Gangnes 'Will Japan's Current Account Turn to Deficit?', in *Japan's New Economy*, cited, ch 3.
29. For an assessment of Japan's economic difficulties see *ibid.*
30. See indications of the Clinton administration's concerns about globalization issues in Julie Soloway and Andrey Anishchenko, 'Agenda Setting for a Millennium Round: Challenges and Opportunities', in Alan M. Rugman and Gavin Boyd (eds) *The World Trade Organization in the New Global Economy*, Cheltenham, Edward Elgar, 2001, ch 3.
31. See comments on increases in mergers and acquisitions in Joseph Quinlan 'No Stopping the Global M&A Train', *Financial Times*, 12 November 2001.
32. On the recent history of the German view see Henning, cited.

33. See symposium on EMU, in *The World Economy*, 24, 10, November 2001, and *Challenges for Economic Policy Coordination within the European Monetary Union*, cited.
34. *Ibid.*
35. See *International Capital Markets, Developments, Prospects, and Key Policy Issues*, cited.
36. See Youri Devuyst 'Transatlantic Competition Relations', in Mark A. Pollack and Gregory C. Shaffer (eds) *Transatlantic Governance in the Global Economy*, Lanham, Rowman and Littlefield, 2001, ch 5.
37. A further problem is that the collapse of a large diversified international firm under irresponsible management can have extensive repercussions, as was evident after the collapse of the US energy trader Enron. See 'Days Enron Shook the World', *Financial Times*, 24 December 2001.
38. German policy has sought to promote the development of such specializations. See Mark Lehrer 'Has Germany finally fixed its high-tech problem? The recent boom in German technology-based entrepreneurship', *California Management Review*, 42, 4, Summer 2000, 89–107.
39. See Dermot Hodson and Imelda Maher 'The open method as a new mode of governance: the case of soft economic policy co-ordination', *Journal of Common Market Studies*, 39, 4, November 2001, 719–46.

3. Alliance capitalism and microeconomic policies

Gavin Boyd and Paul A. Brenton

As industrialized political economies become more knowledge based, through advances in applied technology and the development of complex coordination systems, the nature and patterns of corporate cooperation and rivalry become increasingly significant for the management of microeconomic policies. The tasks of these policies become all the more demanding because the transitions to more knowledge based systems occur with increases in structural interdependence between economies, due to the evolution of often asymmetric production and financial linkages, resulting from increased trade and the operations of transnational enterprises. Nevertheless, underlying economic, social and political systems differ widely even across OECD countries. In this chapter we discuss how such differences may condition the responses of firms and governments to these increasing interdependences, and the nature of alliances between corporations and between corporations and governments that emerge, highlighting the main challenges that currently face policymakers in the US, Europe and Japan.

The common microeconomic objectives are to support, regulate, and guide corporate financing, production and marketing activities, so as to promote balanced growth, with emphasis on enhancing structural competitiveness. In the modern environment, what can be achieved depends very much on the degrees to which home country enterprises, through their cooperative and competitive activities, are able to form dynamic, orderly, and adaptive economic systems, and are oriented toward cooperation with home government policies. Increasingly, however, with the multiplication of international production activities and investment flows, the collaboration of foreign enterprises becomes necessary.

Spontaneous dynamic order in a national economy resulting from corporate cooperation in alliances, networks, and industry groups can be a source of functional inputs into microeconomic policies, and can lighten their tasks, while facilitating adaptation to substantial inflows of foreign direct investment. Without such solidarity based order, a national economy can be seriously disadvantaged in deepening integration: there can be difficult adjustment problems because of uncoordinated relocations of production processes, and other disruptions of sectoral linkages that follow from merger activity and increases in concentration. On a larger scale the internationalization of market failures, as well as efficiencies, can present major challenges. Further, a government's entire policy mix, which can be coherent and functional because of constructive inputs from a broad pattern of corporate cooperation, can be seriously dysfunctional if sufficient constructive inputs are not forthcoming from such a collaborative pattern.

National economic policies are guided in varying degrees by beliefs in the efficiency effects of competition and the associated views on the need for cooperation both between and within the main groups of economic actors: firms, trade unions, and government officials. Policy level recognition of the national and international benefits of competition, however, is typically qualified by mercantilist concerns with the use of state power to enhance relative gains from involvement in the world economy: priority is thus given to trade policy activism and structural policy initiatives. Corporate managements, meanwhile, while affirming the efficiency effects of competition, tend to be motivated primarily by the view that competition generally results in excess capacity and lower profits. Acquisitions and mergers are thus seen as ways of increasing efficiencies, through higher organizational performance and the elimination of excess capacity, while responding to shareholder pressures for higher profits. Alliances and involvement in networks and industry groups can be viewed as means of opening up opportunities for mergers and acquisitions, but there can be enduring relational ties that can sustain such forms of cooperation over long periods. Such ties have been facilitated by technological progress that has undermined vertically integrated structures and stimulated the outsourcing of specific parts of the production process, including the use of processing facilities abroad.[1] In the modern technological age the nature of alliances can play a crucial role in the setting of regulatory standards that, in turn, frame the environment in which innovation and competition take place.[2]

Microeconomic policy management can be challenged by the weakening of home country attachments and loyalties in national firms; by decreases in cooperation between such firms; by extensive shifts of production to foreign locations by those firms; by foreign mergers with and acquisitions of national enterprises; by corporate diversions of resources into speculative rather than productive operations; by the speculative bidding up of stock prices to unsustainable levels; and by functional conflicts within the policy mix. The various dangers will be less serious if there is a well established pattern of solidarity based corporate cooperation. This, however, can be weakened as more instrumental rather than relational cross-border linkages develop in deepening integration: involvement in international technology based alliances becomes necessary, elements of foreign business cultures are absorbed through mergers and acquisitions, and management teams tend to become more multicultural.

The primary challenges for microeconomic policies, as deepening integration continues, are structural and financial. A national economic structure can become increasingly exposed to sectoral disruptions as multinational firms building international production systems shift the locations of production processes while expanding through mergers and acquisitions and driving weaker enterprises into decline. The multinational firms gaining prominence in global concentration trends acquire greater freedom to spread their operations, so as to rationalize them on a world scale.[3] Meanwhile, with the internationalization of financial markets, investments tend to flow to the more prominent multinational firms and the more rapidly growing countries. At the same time the scope for speculation-led stock increases becomes wider, and the asset appreciations tend to become unsustainable. With this problem, which has been evident in the USA's 2001 recession, rent-seeking attractions in financial markets tend to divert funds away from productive use. Moreover, managements in manufacturing and non-financial service firms can be drawn toward risky and highly leveraged speculative ventures, as was illustrated by the failure of the US energy firm Enron in late 2001.[4]

COMPARATIVE ECONOMIC SYSTEMS

Capacities to manage microeconomic policies depend on levels of political development and the nature of institutions, which define how economic actors interact. As industrialized states become more knowledge based there are increasing requirements for orderly performance of macromanagement functions, in a spirit of solidarity focused on the common good. Broadly consensual systems of collegial politics are necessary, rather than adversarial bargaining and the trading of political favours at the expense of the public interest. These requirements cannot be met if political activity is undertaken solely to further individual economic ambitions, with all the opportunism and moral hazards visible in a low trust society. The moral qualities that are needed at policy levels can be matched at corporate levels, and can result in collegial entrepreneurship, with rivalries subordinated to solidarity based cooperation: dynamic and balanced growth can then enable technocratic functions to focus on facilitating further corporate achievements.

Basic contrasts are evident between political economies with cultures and institutions oriented toward trustful relational social cooperation, and those oriented toward intensely competitive activity. The latter type may exhibit higher entrepreneurial vigour, but there can be coordination problems and an emphasis on short-term corporate decision-making, tendencies toward speculative asset appreciation, and adversarial political processes. Weaker entrepreneurial energy may be evident in the more integrated political economy, but with more pervasive coordination functions, more investment in productive rather than rent-seeking operations, and substantially consensual policy making. With these features, moreover, there is likely to be significant spontaneous corporate restraint on concentration trends; considerable corporate stability, associated with stakeholder systems of corporate governance; and orderly adaptation to shifts of production processes to foreign locations. Innovation will tend to be focused on incremental improvements to existing processes and products. In the less integrated political economy, concentration trends will understandably be more active, innovation will focus mainly on the development of new processes and products, with consequent implications for productivity growth, enterprises will tend to lack stable identities, and externalities associated with relocations of production will tend to be disruptive.[5]

The intensely competitive US political economy operates with little institutional support for non-market mechanisms of coordination, with a dependence on market driven relationships.[6] Coordination problems can arise because aggressively individualistic entrepreneurial and political activity prevents the development of institutions that could provide adequate guidance functions in the common interest, and allows little scope for the evolution of a structural policy.[7] Microeconomic policy management tends to be reliant on trade measures, antitrust enforcement, and financial sector regulation. Trade policy interventions are significantly responsive to protectionist pressures from producer groups affected by levels of import penetration attributable mainly to domestic demand in excess of output and to currency appreciation, with the recent imposition of tariffs on imports of steel being a pertinent reminder of these pressures in the US. Antitrust enforcement has exhibited a liberal trend, reflecting in part the importance of funding for political campaigns by large corporations, and has in effect caused firms to engage in tacit cooperation, since litigation has to be based on explicit agreements.[8] Financial sector regulation is difficult because the political influence of the financial community is used to assert much autonomy, citing the competitive advantages of offering an environment more attractive than foreign financial sectors.

Strong propensities to speculative trading in financial assets distinguish the US political economy, especially because irrational investor optimism causes unsustainable asset appreciation, leading to recessions in which growth financed by that appreciation is eliminated, while monetary loosening to finance recovery has limited effects because of continuing diversions of investment into speculation.[9] The speculative propensity is active in concentration trends, contributing to the motivations behind mergers and acquisitions, and these trends are in effect given impetus by the restraints of competition policy on explicit intercorporate cooperation. In external relations the speculative propensity presents a very serious challenge to other industrialized states: their increasing structural interdependencies with the USA entail rising vulnerabilities to its economic downturns.

The US political economy is also distinguished by the orientation of its manufacturing firms toward the use of foreign production locations. This orientation is attributable to strong entrepreneurial compulsions, the availability of resources based on strong positions in the home economy, the higher profitability of foreign operations, the tax advantages associated with such operations, the benefits of spreading risks on a global scale, and the increasing international competition for world market shares. The outward direct investment is undertaken very independently by US firms, as the dynamics of their political economy tend to prevent the development of a structural policy. Hence there are dangers of deindustrialization, and of imbalances in external economic relations.[10] For other industrialized states, meanwhile, there are prospects of losing structural competitiveness in the course of global concentration trends that evidence the effects of the outward US direct investment.

Japan's comparative significance in the world economy has declined because of the severity and duration of its financial crisis: as a coordinated national production system Japanese alliance capitalism has lost status; its previously demonstrated efficiencies, however, had validated the logic of relational intercorporate cooperation, despite the acute deficiencies of its financial sector, and the failures of its political system to provide leadership for effective macromanagement. The pattern of relational cooperation has weakened because of general losses of confidence and because successful outward oriented firms have strong incentives to concentrate on strengthening their own positions in world markets while expanding their foreign production activities.[11] Established microeconomic policies that have enhanced structural competitiveness have become less effective because the development of international production systems has been proceeding with less regard for growth and adjustment problems in the domestic economy.

In Europe, Germany's system is characterized by relationally coordinated production, although it has been somewhat less integrated than Japan's. To protect the national system of relationally coordinated economic activity, the administration is using competition policy measures to prevent foreign takeovers of German firms, and has thus been opposing European Commission efforts to liberalize Union markets for corporate control – efforts that have also been opposed by a majority of the European Parliament. The collegial pattern of German capitalism facilitates the implementation of microeconomic policy measures, especially structural policies designed to enhance overall competitiveness.[12]

The pervasive relational cooperation ensures stability in the German system, but with technological lags for radical innovations and therefore somewhat slower growth, reflecting the relatively conservative influence of banks as major providers of finance; of unions, under co-determination arrangements; and of large concentrations of share holdings. Heavy taxation, moreover, contributes to the slack growth – tax levels were driven up by high unemployment and the costs of rehabilitating the East German economy. Much of the high unemployment has been in that Eastern economy, but a considerable part of it can be attributed to slack growth in the rest of the European Union.[13]

Corporate solidarity in Germany sustains an emphasis on production at home for export. Outward direct investment is at moderate levels, but is increasing in response to opportunities in the Union and in East European states seeking membership, as well as to opportunities in the USA, mainly in medium technology sectors. This expansion into international production has quite limited prospects because of the strong positions of US firms in Europe and the rest of the world, and because excessive diversification by large German firms has tended to prevent concentration on their core capabilities.

For the European Union, which comprises a range of countries with varying degrees of liberal and coordinated mechanisms, a basic trade and structural policy challenge has been to provide a climate in Europe that will enable Union firms to achieve higher efficiencies while serving their single market, so as to ensure more equal structural interdependence with the USA. A common trade policy is implemented, but a common structural policy is not yet possible, mainly because each national administration still seeks to manage independent structural measures.[14] This highlights the difficulties of deep integration between national economies with divergent political and social structures in which coordination within national economies is undertaken with varying degrees of reliance on market mechanisms. Indeed it is becoming apparent that there are limitations on the degree of market integration in Europe.[15] To date the emphasis at the EU level has primarily been on stimulating R&D and, at various times, on encouraging mergers to achieve a competitive size to provide for effective competition with US firms. Nevertheless, alliance capitalism on a Union scale is not in prospect. Germany, accordingly, has to implement structural measures that must remain largely self-reliant and which can therefore reflect the needs and nature of the German economic and political system.

CONVERGENCE AND DIVERGENCE

National systems of corporate competition and cooperation are under pressure to adapt to the intensifying rivalries for world market shares. Institutional factors and management cultures are tending to sustain established patterns of corporate competition and cooperation, but the most notable forms of collaborative capitalism – the German and the Japanese systems – are having to respond to increased global rivalry. The American system, with its greater emphasis on competition, is under much less external pressure to change. The US firms that are becoming more dominant in global concentration trends are becoming more capable of expansion through mergers and acquisitions, as well as being better positioned to develop alliances in preparation for such expansion, and to establish satellite partnering arrangements with suppliers and distributors.

Microeconomic policies are also under pressure to adapt to the global corporate rivalry, through increased emphasis on productive interaction with national and foreign firms, and through reciprocally functional linkages with macroeconomic policies. The pressures for adaptation are severe in the European Union and Japan, and are recognized within established perspectives on governmental economic functions, but with frustrations because of deficiencies in corporate capabilities. The information revolution has undermined the typical sectorally based approach of industrial policy in these countries.

In the USA the perceived pressures are considered challenges for trade policy, rather than structural policy, but the traditionally liberal orientation of macromanagement is considered to be challenged by the problem of excess capacity and weak competitiveness in the steel sector. The liberal policy orientation, moreover, continues to ensure that the strong speculative propensities in the financial sector are given only limited recognition as regulatory issues.[16]

The fragmentation of corporate associations in the USA, the low degrees of trust caused by aggressive individualism, and the influence of the liberal policy tradition, tend to perpetuate the focus of individual managements on their increasing opportunities in the world economy, especially while the prospects for the home economy are very uncertain and the international competition from European and Japanese firms remains weak. Interactions in the fragmented pattern of business interests do not generate active broad concerns to promote intercorporate cooperation at home.[17] While recovery remains uncertain, moreover, managements have to reckon with the probability of sectoral disruptions caused by corporate failures.

Europe, however, has presented a structural challenge as intercorporate and microeconomic policy initiatives have made the Airbus consortium internationally competitive: high technology corporate cooperation has been encouraged and supported by significant government intervention. This very significant example of alliance capitalism has contributed to much diffusion of advanced technology, and has opened the way for corporate and policy level efforts to build a collaborative semiconductor sector.[18] The structural challenge of rationalizing the Union automobile sectors demands more resolute corporate and policy endeavours, but in this area the Union's external challenges, although potent, have not evoked collaborative responses: the automobile sectors remain very significant in the domestic economies of Germany, France and Italy.

Change in the Union patterns of corporate competition and cooperation is developing with shifts to equity financing, an increasingly active market for corporate control, and growing numbers of cross-border mergers and acquisitions. There is intensifying competition between the larger firms that are being formed, and expansion by US firms in Europe is contributing to this rivalry. The German pattern of corporate solidarity is being extended in this process, through individual ventures, and may be weakened through adjustment to collaborative arrangements with other European firms, despite the advantages of generally larger resources, superior technological capabilities, and more efficient administration.

Microeconomic policy change in the Union is occurring to a considerable extent in response to issues of competition regulation, in which member governments interact with the European Commission. The Commission's concern is to facilitate the emergence of strong but not dominant Union firms, and this often results in conflict with member governments supporting expansion by their firms while opposing expansion into their economies by enterprises based in other member states. Competition policy issues are complicated by the involvement of US enterprises in European mergers and acquisitions, often as preferred partners because of superior resources.[19]

Member governments seek to respond individually to the microeconomic policy problems resulting from the pressures of international competition. The logic of evolving a common structural policy is not perceived, and may well be resisted more actively as the Union enlarges. National variations are affirmed in the political processes shaping microeconomic policies, and in these processes informal ties between administrations and national firms tend to be maintained. Cross-border links between corporate associations have developed, for collective representations of interests to the European Commission, but cross-border affiliations between political parties are not developing.[20]

The formation of cross-border connections between corporate associations has been conducive to increased collaboration between EU firms across their borders, but the main effect of market integration has been to increase intra-Union mergers and acquisitions.[21] Meanwhile European firms have sought technology based ties mainly with US enterprises, because of their higher levels of advancement and stronger positions in world markets. The development of these Atlantic technology links is one factor which may be tending to limit European corporate interest in the potential for introducing a common structural policy. Technology enhancement projects sponsored by the European Commission have been on a modest scale that has not been seen to illustrate the feasibility of a Union structural policy, and do not appear to have altered the preferences of European firms for partnerships with US enterprises.

The lack of a common approach to deal with structural policy challenges affects the Union's capacity to deal with problems of external energy dependence. External energy dependence has to be managed with an emphasis on supply of the Union's still fragmented electricity industry, which the European Commission is endeavouring to integrate on a basis of regional liberalization. Pricing issues complicate and hinder cross-border supply within the Union, and in this area of microeconomic policy the manifest need for common management is difficult to meet because of the competing interests of industrial groups linked informally with their national administrations. There are opportunities for cross-border corporate collaboration, but, as in other industrial sectors, the main trend is a development of cross-border mergers and acquisitions. In this industry, functional requirements for very close coordination in generation and supply can be seen to pose imperatives for active corporate cooperation and collaborative regulatory management by member governments; governments supporting and opposing cross-border mergers and acquisitions, however, tend to limit prospects for the regulatory collaboration that would be needed in an integrated liberalized electricity sector.[22]

For the USA, external energy dependence is a more manageable area of microeconomic policy, yet is difficult because of the strongly competitive rather than cooperative corporate orientations in this and other US sectors. The electricity sector has been vulnerable to deficiencies in corporate cooperation affecting external energy dependence, and to regulatory failures – notably in California during the late 1990s. In that experience there was extraordinary regulatory incompetence, and there was no strong system of corporate collaboration extending across the state's industries that could exert sufficient pressure for regulatory reform.[23]

TECHNOCRATIC FUNCTIONS

External and domestic challenges affecting intercorporate systems and the management of microeconomic policies raise questions about technocratic capabilities and commitments. These relate especially to issues of structural interdependence, which, for knowledge based economies losing elements of economic sovereignty to transnational enterprises, require the services of highly dedicated experts. The economic openness of knowledge based political economies, allowing wide scope for cross-border entrepreneurship and, thus, for the internationalization of market failures as well as efficiencies, with imbalances in national gains from world commerce, necessitates knowledge intensive macromanagement tasks. These have to perform structural and regulatory functions in continuous solidarity building exchanges of tacit and codified knowledge with corporate managements. A principal service has to be the provision of assessments of trends in structural interdependence that can facilitate managerial identification of opportunities for entrepreneurial complementarities that can be taken up with relational collaboration.

Extensive relational intercorporate cooperation is necessary in a knowledge based political economy with high levels of structural interdependence. This cooperation has to develop in order to cope with the vulnerabilities and enhance the benefits of interdependence; it can develop autonomously, depending principally on cultural and institutional factors, but it has to be complemented and aided by technocratic consultative services, performed in the common interest, on the basis of developmental concerns broader than those of private consulting firms. Beliefs in the efficiencies and structural optimizing effects of free market forces can prevent recognition of the imperative for technocratic functions, but it must be reiterated that the concentration trends which develop with the operation of free market forces increasingly restrict the scope for such forces. Regulatory responsibilities thus have to be recognized, but these are ineffective against tacit collusion, and this can be overcome through a solidarity based management culture, promoted from the policy level as well as cultivated by corporate associations.[24] More fundamentally, it has to be understood that the scope for entrepreneurial initiatives, as frontier technology advances continue, depends on discoveries of potential complementarities, since firms are becoming more interdependent in the development of their production capabilities; such discoveries will not be sufficiently aided if technocratic responsibilities are restricted to regulatory functions.

Technology enhancement projects initiated by governments have been considered vital for the structural competitiveness of knowledge based economies, and have been assessed mainly with reference to degrees of leadership in home and international markets gained or lost by assisted firms. Major projects in the USA, Japan, and Europe across several high technology sectors are considered to have had mixed results.[25] In question have been degrees of technocratic competence, the degrees to which selections and funding have been politicized, and the durability of the sponsored projects, which can be affected by legislative switching to other ventures, notably in the USA. The significance of balances between competition and cooperation in intercorporate systems has been rather neglected. Because of the widening range of advances in frontier research, however, collaborative explorations of the potential for complementary entrepreneurship have become more necessary in the common interest. International corporate cooperation in research and development is expanding, but in a pattern which is shaped by differences in national balances of intercorporate cooperation and competition, and by the effects of concentration trends. These can push highly specialized firms with small or medium market positions into satellite operations, while making them more vulnerable to takeovers.

The technological leads of US sectors over those in Europe and, more recently, over Japanese industries, have drawn attention to the significance of individualistic entrepreneurial dynamism for structural competitiveness – and as a factor that may more than offset deficiencies in officially sponsored technology enhancement projects.[26] Observations about the costs of an adverse balance between cooperation and competition however have not been invalidated.

Infrastructure sectors, where public goods imperatives are especially evident, have to be served by structural and regulatory policies that depend on corporate cooperation, and cooperation between firms. These policies can be outcomes of awkward political compromises, and the consequences can be all the more serious if the sectors have been liberalized in ways that in effect allow managements to engage in risky expansion, as has been apparent in the bankruptcy of the US energy firm Enron.[27]

A rationale for private competitive provision of infrastructure network services has been widely accepted in the USA and Europe, because of claims of superior efficiencies. Regulatory authorities, however, tend to be established and staffed through the trading of political favours, and in the USA especially can be made somewhat dysfunctional by institutional conflicts; further, even if performed efficiently, regulatory functions may fail to develop with cross-sectoral cooperation. The development and coordination of the sectors has to be a structural policy responsibility, but engagement with this can be difficult if the policy level's commitments to regulated private operations is based on expectations of market driven collaboration within and between sectors. Unified administrative management of the energy, electricity, communications, transport and retailing sectors could facilitate the development of coherent structural policies; in its absence, however, separate sectoral regulatory operations are likely to evolve with politicized orientations at variance with requirements for coordination.

Coordinated development of utilities and services is a public good. If these sectors remain liberalized the imperatives for coordination will become more urgent as structural interdependencies multiply. Technocratic efforts to promote such coordination, moreover, will have to be aided by extensive corporate cooperation across these sectors and in the manufacturing industries which they serve: pervasive collegial capitalism could help solve the coordination problem. The imperative to develop such capitalism, in support of technocratic functions devoted to the public interest, can be seen in critical reviews of the recent history of liberalized utilities and services.[28]

Infrastructure network industries, utilities, and communication and transportation services under private control operate with emphasis on short-term profits, under regulatory pressures to limit price increases, and to seek opportunities for horizontal expansion, within and across borders, with financing from securities sectors that may be supplemented by diverse forms of government funding. The cross-border expansion tends to set up quite vital structural interdependencies which cannot be managed from the policy level without interventions, but the necessary political will may not develop until there is a crisis. Incentives to engage in domestic and cross-border horizontal expansion are generally stronger than those to extend into other infrastructure network sectors, where different regulatory structures function and very different technologies have to be managed. Horizontal expansion, however, does provide resources that can be used for diversification outside the original range of regulatory supervision, as was evident in the Enron case.

The promotion of efficient infrastructure network sector integration, in the common interest, is a basic technocratic responsibility, and requires assessments of the emerging needs of manufacturing industries. For such assessments, information flows about corporate operations and planning are essential and, if there is extensive concerting of entrepreneurial ventures, technocratic efforts to promote the necessary integration of network industries can be assisted. In Europe this is not happening, and the costs of failure are accumulating: a common structural policy for the network sectors is not being adopted, a Union level regulatory authority has not been set up, and member governments are unwilling to collaborate with each other and with the European Commission for the development of a common regulatory mechanism.[29] In the USA a federal level regulatory structure operates, but a structural policy is not evolving, it must be stressed, because of the divisive effects of intense pluralism and the influence of liberal concepts of state economic responsibilities; these, moreover, affect the quality of the regulatory functions, which tend to be politicized.[30]

Manufacturing industries have to develop with supportive technocratic functions related to the coordination of their sectors and to the general requirements for coordinated support from the infrastructure network industries. Coordinated manufacturing development requires management of the production interdependencies between firms and, more fundamentally, the linking of complementarities in their entrepreneurial planning. Here, it must be reiterated, vital technocratic functions are to facilitate and contribute to the exploration of opportunities for entrepreneurial complementarities, especially in response to advances in frontier research. For the necessary consultative interaction, solidarity based management cultures have to develop, in conjunction with solidarity based political cultures.

Competition policies cannot be refined to degrees that could compensate for inadequate corporate commitments to cooperation and for political deficiencies affecting technocratic functions. Competition policy enforcement, it must be reiterated, is ineffective against tacit collusion. The fundamental solution for competition policy problems has to be the development of a collegial management culture. Technocratic authorities can contribute to this while facilitating corporate explorations of opportunities for complementary entrepreneurship. The development of a collegial management culture, meanwhile, can contribute to technocratic learning and dedication to the public interest.

Studies of entrepreneurship in knowledge based political economies have focused on the management of tangible and intangible assets for competitive advantage. This orientation has influenced policy level and managerial perspectives, while little attention has been given to the significance of differing balances between corporate competition and cooperation for the resolution of market failures and the development of systemic efficiencies.[31] The increasing technology based production interdependencies between firms, however, indicate clear requirements for intensive interactions to discern new opportunities for productive development of existing and anticipated operational interdependencies, as more advanced forms of applied technology become feasible. Emphasis on this functional logic, then, obligates recognition of the need for management cultures oriented toward very active corporate cooperation, for entrepreneurial complementarities with soft rather than hard competition.

The public good to be seen in the context of widening and increasingly complex corporate technology based interdependencies can evoke recognition of the growing importance of technocratic involvement in the consultative quests for entrepreneurial complementarities. Individual managements will find it more and more difficult to assess the productive potential of new frontier technologies as these multiply across sectors: broad supportive technocratic expertise must be expected to become more necessary; that is, contributing to and absorbing collegial management cultures.

The technocratic functions, it should be clear, do not have to be performed at arm's length: relational involvement in conferences with managements would be appropriate for the development of solidarity based capitalism. This relational involvement could express expectations of corporate stability and of corporate evolution in line with stakeholder concepts of corporate governance, according with general requirements for emphasis on the formation of human capital. Neglect of human capital, because of managerial emphasis on short-term financial achievements and on maximizing the benefits of location advantages, has to be a technocratic concern.[32] Problems of corporate stability also have to be technocratic concerns, in part because of the importance of accumulations of tacit managerial knowledge in consultative explorations of emerging opportunities for concerted entrepreneurship in the use of advanced research.[33]

MICROECONOMIC POLICY INTERDEPENDENCIES

The development of forms of collegial capitalism would make microeconomic policy interdependencies more manageable. These interdependencies are increasing, notably in Atlantic relations, as liberalized infrastructure network firms expand across borders. The French firm EdF, the world's largest electricity utility, has expanded into Germany, Italy, Austria, Hungary, Switzerland and Britain. Enron, the failed US energy firm, had very extensive international operations, and its demise had adverse effects in European energy sectors. Expansion by manufacturing and financial enterprises is also increasing microeconomic policy interdependencies, again notably in the Atlantic context.

Competition policy issues, particularly between the USA and the European Union, become politically prominent as concentration trends continue, especially because of international expansion by US firms. Intensely competitive orientations activate these trends, and on the European side the absence of strong relational bonds between many Union firms is a source of vulnerabilities. These challenge the European Commission to exert authority by opposing US mergers and acquisitions that would secure significant levels of European and global market dominance, while implementing a Union policy intended to facilitate the emergence of strong but not regionally dominant European enterprises. The US administration does not challenge intra-Union mergers and acquisitions, and tends to accept any adverse European decisions regarding mergers and acquisitions between US firms.[34]

European interests in the policy interdependence are basically defensive, because of the weaker international competitiveness of Union firms, and are asserted with considerable autonomy by the European Commission. The US administration is involved somewhat indirectly, though guidelines from the Department of Justice tend to increase as US firms become more prominent in global concentration trends, but also as European bargaining strengths increase with the Union's deepening integration and enlargement. Frictions in Atlantic trade relations, moreover, influence attitudes on each side, and thus can affect interactions over linked issues, such as questions about the USA's use of tax concessions to export firms.[35]

A spirit of more collegial capitalism in the USA and Europe would make possible more balanced and more dynamic interdependencies in the competition policy area and, more extensively, in Atlantic trade and investment relations, as well as in the structural policy area where problems of excess capacity have to be resolved. Although leadership for the development of collegial capitalism is lacking in the Atlantic context, where cultural and institutional factors are more favourable than elsewhere in the global economy, the range of microeconomic policy interdependencies demanding attention obligates earnest consideration of initiatives that could be taken to promote the development of integrative relational cooperation throughout the pattern of structurally linked industrialized states.[36]

The need for more equitable and more integrative management of microeconomic policy interdependencies between the major industrialized states has to be reiterated with increasing emphasis because of the continuing concentration trends in infrastructure network industries, manufacturing sectors, and international finance, and because of the dangers of speculation-led destabilization associated with the concentration trends. The concentration trends are instances of internationalized market failure, and with them there are externalities affecting employment, sectoral interdependencies, and opportunities for new forms of entrepreneurship. Speculative destabilization – the bidding up of asset prices to unsustainable levels – is another form of market failure that tends to have increasing cross-border dimensions. The issues of efficiency and social justice that thus demand urgent attention do activate knowledge intensive streams of economic advice to governments, and implicit in most of these are motivational imperatives: the advice is intended to be put into effect in a spirit of service to the common good.[37] Corporate managements, then, because of the elements of economic sovereignty which they assume, have to provide constructive inputs into policy, and must themselves serve the common interest, cooperatively, in all the areas covered by microeconomic policies.

The introductory chapter of this volume, focusing on relational assets, indicates how firms, becoming more interdependent in the development of their production capabilities, can manage these to build relational assets, opening up opportunities for complementary entrepreneurship, with security, based on trust and goodwill, thus contributing to overall balances between competition and cooperation that can serve the common interest. The potential for collaborative management of structural interdependencies can thus become evident: the transnational corporations linking national economic structures can establish a collegial system of international capitalism. Greater development of human and social capital would then be possible. Meanwhile the evolution of structural interdependencies could be left more safely to relationally motivated market forces, while the management of microeconomic policy interdependencies would benefit from the constructive political activities of corporate associations. Further, functional linkages with macroeconomic policies would become more harmonious.

Relational assets shared between firms can be seen to have counterparts in relational assets shared between managements and technocrats, sustaining public spirited knowledge intensive exchanges conducive to innovative complementarities. Functional partnering between the two levels is being driven by the multiplication of frontier technologies; it is also being driven by the pressures of competition in world markets, but these can be constructively reoriented if a pervasive spirit of cooperation develops in the management of relational assets.

Thinking about relational assets has to be put into the context of a world economy that is being increasingly integrated, with asymmetries, through rises in levels of structural interdependence. Corporate and policy level emphasis on achieving sector specific competitive advantages, and on enhancing structural competitiveness, is being challenged to become reoriented toward collaborative complementary achievements in uses of advanced technology, and in supportive uses of productive rather than destabilizing rent-seeking investment. Constructive responses to these challenges, increasing internationalized market efficiencies, could overcome internationalized market failures.

The cross-border dimensions of government efficiencies would also be increased, as policy failures were reduced in conjunction with the decreases in market failures. Government failures and market failures tend to interact in perverse reciprocity, notably through policy level deficiencies that in effect facilitate destabilizing speculation-led asset appreciation, and that push up public debt to further the political interests of ruling groups. Public monitoring of macromanagement performance becomes more and more difficult in knowledge based political economies, and accordingly the motivational factors that can activate dedicated corporate cooperation and policy level collaboration become more critical for overall efficiency and social justice.

NOTES

1. For example, in 2000, 25 per cent of EU exports to the US were registered as exports after inward processing. Interestingly, a much smaller share of EU exports to the US (1.5 per cent) were registered as exports for processing in the US. Further details are available in Paul Brenton 'Industrial Fragmentation, Processing and EU–US Trade Relations', mimeo, Centre for European Policy Studies, Brussels, 2001.
2. See, for example, Jacques Pelkmans 'The GSM-Standard: Explaining a Success Story', Working Document 132, Centre for European Policy Studies, 1999.
3. See studies of the expanding international production system in *World Investment Report 2000*, Geneva, United Nations Commission on Trade and Development.
4. See review of Enron's operations in *Financial Times*, 24 December 2001.
5. See Mark Casson *Entrepreneurship and Business Culture*, Cheltenham, Edward Elgar, 1995, chs 7 and 8.
6. See Peter A. Hall and David Soskice (eds) *Varieties of Capitalism: Institutional Foundations of Comparative Advantage*, Oxford, Oxford University Press, 2001.
7. See Casson, cited.
8. See symposium on competition policy in *Oxford Review of Economic Policy*, 9, 2, Summer 1993.
9. See reviews in the International Monetary Fund series *International Capital Markets*, especially the August 2001 issue.
10. The costs of globalization include degrees of deindustrialization, and increases in welfare burdens obligate higher taxes, but international firms reduce tax exposure by increasing foreign production. See Dani Rodrik *Has Globalization Gone Too Far?* Washington DC, Institute for International Economics, 1997. However, there is little to support the view that these considerations are leading to the demise of traditional welfare systems in Europe; see, for example, Duane Swank 'European Welfare States: Regionalization, Globalization and Policy Change', in Thomas Brewer, Paul Brenton and Gavin Boyd (eds) *Globalizing Europe*, Cheltenham, Edward Elgar, 2002.
11. See Magnus Blomstrom, Byron Gangnes and Sumner La Croix (eds) *Japan's New Economy*, Oxford, Oxford University Press, 2001.
12. See Peter A. Hall and David Soskice (eds) *Varieties of Capitalism: Institutional Foundations of Comparative Advantage*, Oxford, Oxford University Press, 2001.
13. The slack growth contributes to a flow of investment to the USA, which in turn limits growth prospects in Europe. See Thomas Brewer, Paul Brenton, and Gavin Boyd (eds) *Globalizing Europe*, Cheltenham, Edward Elgar, 2002.
14. There are some important exceptions in particular sectors and for specific issues. Pelkmans, cited, concludes that the GSM standard 'shows an interesting contrast between the non-cooperative US process of adopting digital mobile standards . . . and the cooperative and open European process' (p. 1).
15. Market integration can proceed provided that legitimate national variation is accepted, but national variation impedes market integration, and the national variations that remain in Europe are likely to be the most intractable. See Peter Holmes and Alasdair Young 'Emerging Regulatory Challenges to the EU's External Economic Relations', Working Paper 42, European Institute, University of Sussex and Paul Brenton, John Sheehy and Marc Vancauteren 'Technical barriers to trade in the European Union', *Journal of Common Market Studies*, **39** (2), June 2001, p. 265–284.

16. This was a factor in delayed monetary policy responses to speculation-led appreciations of stock prices before the 2001 recession. See *71st Annual Report*, Bank of International Settlements, Basel, 11 June 2001.
17. On the representation of corporate interests see W.D. Coleman 'State traditions and comprehensive associations: a comparative structural analysis', *Political Studies*, XXXVIII, 1990, 231–53.
18. On European lags in this sector, see Rose Marie Ham, Greg Linden and Melissa M. Appleyard 'The evolving role of semiconductor consortia in the US and Japan', *California Management Review*, 41,1 Fall 1998, 137–63.
19. See Harvie Ramsey, Neil M. Kay and Jean-Francois Hennart 'Strategic technological partnering by EU firms', *Journal of Common Market Studies*, 39, 1, March 2001, 147–58.
20. See Alistair Cole 'National and partisan contexts on Europeanization: the case of the French socialists', *Journal of Common Market Studies*, 39, 1, March 2001, 15–36.
21. See Ramsay, Kay and Hennart, cited.
22. See symposium on European network infrastructures in *Oxford Review of Economic Policy*, 17, 3, Autumn 2001.
23. Same, and Paul Joskow *California's Electricity Crisis*, National Bureau of Economic Research Working Paper 8442, 2001.
24. On the difficulties of regulating infrastructure network industries see *OECD Economic Studies*, 32, 2001/1 – Special Issue on Regulatory Reform.
25. See David C. Mowery and Richard R. Nelson (eds) *Sources of Industrial Leadership*, New York, Cambridge University Press, 1999.
26. *Ibid.*
27. See Andrew Hill 'Concerns grow over fall-out of Enron collapse', *Financial Times*, 21 December 2001.
28. See *Oxford Review of Economic Policy*, 17, 3, Autumn 2001, cited, and *OECD Economic Studies*, cited.
29. See *Oxford Review of Economic Policy*, 17,3, cited.
30. See references to California's electricity problems, *ibid.*
31. See David J. Teece 'Strategies for managing knowledge assets: the role of firm structure and industrial context', *Long Range Planning*, 33, 1, February 2000, 35–54.
32. This can be argued in the context of a rationale for shifts to stakeholder corporate governance. See Mary O'Sullivan *Contests for Corporate Control*, Oxford, Oxford University Press, 2000, and Margaret M. Blair and Mark J. Roe (eds) *Employees and Corporate Governance*, Washington DC, Brookings, 1999.
33. This theme is implicit in literature on interdependencies in the development of corporate production capabilities: see Nicolai Foss and Volker Mahnke (eds) *Competence, Governance, and Entrepreneurship*, Oxford, Oxford University Press, 2000.
34. See Youri Devuyst 'Transatlantic Competition Relations', in Mark A. Pollack and Gregory C. Shaffer (eds) *Transatlantic Governance in the Global Economy*, Lanham, Rowman and Littlefield, 2001, ch 5.
35. For a review of frictions in Atlantic trade relations see Ernst-Ulrich Petersmann 'Dispute prevention and dispute settlement in the EU–US transatlantic partnership', in *Transatlantic Governance in the Global Economy*, cited, 73–96.
36. At the policy level, several initiatives have been pursued such as the Transatlantic Business Dialogue. Cooperative transatlantic business lobbying was fundamental in pushing the EU and the US to sign a Mutual Recognition Agreement on testing and conformity assessment. For some sectors the agreement appears to work, but for others it has failed, reflecting fundamental differences across the Atlantic in approaches towards the implementation of health and safety regulations.
37. See comments on government responsibilities in *OECD Economic Studies*, cited.

4. Inter-firm R&D partnering in high technology industries

Nadine Roijakkers and John Hagedoorn

Until recently, R&D was not an activity that researchers expected to see carried out in cooperation between different companies. In particular for high technology industries, such as IT and biotechnology, where state-of-the-art research and technological know-how are critical to competitive success, the sharing of R&D activities by competing companies seemed a rather unusual aspect of corporate behaviour. This is probably one of the main reasons why the growth of the number of inter-firm R&D partnerships during the 1980s and the 1990s has attracted so much attention in recent years, both in the academic literature and in the popular press.

We will attempt to contribute to the understanding of inter-firm collaboration in R&D with an analysis of some basic trends and patterns in the forming of R&D alliances in the international biotechnology industry. The biotechnology industry is one of the main examples of current industries where we find a large number of R&D alliances, in particular between large and small companies (Hagedoorn, 1996a; Hagedoorn and Roijakkers, 2002; Kenney, 1986; Powell, 1996). Data from the MERIT-Cooperative Agreements and Technology Indicators (CATI) database (see Appendix 4.1) suggest that over 65 per cent of all the biotechnology R&D alliances are related to pharmaceutical biotechnology. Because of the dominance of this particular sub-sector in the biotechnology industry, with so few alliances found in other biotechnology sectors, our contribution focuses on collaboration between companies in the pharmaceutical biotechnology industry.

Apart from a sectoral restriction we will also limit the analysis to those inter-firm agreements for which the transfer of technology or the creation of new technology through R&D are central to the agreement. R&D refers to the standard research and development activities that are aimed at increasing scientific or technical knowledge and the application of that knowledge to the creation of new and improved products and processes. We will confine the analysis to particular modes of partnering such as joint ventures for which common R&D or technology sharing is a major objective, joint R&D agreements, and minority holdings coupled with research contracts. We have chosen the period from 1975 to 1998 because this covers the years in which inter-firm partnering has risen rapidly, in biotechnology as well as in many other fields of technology and sectors of industry (Hagedoorn, 1996a).

Throughout this chapter we will refer to the biotechnology 'industry' although this is probably an incorrect term as its status as a separate industrial sector is still somewhat unclear. Strictly speaking, biotechnology is not yet a full industrial sector but a hybrid form of an 'industry' with established companies, such as from the pharmaceutical sector, and a wide range of new biotechnology companies that are science based and technology driven but still with relatively few regular products and limited manufacturing capabilities (Powell, Koput and Smith-Doerr, 1996). In other words, when we use the term industry in the following analysis, we recognize that we are mainly analysing the behaviour of a group of companies that are engaged in R&D, innovation and the manufacturing of products and processes that can be labelled as biotechnological activities.

In the following we first present and explain the growth pattern in R&D partnering since 1975. This is followed by a discussion of the major factors that could motivate companies to enter into various sorts of R&D partnerships. Although the rationales for cooperation are numerous we restrict our attention to those rationales that are important for firms in the biotechnology industry (see Hagedoorn, 1993 for a more general overview of motives for R&D partnerships). The next section is devoted to a discussion of the different organizational features of basic categories of modes of cooperation. In that section we also pay attention to the analysis of changes in the distribution of different categories of partnerships. Next, we discuss international patterns of partnering in terms of changes in the historical distribution of domestic and international partnerships, with special reference to the Triad regions (Asia, Europe, and North America). Finally, we pay some attention to the role played by large and small companies in the context of the most R&D cooperation-intensive companies in the biotechnology industry. The closing section presents some conclusions.

HISTORICAL PATTERN OF R&D PARTNERSHIPS

In order to assess the importance and magnitude of alliance activity we examine the number of newly established R&D partnerships as they appear in the CATI database. Figure 4.1 shows the growth pattern of annually newly made R&D partnerships in the biotechnology industry for the period 1975–98. The numbers are calculated as three-year moving averages to show the general trend in the data while correcting for yearly fluctuations.

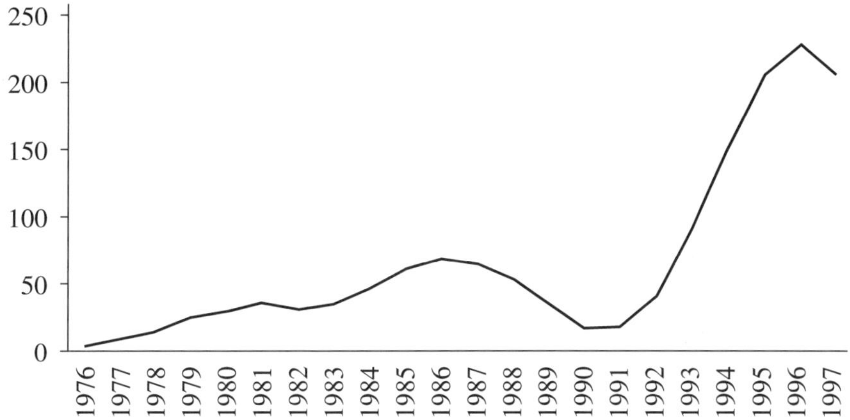

Figure 4.1 *Growth of newly established R&D partnerships, three-year moving averages, 1975–98*

During the second half of the 1970s, there was a gradual increase in the number of newly established R&D partnerships from fewer than five in 1976 to around 15 new agreements in 1978. The end of the 1970s witnessed a rather sudden increase in the number of new partnerships as nearly 25 alliances were established in 1979. This particular growth pattern continued well into the first half of the 1980s. Apart from a small drop in 1982, those years marked a rather steep increase in the number of annually formed partnerships from about 30 in 1980 to nearly 70 new alliances made in 1986. The last couple of years of the 1980s showed a substantial drop in the newly made R&D partnerships to slightly more than 35 in 1989. During the early 1990s the number of newly made alliances dropped even further to fewer than 20 in 1991, after which the number took off again to reach a level of about 230 new partnerships in 1996. At the end of the period of our analysis, the number of annually made alliances was decreasing again to just over 200 new partnerships in 1997. However, this number is still considerably higher than the figures found for most years since the early 1980s.

All in all, the historical data on R&D partnering in the biotechnology industry revealed, despite some irregularities, an overall growth pattern in the number of annually made R&D partnerships since the mid-1970s. During the late 1970s there was a rather steady growth pattern, while the 1980s and particularly the 1990s showed a more accelerated growth trend with clear peaks in 1986 and 1996 as well a significant drop in alliance activity in 1990. This particular, seemingly cyclical, growth pattern is identical to the pattern found for other industries (see Hagedoorn, 1996a).

One possible explanation for the specific pattern in the newly established R&D alliances, found in the MERIT-CATI database is related to the volatility of financial markets during the second half of the 1980s. In the first years of the 1980s venture capital firms invested large amounts of financial resources in capital intensive R&D projects carried out by new biotechnology firms (Hakansson, Kjellberg and Lundgren, 1993; Senker, 1996; Walsh, Niosi and Mustar, 1995). Originally based on university research that led to major scientific and technological changes, nearly all of the new biotechnology companies were founded to commercially exploit promising new technologies such as genetic engineering and cell fusion. For most, if not all, of these small firms, venture capital constituted the single largest source of funding.

After the 1987 Wall Street crash, however, venture capitalists became increasingly hesitant to provide the funds for new biotechnology firms since most of them failed to introduce new breakthrough pharmaceutical products (Barley, Freeman, and Hybels, 1992; Galambos and Sturchio, 1998; Smith and Fleck, 1988; Walsh and Galimberti, 1993). The decreasing availability of venture capital during the second half of the 1980s caused an initial shakeout in the industry with numerous biotechnology firms filing for bankruptcy. The lower number of potential biotechnology R&D partners available to large pharmaceutical companies may provide a tentative explanation for the substantial decrease in the number of newly established partnerships during the final years of the 1980s. Also during these years, the major source of funding for new biotechnology firms shifted from venture capital to large pharmaceutical companies, which shows up in the gradual growth of newly made R&D partnerships during the first half of the 1990s (see also Barley et al., 1992; Senker and Sharp, 1997; Smith and Fleck, 1988).

RATIONALES FOR R&D PARTNERING

In the literature the explanation for the overall increase of alliance activity is generally related to the motives that 'force' companies to collaborate on R&D. Major factors mentioned in that context are related to important industrial and technological changes in the 1980s and 1990s that have led to increased interdisciplinarity of scientific and technological developments, higher risks surrounding R&D, increasing costs of R&D projects, and ever-shortening innovation cycles that favour collaboration (see Contractor and Lorange, 1988; Dussauge and Garette, 1999; Hagedoorn 1993, 1996a; Mowery, 1988; Mytelka, 1991; Nooteboom, 1999; OECD, 1992). In the following we restrict our attention to those rationales that are important for firms that are engaged in biotechnological activities, in particular large established pharmaceutical companies and new biotechnology firms.

For large pharmaceutical companies their motives to enter into R&D partnerships frequently have both a cost economizing background as well as a strategic intent (see also Eisenhardt and Schoonhoven, 1996; Hagedoorn, 1993; Hagedoorn, Link and Vonortas, 2000; Lorenzoni and Lipparini, 1999; Mowery, Oxley and Silverman, 1998). The cost-economizing motivation appears particularly to play a role when we consider the period that covers the first years of the 1980s. Around this time the pharmaceutical industry at large was confronted with a dramatic increase in R&D costs at the same time as there was a declining number of new drug compounds resulting from the more traditional chemical routes to innovation (Grabowski and Vernon, 1994; Pisano and Wheelwright, 1995; Walker and Walker, 1986).

As a result of these developments, large companies such as Bayer, Ciba Geigy, and Eli Lilly were beginning to reposition themselves in an attempt to achieve greater economies of scale and scope in R&D. One of their main goals was to carry out exploratory basic research across a broader range of new scientific and technological areas in order to identify and take advantage of the many commercial opportunities that were opening up in these fields (Galambos and Sturchio, 1998; Hagedoorn, 1995; Hamel, 1991; Walsh and Galimberti, 1993). However, even the largest, well-financed pharmaceutical companies were finding it more and more difficult to finance both basic and applied research across the entire range of relevant new opportunities. This problem induced many of these firms to seek access to external technological research and knowledge by establishing partnerships with others (Barley et al., 1992; Hagedoorn, 1993; Pisano and Wheelwright, 1995; Powell, 1996, 1998).

During the early 1980s pharmaceutical companies began to develop and maintain numerous formal partnerships with external sources of the new technology, i.e. small biotechnology firms, most of them US-based, and research universities in order to gain a window on the scientific advances in molecular biology and genetic engineering (Arora and Gambardella, 1990; Barley et al., 1992; Hagedoorn and Roijakkers, 2002; Powell, 1996). In these cases the strategic intent of R&D partnerships became more apparent. Adopting this strategy allowed these firms to keep their main R&D activities within their own domain while jointly performing R&D with biotech companies in this new, high-risk area of R&D of which the future importance for their technological capabilities was too unclear to justify any sudden changes in the existing research strategy.

If established companies are motivated to enter partnerships mainly to lower the cost of some of their R&D activities as well as to explore new technological opportunities beyond their current domain (Arora and Gambardella, 1990; Doz, 1988; Pisano, 1991; Shan, Walker and Kogut, 1994), small firms in turn primarily have a cost-economizing rationale (Senker and Sharp, 1997). Although biotech firms developed a reputation for their R&D capabilities and applied laboratory research in advanced biotechnology, most of them failed to develop pharmaceutical products for sale to final customers. According to Walsh and Galimberti (1993) this was mainly due to a shortage of funds, an extended development cycle, a lower level of demand than anticipated, and their inability to combine obviously novel forms of technical knowledge with knowledge of approval procedures, production and marketing.

The instability of capital markets in the final years of the 1980s was an important motivating factor for small biotechnology firms to form various kinds of partnerships. As already mentioned, during the first half of the 1980s, the initial capital requirements of US-based start-ups were primarily met by venture capital firms (Hakansson et al., 1993; Senker, 1996; Walsh et al., 1995). Between 1980 and 1983, the most successful biotechnology firms that were founded on the basis of academic breakthroughs, such as Genentech, were the first to go public and launch initial stock offerings (IPOs) (Barley et al., 1992). Some of these had disappointing results, but the stock market boom of 1983 triggered a series of initial public offerings and a period of heavy speculation in the stocks of new biotechnology firms. The strong market for IPOs also stimulated many venture capital firms to provide the funding for large numbers of new start-ups, often on just the promise of a new technology. Besides genetic engineering, the ability to produce, at low cost, large quantities of monoclonal antibodies triggered the founding of many entrepreneurial companies as well as a wave of enthusiasm among investors.

Because development work took longer than anticipated, however, and many new biotechnology-based pharmaceuticals proved to be less promising when subjected to rigorous clinical testing, even the oldest biotechnology firms were slow in introducing new breakthrough products (Galambos and Sturchio, 1998; Smith and Fleck, 1988). Venture capital firms typically receive their financing through partnerships, which are normally based on strict contractual arrangements with respect to payback dates. The low chances of recapturing their investments within a relatively short period of time made these firms less willing to finance costly R&D and clinical trials (Barley et al., 1992). As was previously mentioned, after the stock market collapse of 1987, investors became extremely cautious about the potential for new biotechnology-based pharmaceuticals and their interest in IPOs began to diminish. Unable as yet to produce their own working capital, small firms were consequently experiencing increasing pressure to finance their R&D by entering partnerships with large pharmaceutical firms (Senker and Sharp, 1997; Smith and Fleck, 1988).

Another problem confronting small firms was a lack of the complementary skills, assets and technologies (Teece, 1986) necessary for successful commercial exploitation of the state-of-the-art technological knowledge they clearly possessed. Genetic engineering may provide new routes to existing as well as to new pharmaceuticals, but the required technological know-how must be combined with knowledge of the worldwide market introduction and distribution of safe and effective pharmaceutical products, among others. Such complementary forms of knowledge are possessed by large pharmaceutical companies, which in the past were the dominant innovators in the pharmaceutical industry. In commercial biotechnology it has become common practice for small firms to share their scientific and technical expertise and/or patents in biotechnology with large pharmaceutical firms in exchange for access to the larger firms' financial resources and established organizational capabilities in clinical research, regulatory affairs, manufacturing and marketing (Della Valle and Gambardella, 1993; Hakansson et al., 1993; Larson, 1992; Rothaermel, 2000).

MODES OF COOPERATION

So far we have discussed R&D partnerships in general terms. However, it has to be stressed that in the biotechnology industry R&D partnering takes place through a specific number of organizational modes. In the following we distinguish between a group of equity-based partnerships, such as joint ventures and minority holdings, and a group of so-called contractual agreements, such as joint R&D agreements and R&D contracts. As these modes of cooperation will feature so prominently in the following analysis, we will briefly discuss them further.

Joint ventures are probably the oldest and most well known form of inter-firm partnering (Berg, Duncan and Friedman, 1982; Hladik, 1985). Traditionally, this mode of cooperation accounted for the majority of partnerships in many sectors of industry. In a joint venture, two or more separate parent companies agree to combine their resources and skills in a distinct organizational unit or 'company' that is characterized by shared equity ownership. In the context of R&D partnering, joint ventures have shared R&D as a specific company objective as well as production, marketing, sales, etc. From this brief description of joint ventures it is obvious that equity participation is used in an attempt to lower transaction costs between the parent companies. Because equity participation creates a relatively high degree of organizational interdependence among the participating companies, the chances of cheating on other partners can be reduced to a large extent. If one partner does not behave in a responsible way, then the whole venture suffers and equity diminishes for all parent companies (Buckley and Casson, 1988).

Minority holdings are another type of equity-based partnership where one company obtains a rather small interest (substantially less than 50 per cent) in another. In the biotechnology industry minority holdings are often coupled with technology exchange agreements. In particular, large pharmaceutical companies are well known for investing in small biotechnology companies in order to explore a promising new field of technology without investing the full amount of resources that would be needed for internal development. If the technology of the small firm becomes more important to the pharmaceutical firm, a takeover can be considered.

During the past decades a number of contractual forms of R&D partnering, in particular joint R&D agreements, have become an alternative to equity-based partnerships. We understand joint R&D agreements to cover technology and R&D sharing by two or more companies through the joint undertaking of research and development projects with shared resources. Research contracts are examples of non-equity partnerships that regulate R&D partnering in which one company, usually a large one, contracts another, frequently small, company, to perform particular research projects. Non-equity agreements are used extensively by large pharmaceutical companies in the biotechnology industry in order to raise their ability to switch their research from one technology to another (Barley et al., 1992; Obleros and MacDonald, 1988).

Recent studies have established that non-equity, contractual forms of R&D partnerships, such as joint R&D agreements and research contracts, have become very important modes of inter-firm collaboration as their numbers and share in the total of partnerships has far exceeded that of equity-based partnerships (Hagedoorn, 1996a; Hagedoorn and Narula, 1996). Whereas equity agreements are often established in order to raise mutual dependence, an increasing number of companies prefer a more flexible relationship with other companies. Especially in high-tech industries such as biotechnology that are characterized by the increasing complexity of technologies, rapid technological changes, and the increasing costs of R&D, even the largest firms are no longer able to monitor all the technological developments that are important for their core markets. Cooperation through more flexible types of agreements enables these firms to monitor several technological developments and, at the same time, allows them to concentrate on a few, most promising, projects internally

(Harrigan, 1985, 1988). If certain technologies turn out to be less successful, contractual arrangements can be terminated relatively easily with only a small financial loss.

Figure 4.2 shows the gradual increase in the relative importance of contractual arrangements compared with equity-sharing partnerships, which is in congruence with previous contributions. All numbers are calculated as three year moving averages and expressed as percentages of the total number of annually, newly established R&D alliances.

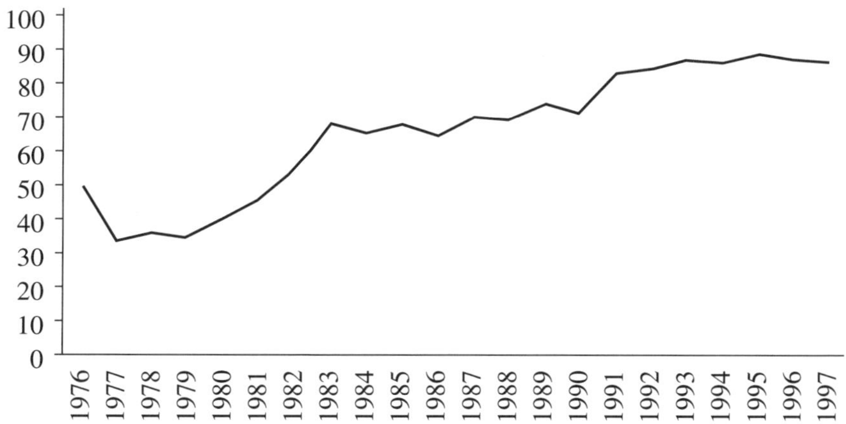

Figure 4.2 Share (%) of contractual modes in all newly established R&D partnerships, three-year moving averages, 1975–98

During the late 1970s, when there were only a small number of R&D partnerships, approximately 60 per cent of new partnerships in the biotechnology industry were equity-based agreements, the majority of these equity-sharing partnerships being of the minority holding type. Fewer than 20 per cent of all the R&D alliances as found in the MERIT-CATI databank were R&D joint ventures. Since the 1980s, the share of contractual arrangements increased from about 60 per cent during most of the 1980s to approximately 85 per cent in the 1990s. In general companies seem to prefer joint R&D agreements to R&D contracts. However, the number of yearly established R&D contracts, found in the CATI database, indicates an increasing popularity of this mode of partnering in recent years.

So far we have presented a general overview of major trends in R&D partnerships in the biotechnology industry since 1975, examining both growth data and the distribution according to major organizational characteristics of these partnerships. These overall trends in inter-firm R&D partnering indicate the following:

- by and large, companies seem to increasingly prefer contractual partnerships to equity-based arrangements,
- the growth of annually newly made R&D partnerships in the biotechnology industry since the early 1980s is primarily caused by an increase in the number of contractual agreements such as joint R&D agreements.

INTERNATIONAL PATTERNS IN R&D PARTNERSHIPS

A considerable number of scholars in business as well as in economics have paid attention to the 'globalization' of the world economy (see e.g. Bartlett, Doz and Hedlund, 1990; Cantwell, 1991; Dunning, 1988, 1993; Hirschey and Caves, 1981; Pearce, 1989; Reich, 1990, 1991; Vernon, 1966, 1979). Globalization is an important and critical feature of today's high technology industries such as biotechnology, where increased international competition between companies forces them to pursue international strategies. Through these international strategies companies do not only seek foreign market entry but also foreign assets (both of a tangible and an intangible nature) and build international inter-firm partnerships for sourcing of R&D, production and supply. Many authors (Contractor and Lorange, 1988; Dunning, 1993; Duysters and Hagedoorn, 1996; Ohmae, 1990; Yoshino and Rangan, 1995) have stressed the critical role that inter-firm R&D partnering plays in the internationalization strategies of a growing number of companies. Consequently, one could expect that the share of international R&D partnerships in the total number of R&D partnerships should have increased during the past two and a half decades.

In this section we will see to what extent inter-firm biotechnology R&D partnerships have become more internationalized, paying special attention to partnerships made between companies from Asia (Japan and South Korea), Europe (the EU and EFTA countries) and North America (USA and Canada). Previous work by Freeman and Hagedoorn (1994) and Ohmae (1985, 1990) revealed that the majority of R&D partnerships are made between companies from within the Triad regions (Japan, Europe and North America). South Korea is mentioned by Freeman and Hagedoorn (1994) and Duysters and Hagedoorn (2000) as a recent 'player' of some importance. In the following, R&D partnerships between companies from Asia, Europe and North America are considered as international alliances, i.e. inter-Triadic partnerships. Intra-European partnerships are seen as regional or domestic partnerships, as are partnerships made within either Asia or North America. All other combinations outside the Triad regions are treated as a miscellaneous category.

Figure 4.3 demonstrates that a large share of the population of biotechnology R&D partnerships was of an intra-regional or domestic nature during the second half of the 1970s as well as the 1980s. However, this share declined over the past decades, from an average of about 55 per cent for most of the 1980s to somewhat higher than 45 per cent during the 1990s. For most of the 1990s, the share of international, inter-Triadic, partnerships was higher than the domestic and regional alliances. During the final years of the 1990s, the share of domestic alliances rose again relative to international partnerships. Also, during the most recent years there was a growth of the share of other combinations to a still relatively small share of around 2 per cent.

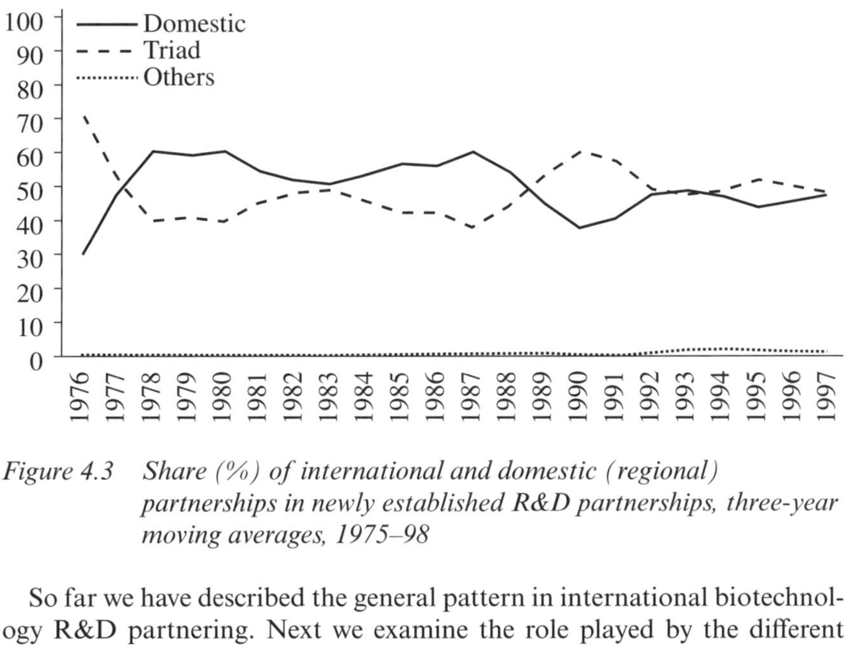

Figure 4.3 Share (%) of international and domestic (regional) partnerships in newly established R&D partnerships, three-year moving averages, 1975–98

So far we have described the general pattern in international biotechnology R&D partnering. Next we examine the role played by the different international economic and trading blocks at a more disaggregated level (see Figures 4.4a–e). If one looks at the overall pattern in R&D partnering during the past two and a half decades, it becomes clear that companies from the Triad participate in over 98 per cent of all R&D partnerships. North America clearly dominates R&D partnering in the biotechnology industry. Over 70 per cent of the R&D partnerships as found in MERIT-CATI for the past two and a half decades have at least one North American partner. During the 1970s and 1980s, the share of partnerships involving at

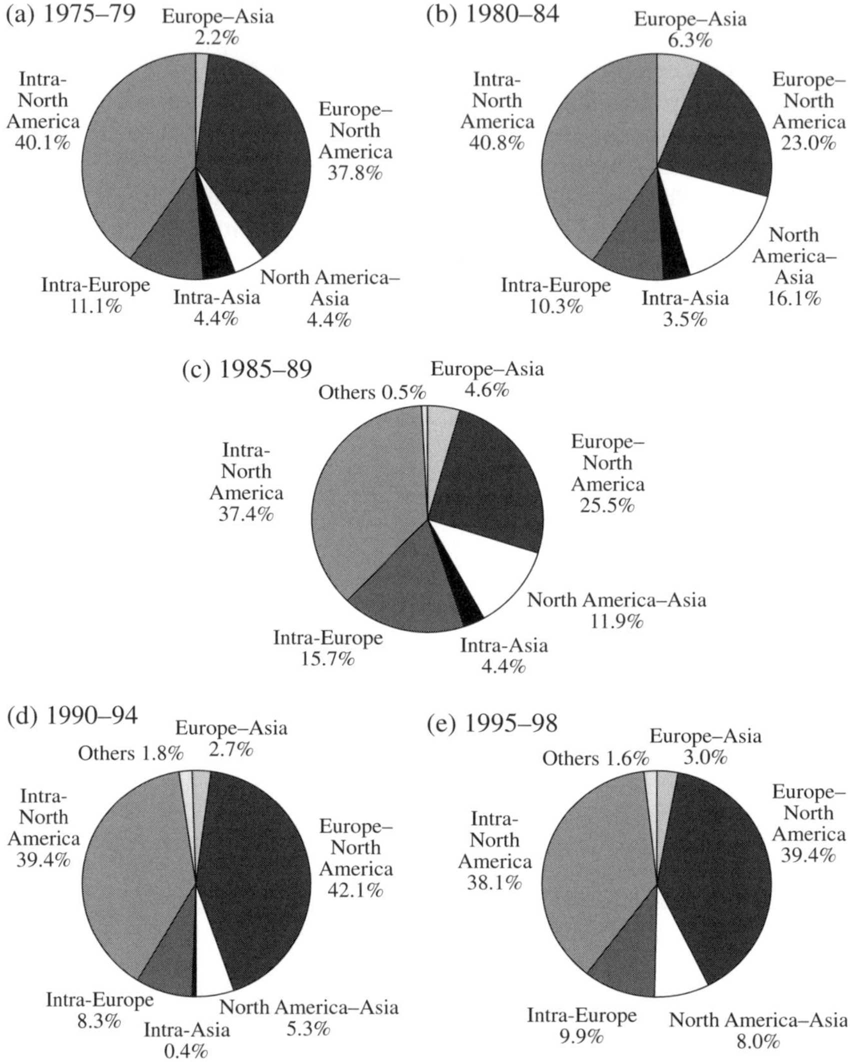

Figure 4.4 International distribution of R&D partnerships; a 1975–79; b 1980–84; c 1985–89; d 1990–94; e 1995–98

least one North American partner gradually eroded from around 82 per cent in the second half of the 1970s to less than 75 per cent in the final years of the 1980s. This share increased again to more than 85 per cent during the 1990s. Partnerships within North America (of which the majority share involves intra-US R&D partnering; US–Canadian partnerships and intra-Canadian partnerships accounting for less than 4 per cent) account for around 40 per cent of all the R&D partnerships in all periods.

During the second half of the 1970s more than 37 per cent of the inter-firm R&D partnerships were made between European and North American companies. This share fell to a level of less than 26 per cent during the 1980s, after which it increased again to over 39 per cent in the 1990s. These shares are substantially higher than the shares found for intra-European R&D partnerships in identical periods. The share of intra-European partnerships dropped from slightly over 11 per cent in the 1970s to around 10 per cent in the early 1980s. The second half of the 1980s marked a sudden increase in the share of intra-European partnerships to nearly 16 per cent. During the 1990s less than 10 per cent of all R&D partnerships were made between two or more European firms.

North American–Asian R&D partnering grew gradually from about 4 per cent during the 1970s to about 16 per cent during the first half of the 1980s. This share eroded to slightly less than 12 per cent in the late 1980s and to only 5 per cent in the first years of the 1990s. The share of R&D partnerships made between companies from North America and Asia reached 8 per cent during the most recent years. Intra-Asian or intra-Japanese R&D partnerships and partnerships between Europe and Asia remained at a relatively low level of less than 7 per cent during the last two and a half decades.

Further analysis of this data (detailed figures are not shown here) reveals some striking developments in the overall distribution of R&D partnerships at the level of countries. First of all, Swiss firms and companies from the UK and Germany played an important role in Europe–US R&D partnering in all periods considered. The overall dominance of R&D partnering between Europe and the US by UK firms is a development that dates back to the late 1980s. During the 1970s less than 5 per cent of these alliances were made between UK-based companies and US companies, and in the first half of the 1980s they accounted for even less than 3 per cent of all partnerships. However, the second half of the 1980s marked a sudden increase in the share of UK–US partnerships to over 7 per cent. This increase continued well into the 1990s and ultimately reached a level of more than 11 per cent. During the last two and a half decades we also saw R&D partnerships between US companies and companies from France, Sweden, and the Netherlands, although these shares have remained relatively low.

Second, while UK-based firms and companies from Switzerland and Germany have dominated Europe–US R&D partnering in the biotechnology industry during the past decades, these firms have also played an important role in inter-firm partnering between two or more European companies. In particular, during the 1980s and 1990s, 2–3 per cent of these partnerships were established within the UK. A few other important country dyads are Switzerland–Germany, UK–Sweden, and Germany–France.

Third, Japan–US partnerships represent the largest share of all Asia–North America biotechnology R&D partnering during the 1970s, 1980s and 1990s. During the 1980s and 1990s, South Korea appeared as a relatively important partner to the US besides Japan.

Fourth, if we take a closer look at the pattern in R&D partnering between companies from Asia and Europe, it becomes clear that companies from Japan, Switzerland, and the UK participated in the majority of these alliances during the late 1970s and the 1980s. During the 1990s, Japan–UK partnerships as well as Japan–Germany partnering and to a lesser extent partnerships between Japanese firms and French companies dominated R&D partnering between Asia and Europe. Besides Japan, South Korea appeared as an important partner for French companies.

LEADING COOPERATING FIRMS

In this chapter an attempt is made not only to understand basic trends in the growth of inter-firm R&D cooperation in the international biotechnology industry, but also to reveal the innovative role played by a large group of cooperating companies, i.e. small, entrepreneurial biotechnology firms and large established pharmaceutical companies.

Our understanding of the role played by these different categories of companies can be clearly placed within the Schumpeterian tradition. The importance of the entrepreneurial company as a major generator of new innovations is most clearly stressed in 'early' Schumpeter (1934). In this early work, entrepreneurial companies are small, independent, and act as major agents of change within new industries. These entrepreneurial companies are innovators that successfully introduce new products of which the development is expected to be largely financed through external sources and not so much through internal financial resources (cash-flow).

Many elements of these Schumpeterian entrepreneurial firms are clearly present in the biotechnology industry. In fact both Kenney (1986) and Powell et al. (1996) depict small biotechnology firms as an ideal type of modern entrepreneurial companies. As mentioned by Arora and Gambardella (1990), Pisano (1991), Barley et al. (1992), and Powell et al. (1996), small new biotechnology companies are frequently financed through venture capital or loans and equity participation of large companies. Originally based on university research that led to major scientific and technological changes, nearly all of the small, biotechnology companies also started as new entrants to the pharmaceutical industry (Kenney, 1986; Pisano, 1990; Powell, 1996).

In terms of their organizational setting and their organizational culture, most of the small biotechnology companies are quite different from the 'standard' company that one finds in traditional industries. New biotechnology companies seem to be driven by scientific discoveries and innovative performance and not only by regular profit-seeking (Lumerman Oliver and Porter Liebeskind, 1997). Also, the 'academic culture' within these innovation-driven and loosely organized companies, with their informal, non-hierarchical structures, sets them apart from many other 'traditional' companies (Pisano, 1991; Powell, 1996).

If we look at the role of large companies in Schumpeter, we have to understand that they play an important part in many of his publications. Specifically the 'older' Schumpeter (1942) pictures a world of 'modern, trustified capitalism' where large science-based companies dominate the innovative environment and where innovation has become routinized in large research laboratories and R&D departments. It is this particular perspective on the role of large companies that for a long period, during the 1950s, 1960s and 1970s, dominated the understanding of the role of large companies as the main source of innovation (see Kamien and Schwartz, 1982; Scherer, 1984).

In the combined biotechnology and pharmaceutical industry, large companies play a dominant role in the more traditional pharmaceutical subsectors (Arora and Gambardella, 1990). Large companies with their extensive R&D activities and their long-term experience with time-consuming clinical trials have come to dominate the innovation process in the traditional pharmaceutical industry. This dominance is based on their leading role in incremental innovation, exploiting their current organic chemical knowledge base and their ability to expand existing portfolios of pharmaceutical products.

Based on the literature discussed, one might expect that the central role of small, entrepreneurial biotechnology firms in R&D partnering, as stressed in the early work of Schumpeter, is likely to be most obvious during the 1980s when many of these new firms introduced major scientific and technological breakthroughs in the pharmaceutical industry. However, as the field of biotechnology has gradually matured, entrepreneurial biotechnology firms have become less important for inter-firm R&D cooperation while large companies may have become more dominant. This more dominant role for large science-based firms in a more routinized innovative environment is particularly stressed in the later writings of Schumpeter. In this section we will see to what extent small firms and large companies play an important role in the context of the most R&D cooperation-intensive companies in the biotechnology industry. Tables 4.1a–e list the ten companies with most R&D links in each Triad region during the past two and a half decades.[1]

For each region it is obvious that many of the leading pharmaceutical companies, such as Roche and Smithkline Beecham from Europe and Merck and Eli Lilly from the US, are well represented. If we look at the leading companies of biotechnology R&D partnering for Asia, we see that in all periods a number of large and medium-sized Japanese companies such as Kyowa Hakko Kogyo and Chugai Pharmaceutical played an important role in inter-firm R&D partnering. In the years 1975–79 the group of most partner-intensive European companies in the biotechnology industry covered a number of leading pharmaceutical companies. We notice that only two small UK-based biotechnology firms, Celltech and British Biotechnology, played a role of some importance during the 1980s, next to large well-established pharmaceutical companies. However, during the 1990s the position of these companies in the rank order of leading R&D partnering firms decreased while several large firms such as Glaxo from the UK entered the top ranking of cooperating companies.

Small firms such as Chiron, Genex and Biogen already held strong positions in the rank order of most intensely cooperating US-based firms during the second half of the 1970s, followed by large companies such as Schering Plough and Merck. During the 1980s these companies continued to hold strong positions in the group of leading R&D partnering firms, while a number of new young biotechnology firms, such as Amgen, Genzyme, California Biotechnology and T Cell Sciences, entered this group. For this time period the top of the list of the most partner-intensive companies located in the US also covered established pharmaceutical companies such as Bristol Myers, Johnson and Johnson and American Home Products. For the 1990s we notice that a number of new biotechnology firms, such as Oncogene Science, Genelabs Technologies, Gensia Pharmaceuticals and Arqule, entered the group of leading companies of biotechnology R&D partnering, however, the position of small firms relative to large companies decreased to some extent.

In congruence with 'early' Schumpeterian views, the results found for the US are indicative of the significant role played by small, entrepreneurial biotechnology firms in innovation, particularly during the 1980s when the new biotechnology first became relevant to the pharmaceutical industry. The 1990s, however, seem to demonstrate a decreasing importance of these small firms in inter-firm R&D partnering if compared with the role of large pharmaceutical companies. These large companies developed into more

Table 4.1a The top ten companies with R&D partnerships, economic regions, 1975–79

Asia			Europe			North America		
Company (size)	Country		Company (size)	Country		Company (size)	Country	
Dai Ichi Kangyo Bank (Large)	Japan	1	Roche (Large)	Switz.	10	Chiron (Small)	US	10
Mitsubishi (Large)	Japan	1	Ciba Geigy (Large)	Switz.	5	Genex (Small)	US	5
Chugai (Medium)	Japan	1	Procordia Nova (Large)	Sweden	3	Biogen (Small)	US	3
Takeda Chemical (Large)	Japan	1	Sandoz (Large)	Switz.	2	Dow (Large)	US	3
Takara Shuzo (Medium)	Japan	1	Schering (Large)	Germany	2	Schering Plough (Large)	US	3
Taiho (Medium)	Japan	1	Smithkline Beecham (Large)	UK	1	Merck (Large)	US	2
Ajinomoto (Large)	Japan	1	Bayer (Large)	Germany	1	Eli Lilly (Large)	US	2
			Boehringer Ingelheim (Large)	Germany	1	Chevron (Large)	US	2
			Pharmacia (Large)	Sweden	1	Innoven (Small)	US	2
			Grand Metropolitan (Large)	UK	1	Amoco (Large)	US	2

Table 4.1b The top ten companies with R&D partnerships, economic regions, 1980–84

Asia			Europe			North America		
Company (Size)	Country		Company (Size)	Country		Company (Size)	Country	
Mitsui (Large)	Japan	7	Roche (Large)	Switz.	18	Biogen (Small)	US	13
Green Cross (Large)	Japan	6	Celltech (Small)	UK	8	Bristol Myers (Large)	US	12
Dai Ichi Kangyo Bank (Large)	Japan	6	Shell (Large)	Neth.	5	J&J (Large)	US	12
Mitsubishi (Large)	Japan	4	Rhone Poulenc (Large)	France	5	Chiron (Small)	US	11
Shionogi (Large)	Japan	3	Ciba Geigy (Large)	Switz.	5	Amgen (Small)	US	9
Kyowa Hakko Kogyo (Large)	Japan	3	Elf Aquitaine (Large)	France	4	Genex (Small)	US	9
Meiji Seika Kaisha (Large)	Japan	2	Procordia Nova (Large)	Sweden	4	Syntex (Large)	US	7
Yamanouchi (Medium)	Japan	2	Smithkline Beecham (Large)	UK	4	AHP (Large)	US	6
Asahi Chemical (Large)	Japan	2	Bayer (Large)	Germany	4	Eli Lilly (Large)	US	6
Dainippon (Medium)	Japan	2	Novo Nordisk (Large)	Denmark	3	Dow (Large)	US	6

Table 4.1c The top ten companies with R&D partnerships, economic regions, 1985–89

Asia			Europe			North America		
Company (size)	Country		Company (size)	Country		Company (size)	Country	
Sumitomo (Large)	Japan	11	Roche (Large)	Switz.	21	Chiron (Small)	US	22
Kyowa Hakko Kogyo (Large)	Japan	7	Smithkline Beecham (Large)	UK	19	AHP (Large)	US	20
Dai Ichi Kangyo Bank (Large)	Japan	7	Celltech (Small)	UK	11	Eastman Kodak (Large)	US	13
Meiji Seika Kaisha (Large)	Japan	6	Pharmacia (Large)	Sweden	9	American Cyanamid (Large)	US	13
Mitsubishi (Large)	Japan	6	Sandoz (Large)	Switz.	9	J&J (Large)	US	13
Mitsui (Large)	Japan	5	British Biotech (Small)	UK	9	Biogen (Small)	US	12
Yamanouchi (Medium)	Japan	5	Procordia Nova (Large)	Sweden	9	Genzyme (Small)	US	12
Toyo Boseki (Large)	Japan	3	Hoechst (Large)	Germany	8	Dupont (Large)	US	10
Green Cross (Large)	Japan	3	Ciba Geigy (Large)	Switz.	7	California Biotech (Small)	US	10
Takeda Chemical (Large)	Japan	3	Rhone Poulenc (Large)	France	7	T Cell Sciences (Small)	US	9

Table 4.1d The top ten companies with R&D partnerships, economic regions, 1990–94

Asia			Europe			North America		
Company (size)	Country		Company (size)	Country		Company (size)	Country	
Eisai (Medium)	Japan	3	Ciba Geigy (Large)	Switz.	13	Chiron (Medium)	US	12
Ono (Medium)	Japan	2	Glaxo (Large)	UK	12	Merck (Large)	US	11
Mitsubishi Kasei (Large)	Japan	2	Smithkline Beecham (Large)	UK	11	Eli Lilly (Large)	US	10
Japan Tobacco (Large)	Japan	2	Rhone Poulenc (Large)	France	10	AHP (Large)	US	8
Chugai (Medium)	Japan	1	Sandoz (Large)	Switz.	7	Pfizer (Large)	US	7
Kyowa Hakko Kogyo (Large)	Japan	1	Hoechst (Large)	Germany	7	Eastman Kodak (Large)	US	6
Takeda Chemical (Large)	Japan	1	Bayer (Large)	Germany	6	Oncogene Science (Small)	US	5
Sankyo (Large)	Japan	1	Roche (Large)	Switz.	6	Genzyme (Medium)	US	5
Mitsubishi (Large)	Japan	1	Astra (Large)	Sweden	5	Genelabs Technologies (Small)	US	5
Dai Ichi Kangyo Bank (Large)	Japan	1	Celltech (Small)	UK	4	Gensia (Small)	US	5

Table 4.1e The top ten companies with R&D partnerships, economic regions, 1995–98

Asia			Europe			North America		
Company (size)	Country		Company (size)	Country		Company (size)	Country	
Chugai (Medium)	Japan	6	Roche (Large)	Switz.	35	Bristol M-Squibb (Large)	US	20
Kyowa Hakko Kogyo (Large)	Japan	5	Smithkline Beecham (Large)	UK	28	Eli Lilly (Large)	US	20
Ono (Medium)	Japan	4	Glaxo Wellcome (Large)	UK	19	Pfizer (Large)	US	18
Takeda Chemical (Large)	Japan	4	Rhone Poulenc (Large)	France	17	Chiron (Large)	US	16
Sankyo (Large)	Japan	4	Bayer (Large)	Germany	11	Warner Lambert (Large)	US	14
Taiho (Medium)	Japan	3	Hoechst (Large)	Germany	11	J&J (Large)	US	13
Yamanouchi (Medium)	Japan	3	Ciba Geigy (Large)	Switz.	10	Schering Plough (Large)	US	13
Shionogi (Large)	Japan	2	Novo Nordisk (Large)	Denmark	8	Arqule (Small)	US	13
Asahi Chemical (Large)	Japan	2	Basf (Large)	Germany	8	Merck (Large)	US	12
Japan Tobacco (Large)	Japan	2	Astra (Large)	Sweden	8	AHP (Large)	US	10

dominant players with multiple partnerships, a change that is clearly more in line with expectations based on the later writings of Schumpeter. However, the findings for Asia and Europe seem to suggest that it was the large pharmaceutical companies, rather than small firms, that were first to explore the new technological area and that these companies have dominated inter-firm R&D partnering more than large US-based companies (see also Saviotti, 1998).

The explanation for these findings is related to the asymmetric international distribution of small firms specialized in biotechnology (Saviotti et al., 1998; Senker and Sharp, 1997; Walsh et al., 1995). By the late 1970s, over 200 biotechnology start-ups had been set up in the US, but a very limited number in Asia and Europe, with the exception of the UK (Rothwell and Zegveld, 1982). The formation of small, R&D-intensive biotechnology firms is generally considered of crucial importance to the early development and commercialization of biotechnology in the US (Kenney, 1986; Grabowski and Vernon, 1994; Orsenigo, 1989). According to Senker (1996, 1998) a similar explosion of small firms was not occurring in Asia and Europe because these regions were lacking a culture which accommodated a close relationship between basic science, private firms and financed entrepreneurship.

Although many large pharmaceutical companies in Europe and elsewhere had already established significant links to university research during the 1940s, 1950s and 1960s, the early development of biotechnology in the US was to a large extent the result of a unique cross-fertilization between venture capital firms and university scientists whose state-of-the-art research led to major scientific and technological changes. Venture capitalists who recognized the commercial potential of scientific research in biotechnology provided the initial investment funds to small start-ups. Their founders and managers were typically academic entrepreneurs who retained their close ties with universities and research institutes while they were getting their new enterprises underway (Barley et al., 1992; Fransman, 1991).

Senker (1998) mentions a number of other factors to explain why Asia and Europe were only slowly taking advantage of the set of new opportunities provided by advances in biotechnology: shortage of venture capital, lack of knowledge of genetic engineering and its commercial potential by existing European and particularly Japanese firms and, compared with the US, a lower science intensity, as well as less frequent cooperation between public research institutions and industry.

From about 1980, European and Asian governments began to adopt policies aimed at remedying these deficiencies and closing the widening biotech gap with the US. They promoted the creation of small venture capital firms and exerted strong pressure on both universities and large companies to collaborate in building up the science base in genetic engineering (Galambos and Sturchio, 1998; Senker, 1998). Lagging behind the US by about five years, small biotechnology firms began to emerge slowly in other parts of the world during the 1980s (e.g. Celltech and British Biotechnology in the UK). However, even today the distribution of small biotechnology firms is very asymmetric: there are still many more in the US than in other parts of the world (Saviotti et al., 1998; Senker and Sharp, 1997; Walsh et al., 1995).

CONCLUSIONS

The increasing costs of R&D projects, the need to search for alternative routes to pharmaceutical innovation, the speed of developments in major scientific areas such molecular biology and genetic engineering, and the high risks surrounding biotechnology R&D describe many of the strategic and cost-related factors that have motivated large pharmaceutical companies to enter into various sorts of R&D partnerships. Major aspects of partnering behaviour of small biotechnology firms can be found in attempts to obtain access to skills, assets and technologies that would complement their state-of-the-art R&D capabilities and make up for a shortage of venture capital. As all these phenomena have become critical in the current process of inter-firm competition in the combined pharmaceutical and biotechnology industry, it is no surprise that the absolute number of R&D partnerships has increased dramatically during the past decades.

This growth is, to a very large degree, caused by the number of contractual agreements, i.e. joint R&D agreements and R&D contracts. Equity-sharing agreements (i.e. minority holdings), once the most prominent form of inter-firm R&D partnering, have largely been replaced by contractual arrangements as about 85 per cent of the recently established partnerships are of a contractual nature. This development suggests that partnering in the biotechnology industry demands organizational flexibility with the actual form of the partnership fitted to the strategic needs of the companies that are involved. In this industry where factors such as the increasing interdisciplinarity of technological fields, rapid scientific advances, and the high costs of R&D projects significantly affect inter-firm competition, companies strive to increase their organizational flexibility by engaging in numerous short-term R&D projects with multiple partners.

As demonstrated, the increase in alliances in the biotechnology industry has also led to a larger number of international or inter-Triadic partnerships. In relative terms the growth of these international partnerships has superseded the increase in the number of domestic partnerships or alliances in the same economic region. An explanation for this specific pattern can be found in the foreign sources of biotechnological know-how that companies seek through international R&D partnerships. In that context the dominance of North America, particularly the US, reflects the important role that this continent plays as a major source of R&D resources and capabilities in pharmaceutical biotechnology. This dominance has not only led companies from other countries, particularly the UK, Switzerland and Germany, to actively search for R&D partnerships with North American companies; the North American dominance of technological development in the biotechnology industry has led to a situation where a large percentage of R&D partnerships are formed between companies within the US.

A major conclusion from the above is that the US has emerged as preeminent in biotechnology R&D primarily on the basis of strong research initiatives on the part of small firms. These research-intensive biotechnology start-ups, an ideal type of modern Schumpeterian entrepreneurs, aided by the large amounts of resources provided by venture capitalists and IPO markets were first to undertake commercialization activities on the basis of the newly acquired knowledge in genetic engineering. In Asia and Europe, however, where the number of small firms is much lower than in the US, it was the large pharmaceutical companies that were first to incorporate the new scientific knowledge into their existing R&D programmes. During the early 1980s, large established firms, particularly from the US and Europe, started to invest heavily in biotechnology research through R&D partnerships with small US start-ups. This largely explains why partnerships within North America and partnerships between European and North American companies account for the majority of all partnerships established during the past two and a half decades.

NOTE

1. Information on size (number of employees) was collected from various sources such as the Institute for Biotechnology Information, the US Securities and Exchange Commission, World Scope Global Researcher, Amadeus, Dun & Bradstreet's Linkages, and Orsenigo (1989). Firms with less than or equal to 500 employees were regarded as small and those having between 501 and 5000 employees as medium sized companies. Firms with over 5001 employees were classified as large companies.

REFERENCES

Arora, A. and A. Gambardella (1990), 'Complementarity and external linkages: the strategies of the large firms in biotechnology', *Journal of Industrial Economics*, 38, pp. 361–79.

Barley, S.R., J. Freeman and R.C. Hybels (1992), 'Strategic alliances in commercial biotechnology', in N. Nohria and R.G. Eccles (eds), *Networks and organizations: structure, form, and action*, Boston, MA, Harvard Business School Press, pp. 311–47.

Bartlett, C.A., Y. Doz and G. Hedlund (1990), *Managing the Global Firm*, London, Routledge.

Berg, S.V., J. Duncan and P. Friedman (1982), *Joint Venture Strategies and Corporate Innovation*, Cambridge, MA: Oelgeschlager, Gunn & Hain.

Buckley, P.J. and M. Casson (1988), 'A theory of cooperation in international business', in F.J. Contractor and P. Lorange (eds), *Cooperative Strategies in International Business*, Lexington, MA: Lexington Books, pp. 31–54.

Cantwell, J. (1991), 'The international agglomeration of technological activity', in M. Casson (ed.), *Global Research Strategy and International Competitiveness*, Oxford: Blackwell, pp. 133–82.

Contractor, F.J. and P. Lorange (1988), 'Why should firms cooperate? The strategy and economics basis for cooperative ventures', in F.J. Contractor and P. Lorange (eds), *Cooperative Strategies in International Business*, Lexington, MA: Lexington Books, pp. 3–30.

Della Valle, F. and A. Gambardella (1993), 'Biological revolution and strategies for innovation in pharmaceutical companies', *R&D Management*, 23, pp. 287–301.

Doz, Y.L. (1988), 'Technology partnerships between larger and smaller firms: some critical issues', in F.J. Contractor and P. Lorange (eds), *Cooperative Strategies in International Business*, Lexington, MA: Lexington Books, pp. 317–38.

Dunning, J.H. (1988), *Multinationals, Technology and Competitiveness*, London: Unwin Hyman.

Dunning, J.H. (1993), *Multinational Enterprises and the Global Economy*, Wokingham: Addison-Wesley Publishing Company.

Dussauge, P. and B. Garette (1999), *Cooperative Strategy – Competing Successfully Through Strategic Alliances*, Chichester: Wiley.

Duysters, G. and J. Hagedoorn (1996), 'Internationalisation of corporate technology through strategic partnering: an empirical investigation', *Research Policy*, 25, pp. 1–12.

Duysters, G. and J. Hagedoorn (2000), 'International technological collaboration: implications for NIEs', in L. Kim and R.R. Nelson (eds), *Technological Learning and Economic Development: The Experience of the Asian Newly Industrialized Countries*, Cambridge: Cambridge University Press, pp. 193–215.

Eisenhardt, K.M. and C.B. Schoonhoven (1996), 'Resource-based view of strategic alliance formation: strategic and social effects in entrepreneurial firms', *Organization Science*, 7, pp. 136–50.

Fransman, M. (1991), 'Biotechnology: generation, diffusion and policy, an interpretive study', UNU/INTECH working paper.

Freeman, C. and J. Hagedoorn (1994), 'Catching up or falling behind: patterns in international inter-firm technology partnering', *World Development*, 22, pp. 771–80.

Galambos, L. and J.L. Sturchio (1998), 'Pharmaceutical firms and the transition to biotechnology: a study in strategic innovation', *Business History Review*, 72, pp. 250–78.

Grabowski, H. and J. Vernon (1994), 'Innovation and structural change in pharmaceuticals and biotechnology', *Industrial and Corporate Change*, 3, pp. 435–49.

Hagedoorn, J. (1993), 'Understanding the rationale of strategic technology part-

nering: inter-organizational modes of cooperation and sectoral differences', *Strategic Management Journal*, 14, pp. 371–85.
Hagedoorn, J. (1995), 'A note on international market leaders and networks of strategic technology partnering', *Strategic Management Journal*, 16, pp. 241–50.
Hagedoorn, J. (1996), 'Trends and patterns in strategic technology partnering since the early seventies', *Review of Industrial Organization*, 11, pp. 601–16.
Hagedoorn, J., A.L. Link and N. Vonortas (2000), 'Research partnerships', *Research Policy*, 29, pp. 567–86.
Hagedoorn, J. and R. Narula (1996), 'Choosing organizational modes of strategic technology partnering: international and sectoral differences', *Journal of International Business Studies*, 27, pp. 265–84.
Hagedoorn, J. and N. Roijakkers (2002), 'Small entrepreneurial firms and large companies in inter-firm R&D networks – the international biotechnology industry', in M. Hitt and D. Ireland (eds), *Strategic Entrepreneurship: Creating a New Integrated Mindset,* Oxford: Blackwell, forthcoming.
Hakansson, P., H. Kjellberg and A. Lundgren (1993), 'Strategic alliances in global biotechnology – a network approach', *International Business Review*, 2, pp. 65–82.
Hamel, G. (1991), 'Competition for competence and inter-partner learning within international strategic alliances', *Strategic Management Journal*, 12, pp. 83–102.
Harrigan, K.R. (1985), *Strategies for Joint Ventures*, Lexington, MA: Lexington Books.
Harrigan, K.R., (1988), 'Joint ventures and competitive strategy', *Strategic Management Journal*, 9, pp. 141–58.
Hirschey, R.C. and R.E. Caves (1981), 'Internationalisation of research and transfer of technology by multinational enterprises', *Oxford Bulletin of Economics and Statistics*, 42, pp. 115–30.
Hladik, K.J. (1985), *International Joint Ventures*, Lexington, MA: Lexington Books.
Kamien, M.I. and N.L. Schwartz (1982), *Market Structure and Innovation*, Cambridge: Cambridge University Press.
Kenney, M. (1986), 'Schumpeterian innovation and entrepreneurs in capitalism: a case study of the US biotechnology industry', *Research Policy*, 15, pp. 21–31.
Larson, A. (1992), 'Network dyads in entrepreneurial settings: a study of the governance of exchange relationships', *Administrative Science Quarterly*, 37, pp. 76–104.
Lorenzoni, G. and A. Lipparini (1999), 'The leveraging of inter-firm relationships as a distinctive organizational capability: a longitudinal study', S*trategic Management Journal*, 20, pp. 317–38.
Lumerman Oliver, A. and J. Porter Liebeskind (1997), 'Three levels of networking for sourcing intellectual capital in biotechnology: implications for studying inter-organizational networks', *International Studies of Management and Organization*, 27, pp. 76–103.
Mowery, D.C. (ed.) (1988), *International Collaborative Ventures in US Manufacturing*, Cambridge, MA: Ballinger.
Mowery, D.C., J.E. Oxley and B.S. Silverman (1998), 'Technological overlap and inter-firm cooperation: implications for the resource-based view of the firm', *Research Policy*, 27, pp. 507–23.
Mytelka, L.K. (ed.) (1991), *Strategic Partnerships and the World Economy*, London: Pinter.
Nooteboom, B. (1999), *Inter-firm Alliances – Analysis and Design*, London: Routledge.
Obleros, F.J. and R.J. MacDonald (1988), 'Strategic alliances: managing complementarity to capitalize on emerging technologies', *Technovation*, 7, pp. 155–76.

OECD (1992), *Technology and the Economy*, Paris: OECD.
Ohmae, K. (1985), *Triad Power*, New York: Free Press.
Ohmae, K. (1990), *The Borderless World*, New York: Harper.
Orsenigo, L. (1989), *The Emergence of Biotechnology: Institutions and Markets in Industrial Innovation*, London: Pinter.
Pearce, R.D. (1989), *The Internationalisation of Research and Development by Multinational Enterprises*, London: Macmillan.
Pisano, G.P. (1990), 'The R&D boundaries of the firm: an empirical analysis', *Administrative Science Quarterly*, 35, pp. 153–77.
Pisano, G.P. (1991), 'The governance of innovation: vertical integration and collaborative arrangements in the biotechnology industry', *Research Policy*, 20, pp. 237–49.
Pisano, G.P. and S.C. Wheelwright (1995), 'The new logic of high-tech R&D', *Harvard Business Review*, 73, pp. 93–105.
Powell, W.W. (1996), 'Inter-organisational collaboration in the biotechnology industry', *Journal of Institutional and Theoretical Economics*, 152, pp. 197–215.
Powell, W.W. (1998), 'Learning from collaboration: knowledge and networks in the biotechnology and pharmaceutical industries', *California Management Review*, 40, pp. 228–40.
Powell, W.W., K.W. Koput and L. Smith-Doerr (1996), 'Inter-organisational collaboration and the locus of innovation: networks of learning in biotechnology', *Administrative Science Quarterly*, 41, pp. 116–45.
Reich, R.B. (1990), 'Who is US?', *Harvard Business Review*, 68, pp. 53–64.
Reich, R.B. (1991), *The Work of Nations*, New York: Vintage Books.
Rothaermel, F.T. (2000), 'Technological discontinuities and the nature of competition', *Technology Analysis and Strategic Management*, 12, pp. 149–60.
Rothwell, R. and W. Zegveld (1982), *Innovation and the Small and Medium Sized Firm*, London: Pinter.
Saviotti, P.P. (1998), 'Industrial structure and the dynamics of knowledge generation in biotechnology', in J. Senker (ed.), *Biotechnology and Competitive Advantage: Europe's Firms and the US Challenge*, Cheltenham: Edward Elgar, pp. 19–43.
Saviotti, P.P., P. Joly, J. Estades, S. Ramani and M. De Looze (1998), 'The creation of European dedicated biotechnology firms', in J. Senker (ed.), *Biotechnology and Competitive Advantage: Europe's Firms and the US Challenge*, Cheltenham: Edward Elgar, pp. 68–88.
Scherer, F.M. (1984), *Innovation and Growth – Schumpeterian Perspectives*, Cambridge: MA, MIT Press.
Schumpeter, J.A. (1934), *The Theory of Economic Development*, London: Oxford University Press.
Schumpeter, J.A. (1942), *Capitalism, Socialism and Democracy*, New York: Harper and Row.
Senker, J. (1996), 'National systems of innovation, organizational learning and industrial biotechnology', *Technovation*, 16, pp. 219–30.
Senker, J. (1998), 'Biotechnology: the external environment', in J. Senker (ed.), *Biotechnology and Competitive Advantage: Europe's Firms and the US Challenge*, Cheltenham: Edward Elgar, pp. 6–18.
Senker, J. and M. Sharp (1997), 'Organizational learning in cooperative alliances: some case studies in biotechnology', *Technology Analysis and Strategic Management*, 9, pp. 35–52.
Shan, W., G. Walker and B. Kogut (1994), 'Inter-firm cooperation and start-up

innovation in the biotechnology industry', *Strategic Management Journal*, 15, pp. 387–94.
Smith, J.G. and V. Fleck (1988), 'Strategies of new biotechnology firms', *Long Range Planning*, 21, pp. 51–9.
Teece, D.J. (1986), 'Profiting from technological innovation: implications for integration, collaboration, licensing and public policy', *Research Policy*, 15, pp. 285–305.
Vernon, R. (1966), 'International investment and international trade in the product cycle', *Quarterly Journal of Economics*, 88, pp. 190–207.
Vernon, R. (1979), 'The product cycle hypothesis in a new international environment', *Oxford Bulletin of Economics and Statistics*, 41, pp. 255–67.
Walker, B. and S.R. Walker (1986), 'Trends and changes in drug research and development', in *Proceedings of the Society for Drug Research, twentieth anniversary meeting*, London, Kluwer.
Walsh, V. and I. Galimberti (1993), 'Firm strategies, globalisation and new technological paradigms: the case of biotechnology', in M. Humbert (ed.), *The Impact of Globalisation on Europe's Firms and Industries*, London: Pinter, pp. 175–90.
Walsh, V., J. Niosi, and P. Mustar (1995), 'Small-firm formation in biotechnology: a comparison of France, Britain and Canada', *Technovation*, 15, pp. 303–27.
Yoshino, M.Y. and U.S. Rangan (1995), *Strategic Alliances*, Boston, MA: Harvard Business School Press.

APPENDIX 4.1 THE MERIT-COOPERATIVE AGREEMENTS AND TECHNOLOGY INDICATORS (CATI) DATABANK

The MERIT-CATI databank (see Hagedoorn, 1993) contains information on nearly 10000 cooperative agreements in various sectors, ranging from high technology sectors such as IT and biotechnology to less technology intensive sectors such as chemicals and heavy electrical equipment. Systematic collection of inter-firm partnerships started in 1987. If available, many sources from earlier years were consulted to establish a retrospective overview. In order to collect detailed information about inter-firm partnerships, various sources are consulted: newspaper and journal articles, books dealing with the subject, and in particular specialized journals that report on business events.

This method of information gathering has some drawbacks and limitations due to the lack of publicity for certain arrangements, and the low profile of certain groups of companies and fields of technology. Despite these shortcomings, which are difficult to circumvent even by extensive and large-scale data collection, we have been able to obtain a clear overview of the joint efforts of many companies. This enables us to perform empirical research, which goes beyond single-firm case studies.

The databank contains information on each cooperative agreement and some information on companies participating in these agreements. Cooperative agreements are defined as mutual interests between independent industrial partners that are not linked through majority ownership. In the CATI databank, only those agreements that involve either a technology transfer or some form of jointly undertaken R&D are being recorded. Information is also collected on joint ventures in which new technology is received from at least one of the partners, or on joint ventures having some R&D programme. Other types of agreements such as production and marketing alliances are not included. In other words, this material is primarily related to R&D collaboration and technology cooperation, i.e. those agreements for which a combined innovative activity or an exchange of technology is at least part of the agreement. We regard as relevant information for each partnership: the number of companies involved; names of companies; year of establishment; and modes of cooperation. Important information on participating companies includes their location, and names of parent companies.

5. Financial liberalization, alliance capitalism and the changing structure of financial markets

Nigel Pain and Desirée van Welsum

INTRODUCTION

For much of the post-war period, financial institutions in North America, Europe and Japan typically operated in highly regulated markets, with controls that affected both the scope and the location of their activities. Many national and local markets remained segmented, with barriers to entry generating excess capacity and productive inefficiencies. But since the 1980s there has been a widespread dismantling of capital and exchange controls and a sustained period of deregulation and liberalization of financial markets in many industrialized economies, with prudential regulation replacing structural regulation. In conjunction with advances in information technologies and the increasing globalization of markets for goods and services, deregulation has generated rapid growth in international capital markets.

Financial market integration has been stimulated by significant consolidation within national markets as well as the rapid expansion in cross-border linkages between firms through both mergers and acquisitions and co-operative joint ventures and alliances. In the period from 1991 to 2000 financial companies accounted for approximately one-quarter of global cross-border mergers and acquisitions (UNCTAD, 2001, Table B10). The capitalization of equity and bond markets has risen significantly over the last 20 years, helped by a growing trend towards securitization within many national economies, and lending by financial institutions has expanded significantly, both in domestic and, more especially, international markets.

These changes are, on balance, likely to be welfare enhancing. National financial markets have become more contestable, with competitive pressures encouraging product innovations and a reduction in excess capacity and operational inefficiencies. The prospects for economic growth are also likely to have been improved, with domestic investors now able to raise finance from a larger volume of savings using a wider variety of financial instruments. But capital market integration may bring costs as well as benefits. Consolidation has been associated with an increasing complexity in the structure of financial institutions across sectors and across countries, and the removal of structural regulation has raised risk-taking incentives. The costs of internal and external monitoring of the activities of such firms have risen accordingly, raising the need for managers and regulators to take action to ensure the provision of timely information to assess solvency and prevent potential systemic risk. Inevitably, internal and external linkages, whether hierarchical or co-operative in nature, raise the potential scale and speed at which events in one location or institution could spread to other parts of the global financial system.

The objectives of this chapter are to examine some of the important forces causing financial institutions to change their corporate strategies and to discuss the wider impact of deeper financial market integration on the major industrialized economies. We begin by providing a stylized representation of the two main forms of financial systems found in most industrialised economies, the Anglo-US market based model and the bank based system commonly found in continental Europe and Asia. The historical evolution of these two models reflected differences in institutional structures as well as in regulatory frameworks. We then describe the main changes seen in the regulation of financial markets in the United States and the European Union over the last two decades, developments which have been reinforced by technological changes and the advent of monetary union in Europe. Next we describe some of the consequences of these and other changes for the internationalisation and integration of financial markets, looking in particular at recent developments in the foreign exchange market, the rapid rise in the number and value of mergers, acquisitions and joint ventures in financial markets, and the growth of cross-border lending by banks located in the major industrialized economies.

Little is known about the impact of joint ventures, particularly across national borders, but, as we discuss in the fourth section, much can be learned from reviewing the factors driving cross-border location in the banking sector and the impact of mergers on the efficiency of the investing banks. Two of the wider consequences of the growth in financial markets – the implications for regulators and the relationships between financial development and growth are considered in the fifth section, where we show that cross-border investments, as measured by foreign direct investment, appear to be more closely correlated with the cross-sectional variation in the growth rates of the major industrialised economies in the 1990s than do other indicators of financial development. Some concluding comments are given in the final section.

In common with related papers on the growth of financial markets we concentrate primarily on developments within the banking sector, partly to keep matters to a manageable length, but also because the majority of the extant literature on financial markets focuses on this sector. However, where possible, we try also to discuss developments in non-bank financial services, such as insurance, securities dealing and asset management, which have become relatively more important over time. For example, whilst the outstanding stock of cross-border bank lending continues to exceed the value of the outstanding stock of international debt securities, the latter has been the most important source of cross-border credit to non-banks since 1999 (Wooldridge, 2002).

DEREGULATION AND FINANCIAL SYSTEMS IN THE UNITED STATES AND EUROPE

For many years the post-war period was characterized by the development of two distinct sorts of relationship between commercial banking and other types of financial activity such as insurance and securities dealing and underwriting. In some countries, most notably the US, legislation ensured that the two activities remained separated. Other forms of structural regulation, such as quantitative restrictions on credit growth or interest rates, also restricted financial activity from time to time. In other countries, especially in continental Europe, universal banking was permitted, with financial institutions allowed to engage in all kinds of financial activities. A common feature of such systems was the development of close links between banks and non-financial firms, either through equity stakes or board participation.

The opportunities for cross-border transactions were also often limited, with many countries having some form of controls in place which artificially restricted the movements of goods, services and capital. Financial markets were particularly affected by the constraints on international capital flows, designed to help maintain currency stability, that existed in many industrialized economies until well into the 1980s.

However, since that time the American and European markets have both seen a gradual deregulation of restrictions that previously acted to segment national and international financial markets. By themselves these regulatory reforms would have generated significant structural changes and the removal of excess capacity; in conjunction with the new trading opportunities made possible by technological improvements they have acted to spur the rapid consolidation of financial institutions by changing the optimal scale of production, and expanding the supply of international financial services (Berger et al., 1999; Cavallo and Rossi, 2001).

Historical differences in national financial systems were also a reflection of differences in the institutional environment within which they developed (La Porta et al., 1998; Tsuru, 2000). In general, countries such as the US and the UK with a common law tradition that supports the rights of shareholders have tended to have a more highly developed and varied market based, or 'arm's length' financial system. Countries whose commercial laws are based on a civil law tradition, such as those in continental Europe, have tended to have bank based (sometimes termed 'relationship based') financial systems.[1]

The distinctive features of market and bank based systems are perhaps more apparent in their forms of corporate governance than in their patterns of corporate finance. In all industrialized countries, internal finance is the dominant source of funds for corporate investment, although the share of external finance in total finance does tend to be larger in countries with bank based systems (Corbett and Jenkinson, 1997).

Under a market based system, a large number of specialized financial markets and institutions provide different forms of financial instruments and perform monitoring functions. Such a framework relies heavily on legal enforcement, as explicit contracts are the sole form of protection for external creditors of a firm. Public information and disclosure requirements are particularly important to help ensure legal enforcement and achieve allocative efficiency.

Agency costs are more likely to arise in this form of financial system, but it is also more likely that finance will be provided to help support new, risky activities at a time of rapid technological changes, such as the development and use of information and communications technologies (Jorgenson, 2001).

Bank based systems have an advantage over securities markets for financing long-term investment projects in mature industries where innovation and uncertainty are low (Allen and Gale, 2000). Such systems provide a good way of overcoming agency costs. But inevitably there are fewer opportunities available for outsiders, reducing the potential for competition. Disclosure requirements tend to be weaker as well, since often only a single external financier needs to acquire information.

The ongoing consolidation in financial markets has begun to blur the distinction between the different kinds of financial system. In the US, deregulation has led to the creation of new integrated financial groups, while in Europe, deregulation has been associated with moves to open up previously segmented markets to external competition and strengthen the provision of finance from securities markets and the role of institutional investors.

Deregulation in the United States

In the United States, restrictions on both intrastate and interstate activities were gradually relaxed over the 1980s and early 1990s. Prior to then banking markets had been fragmented by historical prohibitions on interstate banking and the separation of investment and commercial banking codified in the Glass-Steagall Act of 1933. The Riegle-Neal Interstate Banking and Branching Efficiency Act of 1994 eliminated remaining restrictions on interstate banking and branching as of June 1997, making nationwide banking possible.[2] As we show below, these changes have been associated with significant consolidation in the banking industry. Insurance and securities companies have been less affected, reflecting the absence of previous restrictions on their geographic scope.

A particular feature of the US financial system is the presence of large investment banks such as Goldman Sachs, Morgan Stanley and Merrill Lynch, all of which grew in influence as a result of the historical separation of lending and securities work. Moves to reduce the barriers between commercial banking and securities and insurance activities began in 1987 when the Federal Reserve allowed commercial banks to establish particular forms of subsidiary companies (often termed 'section 20 subsidiaries') in order to underwrite corporate debt and equity, although the permitted scale of underwriting could not exceed 5 per cent of the subsidiary's total revenue. The permitted scale of underwriting was raised to 10 per cent in 1989 and 25 per cent in 1996 (Berger et al., 1999, 2000). The Financial Services Modernisation Act of 1999 (sometimes termed the Gramm-Leach-Bliley Act) removed most of the remaining barriers among banking, insurance and securities activities, although barriers between financial services and non-financial business were retained. In effect this has allowed the market rather than regulators to decide which forms of financial company are viable.

In the two years following the Act, just under 600 new financial holding companies (FHCs) were created, although the majority of these were relatively small. Most of the section 20 subsidiaries were converted into subsidiaries of FHCs (Olson, 2002). Regulatory and accounting differences continue to affect the ability of commercial banks to participate in investment banking markets. For instance, commercial banks book loans at their historical cost whereas investment banks use market prices. Functional regulation still persists, with the direct supervision of financial services firms remaining in the hands of their historic regulators. FHC licences are handed out by the Federal Reserve, which is the traditional regulator of commercial banks. None of the large US-owned investment banks with a global presence have currently chosen to become financial holding companies. This suggests that some of the potential efficiency gains that might be expected from the deregulation of segmented markets within the US may have yet to emerge.

Deregulation in Europe

The Single Market Programme (SMP) and the subsequent formation of monetary union have generated substantial structural changes in European financial markets since the mid-1980s (Gual, 1999). Prior to the advent of the SMP most European countries had fragmented banking systems, with differing national regulations and standards preventing market entry, especially in wholesale banking. The SMP reforms were based on the principle of mutual recognition, with host nations allowing foreign institutions from other EU economies to undertake the full range of activities permitted in their home market. At the same time minimum standards were imposed for all financial institutions in the EU in order to prevent excessive competition for market share through excessively lax rules and regulations which might ultimately raise systemic risk. A detailed summary of the SMP reforms is provided by Murphy (2000). Together they raised market contestability, created incentives for cross-border investments and rationalization of excess capacity, and allowed larger institutions freedom to try to exploit economies of scale and economies of scope by expanding their range of products and services. Banks have been allowed to operate freely across national borders in Europe since 1993, with universal banking becoming the norm. The process of concentration and restructuring has been particularly marked in the smaller EU countries (ECB, 2000); in Sweden and Finland the impetus provided by the SMP was reinforced by restructuring in the aftermath of the Scandinavian banking crisis in the early 1990s.

The historical segmentation of financial markets in Europe also stemmed from the presence of foreign exchange risk and the existence of many legal obstacles to international diversification, such as prudential requirements governing the currency composition of assets and liabilities (Arrowsmith et al., 1997; Gual, 1999). This segmentation acted as a de facto barrier to entry and raised rents for local institutions such as investment banks (often universal banks) which specialised in placing issues in their home country markets. Becoming a pan-European institution involved the creation of a network of local marketing and research teams.

Monetary union has eliminated exchange rate risk for intra-EMU trades and also relaxed the severity of the constraints imposed by asset–liability currency matching requirements. Both these changes would be expected to reduce market segmentation. For example, the costs of building up marketing and research capacity at a pan-European level for investment banks both inside and outside the Euro area have fallen, which should serve to raise the overall contestability of many financial markets. Underwriting fees for bonds denominated in European currencies, which had been almost double those for US dollar denominated bonds prior to 1999, have declined significantly since the start of monetary union (Galati and Tsatsaronis, 2001), and the differential with fees for dollar bonds has disappeared.

Since 1999 the European Commission has begun to pursue a series of further deregulatory measures outlined in the Financial Services Action Plan (FSAP) agreed at the Cologne European Council in June that year. The majority of these are aimed at ensuring greater harmonisation between remaining national standards and regulations, although the continuing existence of barriers to foreign investors in some countries is also a matter of concern. Progress in the first two years is summarised in EC (2001a, b). The introduction of measures aimed at deeper integration of European financial services markets stems primarily from a perception that enhanced financial development will improve the prospects for future economic growth. There are no official estimates of what might be expected from the FSAP, but unofficial estimates by the European Financial Round Table suggest that a properly functioning single financial market could raise EU GDP by 0.7 per cent per annum (Davies, 2002).

Deregulation, technological change, globalization and macroeconomic policies are all exerting pressure in the same direction on the structure of financial markets and the efficiency of financial institutions. Altunbas, et al. (2001) estimate that technical progress reduced costs in European banking markets by an average 3 per cent per annum between 1989–97, with higher gains being enjoyed by the largest banks. In some EU countries these forces have also been supplemented by the impact of the privatization of publicly owned credit institutions and moves towards 'demutualization' of particular institutions, such as building societies in the UK.

TRENDS IN FINANCIAL MARKET INTEGRATION

The worldwide trend towards liberalized financial markets, along with the move to institutionalization, the decline in transactions costs due to new technologies and the development of new financial instruments have all combined to bring a rapid growth in the level of international financial transactions. In this section we look at four measures of the extent of financial integration – foreign exchange and derivatives trading, mergers and acquisitions, joint ventures and alliances, and cross-border bank lending.

Foreign Exchange and Derivatives Markets

The average daily turnover in the global markets for foreign exchange and derivatives is summarized in Table 5.1. The size of these markets has implications for the effectiveness and scope of monetary policy transmission mechanisms. For instance, the scale of trading in the foreign exchange market can affect the extent to which the monetary authorities are able to influence exchange rates through unilateral, and even co-ordinated, official interventions.

Table 5.1 The global foreign exchange and derivatives markets

	1986	1989	1992	1995	1998	2001
Daily foreign exchange turnover ($bn)[a]	188	590	820	1190	1490	1210
As a ratio of:						
World exports of goods and services (%)	*7.2*	*15.8*	*17.3*	*19.0*	*22.0*	*16.0*
World GDP (%)[b]	*1.2*	*2.9*	*3.4*	*4.1*	*5.1*	*3.9*
OTC derivatives turnover ($bn)				200	375	575

Notes:
(a) Average daily turnover on spot, outright forward, and foreign exchange swap transactions, adjusted for local and cross-border double counting and for estimated gaps in reporting, measured at current market exchange rates.
(b) At market exchange rates.

Sources: Galati (2001), BIS (2001), IMF World Economic Outlook Database October 2001.

Average daily turnover in the foreign exchange market rose from around $200 billion in the mid-1980s (almost 1¼ per cent of global GDP) to a peak of $1490 billion (5.1 per cent of world GDP) in 1998. The most recent survey, conducted in April 2001 suggests that turnover was around 19 per cent lower than three years earlier.[3] Even so, turnover was still equivalent to nearly 4 per cent of global GDP and one-sixth of total world trade in goods and services. Some 57 per cent of turnover consisted of cross-border transactions between parties located in different countries, up from 54 per cent in 1995 and 1998 and 50 per cent in 1992.

The decline in turnover between 1998 and 2001 can be partly accounted for by the effects of the formation of the Euro area, which ended trading in the currencies of the former member states, wiping out 6 per cent of total turnover (Galati, 2001). In the 2001 survey the euro entered one side of 38 per cent of all currency transactions, whereas in 1998 the currencies of the Euro area members entered 52 per cent of all transactions. Other factors which may have served to limit turnover include technological changes, such as electronic broking, which are likely to have improved price transparency and the speed with which arbitrage opportunities are exploited, and the lower levels of market participation by many hedge funds whose profitability was adversely affected by their exposures during the emerging markets crises of 1997–99.

Trading in currency derivatives also declined between 1998 and 2001. However this was more than counteracted by rapid growth of trade in interest rate derivatives, and the total average daily turnover in global over-the-counter (OTC) derivatives markets rose by 53 per cent to $575 billion.[4] Cross-border contracts accounted for 58 per cent of total derivatives activity in 2001, compared with 54 per cent in 1995. Around one-third of all turnover in both the derivatives and foreign exchange markets was accounted for by transactions by UK-based institutions, approximately twice the share of the next largest host, the United States.

Financial Mergers and Acquisitions

The number and value of mergers and acquisitions by financial firms in 13 of the 16 largest OECD economies over the period 1991–99 are reported in Table 5.2 and shown as a proportion of nominal GDP in these countries in Figure 5.1.[5] The data are classified according to the country and sector of the acquiring firm. Around 96 per cent of all recorded acquisitions took place in the same countries.

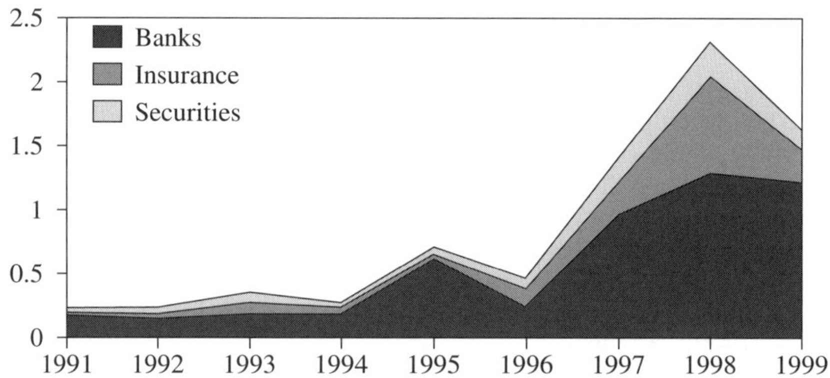

Source: See Table 5.2

Figure 5.1 Mergers and acquisitions (% of GDP)

The upward trend in the number and scale of transactions is readily apparent, particularly after 1994. Acquisitions by banks rose rapidly from 1995 onwards, partly reflecting the timing of legislative deregulation in the United States. Acquisitions by insurance companies and securities firms (a

Table 5.2 Financial mergers and acquisitions (by country and sector of acquiring firm)

World	1991–93		1994–96		1997–99	
	No.	Value ($bn)	No.	Value ($bn)	No.	Value ($bn)
Within border / within industry	1408	117.6	1790	244.4	1849	847.4
Within border / cross industry	251	14.1	387	19.7	440	168.1
Cross border / within industry	165	9.3	303	33.6	396	117.7
Cross border / cross Industry	63	3.4	91	8.3	154	33.8
Regional shares of world total (%)						
North America						
Within border / within industry	46.1	48.4	49.9	47.9	42.4	45.7
Within border / cross industry	5.4	4.5	6.3	3.9	8.5	10.2
Cross border / within industry	2.1	1.3	3.6	2.4	4.9	2.3
Cross border / cross industry	0.8	0.2	0.8	0.3	1.8	0.6
Western Europe						
Within border / within industry	26.1	32.6	17.4	19.1	15.7	20.0
Within border / cross industry	7.4	4.5	7.8	2.2	5.4	4.0
Cross border / within industry	5.8	4.4	7.3	7.5	8.2	7.6
Cross border / cross industry	2.3	2.1	2.4	2.3	3.3	1.9
Pacific Rim						
Within border / within industry	2.4	0.4	2.3	12.9	7.0	7.0
Within border / cross industry	0.5	0.8	0.9	0.3	1.5	0.2
Cross border / within industry	0.8	0.7	0.9	1.1	0.8	0.1
Cross border / cross industry	0.2	0.1	0.4	0.1	0.4	0.4
Industry shares of world total (%)						
Banking						
Within border / within industry	50.5	54.1	49.1	62.8	42.6	57.4
Within border / cross industry	4.3	4.2	5.8	2.6	5.8	3.1
Cross border / within industry	3.2	1.8	4.0	5.6	5.0	4.0
Cross border / cross industry	1.2	0.4	1.8	0.8	1.7	0.5
Insurance						
Within border / within industry	9.3	13.9	7.9	11.7	7.0	9.5
Within border / cross industry	2.0	0.9	2.2	1.0	1.7	8.2
Cross border / within industry	3.4	3.5	4.6	3.3	5.6	4.6
Cross border / cross industry	0.6	0.5	0.4	0.1	1.0	1.2
Securities/other						
Within border / within industry	14.8	13.4	12.6	5.3	15.5	5.7
Within border / cross industry	7.0	4.7	7.1	2.9	7.9	3.1
Cross border / within industry	2.1	1.1	3.2	2.1	3.3	1.5
Cross border / cross industry	1.5	1.5	1.3	1.9	3.0	1.2

Source: Authors' calculations from G10 (2001, Annex A Tables).

category that includes investment banks) began to accelerate from 1997 onwards. The value of the average deal rose significantly over the 1990s, as can be seen from the global totals in Table 5.2. In 1997–99 the number of transactions was 50 per cent higher than in 1991–93, but the total value was more than eight times the size.

Cross-border acquisitions have gradually become more important over time, accounting for 19.3 per cent of the total number of transactions and 13 per cent of the value of transactions in 1997–99, compared with 12 per cent and 8.8 per cent respectively in 1991–93. However it continues to be the case that the average size of cross-border acquisitions remains well below that of within-border acquisitions. Most acquisitions are within-industry, although the share of cross-industry deals has risen over time, especially in value terms. In 1997–99, 20.9 per cent of all deals were cross-industry, accounting for 17.3 per cent of the value of deals. Clearly the average size of cross-industry deals is lower than that of within-industry deals.

In the lower panels of Table 5.2 we report the distribution of the total number of transactions according to the location and industry of the acquiring firm. Over half of all acquisitions are by firms from North America, with the vast majority of these occurring within national borders. The value of within-border cross-industry deals rose sharply in the 1997–99 subperiod, primarily reflecting the formation of Citigroup in 1998 by the merger of Citicorp, a bank holding company, and Travelers, which was a securities and insurance firm. Carow (2001) provides a detailed overview of this merger and its subsequent effects.

Western European firms accounted for around one-third of all transactions, although their combined GDP is under one-quarter of the total sample of countries. In contrast, the share of the Pacific Rim countries, Japan and Australia, during the 1990s was well below their share of GDP. One notable feature is that cross-border acquisitions are much more likely to be undertaken by Western European firms, partly reflecting the size of individual national markets, but also the incentives and opportunities provided by the Single Market Programme and the advent of monetary union.

Around two-thirds of all acquisitions have been by banking sector firms, with the vast majority of the target firms being other banks within national borders. To a large extent this reflects the marked consolidation that has taken place in the US banking industry. The number of banking organizations in the US declined from around 12300 in 1980 to just over 6600 by the middle of 2001 and the share of banking assets held by the largest 25 banks rose from 33 per cent to 61 per cent (Olson, 2002). Acquisitions by insurance and securities firms are more likely to take place across industries and across national borders. However the aggregate rise in the share of all transactions accounted for by cross-border deals stems primarily from the rise in the proportion of banking sector transactions that are cross-border.

The main features of the consolidation process in the EU banking sector from 1995 to the middle of 2000 are analysed in ECB (2000). As the data in Table 5.2 suggest, the majority of M&A activity took place between domestic banks during this period, particularly smaller banks. Approximately four-fifths of all EU mergers were concentrated in the four member states with the largest number of credit institutions – Germany, Italy, France and Austria.[6] Banking sector concentration rose in almost all member states between 1995–99, and was typically higher in the smallest countries. In 1999 the market share of the five largest institutions exceeded 70 per cent in Belgium, Denmark, Finland, Greece, Netherlands, Portugal, and Sweden. Ireland, Luxembourg and Austria were exceptions, the former two because of the presence of many foreign banks and the latter because it has a large number of small credit institutions. Despite this, Austria, along with Denmark, Germany and Italy, is estimated to have the most efficient banks in Europe by Altunbas, et al. (2001).[7]

Looking at international bank M&As, it was found that, numerically at least, the majority of cross-border banking transactions by EU institutions were outside the European economic area, partly reflecting a desire to raise profitability by expanding in emerging markets. The banking sector also appeared to be the driving force behind the formation of financial conglomerates – groups of financial companies operating in different sectors of the financial industry. However, in some EU countries at least, there continue to be significant impediments to foreign ownership of financial institutions (Davies, 2002).

Conglomerates can be set up through mergers or by financial institutions setting up a subsidiary company in another financial sector. Over the period 1997–99 both forms of investment accounted for a roughly equal proportion of national and cross-border conglomerate transactions. Figure 5.2 shows the total number of conglomerate transactions per year since 1995. Just under four-fifths of transactions concerned institutions from five EU countries – Italy, the UK, Luxembourg, Portugal and Greece. With the exception of Italy, most transactions by institutions from these countries involved the establishment of enterprises in new sectors of the financial industry rather than direct acquisitions.

In other countries, notably Austria and Denmark, linkages between different segments of the financial services industry were increased through the establishment of jointly owned enterprises. These offer specialized financial services, such as asset management and stockbroking activities,

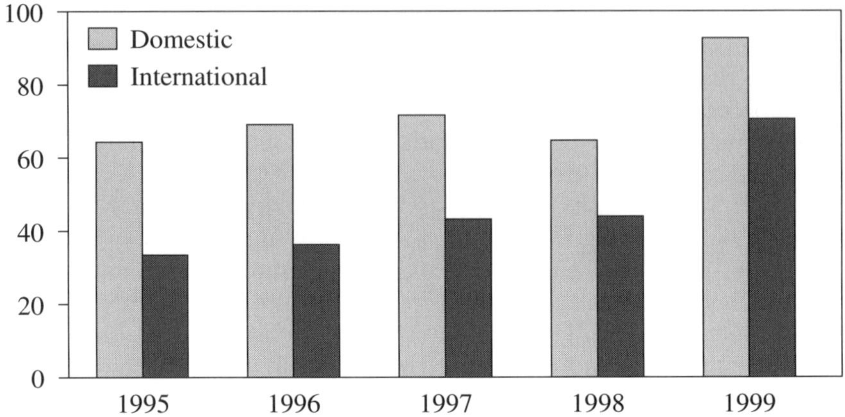

Source: ECB (2000, Tables 2 and 3).

Figure 5.2 EU conglomerate transactions

marketed through all their respective owners which are often within the banking sector.

Financial Joint Ventures and Strategic Alliances

The number of joint ventures and strategic alliances entered into by financial firms is shown in Table 5.3. These data are shown only by number of transactions, so direct comparison with the mergers and acquisitions data in terms of size and industry mix is not possible. None the less the data show the same aggregate trend, with the number of joint ventures rising sharply during the 1990s. The general pattern of the data suggests that joint ventures are much more likely to be undertaken when market entry is difficult, particularly across national borders. Asiedu and Esfahani (2001) provide a detailed analysis of the different factors affecting the host and home country firm share of cross-border joint ventures.

The total number of joint ventures and strategic alliances in 1997–99 was less than two-thirds of the total number of mergers, but the number of cross-border joint ventures was greater than the number of cross-border mergers. Cross border ventures accounted for around 40 per cent of all joint ventures over the sample period, more than twice their share of mergers and acquisitions. The geographical distribution of cross border ventures was remarkably equal by 1997–99, with around one-third of alliances taking place in each of the three main supranational markets. Joint ventures in Western Europe and the Pacific Rim are much more likely to be across national borders than

Table 5.3 Financial joint ventures and strategic alliances (by country of acquiring firm)

	1991–93	1994–96	1997–99
World			
Within-border	214	445	1092
Cross-border	187	257	691
Regional Shares (%)			
North America			
Within-border	28.7	42.6	43.7
Cross-border	16.2	14.1	12.8
Western Europe			
Within-border	19.2	14.0	8.2
Cross-border	24.7	15.7	13.6
Pacific Rim			
Within-border	5.5	6.8	9.4
Cross-border	5.7	6.8	12.4

Source: Authors' calculations from G10 (2001, Annex A Tables).

within national borders, possibly reflecting both average country size and the prevalence of barriers to product market entry in the form of national differences in factors such as regulatory and accounting systems.

Although the number of cross-border mergers by financial firms grew rapidly during the 1990s, firms from this sector were less likely to invest overseas than firms from other sectors. This is illustrated in Figure 5.3, using data from Focarelli and Pozzolo (2001) for 29 OECD economies classified by the sector of the bidder.[8] Financial mergers accounted for over 40 per cent of the total number of mergers over this period, but represented only 27 per cent of all cross-border mergers. Cross-border mergers represented just 15 per cent of all finance mergers, compared with 34 per cent of all manufacturing mergers.

To some extent the difference in the proportion of mergers that involve cross-border transactions in the financial and non-financial sectors stems from the particularly large number of financial mergers within the United States, which serves to reduce the overall proportion of cross-border transactions in the banking sector. Focarelli and Pozzolo (2001, Table 3) show that only 4.2 per cent of all acquisitions by US banks between 1990–99 took place outside the US, whereas 25.4 per cent of acquisitions by non-US banks involved purchases outside the home economy of the purchasing firm.[9]

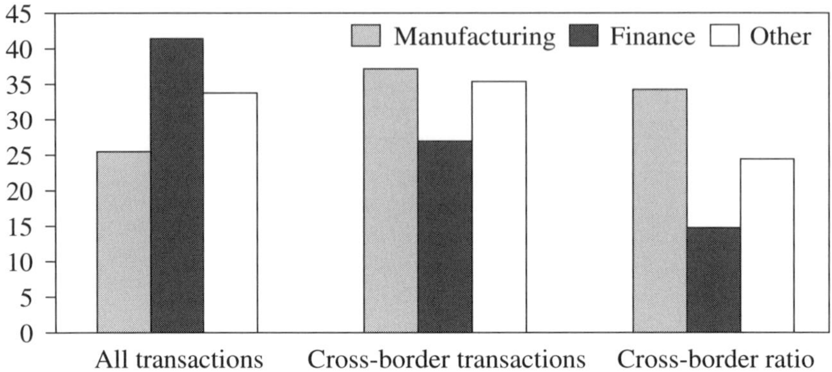

Note: Cross-border ratio is the ratio of cross-border to total transactions in each sector.

Source: Authors' calculations from Focarelli and Pozzolo (2001, Table 1).

Figure 5.3 OECD mergers and acquisitions by sector 1991–99 (%)

Cross-border Banking Transactions

Deregulation and other structural changes have also helped cross-border banking activity to rise rapidly in recent years, especially in the interbank market. For example, cross-border interbank claims between banks located in the Euro area rose from $650 billion in 1995–97 to over $900 billion after the start of monetary union in 1999 (Galati and Tsatsaronis, 2001). Most of this was accounted for by larger banks trading across borders, reflecting their greater expertise at dealing with foreign counterparts, with smaller institutions continuing to operate largely at the national level.

An indication of the aggregate foreign exposure of national banking systems in the major industrialized economies is provided in Table 5.4, which shows consolidated foreign on-balance sheet claims by banks in the BIS reporting area as of the third quarter of 2001. These comprise all cross-border claims by reporting banks incorporated in the respective country, plus local and foreign currency lending by their foreign affiliates. Banks from the 11 countries shown in the table account for 79.4 per cent of all cross-border lending by banks within the Bank for International Settlements (BIS) reporting area.[10] The total claims outstanding were $11.6 trillion (approximately 37 per cent of world GDP at market exchange rates in 2001), of which 80 per cent represented lending to firms, banks and governments in other developed economies. Claims on developing economies represented approximately 11½ per cent of total claims, with the remainder accounted for largely by claims on offshore banking centres in

Table 5.4 Foreign bank lending by nationality of reporting bank in 2001Q3

	Total	Developed economies	Developing economies					Other[a]
			Total	Asia	Africa & Middle East	Latin America	Developing Europe	
Total ($bn)	11579.8	9269.6	1331.3	375.2	142.8	558.4	254.9	979.0
A. SHARE OF TOTAL (%)								
USA	7.3	5.5	19.3	17.1	10.5	28.6	6.8	8.0
Canada	2.7	2.8	2.8	1.5	1.4	5.1	0.3	1.8
Japan	10.8	10.5	6.2	16.4	3.9	2.1	1.6	19.3
Belgium	3.9	4.3	2.2	0.9	1.8	0.4	8.2	2.1
France	7.1	7.3	6.6	6.9	20.8	3.6	5.1	6.0
Germany	19.5	20.9	15.1	12.3	15.9	6.7	37.2	12.8
Italy	2.5	2.4	4.4	0.7	1.8	4.9	10.3	1.8
Netherlands	3.8	3.7	5.4	6.3	4.1	4.7	6.5	2.1
Spain	3.1	1.8	13.2	0.3	1.3	30.6	0.5	1.0
Switzerland	8.9	10.2	2.4	2.9	4.5	1.7	2.1	5.1
UK	9.8	8.2	9.7	15.0	17.9	6.8	3.8	24.6
B. LOANS AS % OF HOME COUNTRY GDP IN 2000								
USA	8.5	5.1	2.6	0.6	0.2	1.6	0.2	0.8
Canada	44.4	36.8	5.2	0.8	0.3	4.0	0.1	2.4
Japan	26.3	20.6	1.8	1.3	0.1	0.3	0.1	3.9
Belgium	199.8	177.8	13.0	1.7	1.2	1.0	9.2	9.0
France	63.8	52.4	6.8	2.0	2.3	1.5	1.0	4.6
Germany	120.7	103.3	10.7	2.5	1.2	2.0	5.1	6.7
Italy	27.4	20.3	5.5	0.3	0.2	2.6	2.4	1.6

Table 5.4 (continued)

	Total	Developed economies	Developing economies					Other[a]
			Total	Asia	Africa & Middle East	Latin America	Developing Europe	
Netherlands	118.1	93.0	19.6	6.4	1.6	7.1	4.5	5.5
Spain	63.7	30.6	31.4	0.2	0.3	30.6	0.2	1.7
Switzerland	425.3	391.1	13.3	4.5	2.7	4.0	2.2	20.9
UK	79.8	53.7	9.1	4.0	1.8	2.7	0.7	17.0

Note: (a) Offshore centres, international institutions and unallocated.

Source: Authors' calculations from BIS (2002) and IMF *International Financial Statistics Yearbook 2001*.

Asia and the Caribbean. Banks from the United States, Germany and Spain are relatively exposed in developing economies, accounting for 13–19 per cent respectively of total lending. Claims on other banks accounted for 46.5 per cent of the total global amount of outstanding claims and 50.3 per cent of claims on the developed economies.

Overall, while banks from the largest economies account for the bulk of total claims, the exposure of all but Germany is relatively small in relation to the size of their home economies. Foreign claims of US banks in 2001Q3 were equivalent to only 8½ per cent of the level of US GDP in 2000 for instance. Several small economies, notably Switzerland, Belgium and Netherlands, have large foreign banking claims relative to the size of their economies and also relative to the size of domestic bank claims on domestic residents, which are shown in Table 5.6 later in the chapter.

The pattern of lending to developing economies is clearly strongly influenced by both historical ties and geographical links. French banks account for over one-fifth of all lending to Africa and the Middle East, German banks for over a third of all lending to developing European nations, and US and Spanish banks together account for almost 60 per cent of lending to Latin America. Japanese banks are relatively prominent elsewhere in Asia, including in offshore centres. British banks also have a strong presence in these centres, accounting for almost one-quarter of total claims in them. The geographical divergence in the spread and scope of exposures means that shocks in particular emerging markets will have differential impacts in different industrialized economies.

The extent to which Spanish banks are exposed to developments in Latin America is particularly striking, with outstanding claims equivalent to 30 per cent of domestic GDP, and around 12 per cent of these representing claims on Argentina. Subsidiaries of Spanish banks are estimated to control around one-fifth of Argentina's banking system. The downturn in the Argentine economy between 1999 and the end of 2001 and the associated build-up of financial pressures, with total deposits in the financial system falling by more than one-fifth in 2001, illustrates the two-way dangers that can arise from such strong linkages. In January 2002 Spain's largest bank, Santander Central Hispano, set aside €1.29bn, an amount equal to the total value of its investment in its Argentinean subsidiary Banco Rio de la Plata (Argentina's third largest bank), to cover potential losses. An additional €1.09bn was set aside to cover potential losses elsewhere in Latin America.[11] BBVA, Spain's second largest bank, also set aside €1.35bn to cover potential losses from its Argentinean subsidiary Banco Frances, Argentina's second largest bank (Crawford, 2002a, b). Taken together these three sets of provisions amounted to 0.6 per cent of Spanish GDP in 2000.

THE DETERMINANTS AND IMPACT OF CROSS-BORDER BANKING MERGERS

Determinants

In practice there are a wide range of factors that may determine the pattern of specialization and location over time. Multinational enterprises arise through a combination of industrial organization motives that result in a number of activities being placed under common ownership and control, and comparative advantage reasons that cause these activities to be placed in separate countries (Krugman, 1995).

Empirical studies of profit maximizing multinational firms point to factors such as market size in the host and home locations, the relative costs of production in different locations, the presence of external agglomeration economies from factors such as skilled labour and clusters of related firms, barriers to the entry of foreign product markets and fiscal instruments such as investment incentives and tax structures as important determinants of the scale, timing and location of investments (Barrell and Pain, 1999; Hubert and Pain, 2002).

Most cross-border investments continue to take place between industrialized economies. This indicates that models of location choice must involve more than just considerations of relative costs. Theories of the multinational firm (Dunning, 1995; Markusen, 1995) and the econometric evidence on the determinants of FDI both highlight the extent to which the decision to establish foreign subsidiaries is influenced by the scope to appropriate the rents accruing from the development of firm-specific knowledge-based assets and practices.

All these factors can be expected to have some bearing on the decisions of profit-maximizing financial companies to invest overseas. Such investments may help to diversify risk and also allow economies of scale and scope to be exploited, especially by financial institutions from countries with a relatively small domestic market. As in many other service sectors, a foreign presence is often essential for successful market entry. Useful summaries of the extant literature are provided by Focarelli and Pozzolo (2001) and Moshirian (2001). Deregulation and technological advances have raised the feasible span of the firm and reduced barriers to market entry, although prudential regulations continue to limit the foreign exposure of some financial institutions.

One clear finding is that larger and more efficient banks are more likely to expand internationally (Focarelli and Pozzolo, 2001; Esperanca and Gulamhussen, 2001). Some key characteristics of a sample of banks in the OECD economies are summarized in Table 5.5.[12] These confirm that large banks are much more likely to undertake acquisitions abroad than are small banks. Conversely, small banks are more likely to be the target for any acquisition, including minority shareholdings, than are large banks. There is also a clear positive correlation between overseas acquisitions and size, with the mean asset levels of banks with foreign shareholdings around 2½ times those without foreign shareholdings. This is true for both large and small banks. However foreign investment does not appear to affect the relative scale of different types of bank. The mean asset level of large banks is around 13 times that of small banks, irrespective of whether they have foreign shareholdings or not.

Table 5.5 Banks' distribution by size

	Large banks	Other banks
Number		
All	260	1888
With shareholdings abroad	114	32
With foreign shareholders	30	246
Mean assets ($bn)		
All	105.9	4.9
With shareholdings abroad	159.4	12.2
Without shareholdings abroad	64.2	4.8

Note: Large banks are ones with assets above $25 billion

Source: Authors' calculations from Focarelli and Pozzolo (2001, Tables 3 and 4).

Locations such as the City of London that offer agglomeration economies arising from the presence of large financial centres are more likely to host international investment (UNCTAD, 2001, Box II.5). Foreign banks now comprise approximately two-thirds of all registered banks in the City of London and in 2000 accounted for over half the combined assets of foreign and UK-owned banks.[13]

A distinctive feature of cross-border investment in financial services lies in the strong interlinkages with cross-border investments by non-financial firms, which in turn reflect the wider process of economic integration within and between supranational markets. Historically, many banks initially entered foreign markets in order to provide services to their home-country clients. Thus the international openness of home economies to trade is often correlated with the extent of international investment by their financial institutions. Moshirian (2001) finds that the location of banking FDI from the US, the UK and Germany is related both to the pattern of bilateral trade between them and host economies and to the level of FDI by non-financial firms from the home economies. Esperanca and Gulamhussen (2001) find that some foreign banks establish branches in the United States because of the presence of non-corporate customers, as measured by the number of immigrants from the home economy. Focarelli and Pozzolo (2001) also find that the ratio of exports to GDP helps to explain the cross-country variation in the degree of internationalization of domestic banks, although this measure becomes insignificant when they consider only a sample of large banks. One explanation for this latter finding is that it is smaller banks who benefit from the activities undertaken by their domestic clients in foreign markets; all large banks already have international firms among their client base.

An under-researched area concerns the policies available to host countries to try to influence the location of international financial institutions within wider supranational markets. This topic is particularly pertinent for the UK at the present time, faced with the decision over whether to enter the Euro area. In 1997 the UK government proposed a series of economic 'tests' that would need to be satisfied before Britain could enter monetary union. One of these concerned the impact on the domestic financial services industry and the City of London. A key issue here, on which there is little empirical evidence at present, is the extent to which the agglomeration economies available in the City will continue to outweigh those available in other financial centres, such as Frankfurt and Paris, which are located in the Euro area and are becoming more important bases for some institutions seeking to undertake pan-European transactions.

The Gains from Mergers

The large literature on the impact of within-border mergers and acquisitions by banks provides little evidence of significant subsequent cost savings, or efficiency improvements on the average transaction (Berger et al., 1999, 2000), although this does not mean that all mergers have been unsuccessful. Indeed the motivation for consolidation is likely to vary between financial institutions according to their primary business and size. Using a panel data set of banks and other financial institutions in France, Germany, Italy, the Netherlands, Spain, and the UK during 1992–97, Cavallo and Rossi (2001) suggest that efficiency in smaller banks is improved by raising their scale of production. For larger institutions, efficiency gains are more likely to be achieved through diversification of their output mix. Altunbas, et al. (2001), using a sample of European banks for 1989–97, confirm that scale economies are widespread for the smallest banks,[14] but suggest that banks of all sizes have scope for cost savings through reducing managerial and other organizational inefficiencies.

There is only a small literature on the impact of cross-border mergers and acquisitions in banking. Although such transactions are predominantly undertaken by larger and more efficient banks, this does not appear to be automatically reflected in the performance of their foreign subsidiaries. Berger et al. (2000) show that only US banks are more efficient than local competitors in the UK, France, Germany and Spain, although in a number of countries foreign banks can be as efficient as domestic banks. Buch and Golder (2001) suggest that foreign banks have a comparative cost disadvantage over domestic banks due to entry costs and asymmetric information about the operations and constraints of the regulatory structure in the host market.

There remains a possibility that the observed differences in the efficiency of domestic and foreign banks are artificially generated through one of two channels – transfer pricing within the firm so that profits are realized by parent companies not subsidiaries, or a failure to control adequately for differences in the types of activity undertaken. For example, domestic banks may have a different cost structure to foreign banks because they have a stronger presence in the retail banking market, allowing them freedom to spread costs over a larger customer base. Ideally, matched sampling or case studies of individual institutions before and after the injection of foreign equity are required to produce soundly based evidence. Case studies are certainly required if anything is to be learned from the wave of joint ventures and alliances recorded in Table 5.3.

An additional gap in the extant literature on the impact of mergers is the relative absence of research that permits an informed assessment of whether the potential benefits from universal banking, either within or across borders, are being realized. For European institutions product diversification is particularly attractive if they wish to concentrate business within the European market, given that monetary union reduces the likely benefits of geographic diversification.

The findings on efficiency gains suggest that foreign banks may find it difficult to gain significant market share in many countries. Indeed it is usual to find that the share of foreign institutions in the total number of banks is much bigger than their share of the total assets of the domestic banking sector in most industrialized economies. Although the benefits of the wave of cross-border transactions and alliances in the 1990s may have been weaker than some participants expected, there are no reasons to believe that the impact of deregulation and the concomitant globalization of financial markets have come to an end. The market for retail banking is inevitably going to retain a strong local bias, but the continued evolution of information technologies and electronic finance is likely to continue to create strong incentives and opportunities for cross-border expansion in wholesale and investment banking, insurance and other specialist financial services. The underlying rationale for cross-border investment – the need for a large distribution platform to cover the costs of developing and offering new products, has not changed. But as the costs of consolidation of large financial institutions rise, strategic alliances and joint ventures may become an increasingly attractive mode of international transactions (G10, 2001).

THE IMPACT OF FINANCIAL MARKET INTEGRATION

The increasing internationalization and integration of financial markets have a number of important policy consequences. In this section we focus on two of the most important – the implications for the regulation of financial institutions and markets and the impact of financial development on the longer-term prospects for economic growth.

Financial Risk and Regulation

If consolidation in financial markets within and across borders has changed the probability that some institutions might fail or become illiquid, then it may also have changed the possibility of systemic risk, given the increasing extent of interlinkages between institutions, either directly or indirectly, via their common exposures to many different national markets. These issues are discussed in detail in Berger et al. (1999, 2000) and G10 (2001). The economic effects of systemic crises can be large; there have, for instance, been several examples of major domestic banking crises in OECD economies since 1980 with the ultimate costs to governments being as high as 9–12 per cent of GDP in the cases of Finland and Mexico, and 3½ per cent of GDP in the United States (*OECD Economic Outlook*, June 1998, Box I.7).

Of course, one of the motives for institutions to expand either their geographic scope or their product range is to try to diversify risk. Identifying activities whose returns have low or negative correlation with those of their core business should improve risk diversification. But this need not necessarily be reflected in the risk of the individual institution. For instance, the gains from diversification may be utilised to make higher risk/return investments. In this case the principal benefits should be reflected in profitability rather than in an overall reduction of risk levels. Joint ventures may offer a better way of reducing some forms of risk than mergers and acquisitions, but they will not remove the costs of adverse selection if an inappropriate partner is chosen.

Equally, risks may rise as institutions become larger and more complex, especially if managers are having to expand the scope of their supervision to include markets or products with which they lack expertise, or attempting to integrate organizations that have very different corporate cultures.[15] The collapse of the (then) British-owned Barings Bank in 1995 stemmed largely from defects in monitoring procedures that allowed an individual employee to conceal trading losses of £1.4 billion arising from complex financial operations in East Asia. The near failure of Long-Term Capital Management, a highly leveraged US controlled hedge fund, in 1998 further underlines the extent to which the increasing complexity of financial activities can complicate financial supervision.

Even if the risks faced by individual institutions have fallen, the possibility of systemic risk may have risen (G10, 2001; ECB, 2000). Consolidation and the increasing complexity of institutions have raised the probability that liquidity problems in one institution could spread to others both within and across national borders, particularly if the same institution is subject to different regulatory regimes in different countries. Contagion might also increase the cost of rescue operations in countries which have publicly backed deposit guarantee schemes. Equally, some institutions might become so large they are considered too big to fail, creating potential moral hazard problems (Berger et al., 2000). A related issue is the extent to which foreign-owned institutions have become an increasing source of potential instability for host countries, especially relatively small ones.

The existence and anticipated continued growth of financial conglomerates is likely to require continued changes in the structure of regulatory systems. National regulatory structures are likely to face greater pressures for convergence in every financial sector, since the health of national institutions will increasingly depend on the effectiveness of the prudential regulations limiting what they can undertake in other countries. Risk-based capital standards are likely to become an increasingly important tool for regulators, as well as for internal monitoring. Increased cooperation will also be required in those countries with separate regulators of banking, insurance and securities markets. Competition policies at a supranational level also have an important role to play, along with measures to force greater transparency and improved accounting practices. An example is the range of measures in the EU Financial Services Action Plan.

In the European economic area the development of cross-border activities and financial conglomerates creates a need for closer supervisory cooperation between member states (ECB, 2000). Memoranda of understanding are already in place to facilitate such cooperation at the bilateral level, while work is under way in the EU and at the wider international level to develop further the prudential regulation of financial conglomerates.

Regulators in the industrialised economies also need to consider the particular problems that might emerge from the exposure of national institutions in emerging markets. The financial crises in South-East Asia, Latin America and Russia during 1997–98 underline the importance of well functioning financial markets and risk management systems for economic performance. One of the problems in each of these developing regions in the build up to the crises was a gradual accumulation of short-term financial commitments (FSF, 2000). Although a high proportion of short-term commitments is common in most countries, it can cause particular difficulties to developing economies who are especially reliant on trade revenues to generate the income required to pay back maturing debt. Short-term capital flows to these countries thus entail liquidity risk, and abrupt changes in sentiment, or sharp fluctuations in primary commodity prices, that lead to portfolio adjustments and debt repayment problems can have systemic consequences.

The proportion of short-term loans in total international bank lending to the developing regions is shown in Figure 5.4.[16] Short-term bank loans are defined as those with a maturity of less than one year. In mid-2001, the proportion of outstanding loans that were short-term was smaller in most developing regions than in developed economies, with the notable exception of Africa and the Middle East.

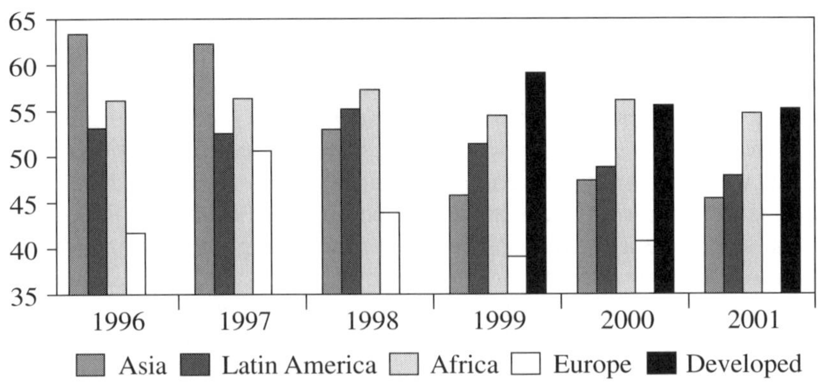

Source: Bank for International Settlements, *The Maturity, Sectoral and Nationality Distribution of International Bank Lending*, various issues.

Figure 5.4 Proportion of short-term foreign bank loans (mid-year, %)

Total bank loans to the developing countries rose from $657 billion in mid-1996 to $828 billion in mid-2001. But it is notable that reporting banks have reduced their short-term exposure to several regions since the mid-1990s. This was particularly marked in Asia, where the proportion of short-term loans declined from around two-thirds in 1996 to under one half by 1999. A gradual reduction in the proportion of short-term loans in Latin America and the transition economies of Central and Eastern Europe is also apparent since 1997–98.

Financial Development and Economic Growth

The relationship between financial development and economic growth has been analysed extensively in recent years. Theoretical modelling and empirical evidence have both suggested that well developed capital markets, typically measured by indicators such as the scale of the banking industry and stock market capitalization, can aid the prospects for sustainable long-run economic growth (Pagano, 1993; Levine, 1997; Levine and Zervos, 1998; Tsuru, 2000).

In a neo-classical world, the form of the financial system might be expected to have little effect on economic growth, with perfect information and few transactions costs obviating the need for financial institutions. Equally, if there were no capital market imperfections the Modigliani–Miller theorems would suggest that different types of corporate financing would not matter for the investment decisions of the firm. But in a world of incomplete information, with potential dead-weight costs associated with bankruptcy, the structure of capital markets may matter.

If savers and borrowers cannot be matched costlessly, financial systems can contribute to the growth process by providing services that help to mobilise and allocate savings, diversify risk and monitor the behaviour of borrowers. If potential borrowers and lenders have asymmetric information, individual investors face agency costs arising from adverse selection (the risk of financing an inherently uneconomic project) and moral hazard (an inability to monitor perfectly the allocation of the funds by the borrower). Securities markets and financial intermediaries such as banks can help to overcome some, although not all, of these costs by undertaking delegated monitoring and assessment (Diamond, 1984). In turn this may help in the development of larger scale and higher return investment projects.

An efficient financial system can simultaneously lower the cost of external borrowing, raise the returns to savers, and ensure that savings are allocated to projects that promise the highest returns, all of which have the potential to affect economic growth rates. However it may also reduce the level of household savings by easing liquidity constraints. This would moderate the effects of liberalization on growth, although not necessarily on consumer welfare.

The ongoing liberalization of the regulations governing institutional investors in the European economic area and North America should raise the level of financial intermediation. This in turn should help to raise the level of investment, and hence the level of output in the world economy as a whole. Greater financial intermediation allows risks to be shared and encourages the global allocation of capital towards projects with the highest marginal product. The expansion of new forms of financial activity, such as venture capital, may also encourage enterprise and innovation, with potential beneficial consequences for future productivity growth. However other developments, such as the consolidation of the banking sector through acquisitions of small, regionally based credit institutions, can at times adversely affect the flow of bank lending to small firms (Berger et al., 1999, 2000).

The evolving structure of national financial systems in Europe towards the US/UK market-based model may be especially important in the light of the possibilities for new investment to utilize recent developments in information and communications technologies. Innovation and entrepreneurship are more likely to be enabled when risk-taking is equity based, through venture capital and other markets, rather than collateral based, as in a bank centred financial system. The latter are more likely to support long term investments for process improvements (where existing fixed capital provides collateral) than the establishment of new firms (who, by definition have little or no tangible collateral) to undertake product innovations.

Empirical Evidence

After controlling for conventional determinants of growth, such as fixed investment and human capital, Bassanini and Scarpetta (2001) find that GDP growth in the OECD economies is significantly related to two indicators of financial development – stock market capitalisation and, to a lesser extent, deposit bank claims on the domestic private sector, both expressed relative to GDP. Leahy et al. (2001) find that both indicators also have a positive and generally significant effect on the level of investment. Taking the two sets of results together, Leahy et al. (2001) estimate that a rise of 10 percentage points in the ratios of stock market capitalization to GDP and private sector credit to GDP will ultimately raise GDP per capita by 3.3 per cent and 1.1 per cent respectively, other things remaining equal.

The plausibility of this finding is difficult to judge. It stems from estimation results which include the relatively smooth expansion in financial development during the 1970s and 1980s. At face value it implies that there should ultimately be a large rise in living standards associated with the recent changes in financial markets in the 1990s. For instance, stock market capitalisation in Switzerland rose from 73 per cent of GDP in 1990 to just over 300 per cent by 2000. The semi-elasticities cited in Leahy et al. (2001) imply that this should eventually be associated with a rise of 75 per cent in GDP per capita. It is difficult to think of economic mechanisms by which this might come about given that Switzerland already has one of the highest per capita incomes of all the industrialized economies.

A further difficulty in interpreting the relationship between growth and financial development lies in the possibility of reverse causality. Financial development may well be led by economic growth, with banks and other financial institutions being attracted to countries in which future economic growth is expected to offer profitable opportunities.

Some key financial indicators for the 13 industrialized economies considered in G10 (2001) are summarized in Table 5.6. There are clear differences across countries in the scale of different forms of financial activity, although the rapid rate of growth of financial market activity, especially in equity markets, is readily apparent in all of them. Cross-border mergers and acquisitions activity is included in the data for the combined total of inward and outward FDI stocks as a proportion of GDP.[17] There was a marked rise in FDI linkages in all countries during the 1990s, with the notable exception of Japan.

The correlations between various forms of financial activity in 1990 and average annual GDP growth between 1990–2000 are shown in Figures 5.5–5.7. These illustrate the difficulties in explaining the relationship between growth and financial development. For instance stock market capitalization is found to be significantly correlated with growth in many empirical studies. Yet two of the countries with the most highly valued stock markets in 1990 – Japan and Switzerland – also had the weakest average annual GDP growth rates during the 1990s. These two observations are sufficient to induce the negative cross-sectional relationship shown in Figure 5.5. Dropping them from the sample brings about a positive cross-sectional relationship between growth and stock market capitalization, although not a significant one. This illustrates how the results from any cross-country empirical exercise could easily be influenced by the range of countries included in the sample, as well as the difficulties of abstracting from cyclical developments.

Switzerland is clearly an outlier among this group of countries. By 2000 the ratio of stock market capitalisation to GDP was well above that seen in any other economy. The amount of private domestic credit advanced by deposit banks in 1997 was higher in relation to GDP than in any other

Table 5.6 Financial development and growth

	Stock market capitalization			Bonds outstanding		Assets of deposit money banks (% of GDP)			Inward + outward FDI stock (% of GDP)[(a)]		GDP growth (% p.a.)
	1980	1990	2000	1990	1997	1980	1990	1997	1990	1997	1990–2000
USA[(b)]	45.2	51.7	151.9	129.0	156.9	72.3	78.3	72.7	21.9	41.1	3.2
Canada	41.0	41.9	109.4	72.5	85.4	45.6	52.1	77.5	34.3	46.5	2.8
Japan	30.2	89.1	70.9	93.0	109.7	97.9	132.4	127.9	6.4	7.5	1.4
Australia	30.9	35.5	102.6	37.0	44.5	38.5	71.8	82.1	34.2	48.3	3.5
Belgium	10.0	30.7	79.7	139.6	159.2	43.5	66.1	137.9	46.5	98.7	2.1
France	8.4	24.1	110.6	60.1	84.6	82.0	102.2	100.0	15.2	26.3	1.8
Germany	9.5	21.8	67.2	57.3	86.5	96.7	111.7	137.9	12.2	23.8	1.9
Italy	4.2	12.7	70.8	100.2	138.6	70.6	64.3	72.3	10.0	29.8	1.6
Netherlands	17.3	39.2	171.8	53.8	67.6	77.0	103.8	125.7	57.5	91.9	2.9
Spain	8.2	21.5	89.4	42.2	62.0	74.9	93.4	101.8	15.7	28.8	2.7
Sweden	9.5	38.6	150.3	78.3	115.9	48.6	64.6	45.1	26.0	54.5	1.8
Switzerland	40.1	64.4	318.3	67.8	75.7	114.3	170.8	181.1	44.8	94.0	0.9
UK	33.2	79.3	187.2	38.0	59.4	32.4	115.8	122.3	42.1	49.0	2.3

Notes:
(a) Year end asset values as a proportion of calendar year GDP.
(b) Stock market figures for 1990 and 2000 are for combined value of shares on NASDAQ and the NYSE.

Sources: Columns 2 and 5–9: World Bank *Database on Financial Development and Structure*; columns 3–4: calculations from International Federation of Stock Exchanges *Market Capitalisation of Shares of Domestic Companies* and IMF *International Financial Statistics Yearbook 2001*; columns 10–12: calculations from IMF *International Financial Statistics Yearbook 2001* and OECD *Main Economic Indicators*, January 2002.

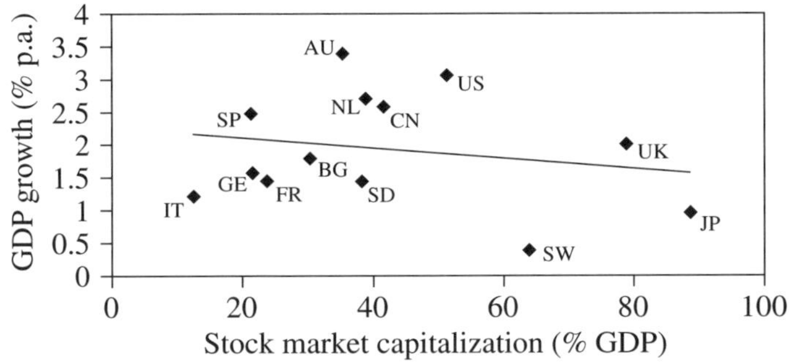

Figure 5.5 Stock market capitalization in 1990 and GDP growth in the 1990s

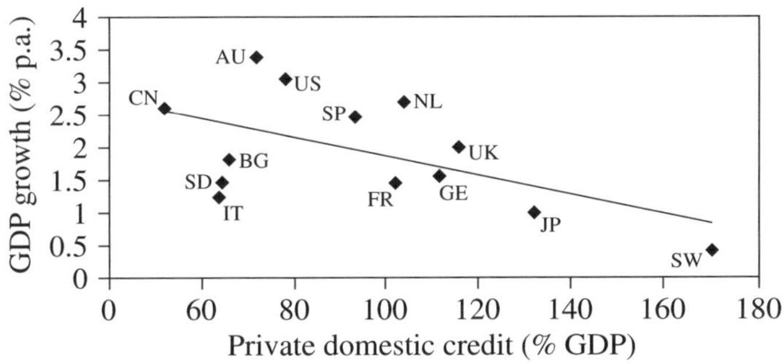

Figure 5.6 Deposit money bank assets in 1990 and GDP growth in the 1990s

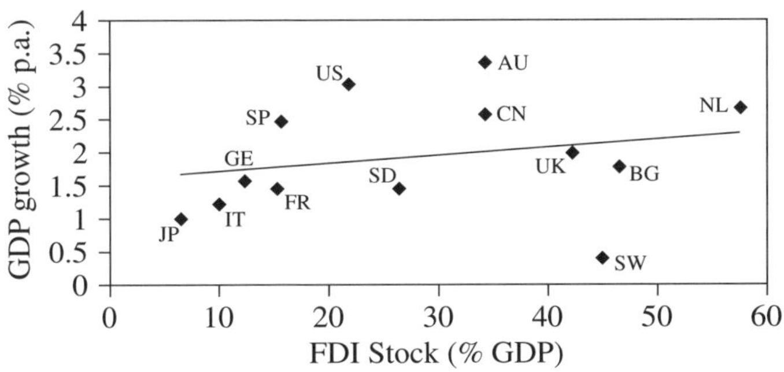

Note: Countries for Figures 5.5–5.7 are Australia (AU), Belgium (BG), Canada (CN), France (FR), Germany (GE), Italy (IT), Japan (JP), Netherlands (NL), Spain (SP), Sweden (SD), Switzerland (SW), the UK and the US.

Figure 5.7 FDI stocks in 1990 and GDP growth in the 1990s

country, and the combined stocks of inward and outward FDI were greater than in all countries apart from Belgium. A similar pattern existed in 1990. Despite the significant scale of financial development, GDP growth through the 1990s was poor, indicating that many other factors need to be included in any detailed empirical exercise to explain variations in cross-country economic performance.

Figure 5.6 shows that there is a negative cross-sectional relationship between the level of private domestic credit and growth in the 1990s, again contrary to the findings from many existing empirical studies. The negative coefficient on credit in a simple linear regression is significant if Switzerland is included, but becomes insignificant if it is dropped from the sample.

A more striking finding apparent from Figure 5.7 is that there is a positive cross-sectional relationship between growth and the size of FDI stocks in 1990. Again this becomes stronger if Switzerland is excluded from the sample. In this latter case the results from a simple linear regression suggest that each 10 percentage point increase in FDI stocks as a ratio of GDP is associated with an increase of 0.21 percentage points in average annual GDP growth (standard error 0.084 percentage points). The cross-sectional variation in FDI stocks in 1990 captures one-quarter of the cross-sectional variation in GDP growth rates during the 1990s. It is difficult to be confident about the scale of any relationship between FDI and growth from a simple partial regression of this kind, although it is consistent with evidence that FDI has raised technical progress in many European countries (Barrell and Pain, 1999; Pain, 2000), and there is nothing to guarantee that it is stable over time. None the less it does suggest that the growing level of cross-border activity during the 1990s should help to improve the prospects for economic growth in the years to come.

Other recent empirical work has sought to examine the specific mechanisms through which financial systems may affect growth, focusing in particular on the importance of financial framework conditions, such as the regulatory environment within which banks and capital markets operate, and on the differential impact across industries within countries according to their dependence on external finance, following the approach pioneered by Rajan and Zingales (1998). A related issue is whether different forms of corporate governance, as proxied by the share of equity held by institutional investors, also matter.

The studies cited above suggest that the size of the banking sector can matter for economic development. A related issue explored by Cetorelli and Gambera (2001) and Cetorelli (2001) is whether the structure of the banking sector also matters. The former consider growth over 1980–90 in a sample of 36 industries in 41 countries, which include some developing countries as well as the OECD economies. They find that higher concentration in the national banking sector has a significant negative relationship with growth. However this effect is much smaller, and in some cases even positive, in those industries which are heavily reliant on external finance. One explanation of this finding is that increased concentration is associated with some general inefficiencies and a reduction in credit availability in imperfectly competitive credit markets. But at the same time relationship banking may be more likely, with larger banks developing closer ties with their client firms.

In a related study Cetorelli (2001) explores the effects of banking structure on the structure of the industrial sector, using a sample of 35 manufacturing industries for 17 OECD economies. Her results suggest that there is a significant positive relationship between average firm size and the concentration of the domestic banking sector.[18] Again this is especially evident in industries which are relatively reliant on external finance. However it is found to be weaker in countries with a higher overall level of financial development.

An implication of these results is that the increasing concentration seen within the US and European banking systems over the past 20 years may offset some of the wider benefits that have resulted from the overall expansion in the size and scale of the banking sector. At the same time, greater bank concentration may be helping to contribute to the formation, and subsequent conduct, of larger industrial companies in at least some industries and countries.

CONCLUDING COMMENTS

Deregulation, technological change and the growing cross-border interdependencies of non-financial firms have all contributed to the rapid growth in the scale and scope of financial institutions over the past 20 years. National markets have become less segmented, and significant consolidation has taken place both within and across national borders. One consequence of these changes is that distinctions between different types of financial systems are becoming weaker. In the United States, financial holding companies operating across a large number of product markets are beginning to emerge, while in many European countries, equity and bond markets are gradually becoming a more important source of finance relative to the previously dominant banking sector. Continuing deregulation, especially in Europe, the impact of monetary union on portfolio allocations and location choice, and the ongoing integration of global markets for goods and services are all likely to provide incentives for further consolidation and growth in financial markets.

A smaller proportion of financial sector corporate deals take place across national borders than in the non-financial sector, despite the greater likelihood that a foreign presence may be required for market entry. This either points to the greater costs of establishing foreign facilities in the financial sector or it suggests that regulatory barriers to entry still remain in some markets (Davies, 2002). Insurance and securities firms are much more likely to invest abroad than banking institutions, although the share of cross-border transactions in the total number of corporate deals undertaken by banks has risen in recent years.

Joint ventures and strategic alliances have become a more common form of cross-border consolidation than mergers and acquisitions, at least in numerical terms. Unfortunately, little information is available to quantify the value, the sector mix or the impact on operating conditions of such alliances. The evidence on the impact of mergers and acquisitions suggests that they are not always successful, at least not when judged in terms of the efficiency of the merged institutions. Larger and more efficient firms are more likely to expand overseas, and smaller companies are more likely to be purchased. Possibly for this reason, or other difficulties such as the work involved in integrating firms with differing corporate cultures that are operating under different regulatory structures, foreign subsidiaries tend to be smaller and less efficient than domestic firms in host markets. Joint ventures provide an alternative mode of market entry that may bypass some of these difficulties and reduce risks; indeed they appear to be more prevalent in those markets that have higher barriers to entry.

In an endogenous growth framework, financial development can promote economic growth via its positive impact on capital productivity or the efficiency with which financial systems convert savings into fixed investment. But the close statistical relationship between financial development and growth found in many studies may not necessarily imply causality from financial development to economic growth, nor that the relationship is constant over time. Looking at the experience of the 1990s, it appears that cross-border transactions, as measured by FDI, may be more closely associated with the cross-country variation in growth rates in the largest OECD economies than either stock market capitalization or bank lending to the private sector.

The rapid growth in the size of some financial institutions may also have other consequences. Increased concentration within the banking sector appears to be associated with increased concentration within non-financial sectors, which has implications for competition policies. Regulators also have to remain vigilant against the increased possibilities of systemic risk and the possibility that some institutions become 'too big to fail'.

The scale of foreign activities undertaken by existing client firms from home markets continues to be one of the key determinants of the decision of banks to expand overseas, as do the external economies available from locating in international financial centres. But the interrelationships between banking and industrial concentration suggest that some industrial location decisions may now be influenced by the location of overseas subsidiaries of financial institutions with whom investing firms do business in their home market. The pattern of international trade in services may also be affected by the location of financial services companies. Further research is called for on these questions.

NOTES

We are grateful to Philip Davis for helpful comments and suggestions and to the UK Economic and Social Research Council for financial support (grant number L138251022).

1. Within the civil tradition there are three major legal families that can be distinguished – French, German and Scandinavian (La Porta et al., 1998). Common law countries tend to offer the best protection for the rights of shareholders, while Germanic-origin countries have a higher quality of creditor rights and Scandinavian-origin countries benefit from strong law enforcement and accounting standards. Investor protection tends to be weakest in countries with a French civil law tradition.
2. Some restrictions remain on mergers and acquisition activity, with the individual share total of bank and thrift deposits that can be reached through mergers capped at 30 per cent in a single state and 10 per cent nationally.
3. The decline was 14 per cent measured in constant April 2001 exchange rates.
4. The OTC market consists of foreign exchange derivatives such as cross-currency swaps and options, plus all interest rate derivatives contracts.
5. The countries are Australia, Belgium, Canada, France, Germany, Italy, Japan, the Netherlands, Spain, Sweden, Switzerland, the UK and the US. Together these economies account for 85 per cent of OECD GDP (at 1995 PPPs) and a little over one-half of world GDP. The three large OECD members excluded from the analysis are Mexico, South Korea and Turkey, all of whom tend to have relatively underdeveloped financial markets.
6. In 1999 there were 3167 credit institutions in Germany, 1143 in France, 951 in Austria and 876 in Italy (ECB, 2000, Table 3.1). The country with the next largest number was the UK, with 494 credit institutions.
7. Altunbas, et al. (2001) use a stochastic cost frontier approach to model total (operating plus financial) costs for a large sample of European banks between 1989 and 1997. A bank is inefficient if its costs are higher than predicted for an efficient bank with the same combination of inputs and outputs and above what can be attributed to statistical noise.
8. The coverage of the financial sector is broader than that in G10 (2001).
9. In the non-financial sector, 18 per cent of purchases by US firms were cross-border, compared with 39.4 per cent of purchases by non-US firms.
10. The remaining lending is by banks from a further 12 countries: Austria, Denmark, Finland, Hong Kong, Ireland, Luxembourg, Norway, Portugal, Singapore, Taiwan, Turkey and Sweden. As the data are measured using market exchange rates, the shares of individual lenders and borrowers will be sensitive to currency fluctuations.
11. At that time the bank had approximately one-third of its assets in Latin America, on which it earned almost half of its total net profits.
12. The sample includes banks with assets of more than $1 billion in December 1997 and

headquarters in one of the OECD economies. Foreign branch activity is included in that of the parent bank, whereas foreign subsidiaries are included as autonomous banks.
13. Foreign competition is important in other financial markets in the UK as well, with foreign controlled companies having 20 per cent of the life insurance market and 43 per cent of the general insurance market (Davies, 2002).
14. Large banks, with the exception of those in Germany, Denmark, the Netherlands and the UK, are found to exhibit constant or decreasing returns to scale.
15. These may be additional reasons why foreign banking subsidiaries do not always appear as efficient as their domestic parents.
16. The figures in the chart and this paragraph exclude claims in local currencies by the foreign affiliates of the reporting banks. These are however included in Table 5.4.
17. The FDI data also include greenfield investments, although these are a relatively small proportion of the total.
18. Banking concentration in this chapter and Cetorelli and Gambera (2001) is measured as the average between 1989 and 1995 of the sum of the market shares of the three largest banks in each national market.

REFERENCES

Allen, F. and Gale, D. (2000), *Comparing Financial Systems*, MIT Press.

Altunbas, Y., Gardener, E.P.M., Molyneux, P. and Moore, B. (2001), 'Efficiency in European banking', *European Economic Review*, 45, 1931–55.

Arrowsmith, J., Barrell, R., Pain, N., Young, G. and Wlodek, K. (1997), *Capital Market Liberalisation In Europe*, Kogan Page: London.

Asiedu, E. and Esfahani, H.S. (2001), 'Ownership structure in foreign direct investment projects', *Review of Economics and Statistics*, 83, 647–62.

Barrell, R. and Pain, N. (1999), 'Domestic institutions, agglomerations and foreign direct investment in Europe', *European Economic Review*, 43, 925–34.

Bassanini, A. and Scarpetta, S. (2001), 'The driving forces of economic growth: panel data evidence for the OECD economies, *OECD Economic Studies*, 33, 9–56.

Berger, A.N., Demsetz, R.S. and Strahan, P.E. (1999), 'The consolidation of the financial services industry: causes, consequences and implications for the future', *Journal of Banking and Finance*, 23, 135–94.

Berger, A.N., DeYoung, R., Genay, H. and Udell, G.F. (2000), 'Globalisation of financial institutions: evidence from cross-border banking performance', *Brookings-Wharton Papers on Financial Services 2000*, 23–125.

BIS (2001), 'Central bank survey of foreign exchange and derivatives market activity in April 2001', Bank for International Settlements Press Release 31/2001E.

BIS (2002), 'International consolidated banking statistics for the third quarter of 2001', Bank for International Settlements Press Release 03/2002E.

Buch, C.M. and Golder, S.M. (2001), 'Foreign versus domestic banks in Germany and the US: a tale of two markets?', *Journal of Multinational Financial Management*, 11, 341–61.

Carow, K.A. (2001), 'Citicorp–Travelers Group merger: challenging barriers between banking and insurance', *Journal of Banking and Finance*, 25, 1553–71.

Cavallo, L. and Rossi, S.P.S. (2001), 'Scale and scope economies in the European banking system', *Journal of Multinational Financial Management*, 11, 515–31.

Cetorelli, N. (2001), 'Does bank concentration lead to concentration in industrial sectors?', Federal Reserve Bank of Chicago Working Paper WP 2001–01.

Cetorelli, N. and Gambera, M. (2001), 'Banking market structure, financial dependence and growth: international evidence from industry data', *Journal of Finance*, 56, 617–48.

Corbett, J. and Jenkinson, T. (1997), 'How is investment financed? A study of Germany, Japan, the United Kingdom and the United States', *The Manchester School*, 65, 69–93.

Crawford, L. (2002a), 'Santander issues ultimatum to Argentina', *Financial Times*, 23 January 2002.

Crawford, L. (2002b), 'BBVA moves to cover potential Argentine losses', *Financial Times*, 31 January 2002.

Davies, H. (2002), 'The Single Financial Market – miracle or mirage?', speech at the British Chamber of Commerce Luncheon, Brussels, March 2002.

Diamond, D.W. (1984), 'Financial intermediation and delegated monitoring', *Review of Economic Studies*, 51, 393–414.

Dunning, J.H. (1995), 'Reappraising the eclectic paradigm in an age of alliance capitalism', *Journal of International Business Studies*, 26, 461–91.

EC (2001a), *Financial Services Political Challenges*, COM(2001)286 final, Brussels: European Commission.

EC (2001b), *Economic Reform: Report on the Functioning of Community Product and Capital Markets*, COM(2001)736, Brussels: European Commission.

ECB (2000), *Mergers and Acquisitions Involving the EU Banking Industry – Facts and Implications*, Frankfurt: European Central Bank.

Esperanca, J.P. and Gulamhussen, M.A. (2001), '(Re)Testing the 'follow the customer' hypothesis in multinational bank expansion', *Journal of Multinational Financial Management*, 11, 281–93.

Focarelli, D. and Pozzolo, A.F. (2001), 'The patterns of cross-border bank mergers and shareholdings in OECD countries', *Journal of Banking and Finance*, 25, 2305–37.

FSF (2000), *Report of the Working Group on Capital Flows*, Basel: Financial Stability Forum.

G10 (2001), *Report on Consolidation in the Financial Sector*, Group of Ten, January 2001.

Galati, G. (2001), 'Why has global FX turnover declined? Explaining the 2001 triennial survey', *BIS Quarterly Review*, December 2001, 39–47.

Galati, G. and Tsatsaronis, K. (2001), 'The impact of the euro on Europe's financial markets', BIS Working Paper No. 100.

Gual, J. (1999), 'Deregulation, integration and market structure in European banking', *EIB Papers*, 4/2, 34–48.

Hubert, F. and Pain, N. (2002), 'Fiscal incentives, European integration and the location of foreign direct investment', *The Manchester School*, forthcoming.

Jorgenson, D.W. (2001), 'Information technology and the US economy', *American Economic Review*, 91, 1–32.

Krugman, P.R. (1995), 'International trade theory and policy', in Grossman, G. and Rogoff, K. (eds) *Handbook of International Economics Volume III*, Amsterdam: Elsevier.

La Porta, R., Lopez-de-Silanes, F., Shliefer, A. and Vishny, R. (1998), 'Law and finance', *Journal of Political Economy*, 106, 1113–55.

Leahy, M., Schich, S., Wehinger, G., Pelgrin, F. and Thorgeirsson, T. (2001), 'Contributions of financial systems to growth in OECD economies', OECD Economics Department Working Paper No. 280.

Levine, R. (1997), 'Financial development and economic growth: views and agenda', *Journal of Economic Literature*, 35, 688–726.
Levine, R. and Zervos, S. (1998), 'Stock markets and economic growth', *American Economic Review*, 88, 537–58.
Markusen, J.R. (1995), 'The boundaries of multinational enterprises and the theory of international trade', *Journal of Economic Perspectives*, 9, 169–89.
Moshirian, F. (2001), 'International investment in financial services', *Journal of Banking and Finance*, 25, 317–37.
Murphy, N.B. (2000), 'European Union financial developments: the Single Market, the single currency and banking', *FDIC Banking Review*, 13/1, 1–18.
Olson, M.W. (2002), 'Observations on the evolution of the financial services industry and public policy', speech at the Sixth Annual Institute on Mergers and Acquisitions, Center for the Study of Mergers and Acquisitions, University of Miami.
Pagano, M. (1993), 'Financial markets and growth: an overview', *European Economic Review*, 37, 613–22.
Pain, N. (2000) (ed.), *Inward Investment, Technological Change and Growth: The Impact of Multinational Corporations on the UK Economy*, London: Palgrave Press.
Rajan, R. and Zingales, L. (1998), 'Financial dependence and growth', *American Economic Review*, 88, 559–86.
Tsuru, K. (2000), 'Finance and growth: some theoretical considerations and a review of the literature', OECD Economics Department Working Paper No. 228.
UNCTAD (2001), *World Investment Report 2001*, Geneva: UNCTAD.
Wooldridge, P. (2002), 'Use of BIS statistics: an introduction', *BIS Quarterly Review*, March 2002, 75–92.

6. Corporate alliances in the world trading system

Gavin Boyd

As national economies become more open to each other, through reductions of trade and investment barriers, and through the economic and political effects of exporting and transnational production activities by firms, as well as through the linking of financial markets, patterns of intercorporate cooperation and competition assume increasing structural significance. The capacities of governments to influence, guide, and regulate the corporate activities shaping economic structures tend to weaken, especially because increasing proportions of the expanding international corporate activity are devoted to the building of cross-border production systems, and exploit investment bidding rivalries between states. Inequalities in the overall spread of gains for the interdependent national economies, however, because of their effects on growth and employment, motivate efforts by governments to adopt methods of trade policy activism, and to enhance structural competitiveness. What can be achieved depends very much on the evolution of forms of cooperation and competition between national firms. Such firms have incentives to expand beyond the borders of their countries, and if they retain strong domestic ties the consequences for structural competitiveness can be quite significant. But in the dynamics of rivalries for world market shares, the home country ties of international enterprises tend to weaken.

Within national economies, governmental and societal restraints limit the scope for corporate collusion to exploit home markets and weaken competitors. These restraints have less significance in the international operations of firms, because of a general lack of competition policy cooperation, and because corporate foreign operations do not assume political prominence for home governments. There is much hard competition between transnational enterprises, and between such enterprises and host country enterprises, although this may be moderated and concealed in order to maintain good relations with host governments.

The dominant trend in the world economy is intensifying hard competition between transnational enterprises for global market shares: mergers and acquisitions are driving international concentration trends, thus changing the structural foundations of the global trading system.[1] In this process arm's length trade is replaced by intrafirm, intra-alliance, and intra-network commerce, with dispersals of different stages of production across national borders. The hard competition does not exclude the formation of alliances and networks for forms of cooperation but these tend to be instrumental, experimental, and short term, although they may become integrative through the development of trust and goodwill. Increasing expansions of world market shares enable the more successful firms to exploit the dependence of weaker collaborators and make them targets of merger and acquisition strategies.

Advances in frontier research with potential commercial applications are motivating the formation of technology based complementary specializations, causing the production capabilities of firms to become more interdependent while they focus on the development of their core competencies. The logic of collaboration however tends to give way to the logic of expansion, through mergers and acquisitions, under pressures for higher profits. As international concentration trends continue the more successful firms have scope to absorb partners in technology based alliances and networks, and indeed to implement diversification strategies that previously might have been less advisable because of competitive pressures to concentrate on their core capabilities.

While the structural foundations of the world trading system are being changed through transnational production, with increasingly significant effects on the spread of gains from commerce, national and international patterns of cooperation and competition undergo changes. A strong relational system of collaboration between firms can ensure substantial and fairly secure sharing in the productive effects of world commerce. Without such a system the involvement in global trade can entail serious vulnerabilities, and it may not be possible to overcome these through trade policy measures. Involvement in the international competition for market shares tends to weaken a national system of relational intercorporate cooperation, because firms engaged in transnational operations have increasingly potent incentives to focus on independent pursuits of their global opportunities, even though these may be aided by well established alliances and networks. An intensely competitive national intercorporate system, in which there are few if any relational ties, tends to experience even more active competition as international rivalries penetrate its economy, and as acquisitions of stronger market positions at home become more significant for its transnational enterprises.

The configuration of the world trading system has been altered by the acute and prolonged financial crisis in Japan: its highly integrated pattern of relational intercorporate cooperation has been weakened.[2] The international economy has thus been dominated to a greater extent by firms operating out of the US intercorporate system, in which there is intense competition, and in which collaboration, on a smaller scale, is generally instrumental rather than relational. European firms are generally weaker rivals in contests for world market shares, but the European Union, because of its size, has very substantial bargaining strength in interactions with the USA, Japan, and other states which provide degrees of governance for the international trading system. Europe has a complex mix of intercorporate systems, and its most important component is that in Germany, which is mainly relational, but which has evolved with less entrepreneurial dynamism than the US system of competitive capitalism.

Competition is becoming more active within the US system as it expands internationally, and its spirit of vigorous rivalry is spreading, notably in Europe. Meanwhile the USA is becoming more firmly established as the leading and largest industrialized state in world commerce. In international bargaining over issues of trade liberalization, however, the US administration has to cope with exceptional problems, attributable in a large measure to failures of coordination in its expanding pattern of corporate rivalries. There are unsustainable trade deficits, resulting from foreign production by US firms at volumes much greater than arm's length and intrafirm exports from the home economy, while domestic output is at levels below internal demand, which is strong because of capital inflows and speculative asset appreciations.[3] Clear imperatives for broad collaboration between firms in the public interest are not being met. This state of affairs has assumed great prominence in the world economy, and it raises questions about the potential for promoting intercorporate cooperation in the USA, and for developing systems of entrepreneurial collaboration in other industrialized states that have to manage structural interdependencies with the USA.

WORLD TRADE GOVERNANCE

International trade is conducted on the basis of agreements for increases in market access negotiated in the Uruguay Round of multilateral trade policy interactions, concluded in the mid-1990s, and on the basis of understandings between the USA and the European Union, as dominant traders, about their interests in open markets and in discouraging restrictive and discriminatory forms of commercial activity by other states. Considerable trade liberalization resulted from the Uruguay Round, but more to the advantage of industrialized states than the developing countries, mainly because of politically significant protectionist pressures in the former.

Multilateral negotiations for further international trade liberalization, which began in November 2001, have proceeded with indications of continuity in the pattern of governance through bargaining between the major contenders, within and outside the World Trade Organization which was established under the Uruguay Agreement.

While the current round of negotiations is in progress, the structural foundations of world trade are being further changed by international corporate operations in which differing mixes of competition and cooperation are active, and these are becoming more significant for governments endeavouring to enhance structural competitiveness, so as to increase overall gains from involvement in world commerce. Meanwhile the patterns of corporate competition and cooperation are sources of representations and advice that contribute to the management of trade policies. In the case of the USA, however, its international firms and those moving into foreign operations have incentives to focus more on their opportunities in external markets than on contributing inputs into trade policy. The representation of corporate interests is fragmented – a reflection of the strongly competitive rather than cooperative intercorporate pattern – and the multilateral trade negotiations are expected to be protracted. European firms are much less active in transnational production but are more organized, in peak economic associations, for representation of their interests in the trade policy functions of the European Commission.[4]

The trade negotiations are expected to take several years because of the difficulties of the bargaining processes that were evident in the Uruguay Round, and because US and European quests for hard and precise agreements, which were to a large extent responsible for slow progress in that round, are continuing. There have been strong tendencies to seek such agreements so that they will provide a basis for the avoidance of, and the settlement of, disputes over the implementation of market opening measures.[5] Maximum concessions have been sought from trading partners in return for carefully defined increases in market access, and there has been reluctance to give the World Trade Organization an independent capacity, as a common institution, to arbitrate on disputes over compliance with the very specific understandings of the hard and precise agreements.

For US international firms, direct interactions with host governments in the building of international production systems are more immediately productive than participation in consultations that may influence US multilateral trade negotiating strategies. For the US administration, however, there are urgent requirements to manage such negotiations in ways that will enhance access to foreign markets for US firms manufacturing at home for export.[6] The promotion of increased cooperation in the intercorporate pattern could induce US enterprises to produce more in the home economy, if external markets became more open, but the spirit of aggressive individualism which sustains the intense competition is distrustful of policy level initiatives.

For the European Union, coping with the disadvantages of weaker international competitiveness, degrees of cooperation in the intercorporate systems of member countries, especially Germany, limit vulnerabilities to penetration by outside enterprises and are sources of resistance to reductions of trade barriers that would result in exposure to stronger competition from non-European enterprises. But the national systems of intercorporate cooperation in Europe sustain oligopolistic market strengths that are being changed by concentration trends, within Union members and in the Union as a whole. Competition policies which the European Commission is endeavouring to implement are intended to facilitate the emergence of Union enterprises with sufficient strengths to operate in world markets, yet in a pattern of regional rivalries conducive to efficiencies that will serve the common interest. The intended international competitiveness, however, may not be attained, despite the latter concern, because of the cumulative effects of slack growth in the European economies. Stronger Union firms are emerging, with strengths spreading across the single market, and are becoming involved in forms of collaboration across the borders of member countries, but mainly on an instrumental rather than a relational basis.

Concentration trends in the USA, and those in Europe, which are being penetrated by the US trends, are increasing oligopolistic strengths in the world economy as it becomes more integrated through negotiated reductions of trade barriers and those resulting from host country treatments of direct investment. In this process of global market transformation, it must be stressed, the terms of competition have been altered in favour of the USA by Japan's economic difficulties. The status of alliance capitalism, as a concept of comprehensive relational intercorporate cooperation exemplified by Japan, has decreased in informed discussions of comparative economic systems. The efficiencies of the US system have received greater recognition, in a way which has encouraged general acceptance of the rationale for greater international trade liberalization, but with qualifications. The prospect of greater oligopolistic strengths in the world economy has increased concerns about problems of international competition policy cooperation. At the same time, dangers of speculation-led destabilization in the USA have become more evident.[7]

International competition policy cooperation in the common interest is difficult to achieve, especially because of the domestic orientation of competition policy in the larger industrialized states, particularly the USA, and because tacit collusion, which is an effective means of evasion in domestic contexts, is more feasible in international operations. A fundamental requirement, then, in the international economy, must be the development of stable forms of corporate cooperation aligned with imperatives to overcome internationalized market failures. In prospect is increasing oligopolistic exploitation of global market strengths; more extensive sectoral disruptions associated with changing strategies in the building of international production systems; a multiplication of informational problems for emerging firms as commercial communications are restricted within exclusive networks; and a public goods issue of great magnitude as general use of methods of hard competition prevent the development of dynamic order in the world economy.[8]

CORPORATE COMPETITION AND COOPERATION

Balances between competitive and cooperative corporate activities, nationally and internationally, are being affected by multiplications of technology based alliances and networks and by mergers and acquisitions which are driving concentration trends, in intense rivalries for world market shares. There is relational logic in the technology based forms of collaboration, in that understandings of the widening range of advances in frontier research, and of the importance of autonomous commercial applications of these advances by independent firms, in the evolution of production interdependencies, can motivate the building of trust and goodwill: the technology based collaboration can thus become self-sustaining. The intensifying competition for world market shares, however, activated especially by the pressures of large investors on firms to achieve higher profitability, tends to force adoption of instrumental methods of managing the technology based forms of cooperation. Use of these methods, moreover, becomes more feasible for large firms gaining prominence and greater resources in concentration trends.

The public goods significance of relational cooperation, within but also apart from technology based arrangements, however, remains important for the development of the world trading system, and indeed is becoming more important. Intercorporate capabilities for adjustment to strains in the international economy are becoming more necessary, and, more significantly, corporate capabilities and motivations for concerting entrepreneurship in complementary ventures are becoming imperative for balanced dynamic growth.

Hard international corporate competition does not produce a balanced pattern of complementary production specializations, but rather a multiplication of cross-border market failures as well as efficiencies. The oligopoly power which results from the unrestrained competition is used to exploit markets and to restrict opportunities for innovative entrepreneurship. Competition policy cooperation, even if it becomes very active, cannot be effective against the tacit collusion which is operative in concentration trends, and this has to be reiterated for understanding of the developmental issues in the world trading system.[9]

Leading-member driven development of the pattern of world commerce and of the World Trade Organization as a bargaining forum is asserted with emphasis on the efficiency effects of competition in an integrating global economy: the ideal is service of open national markets by firms achieving superior performance while forcing less productive ones into decline. This rationale for trade liberalization as a process conducive to world development through gains from trade resulting from specializations driven by corporate rivalries is generally affirmed with reticence about concentration trends and competition policy issues. All this has to be reiterated, but it is also necessary to note that there is typically reticence about problems in exchange rates that can affect international commerce, and about the consequences of changes in business cycles. Stable exchange rates aligned with fundamentals in the structural interdependencies of real economies are clearly required. The avoidance of speculative booms and subsequent declines in major states is also necessary. The dynamics of international trade processes and of trade policy interactions in the unevenly liberalized world trading system, however, do not activate effective corporate and policy level engagement with issues of exchange rate stability or the smoothing of business cycles through restraints on speculation.[10]

The developmental issues of the world trading system and of the World Trade Organization are evident in a context of linkages in which patterns of corporate competition and cooperation became highly relevant for policy making and for the evolution of relevant public goods initiatives by corporate groups. Patterns of integrative intercorporate cooperation, it must be stressed, could contribute structurally and through policy inputs to the development of a more comprehensively productive and more orderly international trading system. But technology based forms of corporate collaboration which could became more relational, it must be reaffirmed, are not leading to integrative cooperation because of the pervasive effects of the intense competition driving concentration trends.

The virtual acquisition of increasing degrees of structural power, as well as cross-border market strengths by established and emerging transnational enterprises, indicates a developmental imperative for collaborative public goods orientations by their managements, in line with the structural policy concerns of their governments, to the extent that these are on a sound basis. Advocacy to this effect can be effective where there are strong peak economic associations, as in Germany, but it has to be made very persuasive where the organization of corporate interests is fragmented, as in the USA, and where corporate attitudes to the policy level are distant and distrustful. Indeed this is all the more necessary in the USA because of the extent to which institutional weaknesses in the major political parties have adverse effects on structural policy capabilities.

The potential importance of concerted corporate dedication to public goods issues in the global trading system and in the bargaining within the World Trade Organization, while evident in the major structural trends associated with expanding trade in manufactured products, is also apparent in the virtual enlargement of market integration processes by the deregulation and privatization policies of governments in services and utilities sectors. Efficiency enhancing competition, with reductions of budget deficits, has been intended, but with considerable tolerance of concentration trends, and acceptance of risks of disruption and destabilization through actual and attempted mergers and acquisitions as well as through imprudent management. In this context public goods issues have been more immediately evident than in the international patterns of trade in manufactures. Partly on this account governments have tended to seek corporate cooperation in the deregulated and privatized sectors through consultations with managements as well as through monitoring and regulatory innovations.[11]

ENTREPRENEURSHIP AND SYSTEMIC DEVELOPMENT

While world commerce is being changed by concentration trends, facilitated by substantial although uneven liberalization, it is also being changed by the transformation of structurally interdependent states into knowledge based political economies. Productive entrepreneurship is becoming a more knowledge based process, setting requirements for wider knowledge sharing, and for the development of complementary specializations, with risk sharing through commitments to solidarity in the common interest. The functional logic of knowledge based entrepreneurship has to develop with multiplications of autonomous complementary specializations. This systemic imperative necessitates restraints on concentration trends, and it must be emphasized that, for this, regulatory methods tend to be inadequate.

Knowledge based entrepreneurship, in the context of extensive complex structural interdependence, has to cope with uncertainties about technological and market trends, and about the implications of production decisions by numerous horizontally and vertically related firms. Capacities to function productively depend not only on very active knowledge sharing but also on shared commitments to collaborative adaptation in response to unexpected challenges. Stable systems of corporate governance with stakeholder features, in a relational intercorporate system, can make it possible to meet the requirements for knowledge sharing and concerted adjustment. Agency type systems of corporate governance, operating with large scale share trading, dominated by major financial enterprises, however, set managerial orientations that prevent the necessary collaboration. Speculation by the major investors, moreover, multiplies the market uncertainties, while in effect imposing financial performance requirements on managements that motivate concentration on hard competition, with minimal information sharing.[12]

Uncertainties about the production decisions of related firms can be reduced by merger and acquisition strategies, and uncertainties about market trends can also be reduced by such strategies, and by diversification. In concentration trends, however, the uncertainties confronting one prominent firm relate more and more to the options of other prominent enterprises. Oligopolistic collaboration can make these uncertainties more manageable but often prepares the way for further mergers and acquisitions.

The increasing prominence of agency type corporate governance, with speculative pressures for financial performance, has broad systemic significance that conflicts with the functional logic of dispersed knowledge based relational entrepreneurship. Efficiency and social justice considerations enter into that logic, while the dynamics of the hard competition deriving from shareholder demands pushes forward concentration trends that increase market exploitation while also driving destructive boom and bust cycles. Firms achieving greater market strengths in the course of concentration trends draw speculative investment for further expansion, thus assuming larger roles in the world trading system, but with risks of failure to sustain growth because of excessive outlays and adverse shifts in market conditions that may be related to declines in investor confidence.[13]

Forms of alliance capitalism that sustain relational intercorporate cooperation, based on stakeholder corporate governance, can restrain concentration trends, limit speculative funding of firms gaining larger market shares, and allow wide scope for autonomous complementary entrepreneurial ventures on a long-term basis, with expectations of concerted adjustment to any strains in production interdependencies. This has to be stressed because of the vulnerabilities of the world trading system to disruptions caused by the weakening and failures of large transnational enterprises attempting risky expansion in the context of hard competition. It also has to be stressed because very high volume trade in financial assets, expanding because of the profitability of speculation, causes uncertainties for the commerce that can increase growth in real economies. These uncertainties affect exchange rates, levels of demand, productive operations, and government finances, especially in economies with industries heavily dependent on funding drawn from hyperactive trade in financial assets, and heavily dependent on efficiencies resulting from intense intercorporate competition.[14]

The recent history of the world trading system is a record of market failures and policy failures in which enterprises engaging in large scale transnational production, independently and in fierce competition, have focused on quests for world market shares without concerns for overall efficiency and equity – concerns that have been considered the responsibilities of governments. Interactions with governments have been managed to further corporate interests, extract tax and other concessions, and avoid exactions that would be consequences of host country political processes forcing fiscal expansion. Where there has been solidarity in groups of transnational enterprises this has been on a national basis, as has been evident in Japanese outward direct investment; no solidarity based international management culture has evolved. Meanwhile, although national political economies have become more knowledge based, with rising levels of policy and structural interdependence, there have been few advances toward the development of an international political culture. The World Trade Organization has remained a bargaining forum operating with adversarial legalism, while its significance as a crude mechanism for governance of the world trading system has been limited by the large scale expansion of transnational production under arrangements between firms and governments in which the former have had increasing leverage.[15]

International cooperation between firms based on technological specializations becomes more functional, in the common interest, as corporations become more knowledge based. A natural evolution is possible in which managements attentive to frontier research become more open to possibilities for complementarities with innovative initiatives by related firms whose independence is necessary for the continued development of their capabilities in areas of advanced applied technology. Recognition of highly specialized forms of human capital and of other intangible assets, as well as of the importance of building trust and goodwill, becomes vital for enlightened management in such contexts.[16]

Much discussion in international management literature however focuses on competitive advantages gained through complementary technological specializations. There is little recognition of the public goods significance of efficiencies driven by integrative cooperation, and of what may be called cooperative competition, in which rivalries are subordinated to common interests in the development of complementary production capabilities. The research focus on competitive advantages is understandable because of pervasive pressures on managements to achieve high short-term profits, but this focus tends to exclude recognition of the widening requirements for entrepreneurial coordination as technology driven specializations develop in the complexities of deepening integration and, therefore, for systems of corporate cooperation to ensure wide ranging coordination. Excluding this functional perspective can reflect the influence of economic thought that anticipates equilibrium, as markets become more open to each other because of efficiencies generated primarily through competition.[17]

CORPORATE COOPERATION AND INTERNATIONAL TRADE DISPUTES

The emphasis on competition in international management studies is also due in part to general awareness of disputes about market access that have been multiplying in the World Trade Organization. These disputes have resulted mainly from groups protesting against forms of import penetration, and from the related efforts of supporting and opposing governments to assert favourable interpretations of the hard and precise terms of commitments under the Uruguay Agreements. The disputes settlement system, as a member driven arrangement, does not command general confidence. The disputes of most significance for overall operation of the world trading system have been between the USA and the European Union, and management of these on each side has been criticized because of the use of adversarial methods that have diverted attention from benefits attainable by wider cooperation.[18]

Constructive suggestions in the trade policy literature have proposed improvements in the disputes settlement system of the World Trade Organization, based on increased understandings of the efficiencies of competition, but also of integrative interpretations of agreed market opening commitments. The significance of inputs by competing interest groups into trade policies has been recognized, but generally without realizing that harmonious evolution of the international trading system will require extensive cross-border interactions of peak economic associations, for transnational interest aggregation and consensus formation, so that trade policies can be managed in the common interest. At a more fundamental level, moreover, developmental imperatives to promote more order, balance, and collaborative dynamism in the structural foundations of world trade have not been given attention, despite general awareness that imbalances in the spread of gains from international commerce are resulting more from transnational production patterns than from arm's length trade.[19]

Alliances between firms have more significance in the expansion of transnational production and in the growth of intrafirm trade than in the evolution of arm's length commerce. Most trade disputes that have been submitted to the World Trade Organization have arisen in arm's length exports, and those of central significance in global commerce have been issues in Atlantic trade. The high profile cases of structural importance have concerned subsidies. One with far reaching implications has been a European Union complaint against the USA's tax treatment of foreign sales as a means of subsidizing exports; rulings against the USA after Geneva hearings have made it possible for the Union to resort to retaliatory treatment of US exports. Political cooperation between US firms at home and in Europe has been given impetus by this case, and the American companies in the Union have been well placed to assert their interests within host corporate associations interacting with the European Commission, but it is unclear whether there have been any direct effects on patterns of US corporate competition and cooperation, regionally and internationally.[20]

Atlantic trade frictions have the general effect of increasing US and European corporate incentives to secure wider and safer market access through direct investment. Greater use of alliances and networks can be advantageous in this context, but such forms of collaboration have not been evident in the fragmented European corporate presence in the USA, and in Europe the political cooperation that has been noted does not appear to have altered individual US corporate orientations toward securing acceptance, in host countries, without affiliations that could appear to be oligopolistic.

A structurally significant issue involving only bilateral interactions has been the European use of large scale subsidies for the Airbus consortium, which has reduced Boeing's still dominant share of the world aircraft market. US complaints about the European subsidies have been restrained in part by a growth of high technology based forms of Atlantic corporate cooperation, as well as by the influence of international security concerns in US policy level deliberations. Within the USA the case against the Airbus subsidies has not been politically prominent.

Trade issues that have assumed some political prominence in the USA, but that have not been structurally significant and have activated only political collaboration between firms, have concerned European restraints on imports of US hormone treated meat and of bananas from US producers in Latin America.[21] A broad pattern of corporate cooperation in medium and high technology sectors, which have high prominence in the USA's external trade and its transnational production interdependencies, could have prevented complaints about the European Union's meat and banana imports.

Proposals for reform of the World Trade Organization have had to acknowledge its decision making problems and the tacit reluctance of the USA and the European Union to facilitate the development of its Secretariat as an institution with autonomous research and surveillance capabilities.[22] Improvement in the conventions for bargaining and the implementation of agreements have thus been the main suggestions, with affirmations of the importance of economic advice to governments that will increase their understanding of the efficiencies to be expected from general trade liberalization. Little attention is given to the beliefs and motivations of corporate managements that influence their orientations toward competitive and cooperative activities. Studies of these orientations have indicated that while technology based affinities, interdependencies, and complementarities between enterprises are recognized in ways that lead to collaborative arrangements, management of these arrangements is difficult and often unsuccessful: strong competitive compulsions cause solutions to be sought through mergers and acquisitions. Reconsideration of this obligates greater awareness of international competition policy problems, which cannot be appropriately entrusted to a bargaining forum.[23] The systemic developmental imperative, then, has to be the cultivation of an integrative international management culture that will help to establish more order, efficiency, and equity in world commerce. Openness to thinking along these lines can develop with reflection on the insights of researchers examining managerial interactions dedicated to complementary entrepreneurship in uses of applied frontier technology.

International management literature, adjusting to the structural significance of expanding transnational production that raises cross-border high and medium technology interdependencies, has to recognize corporate responsibilities for overcoming international market failures, in collaboration with constructive endeavours by governments. Market failures and policy failures demand recognition in the present state of the world trading system, and resolution of these problems is not to be expected through the effects of the hard competition that tends to prevail in international corporate activities.

CONCERTING ENTREPRENEURSHIP AND GAINS FROM TRADE

Problems in the structural foundations of world trade have indicated the fundamental importance of coordination functions that could meet requirements for orderly interdependent growth. The deficiencies have been evident in the interconnected market failures and government failures that have assumed international dimensions while uneven deepening integration has been continuing, with mainly hard competition between transnational enterprises. Asymmetric growth patterns in this vast process, while causing stresses, have nevertheless revealed the potential of multiplying forms of advanced applied technology in interdependent production specializations.

The gravity of coordination deficiencies has been dramatized by excess global steel capacity, which became a more serious challenge during the US 2001 recession.[24] The US administration sought cooperation from foreign governments and firms to reduce production, while planning to restrict steel imports. This intervention strategy was implemented outside the framework of the World Trade Organization, after a new round of multilateral trade liberalization negotiations had begun. The implications for steel-using US manufacturers were unfavourable, and their higher costs were going to affect their international competitiveness, thus raising concerns about the continuation of the nation's very large trade deficits: these were not likely to be reduced while negotiations for multilateral reductions of trade barriers were still in the early stages. A major form of tacitly managed trade was a prominent factor in the larger context, as Japanese exporters of automobiles to the USA were still observing the restraints of an expired 'voluntary' export limitation agreement that had become illegal with the establishment of the World Trade Organization but which could not be exceeded without risking retaliatory protectionist measures.

International production coordination deficiencies become more serious in their effects, and more difficult to overcome, in recessions that follow speculative booms. The gravity of the effects during the 2001 US recession has been exceptional because in this recession investment in international speculative operations has continued at large volumes, with returns considered higher and safer than those expected from funding domestic productive activity, in conditions of generally low confidence. Levels of such confidence, particularly in recessions, depend on degrees of corporate solidarity that are sustained through affirmations of goodwill, information sharing, and commitments to risk sharing. Without significant degrees of solidarity, investors confront greater uncertainties and are thus attracted more to the financial sector's global activities, with their opportunities for tax avoidance.[25]

International production coordination deficiencies can decrease with concentration trends, if there is oligopolistic collaboration. This however may not develop because of the aggressive and distrustful orientations driving hard competition and, if it does occur, it may well be disrupted by the opportunism that typically alters the benefits of corporate alliances and networks. A recession spreading from a major industrialized state will increase international market uncertainties in ways that encourage opportunism by alliance and network partners, unless these are based on strong shared commitments to solidarity.

Conclusions about the difficulties of coordinated recoveries from post speculative boom recessions, drawn from the US experience, can increase understanding of imperatives for wide ranging international corporate cooperation to ensure harmonious development of the structural foundations of world commerce. These foundations are being expanded by transnational production, which is assuming larger proportions outside the framework of the World Trade Organization: since the failure of negotiations for a multilateral agreement on investment in the late 1990s there has been no support for inclusion of investment issues in the Organization's agenda.[26] Direct investment flows are increasing, especially across the Atlantic, due to the attractions of the European Union market for US firms with superior entrepreneurial energies and international competitiveness, and the opportunities for European firms in areas of US industry that are less internationally competitive but more promising than equivalent sectors in the Union. Systemic requirements to promote balanced complementarities in this central pattern of structural interdependencies are evident, and recognition of these, at corporate and policy levels, could provide a basis for initiatives aimed at orderly transformations of commerce that would spread from an Atlantic system of alliance capitalism.

Growth in interdependent knowledge based political economies has to be achieved by concerting complementary specializations in applications of frontier technology. These are not likely to be efficiently concerted through the effects of price signals on hard competition, in contexts in which the funding of productive activity for real economies is subjected to the dynamics of very high volume speculation in financial sectors. The potential for coordinating specializations has to be explored with insights from institutional economics, but research on the implications of deepening integration for institutional economics has been lacking. What have to be investigated are the possibilities for integrating, across borders, cultures, moral systems, and governance structures that can orient transnational enterprises toward complementary forms of entrepreneurship, and that can restrain speculation in financial sectors.

Hard competition, domestically and internationally, under performance pressures generated by high volume speculative trading in financial assets, produces unstable environments, with levels of uncertainty that cause managerial emphasis on self-reliance and manipulative cooperation in alliances and networks, to extract maximum advantages. Opportunism is thus to be expected in any complementary specializations, with strains leading to discontinuities and mergers and acquisitions, thus pushing forward concentration trends and their attendant vicious circles, including failures in vital information flows.[27]

Collegial competition, managed with trust and goodwill based on moral values, and with understanding of shared and common interests served by complementarities, can lead to collegial management of alliances and networks. The intense rivalries for global market shares tend to prevent such collaboration, that is in conjunction with the uncertainties of active markets for corporate control and the risks of instability due to speculative manipulations in financial markets. Altogether, the complex problems of coordination for functional development of the world trading system are thus becoming more difficult to meet.

Systemic developmental imperatives for a high principled solidarity based international management culture thus have to be affirmed in political economy research institutes, in advice to governments, and in statements of purpose by corporate groups. The pervasive stress on the efficiency effects of competition, in economics and management literature, will have to be altered with recognition of the productive significance of collegial rivalries and of the technology based logic of transforming these into forms of alliance capitalism for more integrative collaboration. The public goods requirement, to be emphasized in economic advice to governments, becomes more demanding as transnational enterprises increase the range of their activities that are building international production systems.

ALLIANCE CAPITALISM AND ALLIANCE TRADE POLICIES

The multiplication of cross-border structural linkages shaped with increasing degrees of autonomy by transnational enterprises is constituting a new but underdeveloped commercial system, with problems of coordination and governance; competition driving concentrations increases, with other forms of market failure, while tending to overwhelm processes of spontaneous corporate cooperation based on complementary specializations. In the absence of substantial international competition policy cooperation, trade policies have to be managed with more and more active concerns about the structural consequences of the concentration trends, as well as the related externalities incidental to shifts in corporate relocation and production strategies. Trade restrictions can be attempted, depending on relative bargaining strengths; investment bidding can become more discriminating; and aids to national industries can be increased.

While linkages between policies become functionally more important at the national level, international collaboration between policy makers and corporate managements becomes more necessary for the entire pattern of world commerce. This is difficult because of the strong domestic responsiveness of national trade policy processes. That responsiveness tends to become more active not only because of the disruptive effects of import penetration, but also because of those popularly attributed to the entire process of globalization, in which rationalizations of corporate production capabilities follow mergers and acquisitions. During recessions the domestic responsiveness increases.

Institutional arrangements for intense and continuous interactions between national trade policy communities are clearly necessary, for restraint on protectionist responses to the implications of concentration trends, and more fundamentally for the development of an international elite political culture. Progress in the formation of such a culture could transform national political institutions. A regional elite political culture is beginning to develop in the European Union, because of the degrees to which national political processes are being Europeanized through Union level decision making, but national attachments and loyalties remain strong, especially because of the efforts of member governments to implement structural policies that will enhance the competitiveness of their economies.[28] Frictions in Atlantic relations are causing antipathies toward the USA in the national political cultures, and in the emerging Union level culture, while increasing sensitivities to the competitive strengths of US firms.

In the USA the political culture sustains a traditionally strong orientation toward independent assertiveness in foreign economic relations, with confidence in capacities to maintain technological and competitive leads over Europe and the rest of the world. Corporate distrust of government and emphasis on complete freedom for entrepreneurial initiative contribute to policy level outlooks that are uninterested in opportunities to seek basic political understandings with foreign elites, except on the importance of market openness, and of confining governments to very limited roles in their economies. Beliefs in the efficiencies of market forces tend to be responsible for reluctance to consider the significance of international concentration trends, in which US firms are very prominent. Meanwhile inputs into the trade policy process, in which assertions of constituency interests are very active, tend to drive adversarial legalism in trade liberalization negotiations, to achieve hard and precise agreements. This trend, while reciprocated on the European side, influences trade policy elites in the rest of the world.[29]

Alliance politics across borders, for integrative trade policy management, is not developing, and corporate alliances altering market processes and shaping economic structures are mainly US, US–European, and European ventures in which the logic of complementary specialization gives way to merger and acquisition strategies, under pressures from financial sectors. The public goods issues which thus demand attention, in perspectives on systemic development, however, could well be taken up through enlightened policy level and corporate initiatives inspired by new understandings of the dynamics of technology based complementarities between firms and of the efficiencies of concerted entrepreneurship. This is argued in the final chapter of this volume.

Third world interests, asserted hypocritically by violent protectors at the Seattle and Genoa disturbances, can benefit if a spirit of alliance capitalism is promoted vigorously by US and European elites responding to the severe strains of the largely uncoordinated and ungoverned international trading system. Large and increasing disparities in bargaining strengths on trade and investment issues place third world firms and governments at serious disadvantages in dealing with US, European and Japanese enterprises that are establishing international production systems and gaining advantages in global concentration trends. Hard competition between the multinationals tends to be self-reinforcing, making it likely that any generous treatment of host country firms by a US, European, or Japanese multinational will be exploited by its rivals if these are prepared to drive hard bargains. Atlantic promotion of an integrative international corporate culture, however, although difficult, could open the way for progressively more equal structural links between developing countries and major transnational enterprises, and more equal involvement by those countries in the world trading system.

US, European, and Japanese trade policies toward developing countries, it must be reiterated, have long been discriminatory, hindering the development of export oriented industrialization by those countries, while in effect making them significantly dependent on the attraction of investment by advanced country firms in assembly type manufacturing and resource extraction. In addition to these disadvantages, third world countries have been vulnerable to US and European anti-dumping measures that have been biased against them, and that have tended to make their exporters dependent on sourcing by US and European trading firms that can avoid exposure to anti-dumping charges.[30] US and European enterprises that sell below cost in their home markets are not considered to be thwarting the efficiency effects of free market forces.

China's entry into the World Trade Organization, which has opened the way for deeper involvement in the world trading system, has implications which can be seen to strengthen imperatives for Atlantic and hopefully Japanese endeavours to introduce a spirit of alliance capitalism into corporate and policy level decision making. Opportunities for comprehensively constructive engagement have been neglected in efforts to induce Chinese economic liberalization and acceptance of hard and precise terms of increased involvement in the world trading system. The exposure to international competition has in effect made informal cooperation between Chinese firms, and between those firms in their administration, increasingly important for the regime's structural competitiveness and the limitation of its vulnerabilities to intrusion by foreign enterprises with large resources, as well as its prospective vulnerabilities to external speculative penetration of its financial sector. The latter danger has been made quite evident by numerous western research publications on the East Asian financial crises of the 1990s. While external pressure has sought to weaken intercorporate collaboration in China, foreign investment and trading activity has been intensely competitive rather than cooperative, thus tending to discourage trust and long term partnering. This is not to deny that frustrations have been experienced because of Chinese deficiencies, but it has been clear that the western form of capitalism that has been presented has not exhibited a spirit of solidarity.[31]

The same criticism has to be made about US and European relations with the transitional Russian economy, although its severe problems over the past decade have been due mainly to extraordinary mixes of incompetence and corruption that would have made comprehensively constructive engagement extremely difficult. For Russia, the dangers of acute destabilization through high risk large scale rent seeking in totally competitive capitalism have been made evident by the US recession of 2001. A conclusion that can be drawn from that and from Russia's own experience is that firm central control is necessary in an industrialized state to ensure that the financial sector serves the real economy, and to achieve the structural competitiveness required for effective involvement in the world trading system.[32]

Russia's inferior status as a transitional political economy is being made more evident by the advances of East European states toward membership of the European Union, and by China's entry into the World Trade Organization, which has prepared the way for attractions of foreign direct investment on a rather large scale, as well as for influential participation in negotiations on Russia's entry into that organization. For effective involvement in world commerce, Russia has to seek wide ranging economic cooperation with the European Union, despite the slack growth in its enlarging internal market and its problems of pluralistic decision making. European interest in this connection is being encouraged by awareness of vulnerabilities to destabilization in the US economy, and also of large drifts of European investment to the USA.

POLICY FAILURES AND MARKET FAILURES

Systemic development in the world trading system can be promoted in advance of institutional development in the World Trade Organization if an international management culture of collegial and integrative cooperation is promoted through corporate and policy level initiatives in the USA and the European Union. Optimism is not being encouraged by the accumulation of policy failures and market failures associated with Atlantic involvement in global commerce, but these have to be seen as challenges for highly constructive knowledge intensive endeavours. Such endeavours can start with the logic of seeking a public goods aligned balance between competition and cooperation in corporate activities, and the logic of technocratic sponsorship of conferences on entrepreneurial complementarities tentatively indicated by advances in frontier research, as well as by the evolution of ongoing technology based alliances. The spirit of cooperation that could be promoted could be a source of diffuse restraints on concentration trends, and more importantly of increased dynamic efficiencies in global commerce.

The structural tasks that demand recognition are urgent because of the conjunction of extraordinary dangers of speculation-led destabilization in the USA; increasing concentration in the global corporate pattern; and the expanding roles of transnational enterprises in shaping interdependent economic structures across borders. Market forces in this vast context are not working toward a global balance of dynamic efficiencies in the generally competing specializations. Governments on the whole are tacitly accepting losses of economic sovereignty to international firms while endeavouring to manage interactions with domestic groups asserting trade policy interests. Macromanagement rivalries between governments are not causing convergence toward an optimum system of national capitalism; distributional conflicts associated with the costs of globalization are making macromanagement, with declining economic sovereignty, more difficult, while increasing corporate incentives to develop large scale international production systems, for greater profitability and security.

Understanding of the structural imperatives that require high principled responses for authentic development of the world trading system has to be based on recognition that concepts of individual self-seeking rationality, using whatever means are expedient, have to be revised to take account of the multiplication of coordination functions that is necessary in interdependent knowledge based political economies. These coordination functions have to be fulfilled in firms, industry groups, alliances and networks, in corporate associations and political parties, in national administrations, and in international organizations, including the World Trade Organization. The functional significance of cooperation dedicated to organizational and broader community interests, and of responsiveness to dedicated coordinating institutions, increases as overall levels of operational interdependence rise with introductions of new technology. Relational assets, then, become more important for orderly development of the linked knowledge based national political economies. In the world trading system, accordingly, competition has to become more collegial, and the structural foundations of world commerce have to be built, more and more, through integrative corporate cooperation.

The dangers of speculation-led destabilization in world commerce are becoming more serious, especially because the US financial sector, while maintaining its central role, attracts global investment, and because firms becoming more prominent in global concentration trends are being drawn toward opportunities for risky speculative expansion.[33] The risky speculation can be effective in causing asset appreciations, mainly because much of it is collusive. The fundamental remedy, in a context in which regulation of international financial markets has become very difficult, will have to be the development of the new international management culture that is needed for integrative management of the trade and production links between real economies as these become more knowledge based.

Prospects for the world trading system have to be estimated with reference to trends in structural competitiveness, phases in business cycles, the market opening and restricting effects of trade and investment measures, and changes in the structural foundations of commerce resulting from the expansion of transnational production and from concentration trends. Competition between firms and between governments is usually seen as the principal driving force in the global pattern, increasing market efficiencies but also failures, while causing policy efficiencies and failures. Public goods imperatives for equitable and functional coordination by firms and by governments are evident, but can be considered unattainable. Corporations gaining strength in world markets can be expected to become more intensely competitive, and within states the dynamics of political competition can be expected to force increasing emphasis on quests for advantages in rivalries for greater shares of the gains from world commerce.

In perspectives inspired by public goods concerns, however, the productive potential of *cooperative* as well as competitive advantages can be recognized. The cooperative advantages that firms can develop and use with increasing effect are relational assets explicitly oriented toward partnering. These include status as a reliable and innovative partner, building trust and expressing goodwill; the matching qualities of current partners; shared orientations toward information exchanges for the development of complementarities; intrafirm efficiencies generated through community formation and stakeholder corporate governance;[34] corporate stability maintained through stable shareholding; and solidarity promoted through alliances, networks, industry groups, and associations. Associated with these cooperative advantages are those which may be developed by governments: equitable and supportive policy level treatment of domestic and foreign firms, and considerate management of macro- and microeconomic policy interdependencies with other national administrations.

In the basic analytical levels of institutional economics, when these are related to issues of systemic development in world commerce, the importance of beliefs and values conducive to greater understanding of cooperative rather than competitive advantages becomes more apparent. The multiplication of structural and policy interdependencies, resulting from international corporate activities, sets developmental requirements. To the extent that these are obscured by contested issues, a vital international public good is underprovided. This has to be affirmed with emphasis on the increasing importance of intangibles for the *cooperative* potentials of firms and governments: studies focusing only on the competitive significance of intangibles hinder understanding that, in the larger system of intercorporate relations which is evolving with the expansion of world commerce, the full development of intangibles has to occur through the integrative management of knowledge based interdependencies. The generation of intangible assets through widening cooperation, at corporate and government levels, become potentially more and more important as frontier technology advances continue, that is for efficiencies and equity in global commerce. Substantially efficient production, valuation and use of intangible assets through competitive market processes is difficult: the logic of relational cooperation becomes stronger, in a broad systemic perspective, as the productive significance of new technologies demands more intensive and wider ranging entrepreneurial exploration.[35]

The development of corporate alliances, however, is discouraged by competition policy enforcement, even though this can provide incentives for the formation of such alliances. Merging with or acquiring firms that might otherwise be alliance partners enables the new enterprise to set prices and discriminate between markets in ways that would be open to competition policy enforcement if attempted by an alliance. The threat of such enforcement *can* discourage a large merger or acquisition that would secure an almost dominant market share and thus can motivate the formation of alliances that can be managed in ways that will not be exposed to action by competition policy authorities: but there will be incentives for tacit collaboration to maximize the market benefits obtained from the cooperation. If the danger of competition policy enforcement diminishes, moreover, for example because of political changes or investment bidding, the collaboration will tend to be weakened by opportunism and then ended by mergers and acquisitions.

Trade policy management by the USA, the European Union, and Japan, is being challenged by the transnational production and marketing activities of international firms operating with increasing independence in the exploitation of location advantages and the investment bidding, weak industrial policies, and macromanagement deficiencies of host governments, as well as their failures in international competition policy cooperation. Remedies that have been proposed include active social monitoring and coordinated restraints on the use of subsidies.[36] More fundamental solutions can be sought through intensive technocratic interactions with corporate managements, in which technocratic advising would become influential through contributions to managerial learning about innovative technology based opportunities for entrepreneurial complementarities, and to managerial awareness of collective obligations for systemic development with equity. From the corporate side such productive technocratic engagement can be complemented, with synergies, through wide ranging relational cooperation between firms responsive to the systemic technocratic concerns. Orderly development of the structural foundations of world commerce could then be possible.

NOTES

1. See *World Investment Report 2000*, Geneva, United Nations Commission on Trade and Development.
2. See Magnus Blomstrom, Byron Gangnes and Sumner La Croix (eds) *Japan's New Economy*, Oxford, Oxford University Press, 2001.
3. On US foreign direct investment positions see *Survey of Current Business*, July 2000.
4. US firms in Europe are involved in these organizations: see David Coen 'The Impact of US Lobbying Practice on the European Business–Government Relationship', *California Management Review*, 41, 4, Summer 1999, 27–44.
5. See symposium on trade agreements in *International Organization*, 54, 3, Summer 2000.
6. See Catherine L. Mann, *Is the US Trade Deficit Sustainable?* Washington DC, Institute for International Economics, 1999.
7. For a discussion of the dangers of destabilization see symposium on financial instability in *Oxford Review of Economic Policy*, 15, 3, Autumn 1999.
8. The hard competition tends to accelerate concentration trends: the spirit of this competition is expressed in Ralph E. Gomory and William J. Baumol *Global Trade and Conflicting National Interests*, Cambridge, MIT Press, 2000. See also *US Competitiveness 2001*, Washington DC, Council on Competitiveness.
9. See symposium or competition policy in *Oxford Review of Economic Policy*, 9, 2, Summer 1993.
10. See discussions in *71st Annual Report*, Bank of International Settlements, Basel, 11 June 2001, and *International Capital Markets: Developments, Prospects and Key Policy Issues*, Washington DC, International Monetary Fund.

11. See symposium in *OECD Economic Studies*, 32, 2001.
12. On the pressures on managements see Mary O'Sullivan *Contests for Corporate Control*, Oxford, Oxford University Press, 2000.
13. See reports on the demise of Enron, the US energy firm, *Financial Times*, various issues during December 2001.
14. See symposium on financial instability in *Oxford Review of Economic Policy*, cited.
15. The building of international production systems, reviewed in *World Investment Report 2001*, Geneva, United Nations Commission on Trade and Development, enables firms to assert greater freedom in choosing production locations. See also Thomas A. Gresik 'The taxing task of taxing transnationals', *Journal of Economic Literature*, XXXIX, 3, September 2001, 800–38.
16. Firms tend to become more interdependent in the development of their production capabilities, because of multiplying advances in advanced technology, and this interdependence can be managed best through synergies generated in intensive exchanges of tacit knowledge, which develops through such exchanges. See Nicolai Foss and Volker Mahnke (eds) *Competence, Governance, and Entrepreneurship*, Oxford, Oxford University Press, 2000.
17. On efficiencies generated through cooperation see Peter A. Hall and David Soskice (eds) *Varieties of Capitalism: Institutional Foundations of Comparative Advantage*, Oxford, Oxford University Press, 2001.
18. See discussions of these disputes in Alan M. Rugman and Gavin Boyd (eds) *The World Trade Organization in the New Global Economy*, Cheltenham, Edward Elgar, 2001.
19. This point is implicit in surveys of international production systems, as presented in *World Investment Report 2001*, cited.
20. See Coen, cited.
21. See references in Boyd and Rugman, cited.
22. *Ibid.*
23. International competition policy cooperation has developed, with strains, between the USA and the European Union. See Youri Devuyst 'Transatlantic Competition Relations', in Mark A. Pollack and Gregory C. Shaffer (eds) *Transatlantic Governance in the Global Economy*, Lanham, Rowman and Littlefield, 2001, ch. 5, and Simon J. Evenett, Alexander Lehmann and Benn Steil (eds) *Antitrust goes Global*, London, Royal Institute of International Affairs and Washington DC, Brookings Institution, 2000.
24. See reports of OECD sponsored discussions on excess steel capacity, and on US consideration of import controls, *Financial Times*, 18 and 20 December 2001.
25. Quests by investors for higher returns from speculative operations have been evident in the USA despite the lowering of interest rates to facilitate economic recovery. See articles on hedge funds by Robert Clow *Financial Times*, 9 October 2001 and 4 December 2001, and his comments on Mutual Funds, *Financial Times*, 16 October 2001.
26. See references in Rugman and Boyd, cited.
27. Information failures were evident in the operations of Enron after its collapse. See especially *Financial Times*, 24 December 2001.
28. See references to industrial policies in symposium on infrastructure network industries in *Oxford Review of Economic Policy*, 17, 3, Autumn 2001.
29. See *International Organization* – symposium on trade agreements, cited.
30. See references to anti-dumping in Rugman and Boyd, cited, and comments on third world problems in J. Michael Finger, 'Implementing the Uruguay Round Agreements: Problems for Developing Countries', *The World Economy*, 24, 9, September 2001, 1097–108.
31. Increased disputes are expected in the World Trade Organization because of the complex market opening commitments which the Chinese have been obliged to make. See Will Martin and Elena Ianchovichina 'Implications of China's accession to the World Trade Organization for China and the WTO', *The World Economy*, 24, 9, September 2001, 1205-20.
32. See Lucjan T. Orlowski (ed.) *Transition and Growth in Post-Communist Societies*, Cheltenham, Edward Elgar, 2001.

33. On inefficiencies and instability in financial markets see Alexander Karmann (ed.) *Financial Structure and Stability*, Heidelberg, Physica-Verlag, 2000. See also *Financial Market Trends*, 75, Paris, OECD, March 2000.
34. See Ahmed Bounfour 'Intangible Resources and Competitiveness: Towards a Dynamic View of Corporate Performance', in Pierre Buigues, Alexis Jacquemin and Jean-Francois Marchipont (eds) *Competitiveness and the Value of Intangible Assets*, Cheltenham, Edward Elgar 2000, ch. 2.
35. This can be argued with reference to observations in Gunnar Aliasson, 'Making Intangibles Visible: the Value, the Efficiency and the Economic Consequences of Knowledge', in the same volume, ch. 3.
36. On the public goods problems resulting from the independent operations of transnational enterprises see Keith Cowling (ed.) *Industrial Policy in Europe*, London, Routledge, 1999.

7. Corporate alliances and competition policies

Gavin Boyd and Alan M. Rugman

This chapter explores the reasons for the recent tensions between the European Union (EU) and the United States in the administration of competition and antitrust policies. The growth of corporate alliances between multinational enterprises (MNEs) and other firms based in the EU and North America is basically driven by business and financial efficiencies, but it also poses issues for the respective competition authorities. The corporate alliances involve various forms of cooperation based ultimately on expanding markets and increasing shares of those markets. Yet this process increases the degree of concentration, particularly if the intercorporate cooperation is in the form of mergers and acquisitions. In addition, empirical evidence suggests that, while alliances may develop with sound rationales (based on the advantages of complementary technological specializations, and of combining established or prospective market strengths), they often *fail*, within a few years, because of distrust, conflicts of interest, and opportunism.[1] Mergers and acquisitions thus may become subject to investigation by competition authorities if there are concentrations of market power above certain permitted levels.[2]

Cultures, institutions and established policy orientations in the 'triad' of the United States, the EU, and Japan, influence corporate strategies in the use of opportunities for alliance formation and for mergers and acquisitions. Both types of activities are at high levels in the Atlantic context of complex large-scale structural interdependencies between the United States and the EU. Overall trends in this pattern (together with those in a secondary pattern centred on the still distressed Japanese economy) are having cumulative macroeconomic effects on global markets. These macroeconomic effects include changes in the preferential funding of more competitive firms; rates of technological progress; levels of growth and employment; the relative bargaining power of firms; and in dealings with other enterprises and governments.

Issues of international competition policy cooperation are also becoming prominent, principally in transatlantic relations, and are increasing speculation about possible global competition policy cooperation in the World Trade Organization. Very extensive shared interests in the harmonious development of trade and investment links between the United States and the EU could be expected to motivate cooperation on competition policy issues. Yet this has been difficult, due to opposing pressures from rival international firms, differences in the estimation of market strengths and potentials, and problems in the aggregation of preferences across corporate associations and political groups.

International competition policy issues have structural significance, and thus tend to activate structural policy initiatives, which in turn can complicate and increase competition policy problems. In the EU, competition policy aims, in principle, to facilitate the emergence of enterprises that will be internationally competitive but without sufficient domestic strength to significantly reduce the efficiency effects of corporate rivalries. Decisions made in this context have to be related to estimates of the effects of antitrust enforcement in the United States that have Atlantic and global consequences.[3] In the United States, competition policy management involves considerable institutional pluralism, influenced by administrative guidelines. It is less related to structural issues and structural policy concerns, which can be attributed to a more liberal economic policy tradition.[4] Japanese competition policy, informally tolerant of oligopolistic market strengths, is in effect linked to a very active structural policy. This has international competitive objectives more ambitious than those of the EU. While the US, Canadian and Mexican economies have become much more open to each other, in the North America Free Trade Area (NAFTA), the US economy's trade and investment links with the EU have became very large.

The US–EU link is now the most significant in world commerce. It is being further expanded with the entries of East European states into the EU, as well as with the extension of the EU's preferential trade arrangements, notably with Mediterranean and African countries. Corporate alliances and mergers and acquisitions in Europe have major implications for US MNEs which have a large corporate presence in the EU, and for US exporters to the EU. Strong European corporate interests in collaboration with US enterprises also have major implications for US firms active in transatlantic commerce. The multiplying forms of European corporate involvement in the United States also present challenges and opportunities for US MNEs, although the European presence in the United States is more fragmented and generally less competitive than the US counterpart in Europe.[5]

COMPETITION POLICY IN NAFTA

In NAFTA the competition policy processes of major US structural significance are exercises of regulatory authority by the Antitrust Division of the Department of Justice and the Federal Trade Commission. The former is an arm of the administration, responsive to its economic philosophy. The latter is a nominally independent agency, identified in principle with a popular tradition of opposition to concentrations of economic power. This is a tradition that also influences the Department of Justice. Policy level perspectives, however, have been open to flows of economic advice emphasizing efficiencies achieved by large enterprises that serve the public interest and that can operate competitively in world markets.[6] Despite a strong trend towards concentration resulting from numerous mergers and acquisitions, US antitrust enforcement has continued to discourage many forms of cooperation between firms that could be considered as anticompetitive. Intercorporate alliances thus have had to be managed cautiously, to avoid litigation based on allegations of price fixing or market sharing. Hence there have been incentives to merge with or acquire alliance partners.[7]

Technological advances make firms more interdependent in the development of their production capabilities, and this has implications for their marketing activities. In the US context it is especially important to avoid explicit agreements that could be cited in antitrust litigation because large damages can result. Also alliance partners may have doubtful loyalties, and may undergo changes because of active markets for corporate control. Alliances can be exposed to high degrees of opportunism and low levels of trust. These strains weaken alliances despite increases in interdependence that can make their rationales evident.

Degrees of coherence in US antitrust policy have been affected by complexities resulting from judicial involvement, with successive rulings and appeals.[8] These add to uncertainties that have to be reckoned with in decisions about mergers and acquisitions, and also in those affecting choices regarding the management of alliances. Currently, there is more tolerance of mergers and acquisitions than of methods of increasing the market benefits of alliances. This is reflected in the strength of concentration trends within the United States. In 1999 the total value of mergers and acquisition in the United States was estimated to be about $1.7 trillion.[9]

The structural consequences of the US concentration trend are extremely important for Canada and Mexico. Total factor productivity levels in Canada are lower than those in the United States, and the differences have been tending to increase.[10] Further increases may be expected as a consequences of greater efficiencies associated with the emergence of larger enterprises with more extensive market shares in the United States. These firms will have superior capabilities for the penetration of foreign markets. Canada cannot challenge decisions by US antitrust authorities regarding mergers and acquisitions by US firms, or the management of their alliances; this is possible only for the EU, if it can provide evidence of substantial increases in levels of international market strength.[11] The EU's bargaining strength is comparable with that of the United States; leverage can be exercised on trade and investment issues of vital significance for the United States. This capability is not available to Mexico as there are few European economic links. Mexico, still at a lower level of economic development than Canada, simply has to accept the structural effects of US competition policy decisions. Disparities in the levels of competitiveness and bargaining strengths in this relationship are still large.

Forms of intercorporate cooperation in Canada and Mexico have minor significance for the development of more balanced structural interdependencies with the United States. The US economy exerts powerful attractions which draw entrepreneurial initiatives from both countries, principally to the advantage of large US firms as leading partners in alliances and networks. Passive investment flows complement the movements of direct investment.

Chapter 15 of the agreement which established the NAFTA sets out obligations for the member countries to cooperate in the implementation of their national competition policies; that is, through information exchanges and consultations, especially within a Working Group on Trade and Competition.[12] The activities of this group are understandably affected by asymmetries in information access and in surveillance and research capabilities, as well as in ranges of interests. This is especially because the Canadian and Mexican direct investment positions in the United States are much less significant for US antitrust authorities than are the US direct investment positions in Canada and Mexico for competition policy management in these two countries.

General principles in NAFTA relate to monopolies and state enterprises, but there are no specifics regarding the abuse of dominant positions, collusion, or vertical restraints. Export cartels, however, are exempt from antitrust enforcement in the United States and from applications of competition law in Canada and Mexico. While US firms collaborating in the Canadian and Mexican markets can thus be especially advantaged, under a 1985 Mutual Legal Assistance Treaty the United States and Canadian governments are committed to assist each other in the investigation of cartels and in competition policy enforcement against them.[13]

While engaged in US–Canadian competition policy cooperation, the United States still endeavours to give its antitrust enforcement an extraterritorial reach, in line with guidelines issued by the Department of Justice and the Federal Trade Commission in 1995. These are subject to discretionary interpretation by the Department of Justice, and deal mainly with issues affecting US consumers or the interests of US exporters. Attempts at enforcement have resulted in conflicts with European governments and also with Canada. Accordingly bilateral competition policy cooperation agreements have been sought, as US policy has generally not favoured multilateral competition policy cooperation in the World Trade Organization.[14]

Under the NAFTA agreement, member countries remain free to subsidize the production and trading activities of their firms and to resort to anti-dumping actions against each other, but chapter 19 provides for dispute settlement through binational panels, although these have only review functions. The United States is very active in the use of anti-dumping measures, within NAFTA and in relations with the EU, and its procedures tend to favour the interests of domestic producers. Sentiment among US legislators strongly supports separation of antidumping cases from competition policy issues.[15] Canadian antidumping policy does not have a domestic bias, and is administered with procedures that allow consideration of related competition policy issues, although this has not always been a common practice.

The evolution of forms of intercorporate cooperation and of the concentration trend in the United States has very substantial consequences for the structural foundations of North American commerce, and, thus, for competition *processes* which are changing those foundations and the context of competition policy issues in NAFTA. Intercorporate alliances in the United States, especially to high technology sectors, tend to exert increasingly powerful attractions for Canadian and Mexican enterprises seeking to develop related economies of scale. Opportunities for such firms are limited in Canada and even more limited in Mexico. The Canadian market is under one tenth the size of the US market and Mexico's is about one-twentieth. Industrial policy capabilities in Canada are restricted by partnerships with US firms which influence Canadian managements, and because of the fragmentation of corporate associations in Canada.[16] Also the perspectives of Canadian firms are sensitive to uncertainties about the long-term prospects of the national economy. The persistence of barriers to trade between Canadian provinces also affects those uncertainties. Canada, like Mexico, has become very dependent on the US market, and the failure to develop strong economic links with the EU is having a cumulative effect on Canadian corporate outlooks. Canada's trade, investment, and political connections with Mexico are of minor significance. For the Mexican government and for Mexican firms there are now significant opportunities to develop ties with Latin American states, and the principal challenges for policy and corporate planning in Mexico are to respond to US initiatives for the development of a Free Trade Area of the Americas.[17]

A high proportion of the alliances between US enterprises lead to mergers and acquisitions, approval of which is almost entirely a US process, and is in effect open to challenge only by the EU. If large market positions are involved, the evolution of forms of US intercorporate cooperation tends to be determined mainly by degrees of tolerance in antitrust enforcement, the bargaining strengths of large I75 firms, and the increasing importance of technology based incentives for alliance formation and for mergers and acquisitions. Canadian and Mexican firms seeking linkages with US enterprises have to reckon with increasing asymmetries in the complexities of antitrust changes and continuities, corporate market positions, and technological interdependencies within the US pattern. The overall trend – increasing concentration with stronger technological leads in that pattern – has several implications.

US corporate alliances and mergers and acquisitions, through effects on the interests and opportunities of Canadian and Mexican firms, contribute to changes in the incentives that can motivate Canadian and Mexican competition policy authorities, and legislators shaping those policies. Bargaining strengths of significance regarding those incentives must be expected to undergo further changes if there are more active US initiatives for the establishment of a Free Trade Area of the Americas, and especially if these initiatives seem likely to lead initially to a hub and spoke configuration of trade liberalization arrangements apart from NAFTA.[18] Meanwhile, the domestic administration of competition policy in Canada and Mexico will tend to have diminishing structural significance. Competition policy enforcement intended to facilitate the emergence of internationally more competitive Canadian and Mexican enterprises is becoming less effective. Such firms are drawn into generally subordinate partnering roles in the United States. Also incentives for collaboration between Canadian corporations and Mexican firms are decreasing.

COMPETITION POLICY IN THE EUROPEAN UNION

Competition Policy in the EU is managed with considerable autonomy by the European Commission, on the basis of essentially free market principles accepted by member governments, although with tacit reservations related to their structural policy concerns. Commission decisions can be appealed to the European Court of Justice, and its decisions have overturned Commission rulings, notably regarding forms of marketing collaboration. Explicit forms of marketing coordination are in principle subject to competition policy enforcement, but there are ambiguities regarding coordination occurring through independent decision making without formal understandings. Mergers and acquisitions above certain levels have to be approved by the Commission. It has sought to lower these levels, but has been resisted by member governments.[19] The established Commission orientation is toward facilitating the emergence of competitive EU firms that will not be regionally dominant but that will be capable of managing rivalries with US and Japanese enterprises in world markets. The necessary judgemental decisions are difficult because of the generally weaker international competitiveness of firms that emerge in intraunion consolidation processes, and because of the scope for expansion within the EU by US enterprises, who are attractive partners in alliances, mergers, and acquisitions.[20]

The development of cross-border alliances within the EU, with pricing and market sharing arrangements, can be advantageous between firms seeking to extend their operations, while maintaining independence, and reckoning with the uncertainties of negotiating mergers or acquisitions. Competition policy enforcement by the European Commission discourages explicit agreements for coordinated cross-border marketing. In effect, this allows scope only for mergers and acquisitions in which one major party has large resources for bargaining and risk taking, or in which relatively equal partners have been able to collaborate and build trust with each other while avoiding exposure to EU level competition policy actions through explicit marketing agreements. Large established firms in the more industrialized member states are thus advantaged, and in this category are major privatized utilities. Cross-border mergers and acquisitions by these infrastructure network enterprises challenge member states to assert independence in the management of their own competition policies.[21] Meanwhile, the use of direct and indirect subsidies for national firms, to enhance their competitiveness within the EU, and internationally, tends to be given greater importance by member governments, although this evokes pressures from the European Commission to force reductions of such state aids.

The structural objectives evident in EU competition policy have to be pursued in ways that contend with excess capacity and virtual market segmentation in the automobile sector; oligopolistic retailing in major member countries, accounting for high living costs; and the advantages of collaboration with US firms for European enterprises lacking confidence in their region's prospects. The European Commission's efforts to cope with these problems are understandably affected by the dynamics of its interactions with member governments and in particular by its capacity to articulate persuasively the logic of competition policy enforcement in the common interest.

The development of alliance capitalism, with structural change being influenced by competition policy, is restricted primarily because of cultural and political differences between member countries that are reflected in their structural policy rivalries. Productive informal intercorporate cooperation on a relational basis is extensive mainly in Germany. It avoids exposure to competition policy enforcement by the European Commission because of the absence of explicit agreements. In ventures within other member countries, however, the limited scope for relational dealings encourages emphasis and quests for mergers and acquisitions; German firms have generally larger resources than their rivals in other member countries. Technologically, moreover, German firms also tend to be advantaged: enterprises in other member countries have relatively weaker capabilities for partnering in technology-based alliances.

In the automobile sector the Commission is endeavouring to reduce long-established restrictive selling by requiring the development of more open distribution networks. National industries will be brought into more direct cross-border competition that will force efficient specializations. Structural policy rivalries in this area between member governments are thus being intensified, with major implications for overall industrial development and employment. Cross-border alliance capitalism could contribute to harmonious regional integration of the sector but this is not in prospect. While national automobile markets – principally those of Germany, France, and Italy – remain virtually segmented, the EU as a whole is open to penetration by US and, to a lesser extent, Japanese, automobile firms. The larger resources of these outside MNEs enable them to implement aggressive sales strategies. The German, French, and Italian manufacturers have to cope with market limitations on their capacities to increase their own resources, so they fail to achieve beneficial cross-border economies of scale.

Well established national oligopolistic retailing systems in the larger member states impose considerable supply requirements on producers and benefit from informal political ties with governments similar to those which are important in the structurally more significant automobile industries. The dominant retailing firms implement pricing strategies that maintain costs above US levels, while also keeping employment below what would be possible in a more competitive setting. While the options for suppliers are restricted by the buying strengths of the leading retailers, the opportunities for new entrants are also restricted – all the more so because of complex regulatory requirements in retailing sectors. Regulatory functions tend to be politicized, within national systems of governance, and there is resistance to EU level penetration into this domestic policy area. Cross-border collaboration between leading retail firms is exposed to competition policy enforcement by the European Commission, and accordingly these firms have incentives to resort to merger and acquisition strategies, but these have to contend with the informal political bonds that benefit such firms in their home environments.[22] An important consequence is that entries by such firms into less industrialized member states with weaker retailing sectors are more feasible than entries into each other's established markets.

The advantages of collaboration with US rather than European partners are tending to become more important factors in the regional pattern of corporate strategies because of the continued gaps in competitiveness and rates of growth between the EU and the United States. In the retailing sector the entrenched positions of leading European enterprises are evidently seen to be protected by politicized bias in regulatory systems. For producers, particularly outside the automobile sector, opportunities to collaborate with US firms, offering scope for mergers and the acceptance of acquisitions, are apparently tending to become more significant than collaboration with other European enterprises. The logic of forming technology based alliances – that are likely to lead to mergers and acquisitions – is becoming more compelling. US corporate representation in the articulation of regional business interests to the European Commission is now a major influence on the calculations of European firms seeking wider opportunities.[23]

European corporate interest also motivates quests for mergers and acquisitions in the United States, and these can be preceded by alliances. The targets are mostly in medium and low technology sectors, with small or moderate market strengths, and are of secondary significance for US antitrust authorities. The direct investment and high volume European portfolio flows to the United States contribute to a lower value of the euro against the US dollar, but have special significance for the US current account, because of the size of the US trade deficits.[24]

Controls over mergers between European firms are generally ineffective at the EU level, especially because of the unwillingness of member governments to accept Commission proposals for lowering ceilings under which their competition authorities have responsibility. The Commission has to be notified only when the combined annual worldwide turnover of the parties exceeds €5 billion, and the EU turnover of each of at least two of the parties is more than €250 million, and the parties conduct two-thirds or more of their business within one member country.[25] There are procedures for coordination between the Commission and the competition authorities in member states, but the structural policy concerns about competition policy autonomy in member governments are increasing. Cross-border mergers within the EU require approval by competition authorities in the member states within which the parties operate. Negotiated understandings about the acceptability of the likely structural effects can thus become necessary, and can be influenced by the relative bargaining strengths of member governments. In effect there can be reciprocal restraints, as would appear from the national concentrations of market power in retailing.

Increased efficiencies in competition policy management, it can be argued, would be possible if this were entirely centralized at the EU level. That, however, is not to be expected. The structural policy rivalries which exist prevent the development of a common policy which could engage comprehensively with the problems of lagging performance in European industries. Enlargement of the EU with the admission of East European states will add to the difficulties of collective decision making on structural and competition policy issues. The impetus given to EU commerce by the establishment of monetary union, however, is likely to be reflected in more numerous cross-border mergers made feasible by understandings between competition authorities in member states with superior bargaining strengths, based on size and market positions. The key states will continue to be Germany, France, and Italy. Germany's significance is likely to be strengthened by trade and investment links with the East European entrants, as well as by the persistence of structural policy problems in France and Italy. Relational bonds between German firms, although weakened by strains in the German political economy, will tend to assume greater significance in the structural evolution of the EU.[26]

ATLANTIC COMPETITION POLICY COOPERATION

Competition policy cooperation has developed between the United States and the EU in a context of high structural and policy interdependencies, informal mutual accountability, rough equality in bargaining strengths, and large flows of economic advice to policy levels from research institutes and interest groups. This is occurring despite considerable social distances between legislators, and domestically oriented policy processes.

The structural interdependencies result from large-scale cross-investment and intra-industry trade. Policy interdependencies, attributable primarily to the structural linkages, have been increased by the establishment of the European Monetary Union, as mentioned in Chapter 2. Mutual accountability has developed informally through decades of interaction on macro- and microeconomics policy issues, facilitated by cultural affinities. The EU economy which is similar in size to that of the United States, lags in overall industrial development, but is characterized by an extensive network of preferential trade relationships. Elite communities of economic policy experts and international management scholars activate intensive discussions of policy coordination problems, but at a level somewhat remote from the concerns of legislators. In the EU, domestic preoccupations have become very complex through its system of collective management. In the United States, traditionally intense pluralism has tended to become more domestically focused because of the difficulties of achieving a recovery from the 2001/2 recession and the events of 11 September 2001.

The dimensions of the Atlantic structural interdependencies tend to motivate enlightened policy level and corporate efforts to overcome strains in competition policy cooperation. Such strains develop principally because of the immediate and projected market effects of ongoing concentration trends. Those in the United States are viewed with special concern in the European Commission because of changes in market strengths, transregionally and globally. This affects the fortunes of EU firms in their own market and internationally. Concentration trends in Europe are of less significance for the United States because the scale of these is still limited by the persistence of considerable fragmentation in the EU market, and because their effects within the United States tend to be dispersed in the separate British, German, French, Dutch and other European MNE presences in the United States. Atlantic strains also develop because of corporate marketing activities deemed to be anticompetitive by either side. These can assume additional significance if they are related to concentration trends.[27]

The European Commission and the US antitrust authorities exchange information about current and anticipated market changes associated with mergers, acquisitions, and diverse forms of corporate marketing cooperation. Judgemental considerations, however, influenced by structural as well as market concerns, tend to be especially evident on the European side, on the basis of concerns about weaker competitiveness and about the somewhat liberal orientation of US antitrust enforcement. These concerns are manifest in the marketing area, and one common effect is that, because evidence of diverse forms of marketing cooperation results in vulnerability to competition policy enforcement, collaborating firms are given incentives to unite through mergers and acquisitions. European Commission hopes for the emergence of strong firms in a balanced and dynamic pattern of rivalries within the single market are challenged by intra EU mergers and acquisitions, which, in combination with forms of tacit cooperation, tend to produce an imbalanced pattern of market strengths.[28] Additional challenges are presented by the expansion of the US corporate presence in Europe, through mergers and acquisitions, as well as through informal methods of cooperation, aided especially by a strong direct investment position in financial services and, indirectly, by large flows of passive European investment to the United States.[29]

The record of competition policy interactions between the United States and the EU since the signing of a 1991 agreement between the US administration and the European Commission, indicates active concern, in the European Commission, with the effects of concentration trends involving large internationally competitive US MNEs. There are also indications of openness, however, to complaints by US antitrust authorities about European corporate and policy level discrimination against US enterprises in Europe, notably in air transport sectors.[30] In this industry there are asymmetries of access, as US carriers operate across borders in the EU but European carriers cannot provide services between points in the United States.

European competition policy enforcement has given special attention to US aerospace mergers and acquisitions, which would affect the Airbus consortium's international market interests. This European attention has also been given to concentration trends in other US service sectors (apart from air transport), notably in communications and business services, that have seemed likely to enhance the United States' overall competitiveness in service industries.[31]

European Commission efforts to use regulatory powers for the development of a more active market for corporate control in the EU, which have been opposed by member governments, are in accord with US antitrust policy and with the interests of US firms in Europe, but have not evoked US approval. US MNEs in the EU, as noted, have gained recognition as partners in European business associations for the representation of common concerns to the European Commission and administrations in member states.[32] European firms, moreover, while tending to align with US enterprises for mergers and acquisitions, have been willing to reverse excessive diversifications through divestment strategies acceptable to majority shareholders when there are advantageous terms offered by US acquirers. The perspectives of EU member governments, focused on structural policy issues, but also on the maintenance of domestic political ties, have been complicated by the interests of managements and large shareholders as the EU becomes more closely linked with the United States.

Financial market regulation has tended to become more closely linked with Atlantic competition policy cooperation because of strong concentration trends in world financial markets. The potential for destabilizing speculation has become more significant as became evident with the collapse of Enron, the large US energy firm in early 2002.[33] This historic bankruptcy has made European authorities more sensitive to problems in the regulation of large nonfinancial enterprises that have not been subject to competition policy enforcement even when they have attempted hazardous speculative diversification. And US antitrust agencies have been obliged to consider the destabilizing potential of speculative propensities in the management of large enterprises that become conglomerates.

European financial markets are less developed and less effectively regulated than those in the United States. They are significantly open to entries by US financial enterprises, whose home and international market positions are generally larger and are under more aggressive management.[34] The US enterprises, moreover, have an attractive home market for European investors, while there is a smaller scale of European financial sector involvement in the United States. Cooperative practices developing between European and US competition authorities tend to benefit US financial enterprises expanding their European operations. Relations between the European Commission and US trade policy agencies tend to be adversarial, and thus affect negotiations on the liberalization of trade in financial services.[35]

Efficiency considerations are a basic element in the formal rationale for competition policy cooperation between the EU and the United States. Competitive pressures driving corporate performance in specializations are expected to increase interdependent growth while preventing abuses of market strengths. Potential efficiencies resulting from mergers and acquisitions tend to be secondary considerations in European and US competition policy enforcement, because of the prominence given to assessments of relative market power. On the European side, because of weaker structural competitiveness, efficiency assessments could logically be given greater priority. This would be consistent with Commission endeavours to promote the development of small and medium sized firms, especially in high technology sectors.[36] The efficiency assessments, however, would be highly judgemental, and would require expertise outside the competition policy area. In the Commission such expertise would have to be provided by directorates dealing with industries. These have been oriented mainly toward the encouragement of mergers and acquisitions which would achieve scale economies simply on the basis of larger market power. The promotion of growth by small and medium sized enterprises has been a secondary endeavour. It has encountered difficulties because of the weak technological capabilities of such firms. In the United States, antitrust authorities would also require additional expertise to assess the efficiencies of mergers and acquisitions. They focus on the significance of market power, although the main trend in official guidelines has been increasing recognition of the productive capabilities of large firms for the national economy.[37]

CORPORATE COOPERATION AND COMPETITION POLICY ISSUES

Competition policy cooperation in Atlantic relations, and competition policy enforcement in the EU and in the United States, have led to recognition of the increasing complexity of major issues of efficiency, stability, and social justice in the evolution of corporate alliances, concentration trends, and market practices. Regulative functions intended to ensure efficiencies in the operation of market forces have taken effect in contexts in which market failures have been mixed with the efficiencies, especially because of the concentration trends. Questions about stability and order have assumed prominence because of the scale of speculative activities in financial markets that tend to contribute to unsustainable asset appreciations which can make those trends destabilizing. Externalities associated with the mergers and acquisitions driving the concentration tends can include sectoral disruptions and employment losses.

Engagement with public goods issues is becoming a more necessary and more demanding task for competition policy authorities although they remain charged principally with responsibilities for the maintenance of free market forces. Official capacities for management of those responsibilities have always depended on degrees of spontaneous order and self-regulation in corporate communities, and these now have greater significance because of the difficulties of judgemental determination on competition matters in structurally interdependent knowledge based political economies. If there can be increased relational intercorporate cooperation in the development of international production and marketing systems, with emphasis on initiatives to build entrepreneurial complementarities, concentration trends will be moderated and corporate alliances will become more stable, with greater synergies.[38]

Surveillance of forms of intercorporate cooperation by competition authorities is becoming more difficult because of the multiplication of technology based production interdependencies between firms. This requires numerous exchanges of tacit as well as codified knowledge, and the development of informal understandings about related production and marketing plans, which necessarily involve suppliers and distributors linked in alliances and networks. The rising costs of new investments in advanced technology make the planning of complementary entrepreneurial ventures dependent on understandings about the use of concerted strategies to ensure anticipated sales and revenues. The building of trust and goodwill in alliances and networks depends on collaborative marketing that adjusts to changing demand patterns and to technological breakthroughs.[39]

Collaboration can become collusive. This can be prevented through forms of accountability developing in comprehensive corporate associations, which therefore should be free to form on a relational basis, without restrictive involvement by competition authorities. The order provided by such associations and industry groups can complement competition policy enforcement while limiting its tasks in ways that can provide scope for continuing development of the associations and industry groups and for their productive partnering with structural policy authorities.

The multiplication of technology based production interdependencies between firms, resulting from advances on widening fronts in fundamental research, is becoming more and more international, yet with US scientific institutes at the centre. Collaborative pre-competitive research in the United States can be managed with certification by antitrust authorities, but continuing cooperation for commercial application is possible with only tacit understandings about the terms of procurements and sales. There are advantages in developing such understandings with foreign partners, although binding them with explicit agreements on marketing practices can risk exposure to competition policy enforcement. Risk of this kind adds to the incentives to shift from alliance to merger and acquisition strategies. These can be used with greater effect to restrict competition.

The internationalization of corporate production interdependencies, in conjunction with increases in corporate alliances and mergers and acquisitions, adds to the importance of international competition policy cooperation as a public good. The capabilities of national competition authorities and of systems for their collaboration, however, are being strained by the expanding range of technology based alliances and the widening scope of cross-border corporate collaboration. The regulatory functions tend to be politicized, especially because of their significance in the tacit trading of political favours. The conclusion is that comprehensive corporate associations and industry groups must promote spontaneous order and harmony, to complement the increasingly difficult tasks of competition policy authorities. This is all the more significant in view of the dimensions of the cross-border production interdependencies that have to be recognized. A case for entrusting international competition policy responsibilities to the World Trade Organization, however, cannot be pressed while that body's institutional weaknesses persist. The degree of self-regulation that can become possible for US and European business groups, in close association, is a vital public goods concern, both for Atlantic relations and the international community.

NOTES

1. See Andrew C. Inkpen and Jerry Ross 'Why do some strategic alliances persist beyond their useful life?', *California Management Review*, 44, 1, Fall 2001, 132–48.
2. Simon J. Evenett, Alexander Lehmann and Benn Steil (eds) (2000), *Antitrust Goes Global*, London: Royal Institute of International Affairs and Washington: Brookings Institution, 2000 and P.J. Lloyd and Kerrin M. Vautier, *Promoting Competition in Global Markets*, Cheltenham, UK: Edward Elgar, 1999.

3. See *Antitrust Goes Global*, cited, especially Ch. 2.
4. See *Oxford Review of Economic Policy*, 9, 2, Summer 1993 – symposium on competition policy.
5. See references to Atlantic cross investment in Thomas L. Brewer, Paul A. Brenton and Gavin Boyd (eds) *Globalizing Europe*, Cheltenham: Edward Elgar, 2002.
6. See comments on US antitrust policy in Lloyd and Vautier, cited, and B. Dan Wood and James E. Anderson, 'The politics of U.S. antitrust regulations', *American Journal of Political Science*, 37, 1, February 1993, 1–39.
7. See Lawrence J. White, 'Competition policy in the United States', *Oxford Review of Economic Policy*, cited, 133–51.
8. *Ibid.*
9. See *Antitrust Goes Global*, cited, 60.
10. See Dale W. Jorgenson and Frank C. Lee (eds) *Industry Level Productivity and International Competitiveness between Canada and the United States*, Ottawa: Industry Canada, 2001, and *Economic Survey, Canada*, Paris: OECD, September 2001.
11. See references to Atlantic relations in *Antitrust Goes Global*, cited, and Youri Devuyst 'Transatlantic competition relations' in Mark A. Pollack and Gregory C. Shaffer (eds) *Transatlantic Governance in the Global Economy*, Lanham: Rowman and Littlefield, 2001, Ch. 5.
12. See Lloyd and Vautier, cited, Ch. 6.
13. *Ibid.*
14. See Lloyd and Vautier, cited, Ch. 3.
15. See discussions of antidumping in *The World Economy*, 21, 8, November 1998, symposium on competition policy. Also see Alan M. Rugman and Andrew Anderson *Administered Protection in America*, London: Routledge, 1987 and in *The World Economy*, cited.
16. See William D. Coleman, 'State traditions and comprehensive associations: a comparative structural analysis', *Political Studies* XXXVIII, 1990, 231–53.
17. See Lloyd and Vautier, cited, 116.
18. See Jeffrey J. Schott, *Prospects for Free Trade in the Americas*, Washington, DC: Institute for International Economics, 2001.
19. See references to EU competition policy in *Antitrust Goes Global* and Lloyd and Vautier.
20. See R. Narula (1999) 'Explaining the growth of strategic R&D alliances', *Journal of Common Market Studies*, 37, 4, December, 711–23. There is increasing concentration in European banks – see Jean Dermine 'The economics of bank mergers in the EU', *Journal of Common Market Studies*, 38, 3, September 2000, 409–26, but US financial institutions have a large presence in Europe – see *Survey of Current Business*, July 2001, 27.
21. See symposium on European network infrastructures in *Oxford Review of Economic Policy*, 17, 3, Winter 2001.
22. See Paul Dobson and Michael Waterson 'Retailer power: recent developments and policy implications', *Economic Policy*, 28, April 1999, 135–50.
23. See David Coen 'The impact of U.S. lobbying practice on the European business–government relationship', *California Management Review*, 41, 4, Summer 1999, 27–44.
24. This investment flow has been noted in numerous *Financial Times* articles during the first half of 2001.
25. See Lloyd and Vautier, cited, 65.
26. See discussions of Germany as a coordinated market economy in Peter A. Hall and David Soskice (eds) *Varieties of Capitalism*, Oxford: Oxford University Press, 2001.
27. See discussion in *Antitrust Goes Global*, cited.
28. See Michael Darmer and Laurens Kuyper (eds) *Industry and the EU*, Cheltenham, UK: Edward Elgar, 2000, especially Chs. 2 and 8.
29. See *Survey of Current Business*, July 2001, cited.
30. See *Antitrust Goes Global,* cited, references to EU–US cooperation.
31. See references to these sectors in the same volume.
32. See Coen, cited.

33. See 'Days Enron shook the world', *Financial Times*, 24 December 2001.
34. See Dermine, cited, Table 1, and *World Investment Report 2000*, Geneva: United Nations Commission on Trade and Development, 2000.
35. See references to trade conflicts in Pollack and Shaffer, cited.
36. See Hans Schenk, 'Industrial policy implications of competition policy failure in mergers' in Keith Cowling (ed.) *Industrial Policy in Europe*, London: Routledge, 1999, Ch. 11.
37. See White, cited.
38. Relational intercorporate cooperation can result in emphasis on developing entrepreneurial complementarities through coordination. See Hall and Soskice, cited, and references to corporate cooperation in Shumpei Kumon and Henry Rosovsky (eds) *The Political Economy of Japan*, vol, 3, Stanford: Stanford University Press, 1992.
39. See Inkpen and Ross, cited, and Africa Arino, Jose de la Torre, and Peter Smith Ring 'Relational quality: managing trust in corporate alliances', *California Management Review*, 44, 1, Fall 2001, 109–31.

8. Alliance capitalism in Europe

Sarianna M. Lundan

This chapter explores the interplay between two forms of alliance capitalism: alliance capitalism at the level of the state, which refers to the institutional structure underlying economic activity, and alliance capitalism at the level of the firm, which is concerned with the motivations and modalities relating to cooperative corporate activity. We begin by outlining the main differences between the coordinated and liberal market economics, typified in Europe by Germany and the United Kingdom respectively. We then discuss the extent to which such systemic differences translate into economic performance, and particularly the extent to which they shape the activities of indigenous firms. We conclude the discussion on the institutional level of alliance capitalism by examining the dynamics of such systems, and in particular, the role of multinational firms in effecting change.

From the dynamics of national systems we move on to the level of the firm, and present a theoretical context for multinational corporate activity that covers both the observed growth in mergers and acquisitions as well as strategic alliances. We then review some recent empirical evidence relating to the extent of strategic alliances, and in particular contractual alliances in high-technology sectors, and the clustering of innovative activity in specific regions. We conclude by assessing the implications of this activity to the competence accumulation of European firms, which we see as essential in contributing to the formation of high value-added clusters of business activity, and thus to improving the locational attractiveness of Europe.

We end this chapter with a discussion of the extent to which we should expect a degree of convergence toward a more global (American) business model in Europe, or whether the differences in national business systems within Europe might in fact be reinforced by multinational corporate activity. On the policy side, we will argue that the process of cluster formation needs to be accompanied by a competition policy that permits foreign multinationals to derive asymmetrical benefits from their participation in the local cluster by allowing them to reach a substantial market share in the European context. Alliance capitalism, involving economic activity of a cooperative nature among participants that are known to each other, itself represents a move away from the purely competitive market, and as such requires macro-organizational policies by governments that are neither overly interventionist nor completely laissez-faire. The market-led process of the creation of clusters of economic activity that form hotspots attractive to multinationals is an example of a virtuous cycle of technological accumulation where the role of the government is merely a facilitative one. However, the ability of regions to hold on to investment and to achieve sustained economic growth rests on the ability of firms to derive long-term benefits from their presence in the area, which in some cases may involve the acceptance of a degree of collusion and market dominance.

VARIETIES OF CAPITALISM

At the level of the nation state, institutions such as the relative role of shareholders and banks as sources of corporate finance, and the role of trade associations, chambers of commerce and trade unions, play an important part in shaping the strategies of European firms.[1] In the economic and business literature, the institutional underpinnings of different forms of capitalism have been famously discussed by North (1991), as well as by scholars employing the concept of the national business system prominent in the work of Whitley (1992a, b). Other contributions in this vein have ranged from the largely descriptive account of Vogel (1991), to the more formal comparative approach adopted by Hamilton and Biggart (1988), and the theoretical arguments offered by Jones (1995). In contrast to scholars who focus on a particular aspect of the institutional setting, such as comparative studies on corporate governance and labour relations (see e.g. Cohen and Boyd, 2000; Lane, 1989), these authors attempt to incorporate culture and societal norms into the broad range of institutions that influence economic performance.

A contrasting approach presented by Casson and Lundan (1999) argues that international differences in industrial systems are better seen as a reflection of the different composition of industries found in each country. Each industry has its own particular functional logic, which determines the best-practice style of management, and the most appropriate pattern of ownership. Thus, for example, economies of scale mean that the steel industry in each country is dominated by a small number of very large firms, while diseconomies of scale mean that the printing industry normally consists of a large number of small firms. In general, each industry has its own distinctive 'recipe' (Spender, 1989), which is shared by managers who see it as appropriate for their conditions. The comparative advantage of the country, as determined by natural resource endowments, labour skills, and so on, governs which type of industry dominates the country, and therefore governs which form of organization is typical of that country. In order to account for the differences in performance between economies, one needs not only to focus at the industry level, but also to incorporate the dynamics brought about by multinational activity and the role of entrepreneurship.

In this chapter, we aim to integrate the country-specific view with the industry-specific view, by exploring the dynamics of change within European business systems that arise from multinational activity. In the end, whether international variation dominates inter-industry variation, in other words, whether the same industries are organized differently in different countries, and different industries are organized in a similar way in the same country, is an empirical question. In some cases industry recipes are very strong, and the transformational logic of an industry is sufficient to bring about institutional change at the national level. In other instances, firms continue to reflect the legacy of their home country context. (In practice, the benefit of disaggregation at the industry level is that propositions can be based very closely on primary evidence, whereas propositions based on aggregation are really statements about the average or typical case.)

We will use the classification employed by Hall and Soskice (2001) of coordinated and liberal market economies as the basis of our discussion. In their discussion as well as here, among coordinated economies Germany is pre-eminent in the analysis, although the group also includes the Scandinavian countries, the Netherlands, Belgium, Austria, Switzerland and Japan. Coordinated economies typically enjoy 'patient' debt capital encouraged by the cross-ownership of banks and industrial enterprises and interlocking directorates. In coordinated economies decision-making tends to be consensus based, and in Europe a model of industrial relations involving collective bargaining through peak associations is typically employed. Such economies depend on industry- or firm-specific skills and, due to limited labour mobility, encourage cooperation between firms in a given sector through trade associations or chambers of commerce. Coordination in Germany (as well as in Finland and Sweden, for example) takes place at the level of industry, whereas coordination in Japan and South Korea is done at the level of the business group, or the keiretsu and chaebol respectively.

By contrast, liberal market economies are typified by the United States, but also include Canada, the United Kingdom, Ireland, Australia and New Zealand. These countries feature widespread share ownership and a persistent threat of takeovers, flexible labour markets with the right to hire and fire, and education systems geared towards mobility. Due to rigorous antitrust provisions, knowledge transfer between firms in liberal economies was traditionally conducted through the marketplace by technology licensing agreements or by poaching human resources from the competitors' research laboratories. While in the coordinated market system, continued collaboration within and among firms results in consensus-based standards, in market-based systems standards are formed in a race to the finish, where the winner takes all.

Another interesting feature of the institutional fabric highlighted by Casper (2001) that may systematically influence firm behaviour is the degree to which the legal system allows the kind of freedom of contracting typically enjoyed by US firms. For example, the legal system in Germany operates with much more standardized contractual structures or frameworks that have been brought about by collaboration within the networks of trade associations and firms. Under conditions of incomplete contracts, such a system allows for the courts to intervene when there is an imbalance of power between the contracting parties that would allow the dominant firm to shift risk to the weaker party. Such discretion restricts the range of governance structures that are available to (dominant) firms.

That there are persistent differences in institutional structures is not debatable, but whether such differences systematically influence the key parameters of innovativeness, productivity and competitiveness on a national level is less evident. As much as some key aspects of the economy are shaped by historical circumstances, industries have their own histories and a transformational logic that is complementary to the national level, and implies aggregation from the firm level up rather than the other way around. There are path-breaking firms within coordinated economies, and an institutional explanation of how Nokia has arisen out of an industrial structure that has previously supported industries exploiting forest and mineral resources would require very rapid changes in the institutional fabric. On the other hand, it could be argued that Nokia has tapped into a more general institutional setting in Finland, with high quality engineering education and an informal management culture that is none the less results oriented. If this was the case, the emergence of Nokia could in fact be thought of as an example of entrepreneurial activity uncovering previously underutilized resources within the institutional setting. In the following section we will explore more examples linking firm behaviour and institutional change.

DYNAMICS OF BUSINESS SYSTEMS

Coordinated market economies are particularly well suited to exploiting a highly skilled labour force that enjoys a relative degree of autonomy, and works to achieve incremental improvements in production. By contrast, the liberal market economies are more likely to encourage frame breaking innovation, while they do not always deal well with the requirements related to quality control and continuous improvement. Coordinated market economies also typically provide extensive education and training suitable to the production system. Among others, Hall and Soskice (2001) argue that German firms have benefited from a national system of innovation that is based on inter-firm cooperation within trade associations and consequent gradual improvement in the industry. This is reinforced by two distinct aspects of corporate governance, namely the existence of two-tier boards where workers are represented alongside company executives, and the cross-ownership of firms and banks that ensures 'patient' capital and information exchange, both at the higher and lower levels of the firm.

Indeed, the European patent data presented by Hall and Soskice (2001) seem to indicate quite a clear division of labour, whereby firms in the United States patent much more heavily in the high-technology sectors of biotechnology, new materials, pharmaceuticals and information technology, while the German firms are much more prevalent in areas such as civil engineering, transport and agricultural machines. (These counts compare German and US patents in different sectors in relation to global patenting in each sector.) Furthermore, the evidence cited by Padoan (2002) demonstrates that there are fundamental differences in knowledge accumulation between European countries, so that in the United Kingdom, for instance, knowledge accumulation is sensitive to domestic R&D, and also benefits strongly from high-technology imports and the stock of knowledge of foreign multinationals. By contrast, the results for Germany show moderate sensitivity of patenting to R&D expenditure, a more moderate role of the stock of foreign knowledge, and the higher importance of high-technology imports in enhancing domestic knowledge accumulation. Furthermore, in assessing whether the foreign stock of knowledge originates inside or outside the European Union, not surprisingly it was found that Germany is the only case that shows a strong regional effect. It was also revealed that the regional effects are sector specific, which lends support to the importance of the organic market order of specialization within industries that creates the potential for local clusters of economic activity and the subsequent spillover effects.

This being the case, it might be expected that German firms would be less inclined to engage in strategic alliances with one another, and would rather engage in alliances with companies from the United States, whose knowledge base is sufficiently different owing to the availability of venture capital and an emphasis on entrepreneurship. Indeed, there is evidence to indicate that firms would prefer to collaborate with others that possess a different knowledge base from their own. For example, in a study of the 15 largest electronics firms in Europe, Giarratana and Torrisi (2002) found that

EU-sponsored agreements between European firms, whether in core or non-core sectors, do not have a significant effect on technological performance as measured by patents. Rather, these serve as a forum where firms can influence the future direction of technical standards, for example. By contrast, private research collaborations were found to have a strong positive effect on patenting, particularly in non-core sectors, and particularly with US and Japanese partners. Similarly, Miotti and Sachwald (2002) analyzed the extent of cooperation in R&D based on a sample of manufacturing subsidiaries in France, some of them indigenous French firms, and others the affiliates of other European, US and Japanese firms. They concluded that for the French firms, international R&D partnerships were more efficient than French partners at increasing the firms' innovative capabilities. Furthermore, firms that cooperated with American partners tended to do so in relatively high technology sectors, while also cooperating with EU and Japanese firms.

One could even argue that the relatively low levels of foreign direct investment from Germany as compared with the United Kingdom, for instance, might be due to the fact that in coordinated economies, the institutional setting is an important part of a firm's competitiveness, and as such it poses an impediment to mobility. However, one way for firms to overcome such impediments is for them to transplant the domestic organizational logic to a foreign production location. Japanese firms' successful transplantation of their production system into the United States in the late 1980s is a case in point (see e.g. Cusumano and Takeishi, 1991). Another way is for the institutional structure of the host country to be transformed to better suit the firm. For example, according to Kanter (2000), the decisive factors in getting BMW to commit to locating in Spartanburg in the state of South Carolina had to do with the role played by the local business coalitions in the re-designing of the education and technical training system towards something resembling the German model.

The growth in both acquisitions and alliances involving European firms during the past decade is undoubtedly exerting a transforming influence on European business systems. The evidence presented by Emmons and Schmid (2002) shows that of the total of $720 billion worth of mergers and acquisitions undertaken in 1999, European Union firms were responsible for about $500 billion as buyers, and about $350 billion as sellers, and during the same year three-quarters of the firms involved in the world's ten largest cross-border mergers came from Europe. (This is in spite of the rather dismal track record of the success of mergers, which may be linked to the element of imitation that has created successive waves of merger activity.)

The decline of the continental business model in favour of a model of shareholder capitalism has created conditions where corporate restructuring through mergers and acquisitions has been made possible. Particularly in Germany, France and Spain, where the ownership of large firms by financial institutions and the practice of interlocking directorates have been the norm, a spate of big ticket takeovers most notably of Mannesman by Vodafone in 2000, or indeed the takeover by Daimler Benz of Chrysler which took place two years earlier, have signalled a transition to a new era (see e.g. Canals, 2002; Emmons and Schmid, 2002). Following the European Union regulation on the control of concentration which came into effect in 1990, an analysis by Glais (2000) of a large number of decisions announced over the last ten years highlights the fact that the European Commission has adopted a liberal interpretation of the rather strict competition rules. This interpretation has allowed mergers that meet industrial policy goals not to fall foul of a very orthodox interpretation of the competition rules. This has been particularly pertinent in terms of the definition of the relevant market, since an appropriately wide definition allows for much more substantial market dominance to take place. In addition, potential competition from firms located within or outside the community can be taken into account in accepting a merger, which has proven critical in allowing for the approval of merger projects that promote European economic efficiency even if competition is compromised in the concerned market.

While the hostile takeovers have sometimes been taken as an indication that the institutional context of European economies is about to give way to a global or American kind of capitalism, we would argue that such a judgment is premature, or may only concern the relationship of European firms in connection with the (global) financial markets. Institutional shareholders within Europe, and certainly in the United States, are clearly becoming more demanding in terms of corporate transparency and performance, and this is changing some practices within Europe. One could argue, for instance, that the use of debt financing and close shareholding to protect firms from takeovers are among the non-competitive aspects of European capitalism, and that such practices are ultimately discriminatory towards outsider (foreign) firms.[2] Just as Japan has continued to be under pressure to change its opaque system of insider connections, some of the same transformation is now going on in Europe. However, this does not mean that the functional aspects of the diverse institutional fabric within Europe, whether it be the German apprenticeship system or the French state–business relations, or the combination of liberal markets and corporatism in Britain, would not continue to provide European firms with a source of competitive advantage by mediating information exchange within industries.

To the extent that national institutions in fact contribute to the performance of firms and are not merely a relic carried over from another era, there is no reason why such institutionally distinctive characteristics could not be maintained in the global economy. The institutional structure is functional if it allows firms to derive value from their presence in the area, and in a world of capital mobility this would form the basis on which an international or regional division of labour would occur. It will be argued that such advantages arise from some kind of a distortion of the market, and cannot by definition be beneficial to all market participants. Consequently, policies should be aimed at cultivating regional differences in the creation of such competencies, and not aimed at a pan-European level of competence accumulation. The institutional environment and the differences between countries in Europe are beneficial to some firms, most obviously successful indigenous firms, but also to those foreign firms that are able to integrate themselves into the local setting. Thus while we agree with the basic analysis of the knowledge-based economy and the importance of national or local systems of innovation as presented by Padoan (2002), for example, we would argue that his proposition to create a European system of innovation is overly structuralist, and ignores the origins of the competitive advantage that is derived from local clusters.

The following section will explore the motivations of firms to enter into (cross-border) collaborative activity. This is followed by a review of recent empirical evidence of the patterns of alliance activity and the growth in mergers and acquisitions. We will argue that these patterns are related to the formation of regional clusters of economic activity that both build on, as well as transform, the institutional features of the local economy.

MOTIVATIONS FOR STRATEGIC PARTNERING

One of the oldest and more widely studied forms of inter-firm partnering is joint ventures (see e.g. Berg, Duncan and Friedman, 1982; Hagedoorn, 1996; Hladik, 1985). Joint ventures are organizational units created and controlled by two or more parent companies, and as such they increase the organizational interdependence of the parent companies. Although joint ventures can be seen as 'hybrids' that fall between markets and hierarchies, they do come close to hierarchical organizational structures as parent companies share control over the joint venture. However, joint ventures can also act as semi-independent units that perform standard company functions such as R&D, manufacturing, sales, marketing, etc. It is this semi-independent status that enables companies to apply joint ventures in a broader strategic setting where companies enter into new markets, reposition themselves in existing markets or use exit strategies in declining markets (Harrigan, 1988).

According to the empirical evidence presented by Hagedoorn (1996) and Narula and Hagedoorn (1999), there has been a decline in the popularity of joint ventures when compared with other forms of partnering. It can be hypothesized that the decreasing popularity is probably due to the organizational costs of joint ventures in combination with their high observed failure rate (Kogut, 1988; Porter, 1987). More specifically, problems with the continuation of joint ventures, as discussed in the literature, are related to the risk of sharing proprietary knowledge, the desire for control by one partner, and a divergence of strategic objectives (Harrigan, 1988; Hladik, 1985).

Recent studies have established that non-equity, contractual forms of R&D partnerships, such as joint R&D pacts and joint development agreements, have become very important modes of inter-firm collaboration, as their numbers and share in the total of partnerships have far exceeded that of joint ventures (Hagedoorn, 1996; Narula and Hagedoorn, 1999; Osborn and Baughn, 1990). These contractual agreements cover technology and R&D sharing between two or more companies in combination with joint research or joint development projects. Such undertakings imply the sharing of resources, usually through project-based groups of engineers and scientists from each parent company. The costs of capital investment, such as laboratories, office space, equipment, etc., are shared between the partners. Although these contractual R&D partnerships have a limited time-horizon due to their project-based organization, each partnership none the less appears to require a relatively strong commitment by the companies involved and a corresponding level of inter-organizational interdependence during the joint project. However, if compared with joint ventures, the degree of organizational dependence between companies in an R&D partnership is still smaller, and the time-horizon of the project-based partnerships is almost by definition shorter (Hagedoorn, 1993).

Given the somewhat more informal nature of this form of collaboration, the R&D pacts and joint development agreements cover a wide variety of legal and organizational arrangements. Also, even more than in the case of joint ventures, these contractual R&D partnerships should be seen as incomplete contracts,[3] since it is impossible a priori to specify the concrete results of the joint effort. Consequently, the causes for the popularity of contractual arrangements have to be found in the flexibility that companies achieve through entering into such relatively small-scale projects. Specifically, the costs of both intended and unintended terminations are much lower when compared with the costs of the termination of a joint venture, which involves the dissolution of a separate organization.

In general, it would appear that both a cost-economizing rationale and a strategic rationale play a role in the motivation of companies to enter into different R&D partnerships. The cost-economizing motivation applies when at least one company enters the partnership mainly to lower the costs of some of its R&D activities by sharing these with other companies. The cost-economizing rationale plays a role particularly in capital and R&D intensive industries, such as the telecommunications equipment (capital goods) industry, where the costs of a single, large R&D project are beyond the reach of most individual companies (Hagedoorn, 1993). However, the strategic rationale becomes important if, for instance, companies decide to selectively enter into R&D partnerships that are not related to their core activities, while keeping their primary R&D activities within their own domain (Teece, 1986). The strategic intent of R&D partnerships is also apparent in those cases where companies jointly perform R&D in new, high-risk areas, whose future importance for the partners' technological capabilities remains uncertain for a considerable period of time.

It is apparent from the results of several studies on the motives for inter-firm partnerships, that in many cases the cost-economizing and strategic motivations are intertwined. Most studies on R&D partnerships or similar forms of alliances stress a variety of motivations for these relationships (see e.g. Das, Sen and Sengupta, 1998; Eisenhardt and Schoonhoven, 1996; Hagedoorn, 1993; Hagedoorn, Link and Vonortas, 2000; Lorenzoni and Lipparini, 1999; Mowery, Oxley and Silverman, 1996). The most common motivations (in no particular order) are: the need to monitor and engage in the cross-fertilization of technological disciplines, the need to achieve economies of scale and scope in R&D, the need to share the costs of R&D projects, the need to shorten the innovation cycle, the desire to incorporate complementary technologies, the desire to search for technological synergies, the desire to capture a partner's tacit knowledge and the desire to jointly manage R&D uncertainty.

Although partnerships are a crucial element in the overall strategy of many companies, for others they are a relevant, but still only complementary, part of their strategic activities. There is some evidence to indicate that leading companies (market leaders and technology leaders) seek partnerships outside their core activities, searching for new activities and new technological opportunities beyond their current domain (Hagedoorn, 1995; Hamel, 1991; Hamel and Prahalad, 1994). However, in general one can expect that for many companies their motives to enter into R&D partnerships frequently have both a cost-economizing background and a strategic intent. Furthermore, it is important to realize that there is a dynamic aspect to all of this, as the motives of a company with multiple research programs can change over time due to developments within the company itself, as well as within its environment and the partnership (Harrigan, 1988).

PATTERNS IN ALLIANCE FORMATION AND MERGER ACTIVITY

In this section, we will review the existing evidence of the sectoral and geographical distribution of alliance activity, as well as the (more limited) evidence on patterns of mergers and acquisitions. We will also discuss the extent to which the empirical evidence point to similarities or differences in the use of alliances and mergers in the asset augmenting activity of multinationals. The fact that both mergers and alliances can be used in a similar manner to tap into other firms' knowledge-based assets makes at least some merger and acquisition activity arguably very similar to alliance formation in its motivation.

Since the 1970s, we see an almost exponential growth of strategic technology alliances from less than 50 strategic technology alliances founded each year during the mid-1970s, to nearly 600 founded in the 1990s (Hagedoorn, 1996). During this period of growth, the sectoral distribution of strategic technology alliances changed as well, largely due to the increasing importance of high-technology sectors, such as pharmaceutical biotechnology, information technology and new materials. Gradually, these 'new' industries increased their share in strategic technology partnering to close to 90 per cent of all of the alliances established during the 1990s (Hagedoorn, 1996). A similar concentration of alliance activity is found if one considers the geographical distribution of strategic technology alliances. Freeman and Hagedoorn (1994) report that over 95 per cent of all strategic technology alliances are formed between companies from the developed economies. Not surprisingly, the higher the R&D intensity of the industry, the lower the participation of companies from developing and emerging economies, as such firms are seldom in possession of knowledge-intensive resources that would be attractive to a Triad partner (see also Hagedoorn and Lundan, 2001).

The sectoral and geographical concentration of alliances is testament to the underlying pattern of combining highly tacit capabilities with specific location-bound assets. Research by Hagedoorn and Narula (1996) revealed strategic partnering activity to be more evenly distributed between industrial sectors in more technologically advanced countries (R&D/GDP greater than 1 per cent). Subsequent research by Hagedoorn (1996) revealed that certain regions have attracted clusters of international strategic technology partnering activity, such as in the case of the large number of alliances between European pharmaceutical companies and US biotechnology companies, and the many long-term alliances between European information technology companies and semiconductor and software companies from Silicon Valley. Additionally, although technology partnering is still dominated by the developed economies, there is also some recent evidence that a small group of Asian economies (South Korea, Taiwan, Hong Kong) are gradually becoming interesting partners for companies from the developed economies, also in terms of their technology intensive assets, particularly in electronics and related industries (Duysters and Hagedoorn, 2000).

Although firms of all sizes and different degrees of multinationality engage in strategic alliances, the size of the firm (as measured by the number of employees) was found to be an important factor in explaining the propensity of firms to form alliances (Duysters and Hagedoorn, 1995). Additionally, Hagedoorn (1995) demonstrated that in most industrial sectors, large multinational corporations, mostly those in the Fortune Global 500, are the most active alliance partners. A network analysis of several sectors revealed that many of these multinationals are 'nodal' players in networks of strategic alliances with a variety of alliance partners, with domestic (uninational) firms playing a much more limited role.[4] Furthermore, the choice of contractual alliances or joint ventures is known to vary by sector, with contractual alliances dominating the high-technology sectors (Osborn and Baughn, 1990), irrespective of the country of origin of either partner (Hagedoorn and Narula, 1996).

As regards the sectoral and geographical patterns of merger and acquisition activity, unfortunately the research to date has focused less on historical patterns, and more on financial performance prior to and following the merger. None the less, some general patterns can be discerned. Overall, it seems that mergers and acquisitions are disproportionately concentrated in sectors other than high technology, where strategic alliances are prevalent. Explanations offered by Ciborra (1991), Oster (1992), Hagedoorn and Sadowski (1999) and Yu and Tang (1992) refer to the need for (organizational) flexibility and the importance of learning, as well as the speed of technological change for alliances in high-tech sectors, whereas formal and well institutionalized modes of control (i.e. mergers and acquisitions) are most appropriate in more stable environments.

Data from the *World Investment Report* (UNCTAD, 2001) reveal that cross-border M&As have accounted for most of the growth in international production over the past decade, even allowing for the differences in the way in which flows of M&As and greenfield investment are calculated. In total, flows of M&As accounted for 80 per cent of all FDI in 1999. Less than 3 per cent of mergers and acquisitions are actually mergers, and full acquisitions account for two-thirds of the total, while minority acquisitions are twice as common in the developing countries. Additionally, most cross-border M&As take place between firms in the same industry, and hostile mergers account for less than 5 per cent of the total value.

Research by Hagedoorn and Duysters (2002) also indicates that mergers and acquisitions are still frequently preferred to alliances in the context of strategic asset seeking investments related to the organization's core activities. The extent to which alliances and acquisitions are alike in their strategic motivations depends on the extent to which the resources sourced abroad are complementary or similar to the existing competencies of the acquiring firm. While the aggregate evidence does not typically reveal the extent to which alliances (or mergers) are undertaken in the core of the company's activities, an analysis by Mowery et al. (1996) of the overlap in patenting activity of US and Japanese alliance partners found that alliances can promote increased specialization rather than a convergence of capabilities between the partners, and that equity participation promoted greater knowledge transfer. This would suggest that alliances are a preferred means of accessing complementary resources, while equity participation is more effective in more closely related (and stable) fields of activity. Particularly in cases where the acquisition is undertaken to gain the R&D capabilities of another firm, the primary motivation in both mergers and alliances seems to be the possibility for learning and knowledge transfer, and there is at least some evidence that the creation of a bi-directional flow of information in the context of an acquisition may be more effective than in other forms of inter-firm relationships (see e.g. Bresman, Birkinshaw and Nobel, 1999).

CLUSTERING AND MULTINATIONAL ACTIVITY

In the two recent re-assessments of the predominant model of foreign investment, the OLI paradigm (Dunning, 1995, 2000), there is a clear change in the focus of the argument, where the balance has shifted from the exploitation of ownership advantages abroad – first to improving the efficiency of the existing configuration of activities, and finally to the active acquisition of new advantages. While market or resource seeking motivations will always characterize some portion of investments, there is an increasing role for efficiency seeking and strategic asset seeking investment, which makes mergers and acquisitions as well as strategic alliances critical to the asset augmenting FDI undertaken by multinationals.[5] This is accompanied by a renewed interest in the location of production, and in particular in the 'stickiness' of competitiveness enhancing resources (see Dunning, 1998). The predominance of created assets over natural assets has made it possible for economies to converge not only in terms of GNP per capita, but also in terms of their productive structure, while simultaneously it has also created possibilities for the creation of more localized clusters or agglomerations of innovative activity, leading to the emergence of newly desirable locational assets.[6]

Indeed, considerable empirical evidence has been accumulating on the internationalization of the research and development activities of multinational firms since the 1980s.[7] Particularly in the high-technology sectors, multinationals are engaging in asset augmenting FDI to exploit as well as to build on their home-based competencies, as described by Dunning (1995), Almeida (1996), Dunning and Lundan (1998) and Kummerle (1999). The desire of the multinational to benefit from location-bound 'centers of excellence' is dependent on its ability to effectively coordinate the flows of knowledge within the organization.[8] The research to date has investigated both the agglomeration economies available in particular locations, e.g. Cantwell and Iammarino (2000) and Santangelo (2000), as well as the patterns of control and coordination within multinationals, e.g. Zander (1999) and Pearce (1999).

There is also increasing evidence that the ability of the firm to take part in local agglomerations of activity, whether in enjoying the externalities from the presence of other firms, such as in Silicon Valley, California, Silicon Glen in Scotland or the pharmaceutical cluster in New Jersey, or whether taking part in government-sponsored research networks, has implications for firm performance. The importance of such localized economies is changing the way in which multinationals approach investment location decisions, and this in turn has implications for government policies with respect to investment attraction.

The literature on so-called national systems of innovation has produced some interesting research on the connections between firms and the locally-based national and regional institutions that support them, such as independent research centers, universities and the like (see e.g. Nelson, 1993a, b) on the national level and Cooke and Morgan (1998) on the regional level). A well-functioning network of firms and institutions not only encourages domestic economic activity, but also creates an attractive hotspot for foreign multinationals, eager to benefit from the interaction.[9] In this context the infrastructure includes both the essential elements of the physical infrastructure, such as a reliable supply of electricity, communications infrastructure, roads and other transport, but also a desirable level of social capital that manifests itself in a work ethic that is conducive to economic prosperity (see Peck, 1996).

A constellation of economic activity, such as a cluster of businesses, fulfils the requirements of being difficult to imitate and rare due to the complexity of connections between firms. But more importantly, such groups are exclusionary, and a part of the value of tapping into these networks arises from the fact that they are not universally accessible. They are accessible to insiders and exclusionary to outsiders, and part of their economic value lies in this reprieve from the competitive market (see also Granovetter, 1995 on the rationale for business groups).

A high quality infrastructure is thus necessary but not sufficient in ensuring that from among many potential investors, the investor with the best long-term potential will undertake the project.[10] In order to attract and retain a foreign multinational, the domestic business network has to be open to accept an ever-increasing role for collaboration with multinationals as inside participants. Since the benefits of groups accrue to those on the inside, there is little moral hazard with respect to the multinational once it is allowed in. The more fully the multinational participates in the local network, the more it is in its interest to keep the network functional and exclusionary, which in the long run should result in the kind of value-adding collaboration most governments are hoping to achieve.

However, the price to be paid is that the firm loses its flexibility of relocating (loss of a real option), and this is compensated by market exclusivity or collusion. Indeed, like many of the issues in a liberalized world economy, the issue of investment retention highlights the tension between spontaneous market order on one hand and institutional structure on the other. The tendency is for the doctrinaire neoclassical side to ignore the context of the market and to advocate strict enforcement of competition law, while the institutionalist view is that it is possible to create market order in the absence of the market by providing firms with the correct incentives.[11]

CONCLUSIONS

In this chapter we have explored the changing dynamics of alliance capitalism in Europe on two levels. First, at the level of the nation state we discussed the ways in which national business systems influence economic activity in the domestic market as well as by shaping European firms' activities abroad. We then moved the argument to the level of the firm (or industry) and argued that the dynamics relating to the need for firms to maintain consistently high levels of innovation is fueling both cross-border acquisitions as well as cooperative activity in the form of strategic alliances. The changing nature of multinational activity from asset exploitation to asset augmenting investment, and the growing importance of the internationalization of corporate R&D have reinforced the importance of local clusters of economic activity. As a consequence, in a world with capital mobility, the firms' choices of partners and locations effectively 'choose' between alternative institutional environments as well.

In light of these developments, policymaking within Europe has to be cognizant of two factors that are somewhat contradictory. First, we argued that underlying the partnering activity and recent acquisitions is a desire by firms from outside and from within the European Union to gain access to some location-bound resources held by European firms, whether they be in R&D, product development or market knowledge. Such locally attractive assets are a consequence of industry-specific developments of capabilities that can be aided and supported by governments through funding for public research or targeted education, for instance, but that ultimately arise out of the organic functioning of the market within a given cluster of activity. Because such concentrations of activity are complex and comprise the set of connections between firms, government and independent research institutions, for example, they also offer potential for sustainable growth in the area by virtue of being difficult to duplicate. Such clusters build on the characteristics of the local environment and provide the basis for attracting further investment and resources into the area.

Second, in aiming to attract firms that aid in the technological accumulation in a given area, it must be recognized that the kind of alliance capitalism that is exemplified by the growth in contractual alliances (and acquisitions) implies deviations from market competition to enable investment in location specific resources, whether it be investment in technology or in people. Firms that invest while anticipating an uncertain payoff seek to hedge their exposure by attempting to guarantee a share of the market. In terms of competition policy this may mean that unevenness of investment in geographical terms also results in some unevenness of investment in terms of market concentration. In order to hedge its exposure, the innovating multinational would like a degree of exclusivity related to its sources of competitive advantage. This particular combination of openness and restrictiveness involves openness of entry that does not discriminate against foreign firms that are willing to make a long-term commitment, with a degree of restrictiveness that arises from the network of established relationships within an industry association, the chamber of commerce or a research consortium. As such, our argument combines spontaneous market order with a strong institutional flavour, leading to a two-stage process where aspects of bottom-up spontaneous processes in the marketplace are combined with the top-down influence of strong local institutions. While some institutional features are becoming more homogeneous across borders, others are likely to persist to the extent that they provide competitive advantages, particularly for large industrial firms.

NOTES

1. Institutions also shape the strategies of foreign firms resident in Europe, but we are not aware of empirical evidence on the extent to which foreign investment in Europe has taken on the institutional characteristics of its host location.
2. See Dunning and Lundan (1997) for a similar argument regarding the low levels of inward investment into Japan and the nonexistence of mergers and acquisitions as an entry mode as one contributing factor.
3. It is recognized that, to an extent, all contracts are incomplete and achieve their completeness from the institutions that are involved in their enforcement, including the social capital existing between the parties.
4. See also D'Cruz and Rugman (1993) on the role of the multinational as a flagship firm.
5. From a theoretical perspective, the focus on asset augmenting investment and unique locational resources has a clear connection to the resource-based theory of the firm (see Rumelt, 1984; Barney, 1991; Conner, 1991; Peteraf, 1993; Teece et al. 1994; Wernerfelt, 1995). It is also linked to Nelson's (1991) theory of dynamic firm capabilities. In both cases, the focus is on the efficient use of the firm's unique capabilities, as well as the on the dynamics of asset (and knowledge) accumulation over time.
6. See e.g. Cantwell and Santangelo (1999) on the role of location-bound knowledge intensive assets in internationalizing the R&D activities of the multinational.
7. For a recent review see the special issue of *Research Policy* edited by Niosi (1999). See also Zanfei (2000) and Cantwell and Piscitello (1999, 2000).
8. See also Holm and Pedersen (2000).
9. 'Sticky places in slippery space' as Markusen (1996) put it.
10. To an extent, this is true of any investment, however attracted, due to the sunk costs. In fact, Mudambi (1998) offers evidence that firms with a longer investment duration are more likely to make further investments.
11. This discussion parallels that of Sally (1998) on the tensions between the neoclassical model of perfect markets and perfect knowledge and the institutionalist argument of national and international institutions playing a critical role in fostering economic activity.

REFERENCES

Almeida, P. (1996), 'Knowledge sourcing by foreign multinationals: Patent citation analysis in the U.S. semiconductor industry', *Strategic Management Journal*, 17(Winter Special Issue): 155–65.

Barney, J. (1991), 'Firm resources and sustained competitive advantage', *Journal of Management,* 17(1): 99–120.

Berg, S.V., J. Duncan and P. Friedman (1982), *Joint venture strategies and corporate innovation*, Cambridge, MA: Oelgeschlager, Gunn & Hain.

Bresman, H., J. Birkinshaw and R. Nobel (1999), 'Knowledge transfer in international acquisitions', *Journal of International Business Studies*, 30(3): 439–62.

Canals, J. (2002), 'Corporate restructuring, corporate strategy and European integration', In Brewer, Thomas, Paul Brenton and Gavin Boyd (eds) *Globalizing Europe*. Cheltenham: Edward Elgar.

Cantwell, J. and S. Iammarino (2000), 'Multinational corporations and the location of technological innovation in the UK regions', *Regional Studies*, 34: 317–32.

Cantwell, J.A. and L. Piscitello (1999), 'The emergence of corporate international networks for the accumulation of dispersed technological competencies', *Management International Review*, 39(Special Issue 1): 123–47.

Cantwell, J. and L. Piscitello (2000), 'Accumulating technological competence: Its changing impact on corporate diversification and internationalization', *Industrial and Corporate Change*, 9(1): 21–51.
Cantwell, J.A. and G.D. Santangelo (1999), 'The frontier of international technology networks: Sourcing abroad the most highly tacit capabilities', *Information Economics and Policy*, 11: 101–23.
Casper, S. (2001), 'The legal framework for corporate governance: The influence of contract law on company strategies in Germany and the United States', in Hall, Peter A. and David Soskice (eds) *Varieties of Capitalism: The Institutional Foundations of Comparative Advantage*, Oxford: Oxford University Press.
Casson, M. and S.M. Lundan (1999), 'Explaining international differences in economic institutions: A critique of the "national business system" as an analytical tool', *International Studies of Management & Organization*, 29(2): 25–42.
Ciborra, C. (1991), 'Alliances as learning experiments: Cooperation, competition and change in high-tech industries'. In Mytelka, L.K. (ed.) *Strategic Partnerships and the World Economy*, London: Pinter.
Cohen, S.S. and G. Boyd (eds) (2000), *Corporate Governance and Globalization: Long Range Planning Issues*, Cheltenham: Edward Elgar.
Conner, K.R. (1991), 'A historical comparison of resource-based theory and five schools of thought within industrial organization economics', *Journal of Management*, 17(1): 121–54.
Cooke, P. and K. Morgan (1998), *The Associational Economy: Firms, Regions, and Innovation*, Oxford: Oxford University Press.
Cusumano, M.A. and A. Takeishi (1991), 'Supplier relations and management: A survey of Japanese, Japanese-transplant, and U.S. auto plants', *Strategic Management Journal*, 12: 563–88.
Das, S., P.K. Sen and S. Sengupta (1998), 'Impact of strategic alliances on firm valuation', *Academy of Management Journal*, 41: 27–41.
D'Cruz, J.R. and A.M. Rugman (1993), 'Developing international competitiveness: The five partners model', *Ivey Business Quarterly*, 58(2): 60–72.
Dunning, J.H. (1995), 'Reappraising the eclectic paradigm in the age of alliance capitalism', *Journal of International Business Studies*, 26(3): 461–91.
Dunning, J.H. (1998), 'Location and the multinational enterprise: A neglected factor?', *Journal of International Business Studies*, 29(1): 45–66.
Dunning, J.H. (2000), 'The eclectic paradigm as an envelope for economic and business theories of MNE activity', *International Business Review*, 9: 163–90.
Dunning, J.H. and S.M. Lundan (1997), 'Foreign direct investment in Japan and the United States: A comparative analysis', *The International Trade Journal*, 11 (2): 187–220.
Dunning, J.H. and S.M. Lundan (1998), 'The geographical sources of competitiveness of firms: An econometric analysis', *International Business Review*, 7(2): 115–33.
Duysters, G. and J. Hagedoorn (1995), 'Strategic groups and inter-firm networks in international high-tech industries', *Journal of Management Studies*, 32: 361–81.
Duysters, G. and J. Hagedoorn (2000), 'International technological collaboration: Implications for NIEs', in Kim, L. and R.R. Nelson (eds) *Technological Learning and Economic Development: The Experience of the Asian Newly Industrialized Countries*, Cambridge: Cambridge University Press.
Eisenhardt, K.M. and C.B. Schoonhoven (1996), 'Resource-based view of strategic

alliance formation: Strategic and social effects in entrepreneurial firms', *Organization Science*, 7: 136–50.

Emmons, W.R. and F.A. Schmid (2002), 'Mergers and acquisitions and a globalizing Europe', in Brewer, Thomas, Paul Brenton and Gavin Boyd (eds) *Globalizing Europe*. Cheltenham: Edward Elgar.

Freeman, C. and J. Hagedoorn (1994), 'Catching up or falling behind: Patterns in international interfirm partnering', *World Development*, 22: 771–80.

Giarratana, M. and S. Torrisi (2002), 'Competence accumulation and collaborative ventures: Evidence from the largest European electronics firms and implications for EU technological policies', in Lundan, Sarianna M. (ed.) *Network Knowledge in International Business*, Cheltenham: Edward Elgar.

Glais, M. (2000), 'Merger control law in the European union', in Krafft, Jackie (ed.) *The Process of Competition*, Cheltenham: Edward Elgar.

Granovetter, M. (1995), 'Coase revisited: Business groups in the modern economy', *Industrial and Corporate Change*, 4(1): 93–130.

Hagedoorn, J. (1993), 'Understanding the rationale of strategic technology partnering: Inter-organizational modes of cooperation and sectoral differences', *Strategic Management Journal*, 14: 371–85.

Hagedoorn, J. (1995), 'A note on international market leaders and networks of strategic technology partnering', *Strategic Management Journal*, 16: 241–50.

Hagedoorn, J. (1996), 'Trends and patterns in strategic technology partnering since the early seventies', *Review of Industrial Organization*, 11(5): 601–16.

Hagedoorn, J. and G. Duysters (2002), 'External sources of innovative capabilities: The preference for strategic alliances or M&As', *Journal of Management Studies*, 39(2): 167–89.

Hagedoorn, J., A.L. Link and N. Vonortas (2000), 'Research partnerships', *Research Policy*, 29: 567–86.

Hagedoorn, J. and S.M. Lundan (2001), 'Strategic technology alliances: Trends and patterns since the early eighties', in Plunket, A., C. Voisin and B. Bellon (eds) *The Dynamics of Industrial Collaboration*, Cheltenham: Edward Elgar.

Hagedoorn, J. and R. Narula (1996), 'Choosing organizational modes of strategic technology partnering: International and sectoral differences', *Journal of International Business Studies*, 27(2): 265–84.

Hagedoorn, J. and B. Sadowski (1999), 'The transition from strategic technology alliances to mergers and acquisitions: An exploratory study', *Journal of Management Studies*, 36: 87–107.

Hall, P.A. and D. Soskice (2001), 'An introduction to varieties of capitalism', in Hall, Peter A. and David Soskice (eds) *Varieties of Capitalism: The Institutional Foundations of Comparative Advantage*, Oxford: Oxford University Press.

Hamel, G. (1991), 'Competition for competence and inter-partner learning with international strategic alliances', *Strategic Management Journal*, 12: 83–103.

Hamel, G. and C.K. Prahalad (1994), *Competing for the Future*, Boston, MA: Harvard Business School Press.

Hamilton, G.C. and N. Woolsey Biggart (1988), 'Market, culture, and authority: A comparative analysis of management and organisation in the Far East', *American Journal of Sociology*, 94(Supplement): S52–S94.

Harrigan, K.R. (1988), 'Joint ventures and competitive strategy', *Strategic Management Journal*, 9: 141–58.

Hladik, K.J. (1985), *International Joint Ventures*, Lexington, MA: Lexington Books.

Holm, U. and T. Pedersen (eds) (2000), *The Emergence and Impact of MNC Centers of Excellence*, Basingstoke: Macmillan.
Jones, E.L. (1995), 'Culture and its relationship to economic change', *Journal of Institutional and Theoretical Economics*, 151(2): 269–85.
Kanter, R.M. (2000), 'Business coalitions as a force for regionalism', in Katz, Bruce (ed.) *Reflections on Regionalism*, Washington, DC: Brookings Institution Press.
Kogut, B. (1988), 'Joint ventures: Theoretical and empirical perspectives', *Strategic Management Journal*, 9: 319–32.
Kummerle, W. (1999), 'The drivers of foreign direct investment into research and development: An empirical investigation', *Journal of International Business Studies*, 30(1): 1–24.
Lane, C. (1989), *Management and Labour in Europe*, Aldershot: Edward Elgar.
Lorenzoni, G. and A. Lipparini (1999), 'The leveraging of interfirm relationships as a distinctive organizational capability: A longitudinal study', *Strategic Management Journal*, 20: 317–38.
Markusen, A. (1996), 'Sticky places in slippery space: A typology of industrial districts', *Economic Geography*, 72(3): 293-313.
Miotti, L. & F. Sachwald (2002), 'Patterns of R&D co-operation by European firms: Cost-economising vs. technology-seeking', in Lundan, Sarianna M. (ed.) *Network Knowledge in International Business*, Cheltenham: Edward Elgar.
Mowery, D., J.E. Oxley and B.S. Silverman (1996), 'Strategic alliances and interfirm knowledge transfer', *Strategic Management Journal*, 17: 77–91.
Mudambi, R. (1998), 'The role of duration in multinational investment strategies', *Journal of International Business Studies*, 29(2): 239–62.
Narula, R. and J. Hagedoorn (1999), 'Innovating through strategic alliances: Moving towards international partnerships and contractual agreements', *Technovation*, 19: 283–94.
Nelson, R. (1991), 'Why do firms differ, and how does it matter?', *Strategic Management Journal*, 12: 61–74.
Nelson, R. (1993a), *The Co-evolution of Technologies and Institutions*, New York: Columbia University.
Nelson, R.R. (ed.) (1993b), *National Innovation Systems.* A *comparative analysis*, New York: Oxford University Press.
Niosi, J. (1999), 'The internationalization of industrial R&D: From technology transfer to the learning organization', *Research Policy*, 28(2–3): 107–17.
North, D.C. (1991), 'Institutions', *Journal of Economic Perspectives*, 5(Winter): 97–112.
Osborn, R.N. and C.C. Baughn (1990), 'Forms of interorganizational governance for multinational alliances', *Academy of Management Journal*, 33(3): 503–19.
Oster, S.M. (1992), *Modern Competitive Analysis*, New York: Oxford University Press.
Padoan, P.C. (2002), 'Specialization matters, and so does technological accumulation. The case of Europe', in Brewer, Thomas, Paul Brenton and Gavin Boyd (eds) *Globalizing Europe.* Cheltenham: Edward Elgar.
Pearce, R.D. (1999), 'Decentralised R&D and strategic competitiveness: Globalised approaches to generation and use of technology in multinational enterprises (MNEs)', *Research Policy*, 28(2–3): 157–78.
Peck, F.W. (1996), 'Regional development and the production of space: The role of infrastructure in the attraction of new inward investment', *Environment and Planning A*, 28(2): 327–39.

Peteraf, M.A. (1993), 'The cornerstones of competitive advantage: A resource based view', *Strategic Management Journal*, 14(3): 179–91.
Porter, M.E. (1987), 'From competitive advantage to corporate strategy', *Harvard Business Review* (May–June): 3–59.
Rumelt, R.P. (1984), 'Toward a strategic theory of the firm', in Lamb, R. (ed.) *Competitive Strategic Management*. Englewood Cliffs, NJ: Prentice Hall.
Sally, R. (1998), *Classical Liberalism and International Economic Order. Studies in Theory and Intellectual History*, London: Routledge.
Santangelo, G.D. (2000), 'Inter-European regional dispersion of corporate research activity in information and communications technology: The case of German, Italian and UK regions', *International Journal of the Economics of Business*, 7(3): 275–95.
Spender, J.C. (1989), *Industry recipes: The Nature and Sources of Managerial Judgement*, Oxford: Basil Blackwell.
Teece, D.J. (1986), 'Profiting from technological innovation: Implications for integration, collaboration, licensing and public policy', *Research Policy*, 15: 285–305.
Teece, D.J., R. Rumelt, G. Dosi and S.G. Winter (1994), 'Understanding corporate coherence – theory and evidence', *Journal of Economic behaviour and Organization*, 23: 1–30.
United Nations commission on Trade and Development (2001), *World Trade and Investment Report 2001*, Geneva: UNCTAD.
Vogel, E.F. (1991), *The Four Little Dragons. The Spread of Industrialization in East Asia*, Cambridge, MA: Harvard University Press.
Wernerfelt, B. (1995), 'The resource-based view of the firm: Ten years after', *Strategic Management Journal*, 16: 171–4.
Whitley, R. (1992a), *Business Systems in East Asia: Firms, Markets, and Societies*, London: Sage.
Whitley, R. (1992b), *European Business Systems: Firms and Markets in their National Contexts*, London: Sage.
Yu, C.-M.J. and M.-J. Tang (1992), 'International joint ventures: Theoretical considerations', *Managerial and Decision Economics*, 13: 331–42.
Zander, I. (1999), 'How do you mean "global"? An empirical investigation of innovation networks in the multinational corporation', *Research Policy*, 28(2–3): 195–213.
Zanfei, A. (2000), 'Transnational firms and the changing organisation of innovative activities', *Cambridge Journal of Economics*, 24: 515–42.

9. EU growth strategy and the new economy

Pierluigi Morelli, Pier Carlo Padoan and Lisa Rodano

INTRODUCTION

Over the past decade, US output and productivity grew at high rates, with low unemployment, while growth in Europe was slower and unemployment was higher. There is a general consensus that the USA's exceptional performance has been due principally to the introduction and diffusion of new information and communication technologies, aided by efficiencies in financial markets and by flexible labour markets. The contrast has motivated a concerted European effort to build a new economy: the Lisbon meeting of the European Council in March 2000 launched a growth strategy to make the Union 'the most dynamic knowledge based economy in the world by 2010'. Impetus for this came from the Portuguese Presidency and the European Commission, and implementation accelerated after the Barcelona summit in March 2002.

This chapter examines the basic framework of the Lisbon strategy, especially its economic and political economy dimensions. The former are analysed with reference to economic and social indicators identifying targets for assessment of the performance of member countries. The latter dimensions of the strategy are reviewed with reference to decision making structures and incentives.

The indicators, set out by the European Commission to guide the policies of member governments, are presented in Table 9.1, listed in four groups: employment, research and innovation, economic reform, and social cohesion. These relate to an economic model for higher sustained growth, achieved through increases in innovation and employment, and spread throughout the Union for greater social cohesion. The growth is to be supported by macroeconomic and financial stability, ensured by management of the European Monetary Union and fidelity to the Union's Stability and Growth Pact.

As mentioned, the role of indicators is to provide a framework for the

Table 9.1 Performance and policy indicators

Structural indicators	Type
Employment	
1. Growth rate of employment	Performance
2. Women's employment rate	Performance
3. Employment rate of the elderly	Performance
4. Unemployment rate	Performance
5. Tax rate on low wages	Policy
6. Life-long learning	Policy
Research and innovation	
1. Public expenditure in education	Policy
2. Expenditure on R&D	Policy
3. Expenditure on ICT	Policy
4. Internet access	Performance
5. Patents	Performance
6. High tech exports	Performance
7. Venture capital	Performance
Economic reform	
1. Trade integration	Performance/policy
2. Business investment	Performance
3. Relative prices and price convergence	Performance
4. Prices in network industries	Performance/policy
5. Public procurement	Policy
6. Sectoral state aid	Policy
7. Capital raised in the stock exchange	Performance
Social cohesion	
1. Income distribution	Performance/policy
2. Poverty rates before and after social transfers	Performance (before transfer); policy (after)
3. Persistence of poverty	Performance
4. Jobless families	Performance
5. Regional cohesion (variation in regional unemployment rates)	Performance
6. People leaving school early and not in training programmes	Performance/policy
7. Long term unemployment	Performance

implementation of national policies, based on the comparison of national performances in EU member states, as well as in non-EU economies, so as to identify best practices and benchmarks. The next paragraph is dedicated to the economics of the 'Lisbon indicators'. The paragraph on the political economy aspects discusses the effectiveness of the coordination method adopted in Lisbon (the 'Open Method of Coordination') in guiding national policies.

THE ECONOMICS OF THE LISBON STRATEGY

While the long-term economic goals of the Lisbon Strategy have been identified, it remains to be clarified what the relationship is between the indicators and the working of the underlying growth model. As Table 9.1 shows, the Lisbon indicators can be separated into performance and policy. The question then arises of the relationship between these two groups of variables as well as among each variable. More precisely, are all indicators equally relevant for the strategy? In addition, is the relationship between indicators pointing to a common economic model for EU countries? And finally, to what extent are national specificities relevant? The analysis that follows offers first tentative answers to these questions.

Three main conclusions emerge: (a) not all the variables as identified by the Lisbon indicators show a clear correlation with output and employment growth. There is, however, a common 'framework', based on a strong correlation between output growth, employment and innovation activities; (b) at the same time, and not surprisingly, EU countries show a high heterogeneity in their growth models. To some extent at least EU economies belong to different groups. Cluster analysis identifies three such groups, one (strong structure) includes the large continental countries and the UK, where the employment rate and R&D investment are above average. A second group (weak structure) includes the Mediterranean countries and Belgium, where employment performance has been much less satisfactory. A third group of dynamic catching-up economies (followers) includes the small Nordic countries and Ireland; (c) a process is in place whereby the weaker countries converge to the stronger ones. This last result sends an optimistic message for the success of the Lisbon Strategy.

Principal Component Analysis

Principal component analysis has been applied to a set of variables for the 15 EU countries and some major OECD economies (US, Japan, Canada, Australia, and Norway) over the period 1980–2000, with the aim of identifying a 'common growth model' as captured by the indicators. Data availability has not allowed us to carry out the exercise for all the indicators, and in some cases proxy variables have been used. The variables we have chosen, in addition to real GDP growth (g), can be classified according to the four 'pillars' (in parentheses). The variables are: (employment) activity rate of the population between 15 and 64 years of age (Ir); (innovation) ratio of R&D expenditure to GDP (gerd), employment rate in the R&D sector (Ird), productivity of R&D expenditure as proxied by the ratio between patents and R&D expenditure (tpat), FDI inflows as a share of GDP (fdii); (economic reform) rate of growth of real labour costs (drlc), rate of growth of labour productivity (dprod), social contributions as a percentage of GDP (ssc), ratio of public investment over GDP (ginv), debt to GDP ratio (d), deficit to GDP ratio (def), degree of trade integration (xm); (social cohesion) unemployment rate (u) . All variables have been considered both in levels and in growth rates (when applicable).

Results are as follows. Four of the 23 factors (the number of factors is equal to the number of variables introduced) capture most of the information, and up to 40 per cent of total variability. The first two factors alone account for 30 per cent of total variability.

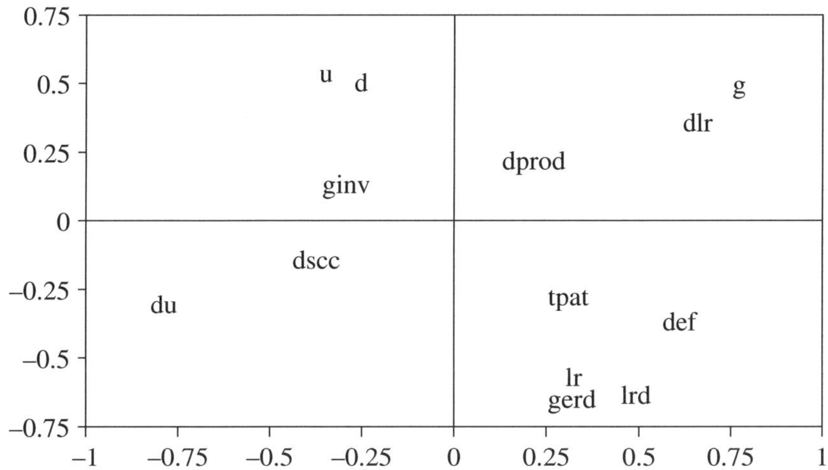

Figure 9.1 Factor analysis

Figure 9.1 describes the relationships between variables. Real GDP (g) is positively correlated with growth of the activity rate (dlr) and both variables are negatively correlated with the rate of growth of unemployment (du) and of social contributions (dssc). These results are intuitive. Somewhat less intuitive, but nevertheless relevant, is the negative correlation with the rate of growth of social contributions.

Figure 9.1 also points to other interesting results. Variables in the fourth quadrant are positively correlated. These are the activity rate and a number of innovation indicators, such as the ratio of R&D expenditure over GDP (gerd), R&D productivity (tpat), and employment in innovation sectors (Ird). All the above variables are negatively correlated with the unemployment rate (u).

In sum, factor analysis offers a first tentative answer to the question: to what extent are the Lisbon indicators based on a common economic model? This extent is limited yet it is intuitive and based on the widely accepted relationship between employment, growth and innovation activities.

Cluster Analysis

Cluster analysis allows us to identify groups of countries that share common features in their economic models. We find three groups of (relatively) homogeneous countries. They are described in Table 9.2.

Group 1: Strong structure

Countries in this group – the US, Japan, the large continental EU countries, and the UK – share a common strong structure identified by variables in levels that present similar values. Important common features are a favourable employment performance, both in terms of overall activity ratio and employment in the innovative sectors, a low (or negative) rate of growth of unemployment (and a high rate of growth of real labour costs), strong innovative activity, as well as sound public finance. The inclusion of the US as well as other advanced OECD economies is justified by the fact that the guiding principle of the Lisbon Strategy is to make the EU advance towards the best performing economies among the industrial countries.

Group 2: Followers

Countries included in this group – the small Nordic countries and Ireland, as well as Australia and Canada – share similar values in the *rate of change* of variables rather than in their levels. Growth rates of both employment and GDP are higher than average. Unemployment grows less and so do social security contributions. Variables above the average level are productivity in R&D and foreign direct investment as a share of GDP.

Group 3: Weak structure

The remaining countries – the Mediterranean countries and Belgium – share a weak structure as indicated by unemployment above average, a low activity rate as well as low employment in innovative activities, low R&D expenditure and low R&D productivity. Public finance is also less sound than average.

These results are not surprising, and in many respects they are consistent

Table 9.2 Cluster analysis

	Above average	Below average	Countries
Group 1: Strong structure	– Activity rate (in % of pop. 15–64) – R&D expend (in % GDP) – Employment rate in R&D sectors – Growth of real labour costs	– Growth of unemployment rate – Deficit (in % GDP) – Govt public debt (in % GDP)	*Germany, France, Luxembourg, Austria, Finland, Sweden, the UK, Norway, the US, Japan*
Group 2: Followers	– Growth of activity rate – GDP growth – Productivity of R&D expenditure – FDI inflows (in % GDP)	– Growth of unemployment rate – Growth of social contributions – Public investments (in % GDP)	*Netherlands, Denmark, Australia, Canada, Ireland*
Group 3: Weak structure	– Unemployment rate – Govt debt (in % GDP) – Public investment (in % GDP) – Govt deficit (in % GDP)	– Activity rate (in % of pop. 15–64) – Employment rate in R&D – R&D expenditure (in % GDP) – Productivity of R&D expenditure	*Belgium, Greece, Spain, Italy, Portugal*

with the view that the EU includes small dynamic economies that are able to exploit the benefits of innovation and a number of other economies, including some large continental countries, that are somewhat lagging behind and/or display both weak public finances and modest employment opportunities.[1] It would be misleading, however, to consider the classification above as static, and established once and for all. Quite the contrary, it is a feature of integration processes, not least the EU one, to be associated with catching-up processes, as well as cases of countries 'falling behind' the top performers. This is also consistent with the basic philosophy of the Lisbon Strategy to upgrade the overall economic performance in the EU and, at the same time, to encourage followers to catch up. That such a process may be realistic is suggested by the analysis of convergence below.

Economic Convergence

Convergence of lagging economies towards higher per capita GDP levels is a very well known phenomenon, both within and outside the EU. The analysis that follows does not add much in this respect. It offers, none the less, some evidence – by adopting a methodology that is different from standard catching up regressions – that countries classified as followers or even weak performers have the opportunity to catch up to strong performers. The evidence is based on the analysis of the probability of transition from one group, as identified by cluster analysis, to another. We have estimated the probability of transition between the three clusters over the period 1980–2000. Probabilities have been computed relating the frequency with which each country shifts from one cluster to another to the total movements from the originating cluster. Results are reported in Table 9.3. Values in the main diagonal are very high, indicating a strong inertia: i.e. the probability of remaining in one cluster is large. In spite of the strong inertia, however, the probability of weak structure countries (group 3) moving on to the group of followers (group 2) is 13 per cent, while followers have a probability of 24 per cent of moving on to the strong structure group

Table 9.3 Transition matrix

	Target cluster		
Cluster of origin	1	2	3
1	81%	18%	1%
2	24%	74%	2%
3	0%	13%	88%

(group 1). The probability of moving directly from group 3 to group 1 is zero. Once a country leaves group 3 it is practically impossible to fall back into it, while there is a high probability – 18 per cent – of falling back from group 1 to group 2.

Given the values of the transition matrix, we have conducted a simulation exercise. Cluster analysis allocates 58 per cent of the countries to group 1, 14 per cent to group 2, and 29 per cent to group 3. Taking into account these initial values and the transition probabilities, we have checked whether the markov process leads countries to converge towards one single cluster or, rather, towards increased diversification. Results are reported in Figure 9.2. They show that a convergence process takes place. At the end of the process the percentage of group 2 countries rises to 40 per cent, while the weak structure group falls to 10 per cent. Group 1 initially shrinks to 44 per cent and, eventually, rises back to 50 per cent.

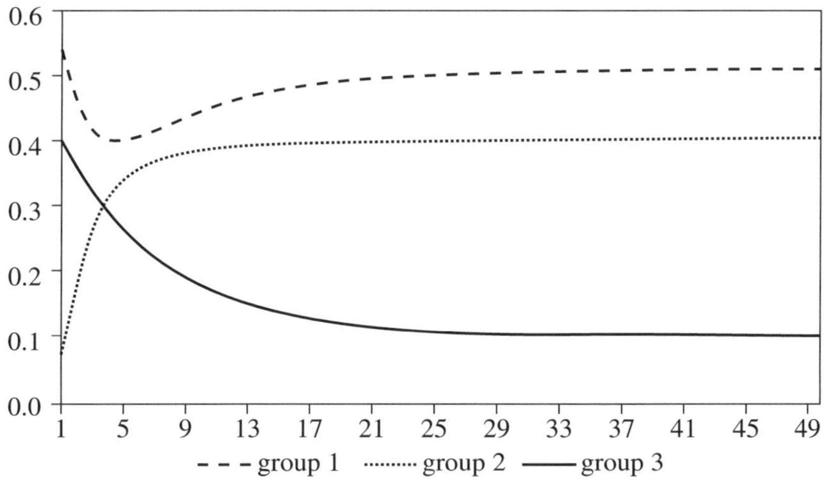

Figure 9.2 Economic convergence

In conclusion, the overall structure of EU economies improves as the share of weak structure countries decreases by two-thirds. However, not all countries converge towards the strong structure group. This last result is quite telling of the problems underlying the Lisbon Strategy. To the extent that our exercise describes convergence as produced by market mechanism it suggests that 'spontaneous' convergence may not be sufficient to bring the EU economy to the best possible levels (we should keep in mind that group 1 includes the 'best world performers'). Policy action is therefore needed. To this issue we now turn.

THE POLITICAL ECONOMY OF THE LISBON STRATEGY

As we know from theory and ample empirical evidence, there are several channels through which catching up takes place. The two most relevant ones are the accumulation of capital and the transfer of technology. Capital accumulation takes place in backward regions because initial capital shortage increases the return to investment with respect to advanced regions. Capital is accumulated both through domestic investment and through capital flows from abroad. Technology transfers also take place through different channels, including trade, capital flows, as well as patent transfers, as returns to the application of technologies that are new for the entrant but old for the incumbents are higher in the former.

Growth convergence can be absolute or, more probably, conditional. In addition, convergence can involve only some of the laggard countries and, finally, convergence is likely to affect regions much more than countries in their entirety. For instance, Padoan (2000, ch. 8) finds that convergence among EU regions excludes some of the poorest regions in some of the Mediterranean countries – thus suggesting the presence of 'convergence clubs' – is conditional rather than absolute, and depends on sector specific rather than country specific characteristics. Padoan (2000, ch. 8) also finds that convergence is faster in those regions where there is a strong presence of both advanced industrial sectors and well developed financial and banking sectors.

Literature on convergence, however, comes to less clear-cut results about the role of policy in accelerating convergence. The Lisbon Strategy also tackles this issue by proposing a new approach to policy convergence and coordination to reach the growth targets.

The Open Method of Coordination

The Lisbon Strategy implicitly assumes that market-led convergence is not sufficient to reach the overall targets of growth and employment and, therefore, it calls for an explicit role for policy based on the so-called 'open method of coordination' (OMC). The basic principle underlying the OMC is that, contrary to what takes place in monetary and fiscal policy in the EU, in many of the other policy areas it is not possible, or desirable, to identify common goals or common instruments and guidelines. Rather, as a form of 'soft coordination', the OMC is based on a process of mutual learning and exchange of best practices.

The OMC includes the following steps: (a) the definition of guidelines at the EU level and the fixing of deadlines for their fulfilment, (b) the definition, whenever possible, of quantitative or qualitative targets and benchmarks vis-a-vis the best world practices, (c) the 'transposition' of EU guidelines into national (and regional) targets that take into account country and region specific factors, and (d) a process of monitoring and peer review. In a nutshell, the OMC is a process of convergence of policies towards best practices, the outcome of which should be the convergence in terms of performance (growth and employment).

The OMC should be seen as a set of policy instruments that are additional to the instruments of directives and EU legislation. It follows a bottom-up approach where, rather than the identification of a common rule (top-down), competition among rules is set in motion.

How is this approach connected to the economics of the Lisbon Strategy we have discussed above? As we have seen the Lisbon indicators include variables that are directly connected to knowledge accumulation (i.e. the variables included the innovation pillar) and to capital accumulation (the economic reform pillar). We can add that variables related to labour market reforms are also conducive to faster catching up to the extent that they allow for higher productivity growth as well as improving the potential for innovation diffusion through human capital accumulation and better work organization.

The Lisbon summit has also clarified the more formal aspects of the coordination process. The key element in this respect is the Broad Economic Policy Guidelines (BEPG) as defined by the Treaty (art. 99). The BEPG is the key document that defines the basic guidelines of economic policy and is set to coordinate the three processes on which EU economic and social policy are based (Luxembourg, Cardiff, and Cologne). The Guidelines are designed so as to provide, over a year-long horizon, a coherent framework for four areas: the macroeconomic policy, public finances in the Stability and Growth Pact, structural reforms (the Cardiff Process), and the labour markets (the Luxembourg Process).

The mechanism was strengthened in 1999. The spring meeting of the European Council had been dedicated to review the process on a regular basis and to set the policy guidelines for the Union in a medium-term perspective, including the framework for the definition of the National Stability Programmes and the National Action Plans as requested by the Luxembourg Process. The Cologne European Council in 1999 added a social dialogue dimension, and the Council of Economic and Financial Ministers (Ecofin) are at the center of the coordination mechanism.

While the design of the institutional structure is sufficiently clear it remains to be seen whether it is also effective, i.e. whether it generates pressures and incentives that will deliver the necessary policy action. There is no clear cut answer to this question, mainly because there are significant differences among the components of the policy process envisaged in the Lisbon Strategy and the incentives and policy mechanisms that are involved in the policy areas are largely different themselves. This suggests that to cope with policy complexity some form of simplification is necessary, given that the Lisbon Strategy is about both economic convergence and policy convergence.

What kind of governance mechanism does the Lisbon Strategy need to be successful? In discussing this point it is useful to compare the macro- and microeconomic domains. The reason for the comparison is that, while the Lisbon Strategy is largely, if not exclusively, about microeconomic and structural issues, it is in the macroeconomic domain that the most significant progress in policy convergence has been achieved in the EU. It is useful to explore, therefore, what lessons, if any, can be drawn from one domain towards the other, keeping in mind the relevance of different mechanisms and rules, i.e. different, yet interacting, policy regimes.

In what follows we look at the macroeconomic (monetary-fiscal) regime and at one specific microeconomic regime, employment policies (the Luxembourg Process) as this represents one of the few areas where some evidence of performance and of the practical operation of the OMC is available.

The Macroeconomic Regime

When one looks at policy regimes – understood as sets of norms, institutions, and regulations that govern market performance – one question to ask is, are they stable? That is, are the regimes based on a structure of incentives that leads to mutually consistent behaviour of the actors involved, both policy and market agents? In the case of the macroeconomic regime the issue is whether agents' behaviours are consistent with monetary union. As has been discussed elsewhere (Padoan 2002) monetary union generates pressure to change both in markets and in policies, in a way that may lead to an incentive structure that supports monetary union itself. This stems from two factors. First, the creation of a supranational institution in one policy area (the European Central Bank) generates pressures for change in other policy areas. Second, to the extent that a 'mixed' model of economic policy emerges – i.e. both national and supranational – it must be based on a coherent set of policy incentives to produce consistent and stable outcomes. To see the point it is useful to reconsider the evolution of the macroeconomic policy regime in Europe from the European Monetary System (EMS) to EMU. This is because one of the main (economic) justifications for the move to a single currency and away from a fixed exchange rate regime was that the latter was becoming increasingly unsustainable in the presence of full capital mobility.

The EMS can be described as a 'weak hegemonic regime' based on an asymmetric distribution of policy incentives between the key country (Germany) and the periphery. The incentives for the latter to participate in the EMS were determined by the import of monetary discipline, or by the exploitation of the public good of monetary stability provided by the centre economy. The incentives for the key country to participate in the regime were the control of monetary stability domestically, and the support of its international competitiveness by preventing or limiting exchange rate devaluations in the periphery. The stability of the regime was obtained to the extent that national policies converged towards the monetary policy stance of the centre. The regime collapsed when, after unification, the core country was not willing (or able) to bear the cost of supporting the weaker (more inflation prone) economies, and the periphery was not willing to make the (deflationary) adjustment necessary to support the exchange rate regime required to cope with relevant changes in market behaviour as a result of capital liberalization. The policy regime proved to be effective as an anti-inflationary mechanism, but it produced limited, if any, policy spill-overs towards other areas (especially fiscal policy). Its crisis showed that policy convergence had to extend to other areas, beyond monetary and exchange rate policy, if it were to pass the judgement of the markets. As long as it succeeded, it proved that an 'intergovernmental' approach to macroeconomic policy requires leadership but that there are limits to such a structure when market integration deepens beyond some critical threshold.

The move forward from the EMS to EMU has led to a major change in the policy regime convergence process in Europe. Policy convergence has affected both monetary and fiscal policy but, what is more important, it has shifted towards a more symmetric configuration. The greater symmetry, however, has required two additional conditions to make the regime effective: (a) the move from a national (hegemonic) leadership structure to a supranational one; (b) the imposition of high entry costs (fulfilment of the Maastricht convergence conditions under the threat of exclusion) as well as high exit costs (the costs associated with the possibility of one country leaving the single currency). In this respect monetary union can be described as a club good with an entry fee (Padoan 1997). Both conditions have represented major changes in the macroeconomic policy regime but neither of them is expected to take place, in the foreseeable future, in the microeconomic regime.

The Microeconomic Regime

The Stability and Growth Pact guarantees that, once monetary convergence has been obtained and a single monetary policy becomes feasible, national fiscal policies are managed according to common guidelines (and hence fiscal policy convergence is also obtained). However, the sustainability of monetary union requires that some adaptation towards the configuration of an optimum currency area is obtained. Consequently, as one cannot rely on market forces alone to produce this convergence, monetary union requires the adoption of appropriate micro (structural) policies to overcome labour and product market rigidities. The extent of harmonization or convergence of micro policies towards common standards required by EMU remains to be seen. The Luxembourg and Cardiff Processes deal with micro and structural aspects. However, they are based on procedures that, so far, while based on principles of 'soft coordination' have provided limited convergence. The Lisbon Strategy is a step forwards as, in a way, it aims at providing, through the open method of coordination, a 'soft solution' to the establishment of microeconomic regimes appropriate for the functioning of a knowledge based economy in a monetary union and in the absence of either supranational policy authorities and of hard binding rules and incentives such as those associated with the Maastricht convergence process to EMU membership. In other words, contrary to EMU, the Lisbon Strategy is based on the idea of 'clubs without entry fees'.

To explore the implications of such an approach we consider the case of employment polices within the Luxembourg Process, which has been recognized as one early example of the OMC. In a nutshell, the EU employment policy framework operates as follows. Each year every EU member state sets out its National Action Plan (NAP) which contains the policy actions it has taken towards the improvement of employment opportunities. The general philosophy of the approach is that flexibility and activity rates in European labour markets can be enhanced by moving away from 'passive' employment policies, such as, for example, unemployment benefits, towards 'active' policies, such as welfare-to-work schemes and active learning and retraining. Within the process, however, a wide range of polices are considered, including policies targeted at supporting small and medium enterprises. Policies are implemented at the national level, as national governments only have jurisdictions over such policies, and are classified according to a (long) list of 'policy guidelines' set out by the Commission and grouped under four headings: employability (employment polices in a strict sense, such as the implementation of placing agencies), adaptability (polices aimed at adapting workers to the new market conditions, such as retraining policies), entrepreneurship (policies aimed at improving the demand side of the labour market, such as incentives for small business), equal opportunity (policies aimed at increasing the employment opportunities for women).

Each year NAPs are presented to the Commission and reviewed by member states through a 'peer review' procedure. A final 'score' is assigned to each government by looking at the degree of fulfilment of policy guidelines as well as the identification of best practices. Policy recommendations are then directed to each member country by the Commission and the Council.

As mentioned, national governments retain full control of policy and are not subject to any explicit obligation,[2] and failure to follow recommendations is not associated with any punishment and/or exclusion threat, as was the case with the entry conditions in monetary union. In other words, as we move away from policies in which the supranational element prevails, the strength of the convergence process weakens.

It would inappropriate, however, to jump to the conclusion that, in areas where there is no explicit obligation to adjust to an EU rule, there are no incentives for national policies to change. Two distinct incentive sets would be operating in such a case: a 'competition' incentive and a 'cooperation' (regime building) incentive. The competition incentive derives from both the policy arena and the market. A poor performing country in, say, improving its employment policies would see its reputation weaken and, consequently, its leverage in the design and implementation of EU policies at large would diminish. This would be particularly worrying whenever the intergovernmental dimension was relevant. In addition, markets would punish a poor performer to the extent that inefficient policies would make that country less attractive for investment, while good performers would presumably enjoy larger investment as their perceived profitability would be enhanced. This aspect is increasingly relevant in a world of high capital mobility. In short, institutional competition may well produce a healthy improvement in EU economic performance as long as it takes the form of exchange of best practices and provides content to the principle of subsidiarity.

The cooperation incentive is relevant to the extent that poor performance in any member of EMU weakens the performance and attractiveness of Euroland as a whole vis-a-vis the rest of the world. In other words, poor policy and economic performance in any one member of the club decreases the quality of the club good, generating a negative externality on the other club members. This will presumably lead to strengthened peer pressure on the poor performer from the rest of the club members (and from the Commission). In this case both the supranational and the intergovernmental dimensions would be relevant. To the extent that such an incentive structure strengthens, therefore, policy convergence could well be the result of the interaction of intergovernamentalism and supranationality.

CONCLUSIONS

The 'new economy' is not simply an economy based on the exploitation of the information and communication technologies. It requires changes in both labour and product markets. The Lisbon Strategy aims at making Europe the 'best knowledge based economy in the world by 2010'. To this end the EU has identified a set of indicators to provide benchmarks and suggest best practices for national policies in EU member states. As our preliminary analysis suggests these indicators are, to some extent, based on a widely accepted economic model that relates output growth to innovation and employment growth. Our analysis also shows that not all EU countries have, so far, experienced the same performance in this respect. Rather, they can be grouped between strong, weak, and catching-up economies.

Economic convergence towards a strong structure for all countries is possible, yet it requires appropriate policy action by EU member states in microeconomic and structural domains. As these policy domains are not governed at the supranational level (as the common monetary policy is) and as there are no binding obligations for countries to adopt specific policies (as was the case for the Maastricht convergence process), some form of policy coordination is needed. This is the role of the open method of coordination; that is, based on soft incentives, exchange of best practices, benchmarking, and peer pressure. While such a policy regime is not as strong as the one that has led to monetary union, it could provide sufficient policy convergence through a combination of market and policy incentives. The early experience of the employment policies (the Luxembourg Process) allow some moderate optimism in this respect.

NOTES

We would like to thank the participants in the conference on Alliance Capitalism and the editors of this volume for many helpful suggestions. The IMF is not responsible for the contents of this chapter.

1. See for instance European Commission (2000).
2. In some areas, of course, national governments must fulfil obligations emanating from Commission Directives such as those related to the prohibition of implementing state aids.

REFERENCES

European Commission (2000), *Competitiveness Report*.

Padoan Pier Carlo (1997), 'Regional Agreements as Clubs, The European Case', in E. Mansfield and H. Milner (eds) *The Political Economy of Regionalism*, Columbia: Columbia University Press.

Padoan Pier Carlo (ed.) (2000), *Monetary Union, Employment and Growth*, Edward Elgar: Aldershot.

Padoan Pier Carlo (2002), *EMU as an Evolutionary Process,* forthcoming.

10. American alliance capitalism

Claude E. Barfield and Cordula Thum

INTRODUCTION

One of the particularly interesting features of the leading market economies of recent years has been the extent to which the hierarchical form of governance of both private and public organizations has been complemented with, and in some case replaced by, a variety of inter-organizational cooperative agreements. This has caused scholars to suggest that the present stage of capitalism may best be described as alliance capitalism.[1]

What is unique about the current stage of capitalism is the use of alliances to undertake innovative activity, and doing so not just at a centralized location but in international locations, often with international competitors. The emergence of these corporate alliances is an indicator of the deep changes currently transforming the world economy, as well as the domestic one.

Although alliances themselves are not a new phenomenon, compared with the 1980s, the 1990s saw a significant growth in international strategic alliances, paralleling the increase in cross-border mergers and acquisitions (M&As).[2] The number of international alliances grew more than five-fold between 1989 and 1999. This prompted suggestions that economic activity through inter-firm alliances is no longer an inferior option to the use of hierarchies, and that in many cases is regarded as the first best option (Ciborra, 1991). Alliances are being formed across a broad range of sectors, including chemicals and pharmaceuticals, computers and electronic equipment, and financial and business services. A greater number of partnerships are for joint marketing and R&D rather than production; this partly reflects the increasing role of service firms in international alliances. In order to achieve global scale in operations, enterprises are choosing international alliances, along with M&As and greenfield investment.

Driving Forces of Alliance Activity

Driven by globalization, which has manifested itself through, inter alia, faster technological change and intensified competition, firms have shown a growing propensity to link up with other firms – often competitors – in order to survive in an increasingly global market place. Alliance activity has become common in industrialized economies; it has an increasingly strategic aspect and many alliances are made to protect or enhance corporate technological assets; further, pressures due to technological developments and globalization cause alliances to be contracted for increased competitiveness and innovation-led growth. This activity exhibits several characteristics:

1. First, alliance activity is no longer a phenomenon peculiar to certain countries such as Japan (see Gerlach, 1992), but typical of most advanced industrialized economies.
2. Second, there is an increasingly strategic aspect to this activity, as alliances are no longer simply undertaken as a means of avoiding transaction and coordination costs of markets (a second-best, exit response), but rather as a first-best 'voice' strategy to reduce market failure due inter alia, to barriers to entry.[3]
3. Third, while agreements were primarily made to enhance or achieve market entry or presence (i.e. asset-exploitation), an increasing number of alliances is made to protect or enhance the technological assets of firms (i.e. asset-creation or acquisition).
4. Fourth, inter-firm alliances are increasingly being undertaken, as a direct response to pressures brought about by contemporary technological developments and globalization. Their growing significance as an inter-organizational form for participating firms to enhance competitiveness and to generate innovation-led growth.
5. Fifth, an increasing number of alliances are being undertaken to protect or enhance the created assets of the participating firms.

Structure

Accordingly this chapter will raise the following questions:

- What are the characteristics of alliance activity involving US firms? At an international as well as domestic level? Are there differences between European and Japanese on the one side and American alliance activity on the other?
- How does the US government shape the formation and content of alliances? What role does the US antitrust law play in domestic alliance formation? Have US firms a disadvantage compared with European or Japanese ones? Are there other structural issues that influence alliance formation of US firms, e.g. the setting of technical standards?
- How do the US trade and investment policies influence international strategic alliances that involve US firms? What role do non-tariff barriers play in the formation of international strategic alliances?

Key Definitions and Distinctions

Several definitions and distinctions are useful in setting the stage for answering our main questions. Since there remains considerable ambiguity as to what constitutes an alliance (Narula and Sadowski, 1998), we start with the definition of the term 'alliances'. Recent work by Madhok (2000)[3] has provided a basis to make a clear distinction, and thereby set the ground for our ensuing discussion. The standard definition used for strategic alliances is that they refer to modes of governance that result in some organizational interdependence between the firms involved, such that there is a strategic benefit that accrues to either partner as the result of shared capital, technology or other resource. In other words, there must be some expected long-term effects of the agreement on the product-market positioning of at least one of the partners (Hagedoorn, 1993). This definition, however, remains imprecise, for the term 'strategic' is open to interpretation. Our view, following that of Dunning (1997) and Madhok (2000) is that both transaction cost minimizing and value-enhancing reasons underlie most of the behaviour of firms.[4]

More than other forms of internationalization, international strategic alliances provide firms with strategic flexibility, enabling them to respond to changing market conditions and the emergence of new competitors. They are prompted by a range of motives, including economizing on production and research costs, strengthening market presence, and accessing intangible assets such as managerial skills and knowledge of markets. In high-technology sectors like pharmaceuticals, soaring research costs and time lags to commercialization are driving partnerships. In telecommunications equipment and other wireless 'network' device manufacturing sectors, alliances are directed to developing a New World product or systems standard. In automobiles and many manufacturing industries, achieving economies of scale in production on a global scale may be the prime motive. And in service sectors such as airlines, alliances are aimed at sharing a partner's sales and distribution outlets. In all cases, international strategic alliances are being driven by the economic demands of global markets, the costs of keeping up with fast-changing technologies, and the opportunities provided by government deregulation and liberalization initiatives.

AGGREGATE CONCENTRATION TRENDS: MERGERS AND ALLIANCES

The political/social concerns about the economic, political, and social power that might be a consequence of the presence and relative growth of mergers or alliances in the US economy have a long history. They extend back at least to the populist movement of the late 19th century. One manifestation of the populist concern about the economic power of large companies was the US antitrust laws, notably the Sherman Act of 1890 and the Clayton Act of 1914.

Mergers and Alliances in Telecommunication: Global Oligopolies?

The global mega-mergers and breakups of telecommunications companies have captured the attention of businesses and governments. Many people have expressed concern that mergers and alliances such as Global One and Concert indicate the emergence of global oligopolies that will control markets and impede competition. This view misses the essence of global telecommunications and the positive impact this remaking of companies can have on markets worldwide.

Understanding the drivers of global telecommunications is key to grasping its effects. Customers are driving telecommunications companies to become global. Multinational customers, whose multiple voice and data service needs require end-to-end service across multiple countries, have the biggest impact. National customers, who need nationwide end-to-end services, are also candidates for the global carriers' advanced services. Local customers, whose needs are primarily network access and use, were important drivers in developing countries. Now these customers are primarily beneficiaries of the domestic competition that global competition is creating. Multinational rivalry increases companies' incentives to build local infrastructure in multiple countries. Building this infrastructure lowers the cost of entering markets to compete for local customers.

The large, developed economies are the primary markets that are driving global telecommunications businesses. The five largest countries for telecommunications – Japan, the US, Germany, the UK, and France – provide 69 per cent of the total world's telecommunications revenues. Japan and the US alone provide 48 per cent of the world's telecommunications revenues. These large economies are also the primary locations for multinational customers. A recent study by the FCC staff showed that 72 per cent of all multinational corporations' headquarters are located in the US (30 per cent), Japan (26 per cent), Germany (8 per cent), the UK (8 per cent), and France (6 per cent). Other markets – primarily those of Latin America and Asia – are growing in importance, and global companies often compete aggressively for footholds when licenses become available.

With the exception of Japan and, to a lesser extent, the US, these countries' incumbent telecommunications companies are the primary players in the global markets. These countries are homes for 15 of the 20 largest telecommunications companies in the world. Global One, which is the largest in terms of combined revenues of the partners, includes Deutsche Telekom, France Telecom, and Sprint, and has almost 15 per cent of the world's telecommunications revenues. Concert, which now includes British Telecom and AT&T, has over 12 per cent. With the defection of AT&T from World Partners, this alliance may fold or be absorbed by Unisource. NTT and US LECs (with the exception of Sprint) are conspicuous by their absence in global M/As. NTT has been slow to enter because, until recently, Japan restricted NTT from offering international services. Also, Japan has been restructuring NTT. With 14 per cent of the world's telecommunications revenues, NTT by itself is on the scale of the global M/As. In the US, the BOC interLATA restrictions keep them from forming global M/As. By themselves, the BOCs are small in comparison to the global M/As. A combined Bell Atlantic/GTE would have only 7.8 per cent of the world's telecommunications revenues. A combined SBC/Ameritech would have only 5.8 per cent.

Developing global mergers and alliances has both pluses and minuses for companies. In addition to addressing particular customers' needs, companies benefit from expanding markets, positioning themselves for future markets, increasing market presence, gaining greater control of industry direction, and counterattacking entry into core markets. This counterattacking is one way that global rivalry increases domestic rivalry. On the minus side, the global mergers and alliances have been frail and costly. Concert has suffered multiple defections and financial losses continue to trouble Global One. There are two reasons for these problems. First, creating a global management system is difficult, especially when it involves former state-owned enterprises. Also, global M/As tie together the futures of companies whose interests and perspectives may be at odds at critical times.

Global mergers and alliances' net effects on customers and markets are positive because they increase domestic rivalry, give entrants stronger positions for negotiating interconnection, and are too frail to exert market power. M/As increase domestic rivalry by improving the economics of domestic market entry and through the cascading industry dynamic. When a global merger or alliance enters a market, it has greater negotiating power than a stand-alone entrant does because the incumbent often needs to interconnect with the merger or alliance entrant. The constant churn in Concert and World Partners demonstrates the difficulty a global merger or alliance would have in exerting market power, assuming it had any.

Public policy has tended to discourage global mergers or alliances even though they have positive effects on customers and markets. As FCC Commissioner Furchtgott-Roth correctly observed, US markets are often constrained by other nations' policies and our own outdated paradigms. Because of concerns over global industry consolidation, the US

Department of Justice imposed restrictions on British Telecom's early investment in MCI and on France Telecom's and Deutsche Telekom's investments in Sprint. Likewise, the European Union required divestiture of Internet assets in WorldCom's recent purchase of MCI.

THE ROLE OF US-FIRM ALLIANCES IN AN INTERNATIONAL PERSPECTIVE

Most strategic alliances (both domestic and international) involve firms from North America, Asia and Europe, as seen in Figure 10.1. North American firms were involved in about 65 per cent of world strategic alliances during 1990–99, while Asian and European firms were involved in 33 per cent and 28 per cent, respectively.

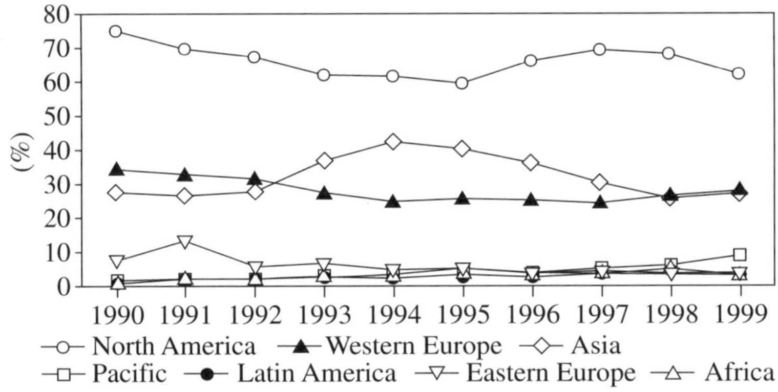

Note: Alliances between different regions are counted more than once (e.g. one for North America and one for Asia, etc.). Regional distribution (%) is calculated by dividing the number of regional alliances by the world total.

Source: Thomson Financial Securities Data.

Figure 10.1 Regional distribution of strategic alliances (%), 1990–99

Strategic alliances increased rapidly in Asia in the first half of the 1990s from 1034 in 1990 to 3654 in 1995, while they decreased to less than 2000 in 1999 (Table 10.1).

Table 10.2 describes regional relationships in strategic alliances in the 1990s. The majority of alliances involving North American firms took place within North America, where North America–Asia alliances and North America–Europe collaborations accounted for 20 per cent and 16 per cent, respectively, of the total. A major portion of the gap between total alliances

Table 10.1 Regional distribution of strategic alliances, 1990–99[5] (number of deals)

	1990	1991	1992	1993	1994	1995	1996	1997	1998	1999	90–99
Asia	1034	1629	1688	2546	3538	3654	1562	1576	1279	1917	20423
Pacific	83	154	129	228	309	481	181	292	311	637	2805
Western Europe	1280	2018	1922	1926	2089	2357	1101	1286	1315	2008	17302
North America	2777	4271	4046	4289	5149	5388	2852	3604	3391	4355	40122
Eastern Europe	289	807	319	459	402	443	164	189	187	216	3475
Latin America	39	123	141	170	223	230	118	221	267	245	1777
Africa	51	103	135	226	218	313	115	197	178	197	1733
OECD	3360	5997	5766	6281	7465	8002	3962	4859	4647	6511	56850
World total	3729	6161	6041	6942	8382	9113	4339	5218	5000	7034	61959

Source: Thomson Financial Securities Data.

Table 10.2 Regional correlation: total alliances, 1990–99 (number of deals)

	Asia	Pacific	Western Europe	Northern America	Eeastern Europe	Latin America	Africa
Asia	7569	673	3534	8216	379	126	326
Pacific	673	919	416	786	44	34	68
Western Europe	3534	416	5018	6437	1639	337	431
North America	8216	786	6437	22374	1088	1108	631
Eastern Europe	379	44	1639	1088	396	11	69
Latin America	126	34	337	1108	11	233	12
Africa	326	68	431	631	69	12	277
Total	20423	2805	17302	40121	3477	1777	1733

Source: Thomson Financial Securities Data

in North America (40 000), Asia (20 000) and Europe (17 000) is attributable to significant differences in the number of intra-regional alliances in each area. While intra-Asia and intra-Europe alliances are 7500 and 5000, respectively, intra-North American collaborations are more than 22 000. As for primary alliance partners, North American firms are the first choice for both Asian and European enterprises, followed by intra-regional alliances.

Following this introduction about the share of alliances involving US firms in the world economy, we will analyze the characteristics of US domestic and international alliances.

CHARACTERISTICS OF ALLIANCES INVOLVING US FIRMS

A review of the theoretical studies on alliances shows there are three fundamental issues and relations to be analyzed concerning US firm alliances.

1. There is a broad correlation between the number of domestic alliances and the size of the national economy, what Narula and Hagedoorn (1997) describe as the country-size effect.
2. Several contributions suggest that the domestic or international character of an alliance influences the particular organizational mode being chosen.
3. There seems to be also a correlation between the technical sophistication of a sector and the particular organizational mode being chosen (equity versus non-equity).

What constitutes the US context in this regard?

Country-size Effect: The Relevance of Domestic Alliances in the US Market

The extent of domestic or international strategic alliances varies significantly from one country to another according to scale, scope and structure. Small countries tend to have a higher involvement in international investment and overseas production compared with large countries. This is because local demand is often (as in the case of the US) sufficient to achieve economies of scale in large countries (Narula, 1995). The reasons for a large number of US domestic alliances include the significant national market in terms of both size and competition,[6] the broader technological and research bases, and the existence of a large number of leading enterprises in various sectors with rich tangible and intangible assets. Therefore, the US possesses comparative advantages in several industries, and is home to agglomerate clusters in most of these.

Table 10.3 Strategic alliances in OECD countries, 1990–99 (number of deals)

Selected countries	Cross-border alliances A	Domestic alliances B	A/(A+B) (%)	B/(A+B) (%)
Australia	2271	770	74.7	25.3
Canada	4064	1057	79.4	20.6
Germany	4062	501	89.0	11.0
Japan	9430	1306	87.8	12.2
United Kingdom	5966	917	86.7	13.3
United States	22293	19141	53.8	46.2
OECD total	38744	25005	60.8	39.2

Source: Thomson Financial Securities Data.

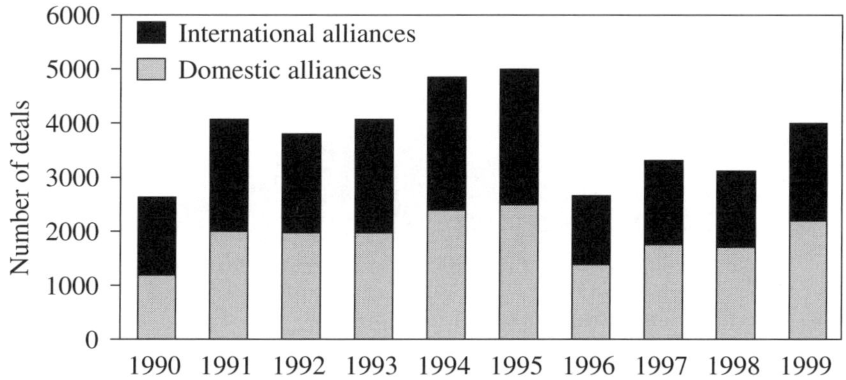

Source: Thomson Financial Securities Data.

Figure 10.2 Strategic alliances in the United States, 1990–99

As shown in (Table 10.3), US alliances tend to be more domestic-oriented than those of other countries.

The majority of US alliances (54 per cent) are domestic partnerships including only US-based companies. Cross-border alliances involving foreign partners represent 46 per cent of US total alliances (Figure 10.2).

International Joint Ventures and the Dominance of Non-equity Ventures

The dominance of non-equity agreements by US firms is not entirely unrelated to the fact that the US has the smallest percentage of international alliances. Research by Gulati (1995) and Hagedoorn and Narula (1996) indicates that international alliances are more equity oriented, whereas a disproportionate share of domestic alliances are of a contractual nature.

Enforcing a contract in an unfamiliar environment is rather difficult compared with enforcing partial control through an alliance in which equity-sharing gives a firm at least some degree of ownership advantage (Dunning, 1993).

Narula and Hagedoorn (1997) note that US firms have a low propensity to use equity for intra-US alliances and a higher level for international alliances.[7] The following graph (Figure 10.3) shows that about 43 per cent of international alliances involving American firms during 1990–99 were joint ventures.

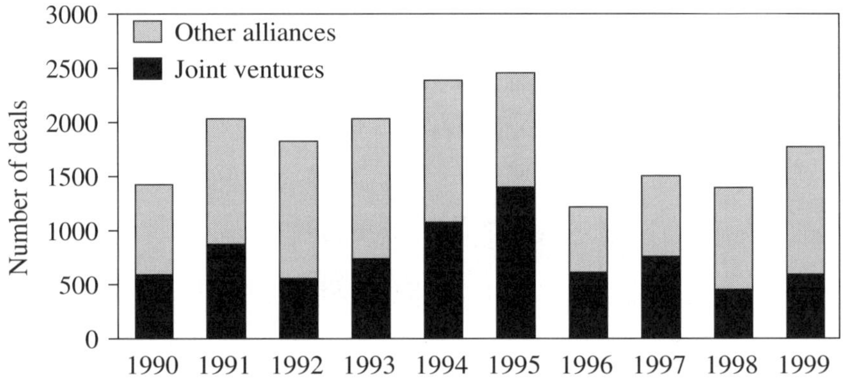

Source: Thomson Financial Securities Data.

Figure 10.3 Types of US international alliances, 1990–99

TECHNOLOGY AND THE ROLE OF R&D INTENSIVE SECTORS IN THE US

A number of studies reveal that the level of technological sophistication of industrial sectors also affects the distribution of equity or non-equity modes of strategic technology partnering. According to Harrigan (1985 and 1988) rapid technological change in sectors of industry induces the formation of somewhat informal forms of cooperation such as non-equity agreements, which are in some ways a 'superior mechanism to undertake technology development in high-tech sectors' (Hagedoorn and Narula, 1996). As industries become mature, more formal modes of cooperation such as joint ventures become the preferred form of collaboration. Osborn and Baughn (1990) suggest that the technological instability of industrial sectors is a crucial factor in explaining different patterns for equity and non-equity partnerships. R&D intensive sectors with short product-life cycles and an innovative industrial climate are expected to demand more organizational flexibility, leading to a general preference for contractual agreements. In sectors with low degrees of R&D intensity and little innovative turbulence where organizational flexibility is also less crucial, technology partnering agreements are expected to be dominated by joint ventures (Yu and Tang, 1992; Hagedoorn and Narula, 1996). This line of reasoning is as follows: high-tech industries, characterized by risk and flexibility, favour strategic alliances to M&As, whereas M&As are expected to be more popular in mature sectors.

In general, though, it would appear that the choice of particular mode of cooperation varies with the technological characteristics of sectors of industry. Equity agreements are preferred in relatively mature sectors, while non-equity agreements are utilized in high-tech sectors (Hagedoorn and Narula, 1996). In the biotechnology sector, the type of alliance depends upon the relative sizes of the firms as well as the extent of appropriability of the innovation. In respect to size, contractual agreements are more likely to involve small companies, while equity agreements were more common among alliances between large firms. In industries where appropriability of innovation (whether through patenting or other means) is more effective, and technologies are close to existing competencies and contractual agreements are more feasible.

It seems that within strategic technology partnering (STP), a particular kind of alliance, there has been a gradual shift away from equity-based partnering to non-equity forms of agreements (Hagedoorn and Narula, 1996). This change in preference reflects the fact that equity agreements tend to be much more complex to administer and control, and take longer to establish and dissolve (Harrigan, 1988).

The growth of knowledge capitalism has led to an explosion of inter-firm alliances. Data on mergers and acquisitions (M&As) and collaborative non-equity coalitions suggest that, whether by FDI or by cross-border licensing, or franchising or other agreements, alliances have been most pronounced, and increased the most, in knowledge-intensive sectors (UNCTAD, 2000).

US alliances tend to have a higher R&D orientation than other countries, compared with a world average of 17 per cent of the total. These alliances also have a different international orientation according to the purpose of the alliance (Table 10.4).

As for marketing and R&D alliances, North American firms are active, reflecting large markets and the broad technology and research bases in the region (Tables 10.5 and 10.6).

Table 10.4 Share of international alliances in US total alliances (share of deals, %)

	1990	1991	1992	1993	1994	1995	1996	1997	1998	1999	90–99
Manufacturing	68	69.34	61.26	65.48	65.51	65.09	63.27	64.79	58.21	59.53	64.298
Marketing	54.19	50.35	48.98	51.6	50.15	47.35	46.28	45.33	39.1	44.69	49.369
R&D	43.93	43.17	37.71	37.9	36.64	40.26	38.56	39.15	40.57	51.21	40.515
Other	52.08	42.91	48.72	9.091	55.13	46.34	40.65	41.62	43.43	40.87	41.538
Total	53.85	50.64	47.57	50.22	49.48	49.42	46.3	45.85	44.77	44.7	48.341

Source: Thomson Financial Securities Data.

Table 10.5 *Regional correlation: marketing alliances, 1990–99 (number of deals)*

	Asia	Pacific	Western Europe	North America	Eastern Europe	Latin America	Africa
Asia	1472	106	897	3235	66	21	46
Pacific	106	98	66	156	9	3	10
Western Europe	897	66	989	2190	300	64	80
North America	3235	156	2190	7710	237	233	185
Eastern Europe	66	9	300	237	55	3	3
Latin America	21	3	64	233	3	30	3
Africa	46	10	80	185	3	3	47
Total	5786	433	4511	13 871	651	348	364

Source: Thomson Financial Securities Data.

Table 10.6 *Regional correlation: R&D alliances, 1990–99 (number of deals)*

	Asia	Pacific	Western Europe	North America	Eastern Europe	Latin America	Africa
Asia	584	24	335	1542	26	4	13
Pacific	24	50	31	80	1	1	4
Western Europe	335	31	473	1489	58	10	17
North America	1542	80	1489	5822	101	41	87
Eastern Europe	26	1	58	101	10	1	2
Latin America	4	1	10	41	1	2	0
Africa	13	4	17	87	2	0	15
Total	2473	179	2349	9096	187	55	133

Source: Thomson Financial Securities Data.

These alliances are especially driven by market entry and technology transfer motives. Interestingly, the share of Asian firms in each type of cooperation is decreasing (from 34 per cent in total manufacturing alliances, 22 per cent in marketing and 17 per cent in R&D) while the share of North American firms indicates an opposite pattern (32 per cent in manufacturing, 53 per cent in marketing and 62 per cent in R&D alliances). For European firms, the share in manufacturing alliances (22 per cent) is slightly larger than that in marketing (18 per cent) and R&D alliances (16 per cent).

Marketing alliances accounted for 37 per cent of US international alliances in the 1990s, while manufacturing and R&D alliances represented 25 per cent and 20 per cent, respectively (Figure 10.4).

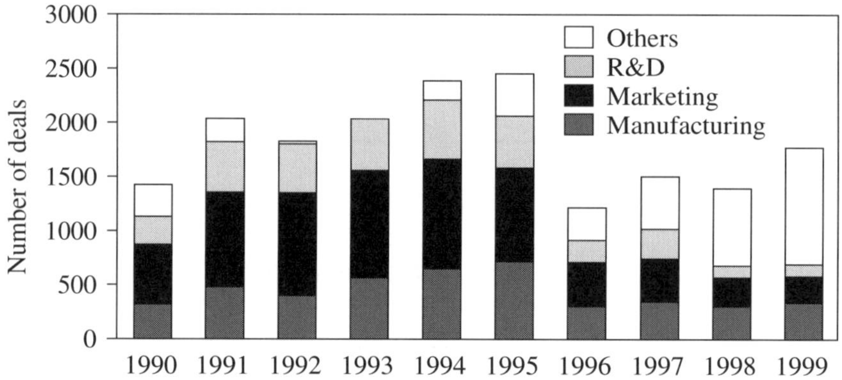

Source: Thomson Financial Securities Data.

Figure 10.4 Purposes of US international alliances, 1990–99

REGIONAL PREFERENCES AND INTERNATIONAL MANUFACTURING ALLIANCES

As for regional preferences, US alliances with Asian and European firms accounted for almost 75 per cent of their total international partnerships (Table 10.7).

The top American firm choice for partners is companies from Japan, the United Kingdom, Canada, Germany and China, which together account for about 60 per cent of US cross-border alliances (Table 10.8).

Moreover, there are also differences in the purpose of alliances by region.[7] In the case of manufacturing alliances, the share of alliances involving Asian firms tends to increase significantly for all major regional

Table 10.7 Regional distribution of US international alliance partners (number of deals)

	1990	1991	1992	1993	1994	1995	1996	1997	1998	1999	90–99
Asia	623	872	823	921	1219	1135	526	555	455	631	7760
Pacific	21	52	36	46	70	110	38	78	70	142	663
Western Europe	589	708	597	631	641	737	398	495	488	639	5923
North America	89	176	178	208	238	242	148	196	207	234	1916
Eastern Europe	116	205	94	121	125	108	52	65	46	48	980
Latin America	19	66	88	98	124	136	68	121	137	96	953
Africa	20	40	47	73	63	91	40	68	60	54	556
US total	1428	2051	1822	2029	2399	2473	1231	1523	1408	1787	18151

Source: Thomson Financial Securities Data.

Table 10.8 Top ten countries of US international alliance partners (number of deals)

	1990	1991	1992	1993	1994	1995	1996	1997	1998	1999	90–99
Japan	503	703	638	584	665	447	224	231	211	254	4460
United Kingdom	198	210	193	188	215	257	163	178	197	236	2035
Canada	88	171	173	197	227	234	143	183	197	222	1835
Germany	101	127	108	121	121	135	67	95	76	96	1047
China	19	38	51	131	218	192	103	87	83	84	1006
France	91	115	82	105	96	101	50	72	51	74	837
Australia	17	43	28	42	65	95	36	69	61	125	581
Netherlands	57	55	46	62	49	47	23	34	37	48	458
Korea	48	38	32	30	58	52	41	46	36	74	455
Italy	41	63	43	53	49	50	18	24	19	39	399
OECD	1247	1718	1519	1531	1716	1603	856	1049	102	1343	12684

Source: Thomson Financial Securities Data.

Table 10.9 Regional correlation: manufacturing alliances, 1990–99 (number of deals)

	Asia	Pacific	Western Europe	North America	Eastern Europe	Latin America	Africa
Asia	3241	200	1718	2522	173	54	134
Pacific	200	77	76	92	14	7	10
Western Europe	1718	76	1161	1274	761	124	148
North America	2522	92	1274	2852	374	271	161
Eastern Europe	173	14	761	374	150	3	26
Latin America	54	7	124	271	3	65	1
Africa	134	10	148	161	28	1	63
Total	7942	460	5141	7431	1465	503	527

Source: Thomson Financial Securities Data.

blocks (Table 10.9). This pattern partly reflects the role of Asia as a world manufacturing centre.

For manufacturing alliances, US firms prefer foreign partners to domestic firms; however, they tend to prefer domestic partners for marketing alliances and, in particular, for R&D alliances. National technological levels are major influences on the development of strategic technological partnerships, and domestic sectoral structures are important determinants of the scope for such partnerships. Large firms, which dominate US industries, are more active in R&D, and are more likely to initiate strategic technology-based partnerships. Narula and Hagedoorn (1997) note:

> First, the level of technological sophistication of the country plays a key factor in the propensity of its firms to undertake strategic technological partnerships (STP), both in terms of undertaking high levels in R&D activity, as well as being involved in high-tech (and therefore high R&D intensity) sectors. Second, the structure of the domestic sector plays an important role in determining the ability to undertake STP (firm size: sales and employees). The US, e.g., tend to have larger firms dominating the industrial landscape. This is important since large firms tend to undertake more R&D activity, and thus are more likely to undertake STP.

Alliances involving American manufacturing firms accounted for about 48 per cent of the total US alliances during 1990–99, while services and primary sectors represented 43 per cent and 5 per cent, respectively (Figure 10.5).

In the manufacturing sector, strategic alliances were concentrated within

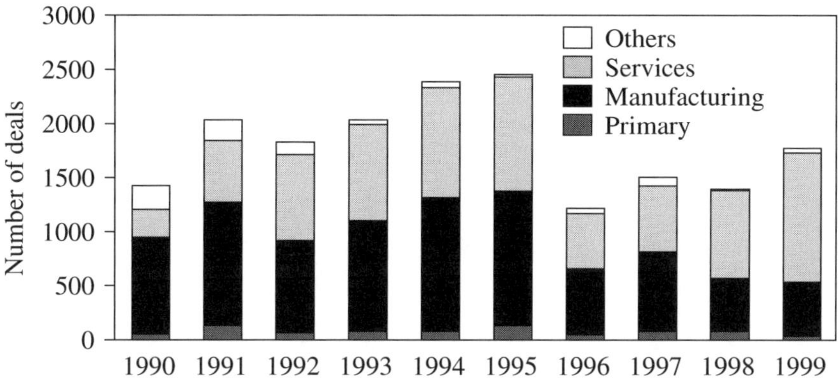

Source: Thomson Financial Securities Data.

Figure 10.5 Sectoral distribution of US international alliances, 1990–99

relatively few industries such as pharmaceuticals, electronics and electric equipment, chemicals, pre-packaged software, communications equipment and computer equipment, which together accounted for more than 70 per cent of manufacturing alliances (Table 10.10).

These industries characteristically display substantial operating risks, high entry costs and rapidly changing technology. However, more and more alliances are taking place in service industries. The share of manufacturing firms in US cross-border alliances continued to decrease, from 63 per cent in 1990 to 27 per cent in 1999, while that of service firms increased from 18 per cent to 67 per cent during the same period. The increase in service industry alliances in the United States can be traced primarily to surges in alliance activity within the business services, trade and financial services industries.

INTERCORPORATE INTERACTIONS: STRUCTURAL ISSUES

Governments shape the formation of domestic and international strategic alliances in a number of ways:

1. Governments can alter the parameters of alliances by influencing firms' partnering decisions.
2. A second area where government regulatory policies influence international corporate alliance formation is in the setting and adoption of technical standards.

Table 10.10 Industrial distribution of US international alliances (%)

	1990	1991	1992	1993	1994	1995	1996	1997	1998	1999	90–99
Primary	3.7	6.7	4.0	3.8	3.5	5.9	4.8	5.9	6.3	2.8	4.7
Manufacturing	62.7	55.3	46.3	50.6	51.6	49.7	47.9	47.7	33.5	27.3	47.6
Pharmaceuticals	12.5	10.3	8.0	7.5	8.2	5.4	7.8	7.4	2.8	1.1	7.1
Electronic	8.8	6.5	6.5	6.8	5.8	5.4	5.7	5.3	3.3	3.1	5.7
Chemicals	2.7	3.4	3.2	6.3	5.2	3.5	3.6	3.2	2.3	2.6	3.7
Software	8.6	6.7	4.8	4.7	6.2	8.4	8.9	9.8	7.4	6.3	7.0
Communications	3.9	3.9	2.9	5.0	4.1	3.7	3.0	3.6	2.0	1.3	3.4
Computer	7.6	6.1	3.2	3.3	3.4	2.3	2.8	2.7	1.4	1.0	3.4
Services	18.1	27.8	43.9	43.8	42.7	43.1	43.1	40.4	59.3	67.1	42.9
Trade	5.0	12.6	25.9	23.0	19.1	12.5	14.4	8.5	5.8	6.8	14.0
Financial	4.4	3.2	2.2	3.6	4.3	6.7	5.7	6.6	18.9	15.2	6.7
Other services	8.7	12.0	15.8	17.2	19.3	24.0	23.1	25.3	34.6	45.1	22.2
Other sectors	15.5	10.1	5.9	1.8	2.3	1.2	4.1	6.0	0.9	2.9	4.7
Total	100	100	100	100	100	100	100	100	100	100	100

Source: Thomson Financial Securities Data.

3. Differences in trade, industrial, and regulatory policies have created a market for the exchange of strategic assets among multinational firms. To compete internationally, US firms are using international strategic alliances to transform and alter their portfolios of strategic competencies and assets.

Strategic Alliances under US Antitrust Laws

Generally, US law treats horizontal agreements, as distinguished from vertical restraints which refers to agreements and practices that may affect relationships between businesses and their supplier, customers or distributors, more strictly than it does agreements among non-competitors.[8] In this context, many analysts argued that because US antitrust laws are far tougher than those in Europe or Japan, US multinational enterprises are at a comparative disadvantage domestically, and were thus more likely to form strategic alliances with foreign companies (see, further, Laurence White, 1999).

Joint ventures among competitors are illegal per se if their purpose is illegal – for example, steel companies cannot establish a joint venture to set steel prices. Exceptions may be cited, notably the treatment of R&D alliances.

The interest of US policy makers in industrial collaboration in R&D arose from a concern over the shrinkage of the technological gap between the US and the rest of the world and the gradual loss of global market share by American firms in technology intensive industries. It was widely held in the early 1980s that, in addition to outmoded managerial attitudes, American firms suffered from an overly regulated domestic environment. Many proposed that the long recognized market failure in allocating resources for technological innovation is accentuated by the overly restrictive antitrust system.

The response to this disadvantage, particularly as a result of US semiconductor industry, led to the enactment of the National Cooperative Research Act (NCRA), 1984, on the basis that domestic alliances in pre-competitive research would improve US international competitiveness in high-technology industries. The rationale for allowing collaboration in the 'earlier' stages of R&D relied on traditional arguments emphasizing the insufficient incentives of individual firms to undertake basic and pre-competitive research at socially optimal levels. However, this view was subsequently challenged as being too restrictive (United State Senate, 1991). Jorde and Teece (1990) dismissed the existence of any clear division between pre-competitive research, development research and production activities in terms of when each activity occurs and how information flows.

Over the past decade antitrust enforcement has had to respond to an internationalization of R&D activity.[9]

The NCRA was amended in 1993 by the NCRPA, which also included production. The prerequisites for collaboration in production were that the joint venture participants cooperated in research as well, and that they would not exclude independent activities in the same field. As with the original NCRA, the NCRPA maintained a rule-of-reason approach in evaluating each research joint venture and kept the potential liability of parties to actual damages instead of the usual treble damages under US antitrust law.[10]

Despite the NCRA's passage, various US corporations have maintained that the threat of US antitrust action still imposes a chilling effect on domestic alliance formation. Citing the antitrust suit filed against Microsoft[11] and Intel, many US computer firm managers say it is simpler and less risky to team up with foreign partners. Incoming investment, takeovers, and joint ventures in the United States have always been subject to antitrust review, but as a rule, only horizontal combinations (for example, between two stainless steel producers) were subject to challenge (Cowhey and Aronson, 1991).

The legislative amendments introduced in 1993 with NCRPA have had an effect on the 'propensity to collaborate' of American industry. As noted in Vonortas (1996, p. 593), the numbers of newly registering research joint ventures (RJV), which had been increasing steadily between 1986 and 1993, dropped for the first time in 1994 and staged an unprecedented recovery in 1995. Another area where US antitrust and regulatory policies have played an indisputable role in strategic alliance formation is the dramatic restructuring of the US telecommunications industry during the late 1970s and early 1980s. Deregulation of the US telecommunications equipment and services markets – the world's largest – and the 1984 divestiture of AT&T, arising from US antitrust litigation, stimulated numerous international strategic alliances.

The Setting of Technical Standards and US Firm Alliance Formation

A second area where government regulatory policies influence international corporate alliance formation is in the setting and adoption of technical standards. An example of the importance of standard setting for strategic alliances is the international race to develop and commercialize high-definition television technology (HDTV). The US Federal Communications Commission's 1991 decision to adopt a digital standard shifted various memberships in rival strategic alliances.

Trade and Investment Policies: Incentives for US Firm Alliances

Government control over market access, via trade and investment policies, has greatly encouraged international strategic alliances. First, governmental moves to non-tariff barriers have created strong incentives for international corporate alliances. One scholar argues that tariffs tend to encourage FDI and joint production arrangements as a means of market penetration, 'nontariff barriers favour the use of collaborative ventures that incorporate product research, development, as well as manufacture' (Mowery, 1989, p. 24). Non-tariff import and export restrictions, such as those permeating the automotive and semiconductor industries, have led to increased collaboration between US and foreign firms for reciprocal market access. One prominent analyst links the escalation in strategic alliances in the 1980s between US and Japanese automakers to Japanese concern over future US trade barriers (Reich and Mankin, 1986, p. 83).

Second, continued Japanese and, to a lesser extent, European government restrictions on FDI – especially in high technology – encouraged firms to enter into strategic alliances. US–Japanese alliance activity in key strategic sectors, such as aircraft and telecommunications, are obvious cases. Finally, because government procurement practices often restrict domestic market access, they encourage international strategic alliances. In Europe and Japan, especially, the prominent and continued role of government ministries as both purchasers and regulators of their telecommunications industries means that US firms must establish alliances with foreign partners, who can then provide them with a national 'cloak' in order to gain market access.

NOTES

1. Sometimes referred to as 'relational', 'collective', 'collaborative and associational' and 'stakeholder' capitalism. For a review of these and similar concepts, see Dunning (1997) and Cooke and Morgan (1998).
2. Indeed, there is a strong link between M&A and strategic alliances, so that firms often establish a strategic alliance with a prospective M&A target.
3. Alliances are defined here as an organizational mechanism to govern an incomplete contract between two separate firms without giving either firm complete control over decision making (Gomes-Casseres, 1996).
4. Decisions to vertically integrate through collaboration or to acquire with suppliers may tend to be primarily cost economizing, but also have a strategic element to them, in that by collaborating with the supplier firm you have pre-empted a similar move by a competitor. This may be defined as a network, which will not be the main focus of this chapter.
5. Figures in these tables include both domestic and international alliances unless otherwise indicated.
6. Countries with outward-oriented economies strongly based on external trade relative to

their size tend to seek more alliance partners outside their own countries. For example, the Netherlands, Italy, Switzerland and Korea are more international in their choice of alliances.

7. Among other things, (a) EU firms have a higher propensity to engage in alliances in sectors in which they lack a comparative advantage relative to US and Japanese firms, (b) strong EU and Japanese firms seek weak partners, so looking for markets and technology while controlling potential competition. See Hagedoorn and Narula (1997).
8. For more details about antitrust in the US, EU and Japan, see Morici (2000, pp. 21–106).
9. On the international dimensions of antitrust enforcement, see Evenett, Lehmann and Steil (2000).
10. Both original research joint venture notifications and subsequent notifications of any changes should be filed with the US Attorney General and the Federal Trade Commission. Both kinds of filings are being posted in the Federal Register.
11. See Richard J. Gilbert and Michael L. Katz (2001).

REFERENCES

Ciborra, C. (1991), 'Alliances as learning experiments: cooperation, competition and change in high-tech industries', in L. Mytelka (ed.) *Strategic Partnerships and the World Economy*, London: Pinter, pp. 51–77.

Cooke, P. and K. Morgan (1998), *The Associational Economy*, Oxford: Oxford University Press.

Cowhey, Peter F. and Jonathan D. Aronson (1991), *Managing the World Economy. The Consequences of Corporate Alliances*, New York: Council on Foreign Relations.

Dunning, John H. (1993), *Multinational Enterprises and the Global Economy*, Wokingham: Addison Wesley.

Dunning, John H. (1995), 'Think again, Professor Krugman: competitiveness matters', *The International Executive*, 37, pp. 461–91.

Dunning, John H. (1997), *Alliance Capitalism and Global Business*, London: Routledge.

Evenett, Simon J., Alexander Lehmann and Benn Steil (eds) (2000), *Antitrust Goes Global*, London and Washington DC: Royal Institute of International Affairs and Brookings Institution.

Gilbert, Richard J. and Michael L. Katz (2001), *An Economist's Guide to U.S. vs. Microsoft*, February 2001.

Gomes-Casseres, Benjamin (1996), *The Alliance Revolution: The New Shape of Business Rivalry*, Cambridge, MA: Harvard University Press.

Gulati, R. (1995), 'Does familiarity breed trust? The implications of repeated ties for contractual choice in alliances', *Academy of Management Journal*, 38, pp. 85–112.

Hagedoorn, J. (1993), 'Understanding the rationale of strategic technology partnering: inter-organizational modes of cooperation and sectoral differences', *Strategic Management Journal*, 14, pp. 371–385.

Harrigan, K. (1988), 'Strategic alliances and partner asymmetries', in F. Contractor and P. Lorange (eds), *Cooperative Strategies in International Business*, Lexington: Lexington Books.

Harrigan, K.R. (1985), *Strategies for Joint Ventures*, Lexington: Lexington Books.

Jorde, Thomas M. and David J. Teece (1990): 'Innovation and cooperation: impli-

cations for competition and antitrust', *The Journal of Economic Perspectives*, 4. 3, Summer.
Madhok, Anoop (2000), 'Inter-firm collaboration: contractual and capabilities based perspectives', in Nicolai Foss and Volker Mahnke (eds) *Competence, Governance and Entrepreneurship*, Oxford: Oxford University Press.
Morici, Peter (2000), *Antitrust in the Global Trading System: Reconciling U.S., Japanese and EU Approaches*, Washington, DC: Economic Strategy Institute.
Mowery, David C. (1989), 'Collaborative ventures between U.S. and foreign manufacturing firms', *Research Policy*, 18, 1, February.
Narula, Rajneesh (1995), *Multinational Investment and Economic Structure*, London: Routledge.
Narula, Ranjeesh and John Hagedoorn (1996), 'Choosing modes of governance for strategic technology partnering: international and sector differences', *Journal of International Business Studies*, 27(2), 265–84.
Narula, Rajneesh and John Hagedoorn (1997), *Globalization, organizational modes and the growth of international strategic technology alliances*, MERIT Research Memorandum 97–017, Department of Economics, University of Maastricht.
Osborn, R.N. and C.C. Baughn (1990), 'Forms of interorganizational governance for multinational alliances', *Academy of Management Journal*, 33, pp. 503–19.
Reich, Robert B. and Eric D. Mankin (1986), 'Joint ventures with Japan give away our future', *Harvard Business Review*, 86, 2, March–April.
United Nations Commission on Trade and Development (2000), *World Investment Report*, Geneva: UNCTAD.
United States Senate (1991), *The National Cooperative Research Act Extension of 1991*, Bill No. 479.
Vonortas, Nicholas S. (1996), 'Research joint ventures in the US', *Research Policy*, 26, pp. 577–95.
White, Laurence J. (1999), *The Antitrust Revolution: Economics, Competition, and Policy*, New York: Oxford University Press.
Yu, C.-M. J. and M.-J. Tang (1992), 'International joint ventures: theoretical considerations', *Managerial and Decision Economics*, 13, pp. 331–42.

11. Japan's network capitalism in evolution

Terutomo Ozawa

INTRODUCTION

Japan once formulated and maintained a highly effective brand of capitalism and corporate management in the post-World War II period – up until the late 1980s. Gerlach (1992) identified it as 'alliance capitalism' (along with the subtitle of 'the social organization of Japanese business'). That particular brand was created out of the tattered economic regime at war's end to reconstruct and build up domestic industries, especially the heavy and chemical industries that Japan had already established in the prewar days but that had become dilapidated during the war. Dunning (1997a, b) adopted the term alliance capitalism when he explored in more general terms the implications of this mode of capitalist pursuit of business goals by modern corporations across national borders.

The themes of this chapter are (i) that Gerlach-type alliance capitalism – or, for that matter, any other type in Japan – has proved to be merely a *transitory* regime that was suitable and instrumental only for a particular stage of Japan's structural upgrading, (ii) that networking is the underlying principle of social organization in Japan, (iii) that G.B. Richardson's (1972) trichotomy model of how economic activity is coordinated (by market, hierarchy, and network) needs to be modified to explain the evolution of Japanese-style industrial organization, (iv) that Japan is presently groping for ways to transform its business model once again into something new, something closer to the American model of 'open-systems integration', and (v) this sequence of institutional transformation is fundamentally a function of the stages of economic growth and structural upgrading.

EVOLUTIONARY TRANSFORMATION

Trichotomy of Economic Coordination

As illustrated in Figure 11.1, it was Adam Smith (1776) who first saw inefficiency in government involvement (that is, 'government failure') in economic affairs and advocated market-driven coordination as a way of maximizing the wealth of nations because 'the Government of Smith's day was corrupt and incompetent; it often peddled monopoly privilege' (Letiche, 1960: 68). Put in modern parlance, Smith was clearly making a distinction between 'market' and 'organization/hierarchy' (i.e. government in his day) in coordinating economic activities. And the modern economics embedded in the market mechanism thus originated with Smith's work. His notion of the 'invisible hand' epitomizes the market, a system of arm's length exchanges based on 'higgling and haggling' in primitive society but on contractual relations in modern society. In other words, a modern market economy is built on a system of jurisprudence (but with its possible downside effect of developing into a high litigation society).

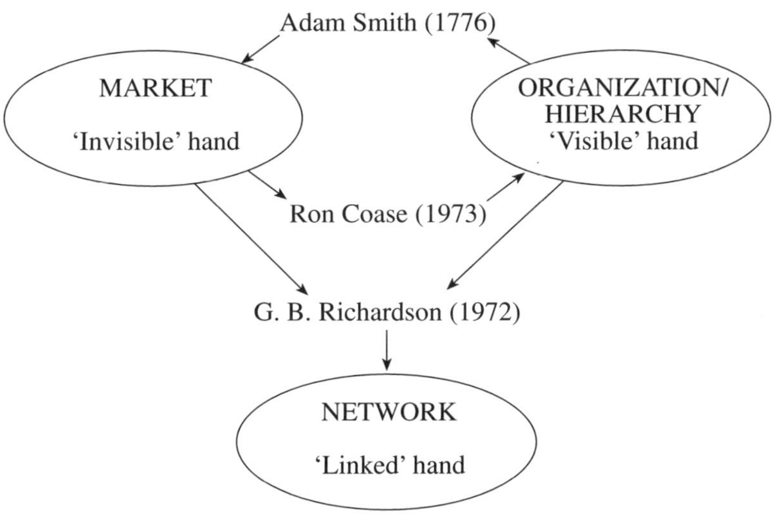

Figure 11.1 Trichotomy of economic coordination

One hundred and sixty one years later, however, Ronald Coase (1937) theorized exactly the opposite situation; that is, why markets might be replaced by organization/hierarchy because of high transaction costs associated with the former (that is, 'market failure'). Market transactions came to be no longer perceived as costless; in fact they are often prohibitively costly when the market fails. And transaction cost economics came into existence, as elaborated most extensively by Oliver Williamson (1975, 1985).

This dichotomy between markets and hierarchies then became popular in the economics of industrial organization. But it was not long before another coordination mechanism (which had actually been known in other sciences) was brought to economists' attention for the first time by G.B. Richardson (1972):

> I was once in the habit of telling pupils that firms might be envisaged as islands of planned co-ordination in a sea of market relations. This now seems to me a highly misleading account of the way in which industry is in fact organised. (p. 883)

He then introduced the concept of networking as the third modality of economic coordination by pointing out 'the dense network of cooperation and affiliation by which firms are inter-related' (1972: 883). Consequently, the trichotomy of market (the 'invisible hand'), hierarchy (the 'visible hand'), and network (the 'linked hand') has come to be widely accepted.[1]

These three modalities of economic coordination are driven by different enforcers of order and stability in economic activities and relations. The market is basically driven by 'enlightened self-interest' (non-opportunistic and responsible pursuit of self-interest), the hierarchy by 'command and control', and the network by 'reciprocity, trust, and obligations' *a la* Polanyi (1944).

It should be noted in passing that while Richardson stressed the notion of *inter-firm* networking at the firm level, Karl Marx (1867) had much earlier stressed the notion of *inter-operative/agent* networking at the individual level in terms of the synergy of collective action among 'social animals' (Marx, 1867).

Gerlach-type Alliance Capitalism

Using data covering the period from the late 1960s and comparing these with data available for US industry, Gerlach (1992) depicted the Japanese structure specific to that period in the following way:

> Japanese business networks are shown to be strongly organized by *keiretsu* across three types of ties (dispatched directors, equity shareholding, and bank borrowing) and more weakly organized in a fourth (intermediate product trade). In all cases but product trade . . . the proportion of transactions taking place with firms in the same group is over ten times higher than the average with firms in other groups, indicating an extremely strong pattern of *preferential trading* that clearly has important implications for how we understand the nature of

> Japanese markets . . . Although *a variety of alliance forms* are discussed in the study, it is the diversified groupings linking *major banks and industrial enterprise* that receive special attention. The large corporation occupies a central position in industrialized economies, especially in strategic sectors such as finance, basic manufacturing, and international trade. Even in Japan, where the medium-and-small-firm sector constitutes a substantial percentage of total employment, it is the large firm sector that has been the primary source of Japan's financial capital, its imports and exports, and its major technological and organization innovations. (Gerlach, 1992: 246–7, emphasis added)

What Gerlach was describing is basically the *keiretsu*-dominated structure funded by main banks and dominated by large corporations, a system that existed from the late 1960s into the 1980s, exactly the same period on which his empirical study was focused. It was, however, a *transitory* (though relatively long) period for Japan's structural transformation (as will be made clear below).

As to the effectiveness of the *keiretsu*-controlled structure, he raises the issue:

> Rationalized markets have long been considered efficiency-generating institutions, yet the Japanese economy has out-performed any other major industrial economy for much of the postwar period. If . . . Japan's alliance structures of industrial organization represent clear deviations from textbook models of market organization, the question becomes whether the Japanese economy has performed as well as it has despite these deviations or because of them. (Gerlach, 1992: 247, emphasis added)

He then characterizes the Japanese system as 'a balancing of benefits and costs', in which the benefits far exceed the costs for the economy as a whole, whereas the reverse is true for the rest of the world. Gerlach, however, did not define the benefits and costs involved, nor did he explain theoretically how the net benefit accrues to the economy. This question will be explored later in the 'knowledge creation' vs. 'knowledge diversion' section.

Although Gerlach's analysis cites and draws on Richardson's principle of networking, he describes Japanese-style alliance capitalism as *sui generis* – that is, not totally explainable by such a principle alone. Those who accept the Richardson's trichotomy are probably perplexed by the thick *confluence/fusion* of hierarchy (*keiretsu*) and network (alliance) in what is presented by Gerlach as the unique Japanese industrial organization. But this puzzle is solved by the work of Kumon (1992) and Imai (1992) below.

Networking as the Underlying Principle of Social Organization

Kumon (1992) treats networking as a form of *information/knowledge management* at the corporate level and expounds a theory of networking (abstracted from the Japanese experience as distinct from – and without any reference – to Richardson's conceptualization):

> . . . a network as a generic social system is one in which, no matter whether it is a complex actor or a societal system, the major type of mutual acts is *consensus/inducement-oriented* [as opposed to *threat/coercion-oriented* or *exchange/exploitation-oriented*]. Networks are organized under the premise that *information rights* are legitimately established in some form or other and at the same time *partially restricted within themselves*. The main reasons for individual actors to join in a network are to share useful information/knowledge with other members, to achieve better mutual understanding, and to develop a firm base for *mutual trust* that may eventually lead to collaboration to achieve actors' individual as well as collective goals. (Kumon, 1992: 109–41, emphasis added)

For Kumon, the market is thus perceived as 'exchange/exploitation-oriented', the hierarchy as 'threat/coercion-oriented', and the network (here only of the Japanese genre) as 'consensus/inducement-oriented'. To stress and explain the Japanese genre, he then presents two classifications: '(1) those that are simultaneously organizations [or hierarchies], and (2) those that are not organizations – namely, those that are societal systems', the former being called 'network organizations' and the latter 'societal networks'. In Kumon's conceptualization, then, there is *no* clear-cut Richardsonian trichotomy of markets, hierarchies, and networks. The three modalities are intricately and functionally combined as complements – *not* as substitutes or alternatives. And his principle of networking applies to *both* markets and organizations, as well as to inter-firm/organization relations and higher-order societal systems at large. Everything is rolled into one integrative whole, and networking is the basic organizational glue everywhere: 'Japanese society can be characterized as a society in which such networks are ubiquitous, not only informally but also in a formally institutionalized form' (Kumon, 1992: 109–141). In short, *networking permeates Japan's society at its core as a major governing principle*.

Adopting the same notion of Japanese-style networking, Imai (1992) argues that Japan first organized *zaibatsu* in the pre-World War II days and then, after the war, 'business groups', and most recently 'network industrial organizations'. By business groups he specifically means *keiretsu*, which Gerlach called alliances. The combined arguments advanced by Kumon and Iami are schematically illustrated in Figure 11.2. Basically, Japanese society is extremely intensive and thick in networking, to facilitate exchanges of information and knowledge. The ubiquitous principle of networks underlies the evolution of Japan's industrial organization. *Zaibatsu* (hierarchy) first emerged as a *manifestation* of Japan's network-woven society in that particular organizational form because of market failures – that is, simply because no well-functioning market existed in an underdeveloped Japanese economy. It was not a matter of rational choice, *zaibatsu* had to fill the lacuna of the market:

> . . . the *zaibatsu* as a large-scale, family-owned conglomerate represents the institutionalization of an organizational mechanism to compensate for the *incompleteness of the market* in developing economies. In addition, the role of *zaibatsu* can be interpreted as providing organizational innovation to retain internally the profits from mutually supporting and cooperative activities in an immature market. (Imai, 1992: 203, emphasis added)

The *zaibatsu* were, in Imai's words, both 'coordinating mechanisms' and 'market-like organizers' of economic activities. And additionally, they were effective in capturing and internalizing the synergistic benefits of collective activities. The 'market-like organizers' are also called 'quasi-markets' by Imai – and 'paramarkets' by Kumon. *Zaibatsu* were at the same time, 'control networks' where their holding companies (family-owned) exercised direct control over a diversified range of industries.

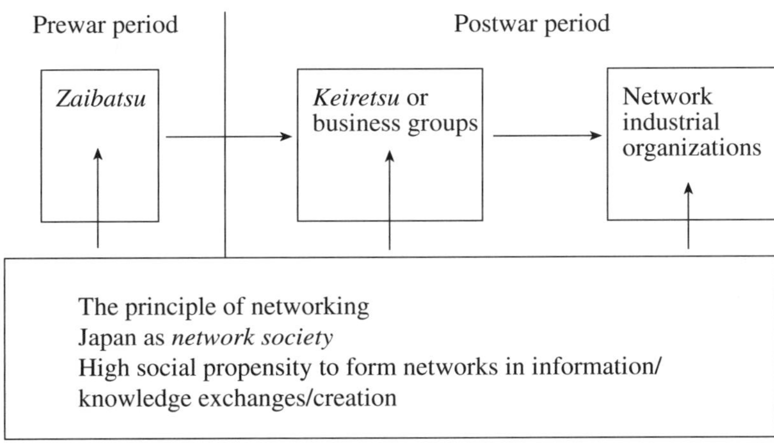

Figure 11.2 Japan as a network society and its manifestations in business organization

Then, shortly after World War II came the 'business groups' or *keiretsu*. Imai emphasized that this new organization was characterized by:

1. the use of 'presidents' clubs' as the core place for periodic exchanges of information

2. intercorporate holding of stock to prevent hostile takeover bids by outsiders
3. the main bank system under which a large city bank served as the key lender and overseer of each group's activities
4. a general trading company at the center of each group's trading, facilitating information gathering and dissemination about market conditions, especially overseas.

According to Imai, furthermore, a crisis was the major trigger mechanism to induce a decisive transformation from one dominant form of industrial organization to another:

> the worldwide industrial reorganization that followed the recession of the 1880s contributed to the formation of the *zaibatsu*, while the dissolution of the *zaibatsu* [after WWII], which was generally regarded as a crisis, produced the competitive postwar reorganization. Similarly, the oil crisis created a new industrial organization. (Imai, 1992: 218)

The oil crisis of 1974 was a blessing in disguise in compelling Japanese industry, especially in the then rapidly emergent electronics and other assembly-based manufacturing, to mold a new form of business organization, which Imai calls 'network industrial organization':

> In this type of work-force specialization [in the wake of rapid technological progress and dissemination] . . . units retain autonomy and yet remain closely interdependent. Unlike the hierarchical division of labour typical in automobile manufacturing, this type of specialization is characterized by self-organizing . . . This specialization of the work force has been noted by M.J. Piore and C.F. Sabel of [MIT], who refer to it as 'flexible specialization.' . . . a more highly specialized work force necessarily creates spontaneous linkages among firms engaged in related types of specialized work. This is because when individual enterprises perform highly specialized work in the age of *system technology*, they cannot reach their full potential *unless mutual progress is made as a network*. This requires *a sharing of information among related firms that is beyond the simple information exchange in the market*. Hence, network activity, or activity with consideration for one's 'position' in the network and 'distance' from others, is the mode of action (Imai, 1992: 218–19, emphasis added)

Given the argument that networks are the warp and weft of the fabric of Japanese society, so to speak, Imai's use of the nomenclature 'industrial network organization' (that is, network-cum-organization/hierarchy structure) is somewhat confusing to those who are accustomed to Richardson's clear-cut trichotomy. Kumon instead calls this combined structure 'a more genuinely network-oriented form' (Kumon, 1992: 109–41). What they are really arguing is that the prewar *zaibatus* and the postwar *keiretsu* or business groups should be regarded merely as the manifestations (derivatives) of network Japanese society.

In short, Japan's business structure has gone through metamorphoses, each of which has been triggered by a certain crisis (as posited in Imai's 'crisis-triggered metamorphosis' theory). And in Imai's view, the path of metamorphosis has so far traced out a three-stage sequence of *zaibatsu* → 'business groups' (or *keiretsu*) → 'network industrial organizations' with the principle of networking as their underlying organizational mechanism. (As will be seen later, however, this sequence will be further elaborated on and extended to the postwar five stages of 'make-shift structure' → 'keiretsu, Mark I' → 'keiretsu, Mark II' → 'systems integration, Mark I' → 'systems integration, Mark II').

WHY NETWORKS HAVE BEEN SO UBIQUITOUS

Legacies of Feudalism[2]

One naturally wonders why the principle of networking has been so pervasive in Japanese society. This has a lot to do with how Japan came out of 200 years' seclusion under feudalism and then plunged into modernity in the mid-19th century – largely under pressure exerted from outside.

According to Veblen (1934), feudalistic traditions or experience play a positive role in economic transformation. This line of reasoning is in full agreement with a widely recognized view that feudalism contributed to the development of democracy, capitalism, and modern civilization in the western societies, for it introduced an orderly social system based on contractually specified relationships. Some even regard feudalism as a prerequisite to civilization. Early on, indeed, feudalism in England gave rise to the practice of covenanting or contracting by specifying and formalizing a system of governance by the rule of law (Prawer and Eisenstadt, 1968). And, in the end, contractual relations, the central mode of governing interpersonal commercial relations and transactions between independent operative units in modern times, have come into existence as a legacy from the evolution of feudalism. The practice of contracts (formal specifications of rights and duties among transacting parties) liberated individuals from the shackles of arbitrariness and exploitation by the powerful lords who bound their vassals in informal and often charismatic relations.

In sharp contrast, the Japanese brand of feudalism had different evolutionary traits that have survived:

> Japan's feudalism differed from the European pattern in several important respects: (1) the continuous importance of the imperial center in spite of its loss of political function; (2) the weakness, perhaps even total absence, of contractual elements in the relations between lords and vassals; (3) the full, personal, familistic expression of these relations; and (4) the lack of any representative institutions. (Prawer and Eisenstadt, 1968: 400)

For our analysis, the second and third features, 'the weakness, perhaps even total absence, of contractual elements in the relations between lords and vassals' and 'full, personal, familistic expression of these relations', are crucial in understanding the social system in Japan's post-feudal period and why trust-based networking has permeated Japanese society. The economies in both the West and Japan are derived from their respective brands of feudalism, but with different ways of coordinating economic transactions and interlinking relations. In the former the behaviours of micro-agents are contractually specified and explicitly rule-governed, while in Japan they are less legally particularized and bound but are more generally governed by personal ties or connections that distinctly characterize Japanese society. The Japanese operate largely on the basis of unwritten, noncontractual relations. In this respect, the Japanese modality of organizing economic transactions has some affinity with what Polanyi (1944) describes as a system of 'reciprocity' as opposed to a system of 'exchange'. In the former system, goods and services are circulated 'on the basis of familial or political obligation, reinforced by ritualistic or religious principles' – in contrast with 'the two-way transfer of equivalent values motivated by self-interested calculation that is characteristic of market exchange' (Stanfield, 1986: 20).

In the western market economies, legal contracting and litigation are the major governing mechanisms that enforce transaction promises between economic agents. By comparison, economic transactions in Japan more strongly involve personal commitments, trust, duties, and obligations – in other words, they are treated more often as *social exchanges* rather than as *pure economic exchanges*. The Japanese are eager to build long-term relationships. Consequently, an atmosphere of patronage and reciprocity *a la* Polayni rather than that of suspicion and threat pervades the exchanges.

In this respect, as pointed out in Kay (1991), Casson's (1987) emphasis on trust and goodwill and Buckley's (1988) on forbearance and cooperation are more appropriate for Japanese-style transactions than Williamson's (1985) on opportunism, though opportunistic behaviour is certainly not non-existent in Japanese society.

What is more, another important legacy of many centuries of secluded feudalism in Japan is manifested in cultural attributes stemming from paddy rice cultivation. This type of farming, particularly in Japan's natural disaster-prone climate (such as frequent typhoons and flooding), necessitated collective control over, coordinated use of, and mutual help in irrigation among the village farmers. Aoki (1988), for example, stresses this point:

> There is no doubt that through centuries of agrarian experience up to as recently as a generation ago, the Japanese developed the customs of mutual help, collective coordination, risk sharing, ad hoc and flexible adaptation to continual and incremental environmental changes, diligent work habits, and penetration of communal life into the private spheres, which are now viewed as characteristics of modern Japanese factory life. (p. 307)

In short, the unique evolution of Japan's feudalism, along with its heavy dependence on wetland farming as the major economic base, left indelible marks on how the Japanese interact with each other not only in economic affairs but also in all other types of activity. The Japanese principle of networking thus derives from deep cultural roots.

SYSTEMS INTEGRATION

An important question still remains unanswered: *Is the Japanese-style of networking, based on intra-group trust and cohesiveness, really equally as information/knowledge-enhancing, hence economic efficiency-increasing as is its American counterpart?*

Open vs. Closed

Analyzing the resurgence of Route 128 and the recent information and communications technology (ITC) revolution in the United States, Best (2000) introduces the new concept of 'open-systems integration' as opposed to what may be called 'closed-systems integration':

> System integration is a static concept with respect to component design rules; it does not imply openness to innovation or technological change. In fact, the challenge of system integration exerts pressure to freeze technological change. *Kaizen*, or continuous improvement management, pursues experimentation and technological improvement but *holds basic technology design rules constant* . . . The process of integrating subsystems have dynamic feedback effects . . . Intel built a business model based on the concept of design modularization. Leading Japanese companies have substantial systems-integration capabilities. They, like Intel, integrate new product development with process reorganization. But *the Japanese leading electronics companies have not redesigned their business system to capture the innovation potential offered by the principle of systems integration. To do so would mean moving from a closed to an open-systems model of supplier relations and industrial organization.* (Best, 2000: 470–1, emphasis added)

For Best, Japanese incremental technical improvement, *kaizen*, is a rather static approach which cannot alter the basic technological paradigm. And the Japanese are still operating under closed-systems integration, unlike their American counterparts who benefit more substantially from open-systems integration. In other words, what Imai identified above as 'network industrial organization' is basically closed-systems integration. In order to stress the importance of transition from the closed type to the open type, we will call the former 'systems integration, Mark I', and the latter 'systems integration, Mark II'.

'Knowledge Creation' vs. 'Knowledge Diversion'

The benefits and costs of open- vs. closed-systems integration can be theorized on a comparative basis in terms of two opposing effects: 'knowledge creation' and 'knowledge diversion'. These effects are analogous to Viner's (1960) distinction between 'trade creation' vs. 'trade diversion'. Knowledge creation occurs within a closely knit network, as information flows unhindered and smoothly in such a group, leading to a successful synthesis and synergy in idea generation. This benefit is, as seen earlier, stressed in both Imai (1992) and Kumon (1992). Simultaneously, however, knowledge diversion may result from the introversive focus of the group, neglecting and slighting ideas and practices outside the group. Kumon (1992) also touches on this undesirable aspect of the closed type of networking:

> . . . in networks, success tends to lead to complacency in and closedness of the system, with members becoming more introverted. Of course, they will show some interest in the outside world insofar as it continues to be the source of some useful information, or other goods and services, but they will have little genuine interest in, or sympathy for, the outside world as such. (p. 109–41)

So long as the knowledge creation (positive) effect outweighs the knowledge diversion (negative) effect, the group as a whole benefits. Ironically, however, the greater the knowledge creation effect, the more introverted and hubristic the group may become; the upshot then is a greater knowledge diversion effect, which eventually ossifies network relations. As will be discussed below, in the early stages of Japan's catch-up growth, the *keiretsu* groups were able to maximize the positive effect, but eventually they were overwhelmed by the negative effect as the nature of industrial technology became more sophisticated and the scope of business operations was increasingly globalized.

This conceptualization of two opposing effects is thus useful in interpreting in theoretical terms what is meant by Gerlach's 'balancing of benefits and costs' as mentioned earlier.

From Comparative to Competitive Advantage

To explain the nature of Japan's network society, the theory of comparative advantage can also be used when we interpret it as the principle of *intra*-unit specialization and *inter*-unit division of labour, whether the unit happens to be a country, a network group or an individual. The trade doctrine of comparative cost advantage originally expounded by David Ricardo (1817) looks at an individual country (entire economy) as a unit of analysis. Trade takes place because of a difference in comparative costs, inducing an expansion of comparatively advantaged (relatively higher labor productivity) industries and a contraction of comparatively disadvantaged (relatively lower labor productivity) industries. This causes a better reallocation of resources, a phenomenon called 'allocative efficiency', resulting in higher outputs and higher living (consumption) standards in trade-participating countries. According to this doctrine, even a *weak* (non-competitive) country, a country that has no absolute advantage in any single industry, can still participate in and gain from trade. In other words, it is clearly a theory of *inclusion and coexistence, not exclusion and rivalrous elimination.*

In this perspective, each *keiretsu* group can be interpreted as an organization which is built on the doctrine of comparative advantage – in the sense that each group comprises several leader companies and a large number of their respective follower/affiliated companies, especially in vertical supply (input procurement and output distribution) chains. This characteristic is popularly called '*gosoh sendan* [convoy formation]' in which a group of affiliated companies/banks, large and small, advance together in mutual protection and cooperation. Strong major companies are supposed to assist and foster their closely affiliated weaker companies. In other words, each *keretsu's intra*-group transactions are based on the doctrine of comparative advantage or the principle of inclusiveness and mutual existence – and not on the doctrine of absolute advantage or the principle of exclusion and rivalrous elimination. For example, a major company in one *keiretsu* may find supplies cheaper if it purchases from a company in another *keiretsu*, but the former refrains from doing so (and the latter may refuse to deal with such an out-of-group customer). Instead, the major company continues to procure whatever it needs from its own affiliated suppliers, while providing any necessary assistance (technical and financial) to make the affiliate more productive and equally competitive. In short, the idea of comparative advantage-based specialization is applicable to, and useful in, delineating the strength of intra-*keiretsu* cooperation.

CATCH-UP IN STRUCTURAL UPGRADING AND BUSINESS ORGANIZATION

The postwar progression of Japan's network-based industrial organization can be juxtaposed with its sequential stages of structural upgrading, since the former has occurred *pari passu* with the evolutionary changes in Japan's industrial composition punctuated by the growth of a certain leading sector in each stage (as shown in Figure 11.3).

The industrial progression is the sequence of 'make-shift structure' → '*keiretsu*, Mark I' → '*keiretsu*, Mark II' → 'systems integration, Mark I' → 'systems integration, Mark II', as suggested earlier. Each type of industrial organization will be explained below. As introduced elsewhere (Ozawa, 1993, 2001a), the stages of structural upgrading to be used here consist of

1. the 'Heckscher-Ohlin' *factor*-driven stage (labour-intensive goods – 'factor goods' – such as textiles, apparel, toys, and sundries produced and exported mostly by small- and medium-sized enterprises) throughout the 1950s,
2. the 'non-differentiated 'Smithian' *scale*-driven stage (capital-intensive goods – 'scale goods' – such as steel, basic chemicals, heavy machinery, and ships) from the mid-1950s through the 1960s,
3. the 'differentiated 'Smithian' *assembly*-driven stage (parts/components-intensive goods – 'assembly goods' – such as automobiles and first-generation electronics – TV sets and pocket calculators) throughout the 1970s,
4. the 'Schumpeterian' *R&D*-driven stage (knowledge-based goods – 'R&D goods' – such as micro-chips, computers, telecommunication equipment, and bioengineering) in the 1980s, and
5. the 'McLuhan' *information*-driven stage (Internet-based goods – 'information goods' – such as e-mail, websites, and e-commerce) from the mid-1990s onward.

Since these five tiers of main sector-led upgrading have appeared in successive waves, a pattern similar to a flying formation of wild geese, their tandem growth is thus in the tradition of the so-called 'flying-geese' theory of economic development (Kojima 2000; Kojima and Ozawa, 1985; Ozawa, 2001b). The transition from one stage to another, however, is certainly not clear-cut but rather overlapping as the dominant sector in one stage gradually phases out, while a new sector rises to prominence in the subsequent stage. This developmental stages model is basically a 'leading growth sector' model *a la* Schumpeter (1934), in which a sequence of growth is punctuated by stages in each of which a certain industrial sector can be

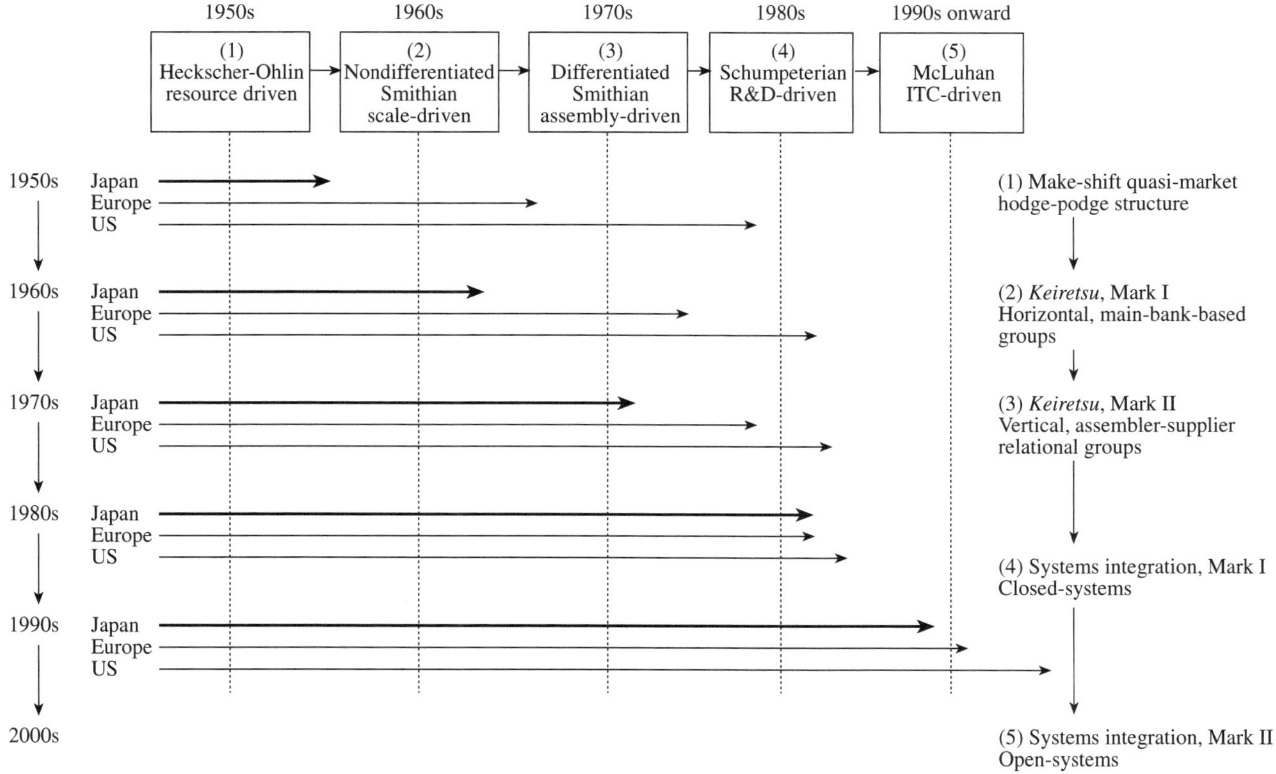

Note: Arrows indicate the relative positions of each economy in stages of growth during different postwar decades.

Figure 11.3 Japan's catch-up in structural upgrading under different forms of business organization

identified as the main engine of structural transformation, and through which one leading sector is rendered 'obsolete' (macro-structurally incongruous) and replaced by a new one in a process of 'creative destruction'.

The upgrading effectiveness of each type of industrial organization is schematically illustrated in terms of how successfully Japan has performed vis-a-vis Europe and the United States (used as reference points) during the different decades since war's end, starting with the 1950s. In the early postwar period (the 1950s and 1960s), Japan was clearly way behind the West. In the 1970s, Japanese industry quickly succeeded in initiating consumer electronics as its leading growth industry (as best exemplified by the successful innovation of pocket-size transistor radios[3]). Thanks also largely to the oil crises of 1974 and 1979, Japanese-made small subcompact cars became popular because of fuel economy, providing Japan's automobile industry with a foothold in the western markets. And by the end of the 1980s, Japan on the whole had caught up with both Europe and the United States in overall industrial and technological levels. In fact, the phrase 'the Triad' that came into vogue in the 1980s mirrored Japan's newly acquired status as an equal economic power in the global economy.

Yet, following the burst of the asset bubble of 1987–90, Japan plunged into stagnation, mainly because of its political inability to solve the banking crisis. Japan today is incapacitated because it is unable to decisively force the banks to cut off their 'zombie' borrowers, especially in the 'pork-barrel' industries such as construction and distribution (Ozawa, 2001b). In the meantime, the United States quickly regained its leadership and forged ahead with the information and communications technology (ICT) revolution.

These outcomes of Japan's catch-up growth at the different stages have been brought about by the efficacy of industrial organization specific to each stage. In the immediate postwar period when economic disruption and chaos initially prevailed, a 'make-shift' structure of industrial organization (whatever way they were able to organize corporate activities) was improvised. And it sufficed for the Heckscher-Ohlin stage of labour-driven economic recovery and reconstruction. *Zaibatsu* was dissolved by the order of the Occupation authorities, and *keiretsu* formation was still inchoate. In order to earn precious foreign exchange, Japan exported whatever manufactures it was capable of producing with an abundance of relatively well trained, disciplined, and low-cost labour in the aftermath of wartime destruction and defeat. Japan's famous 'life-time employment' was still inchoate, and so was the 'main bank' system of corporate finance and governance.

The 1960s began to witness the birth and rapid growth of the six main bank-based groups (Mitsui, Mitsubishi, Sumitomo, Fuyo, Sanwa, and

DBK), a form of industrial organization that may be identified as '*keiretsu*, Mark I'. They were *horizontally* conglomerated and diversified in industrial activity under the so-called 'one-set' principle which compelled each *keiretsu* group to vie vigorously with each other in establishing an almost identical set of key industries, such as steel, heavy machinery, shipbuilding, petrochemicals, and trading (in the form of *sogo shosha* [general trading companies]) – all in an oligopolistic fashion. *Keiretsu*, Mark I proved effective for the non-differentiated Smithian stage of scale-driven heavy and chemical industrialization.

These groups were also financially governed by their respective main banks, which were in turn controlled by the Bank of Japan – that is, by the Ministry of Finance because of the lack of independence of Japan's central bank. But *keiretsu*, Mark I soon began to evolve into '*keiretsu*, Mark II', as assembly-based industries such as consumer electronics and automobiles emerged as the leading growth sector in the 1970s. They grew more *vertically* conglomerated through the supply chains of parts, components, and accessories. *Keiretsu*, Mark II was thus specific to the differentiated Smithian stage of assembly-based manufacturing.

As electronics became increasingly more sophisticated with rapid product/process innovations, however, systems integration emerged as a new form of industrial organization. Computers began to be applied to online order placement and procurement and 'just-in-time' delivery. But this new form of industrial organization, 'systems integration, Mark I', was carried out within the closed system of the *keiretsu* tradition – and was, therefore, accompanied by the negative effect of knowledge diversion (as discussed above).

In the past few years, however, the landscape of Japanese industry has begun to change dramatically. The *keiretsu* has started to break down in its original formation. First of all, the six main banks, which used to lead and jealously guard their respective *keiretsu* groups, have merged with each other into mixed-up entities. Sumitomo Bank (the flagship bank of the Sumitomo group) merged with Sakura Bank (the Mitsui group) to create Sumitomo Mitsui Banking Corp., and Fuji Bank (the Fuyo group) joined forces with Dai-Ichi Kangyo Bank (the DKB group), along with Industrial Bank of Japan and Yasuda Trust, to form Mizuho Holdings, the world's largest bank in assets.

Left in the lurch, group companies themselves began to engage in inter-*keiretsu* tie-ups. For example, Sumitomo Chemical merged with Mitsui Chemical. Strategic alliances have been forged between Kawasaki Steel (the DKB group) and NKK (the Fuyo group), and between two of Japan's largest *sogo-shosha*, Marubeni Corporation (the Fuyo group) and Itochu (the DKB group), in steel trading. Although the *keiretsu* firms are still not yet as uninhibited and as flexible as American firms, they are becoming more profit-conscious than loyalty-bound. Their networking is now pragmatically extending beyond and across their group affiliations.

Some may regard this new business restructuring merely as a regrouping of *keiretsu*, but it is more appropriate to view it as a move toward the new and more flexible form of 'systems integration' pioneered by the electronics industry where rapid technological progress is crucial for business survival and where the forces of globalization and competition are relentlessly compelling the producers to restructure through strategic alliances. They can no longer operate under the principle of comparative advantage (inclusiveness and coexistence) but must perform on the basis of competitive advantages. Yet, they have not yet quite graduated from closed-systems integration, 'systems integration, Mark I'. With deregulation and trade liberalization, Japanese industry is clearly in search of a new business model, 'systems integration, Mark II', which is closer to, if not identical with, American-style, market-driven, open-systems integration. The 'McLuhan' information-driven stage of growth requires a flexible and open business model in order to survive in ever-intensifying global competition in this age of the information and communications technological revolution (Ozawa, 2001a).

SUMMING UP

Japan's network capitalism has evolved, and is still evolving, taking different transitory shapes in industrial organization. Gerlach's description of *keiretsu* as alliance capitalism fits only one form of evolutionary manifestation of the Japanese principle of networking, a form that prevailed mostly during the Smithian (both non differentiated and differentiated) stages of scale- and assembly-driven industrialization (mid-1950s through 1970s), involving the 'metal-bashing' type of production of steel, basic chemicals, heavy machinery, and early-generation automobiles.

The Schumpeterian R&D-driven stage was initially accommodated by 'systems integration, Mark I', especially in electronics and other high-tech industries where technological progress is pronounced and the product cycle is increasingly shortened. Yet the advent of the ITC revolution and its accompanying 'McLuhan' stage calls for a more open and flexible organizational structure, 'systems integration, Mark II'. Japan is clearly in the throes of transition to this new phase. The principle of networking is, nevertheless, the governing doctrine of Japanese society in all walks of life, and the different business models have been reflective of the structural requirements of their respective corresponding stages of industrial transformation.

The notions of 'knowledge creation vs. knowledge diversion' and 'inclusiveness vs. exclusiveness' were introduced as the analytical frameworks within which to evaluate the benefits and costs of Japanese-style networking based on intra-group trust and cohesiveness.

NOTES

1. The phrase, 'visible hand', is adopted from Chandler (1977).
2. This section draws in part on Ozawa and Phillips (1994).
3. OECD (1970) recognized that small transistor radios were Japan's first significant innovation after WWII.

REFERENCES

Aoki, Masahiko (1988), *Information, Incentives, and Bargaining in the Japanese Economy*, Cambridge: Cambridge University Press.

Best, Michael H. (2000), 'Silicon Valley and the resurgence of route 128: Systems integration and regional innovation', in John Dunning (ed.), *Regions, Globalization, and the Knowledge-based Economy*, Oxford: Oxford University Press: 459–84.

Buckley, Peter J. (1988), 'Organisational forms and multinational companies', in S. Thompson and M. Wright (eds), *Internal Organization, Efficiency and Profit*, Oxford: Philip Allen.

Casson, Mark (1987), *The Firm and the Market*, Oxford: Blackwell.

Chandler, Alfred D. Jr (1977), *The Visible Hand: The Managerial Revolution in American Business*, Cambridge, MA: Harvard University Press.

Coase, Ronald (1937), 'The nature of the firm', *Economica*, 4: 386–405.

Dunning, John H. (1997a), 'Advent of alliance capitalism', in John Dunning and Khalil Hamdani (eds), *The New Globalism and Developing Countries*, New York: United Nations University Press: 1–11.

Dunning, John H. (1997b), *Alliance Capitalism and Global Business*, London: Routledge.

Gerlach, Michael L. (1992), *Alliance Capitalism: The Social Organization of Japanese Business*, Berkeley: University of California Press.

Imai, Ken-ichi (1992), 'Japan's corporate networks', in Shumpei Kumon and Henry Rosovsky (eds), *The Political Economy of Japan, Vol. 3 Cultural and Social Dynamics*, Stanford: Stanford University Press: 198–230.

Kay, Neil M. (1991), 'Multinational enterprise as strategic choice: some transaction cost perspectives', in Christos Pitelis and Roger Sugden (eds), *The Nature of the Transnational Firm*, London: Routledge: 137–54.

Kojima, Kiyoshi (2000), 'The "flying geese" model of Asian economic development: origin, theoretical extensions, and regional policy implications', *Journal of Asian Economics*, 11(4) (Winter): 375–401.

Kojima, Kiyoshi and Terutomo Ozawa (1985), 'Toward a theory of industrial restructuring and dynamic comparative advantage', *Hitotsubashi Journal of Economics*, 25(1): 1–20.

Kumon, Shumpei (1992), 'Japan as a network society', in Shumpei Kumon and Henry Rosovsky (eds), *The Political Economy of Japan, Vol. 3 Cultural and Social Dynamics*, Stanford: Stanford University Press: 109–41.
Letiche, J.M. (1960), 'Adam Smith and David Ricardo on economic growth', in Bert Hoselitz (ed.), *Theories of Economic Growth*, New York: Free Press: 65–89.
Marx, Karl (1867), *Capital, vol. 1, A Critical Analysis of Capitalist Production*, London: Swan Sonnenschein, Lowry & Co (reproduced by International Publishers, 1967).
OECD (1970), *Gaps in Technology: Analytical Report*, Paris: OECD.
Ozawa, Terutomo (1993), 'Foreign direct investment and structural transformation: Japan as a recycler of market and industry', *Business & the Contemporary World*, 5(2) (Spring): 129–50.
Ozawa, Terutomo (2001a), 'Japan in the WTO', in Alan Rugman and Gavin Boyd (eds), *The World Trade Organization in the New Global Economy*, Cheltenham: Edward Elgar: 191–215.
Ozawa, Terutomo (2001b), 'The "hidden" side of the "flying-geese" catch-up model: Japan's *dirigiste* institutional setup and a deepening financial morass', *Journal of Asian Economics*, 12: 471–91.
Ozawa, Terutomo and Ronnie J. Phillips (1994), 'Persistence of the Veblenian "Old Japan": organizational efficiency as a wellspring of competitiveness', *Rivista Internazionale di Scienze Economiche e Commerciali*, 41: 721–40.
Polayni Karl (1944), *The Great Transformation: The Political and Economic Origins of Our Time*, Boston: Beacon Press, 1957.
Prawer, Joshua, and Samuel N. Eisenstadt (1968), 'Feudalism', in *International Encyclopedia of the Social Sciences*, Vol. 5, New York: Crowell Collier and Macmillan.
Ricardo, David (1817), 'Principles of political economy and taxation', in J.R. McCulloch (ed.), *The Works of David Ricardo*, London: John Murray: 1–584.
Richardson, G.B. (1972), 'The organisation of industry', *Economic Journal*, **82**(327) (September): 883–96.
Schumpeter, Joseph A. (1934), *The Theory of Economic Development*, English translation by Redvers Opie, New York: Oxford University Press, 1961.
Smith, Adam (1776), *An Inquiry into the Nature and Causes of the Wealth of Nations*, London: Routledge, reproduced New York: E.P. Dutton (1908).
Stanfield Ron J. (1986), *The Economic Thought of Karl Polanyi*, London: Macmillan.
Veblen, Thorstein (1934), *Essays in Our Changing Order*, New York: Viking Press.
Viner, Jacob (1960), *The Customs Union Issues*, New York: Carnegie Endowment for International Peace.
Williamson, Oliver E. (1975), *Markets and Hierarchies: Analysis and Antitrust Implications*, New York: Free Press.
Williamson, Oliver E. (1985), *The Economic Institutions of Capitalism: Firms, Markets, Relational Contracting*, New York: Free Press.

12. Alliance capitalism, FDI and developing countries

Stephen Young and Neil Hood

The objective of this chapter is to assess the dimensions of and future prospects for alliance capitalism in developing countries. The subject is tackled through the lens of an alliance-based approach to foreign direct investment (FDI), mainly involving multinational enterprises (MNEs) and governments. It focuses on three main questions:

- What evidence exists of alliance capitalism in developing countries?
- What would be required of firms and governments to achieve or extend alliance capitalism in developing countries?
- What would be the benefits of promoting alliance capitalism in developing countries?

The definition of alliance capitalism used here follows Dunning (1997a) and Cohen and Boyd (2000) in requiring deep structural interdependence between all stakeholders; and the notion of Berglof and von Thadden (2000) that the stakeholder concept of corporate governance should be generalized to a model of multilateral negotiations. Within the narrower perspective of the present chapter, the analysis of alliance capitalism concerns collaborative relationships between firms, and governments and multilateral organizations. In a 1994 paper, Stopford had emphasized the growing interdependencies between MNEs and governments; and questioned whether MNEs should take a more active and positive role as diplomats and partners in relations with governments, which had traditionally focused upon bargaining.[1]

The interest in this chapter is in the less developed countries (LDCs); that is, countries other than the newly industrialized economies (NIEs) of East Asia and South America and the transition economies of Central and Eastern Europe. Some commentary on the latter is inevitable, however, because of the previous emphasis in research: it should be noted that Dunning and Hamdani (1997) and other authors have suggested that the impact of globalization and alliance capitalism is likely to be marginal in the LDCs. Many LDCs do not have the communitarian cultures and degrees of institutional development that have made possible the development of alliance capitalism in the NIEs (see Hobday, 1995, on the lessons of the East Asian experience).

Finally, the analysis focuses on international strategic alliances, principally in their equity joint venture form, which is still a major form of arrangement in developing countries. This is consistent with Dunning (1997a), Inkpen and Beamish (1997) and Inkpen (2001). Here equity joint ventures (JVs) are viewed as a hierarchical type of alliance with a high degree of interorganizational interaction, within a spectrum which extends to technical training and industry consortia as the lowest forms of commitment and interaction. In the LDCs, many of these equity JVs will still involve partnerships between MNEs and governments.

STRATEGIC ALLIANCES IN DEVELOPING COUNTRIES

The literature on strategic alliances, principally in their equity joint venture form, is extensive. A collection of significant contributions is contained in Beamish (1998), and a concise summary of the literature in Inkpen (2001). Much of the literature on JVs in developing countries *per se* stems from the work of Beamish and his colleagues at the University of Western Ontario.

Joint Venture Characteristics and Performance

In early work (Beamish, 1988) comparing joint venture characteristics in developed and developing countries, significant differences were identified in the reasons for joint venture creation – one partner's needs for the other partner's skills in developed country JVs; and government persuasion or legislation in developing country JVs. (For more recent work on the partner selection process see Saxton, 1997, and Hitt et al., 2000.) Other characteristics of joint ventures in developing countries included a smaller equity stake; a higher association with government partners; a higher instability rate; and greater managerial dissatisfaction with performance.

Analysing high-performing developing country joint ventures specifically, the emphasis was on long-term relations, with local partners providing management (general and functional), knowledge of local business and of the local economy, politics and customs (Beamish, 1988). By contrast in low-performing joint ventures, partners' contributions were regarded as primarily short term, concerning meeting government requirements and avoiding political intervention. Commitment emerged as a major factor in the successful management of JVs, and was reflected in the adaptation of products to local market needs; the increased employment of nationals; and regular visits and the supply of special skills where needed. Committed companies also favoured a sharing of decision-making and greater contributions from their partners.

Some more recent studies have continued to emphasize the problem areas in establishing and managing JVs in developing countries. For example, work by Miller et al. (1997) focused on the fragility of the ventures, and on the difficulties both in negotiating agreements and in subsequently holding the ventures together. In respect of *negotiations*, particularly important and difficult issues concerned the equity structure, and the conditions for technology transfer. Once JVs were *operational*, difficulties identified related to multinationality (export rights, tax issues, dividend and investment policies); ownership and control; or to disputes over product or technology issues; and cultural problems. The overall conclusions were that even committed partners could expect conflicts; that agreements needed to contain detailed provisions but also to be considered as 'living' documents; and that resolution of technology transfer difficulties needed goodwill and understanding.

Despite these findings, Hyder's (1999) small-scale investigation found important differences between developed and developing country joint ventures. In the latter, there was more complementarity of motives, less disagreement, the ownership level was less significant for control, and relationships were more informal. The review of 19 studies by Beamish and Delios (1997) indicates a moderate increase in the performance of international joint ventures in developing countries over time; and a higher level of performance for JVs in developing as compared with developed countries. In a similar vein, Tatoglu and Glaister (1998) found that while Turkish partner firms and western partner firms evaluated the performance of their international joint venture operations equally favourably, the Turkish partners were more satisfied with JV performance compared with host country competitors and home country firms.

Culture and Joint Venture Performance

Studies have shown that differences in the cultural backgrounds of the parents have generally been perceived as a threat to the survival of international joint ventures (for example, Harrigan, 1988; Shenkar and Zeira, 1992). Consistent with this view, Barkema et al. (1996, 1997) and Li and Guisinger (1991) found that the chances of survival of JVs are lower when the cultural distance between the home country of the expanding firm and that of the host country is large. Greater cultural distance increased the incidence of JVs (relative to wholly owned subsidiaries). Recent work by Barkema and Vermeulen (1997) in a study of Dutch MNEs indicated that uncertainty avoidance and long-term orientation were the main cultural problem areas. Interestingly, the effects of cultural distance had not decreased over the three decades to the mid-1990s. Li et al. (2001) investigated the influence of parent culture on JVs in China. They found that oriental collectivist culture was valuable for East Asian firms in terms of efficiency and rapid market entry; but such firms failed to achieve better performance than companies from individualistic cultures.[2]

Patterns of Strategic Alliances in Developing Countries

Vonortas and Safioleas (1997) analysed inter-firm alliances (defined to include mergers and acquisitions (M&As) in information technology (IT), in which one partner was from a developing country (i.e. a non-OECD country), for the period 1984–94. NIEs and transitional economies dominated alliance activity among developing countries, with telecommunications and computers as the most important sectors. The countries of the former Soviet Union registered more alliances than any other nation, followed by China and then Hong Kong and Korea. Telecommunications was the most important sector in a range of countries. For Hong Kong firms, telecommunications alliances represented a way to capitalize on their existing capabilities and diversify; while, elsewhere, the main role of such alliances was to upgrade their telecommunications infrastructure to widen access, improve service delivery and cost, and facilitate the attraction of FDI. A small number of companies from the NIEs dominated alliance activity: thus six Korean firms participated in 232 alliances – about two-thirds of all alliances involving developing country enterprises.

The Vonortas and Safioleas (1997) work indicated that the share of alliances involving at least one participant from a non-OECD country increased from 6 per cent in 1988 to nearly 13 per cent in 1994. By comparison, Narula and Sadowski (1998), in their investigation of strategic technology partnering, indicated a much smaller increase in the share of agreements in developing countries between the periods 1980–87 (5.5 per cent) and 1987–94 (6.9 per cent). But their definition excluded M&As, and their data base was biased towards new and emerging technologies. Their conclusion in terms of patterns *within* developing nations was, however, similar. Thus there was a dominance of Eastern European nations and the East Asian NIEs; and the percentage of alliances in Africa and the non-NIE countries of Asia and Latin America declined between the two periods. Differences between these two groups of countries were also evident in the nature of agreements, with equity modes still overwhelmingly dominant outside the NIEs. Explanations for the patterns in the LDCs were suggested to relate to low levels of economic development, a focus on low technology sectors, and indigenous companies that possess few competitive advantages.

Other Evidence[3]

An investigation of studies available at the country level indicates considerable variety in the nature of FDI and modes of market servicing in the LDCs. By and large the data tend to suggest conventional (hierarchical) relationships between MNEs and LDC partners, with privatization as an important influence on FDI inflows in the recent past. However, even in Africa, there are signals emerging and case-specific evidence which are indicative of changing attitudes, relationships and behaviour patterns. Examples include:

- The evolution of affiliates of developed country MNEs from a domestic market to a regional market orientation, with product specialization programmes among affiliates and the introduction of regional product mandates.
- The establishment of collaborative joint ventures between MNEs and indigenous enterprises to permit the latter to upgrade technologies and facilitate expansion domestically and internationally.
- The network-based regional expansion of indigenous MNEs. Illustrations include the involvement of Mauritian-based MNEs as, for example, participants in privatizations in host countries, and through linkages with the Mauritian diaspora. Similarly there are examples of regional expansions of Egyptian construction companies in power and other projects.
- Multiple nationality foreign investment projects in infrastructure (power generation, telecommunications, etc.), and the exploration and exploitation of natural resources in association with host governments.
- More generally, the wide variety of forms of foreign participation in infrastructure projects (performance contracts, management contracts, service concessions, BOT, lease) means that host governments and domestic enterprises are having to learn different ways of working with and relating to multinational enterprises.

Aside from these, admittedly limited, indicators of alliance activities, external institutions also are playing a significant role in supporting and encouraging collaboration. Thus the International Finance Corporation

(IFC) is an important player in the co-financing of major FDI projects. IFC involvement provides security to foreign investors, and encourages collaborative relations between foreign and indigenous partners and governments. Some companies play a similar role, an interesting illustration being the UK-based CDC Group: with a long history in Africa, this enterprise now operates as a foreign venture capital investor and plays a major facilitating function in a diverse range of projects – from agriculture and food to minerals, oil and gas, and financial services and ICT.

It is also true that some MNEs, because of sector-specific characteristics as well as company policies, are more closely aligned to an alliance capitalism model. Examples include Coca-Cola and Pepsi International through their extensive franchise networks; and hotel chains, where the Accor Group of France is prominent in encouraging collaboration with and active investment from the private sector in host countries.

Synthesis

The literature review suggests an improving picture with respect to JV performance in developing countries. Long-term relations and commitment were important for success, both being factors which would be indicative of an alliance-based approach (Lane and Beamish, 1990). With some notable exceptions, however, arrangements in LDCs were largely similar to the traditional JVs of earlier periods, with similar management challenges, posed *inter alia* by cultural differences. Even so, as the following section will show, liberalization has encouraged a more welcoming attitude to FDI which could be the beginnings of alliance capitalism. In that sense, at least, the ventures of the last 15 years are different to those of the 1960s and 1970s.

PUBLIC POLICY AND ALLIANCE CAPITALISM

National Government Approaches

A policy emphasis on open markets and trade and investment liberalization has been a dominant trend in the global economy in recent times. Although the process is far from complete in the LDCs in particular, many countries have abandoned their former state-led, inward-oriented development strategies.

FDI attraction and privatization

In the new environment, the attraction of FDI became in effect the principal mechanism by which countries attempted to capitalize on liberalization. FDI attraction was either direct or indirect, the latter linked to privatization, which became a widespread policy prescription in the 1980s and 1990s; and the process is continuing in Africa, for example, into the 2000s. Aside from differing timescales, the extent, objectives and methods of privatization have differed between countries, as has the importance of foreign investment (OECD, 1998). Objectives have included improving efficiency, encouraging private sector development, attracting FDI, raising revenue to reduce debt levels, and redistributing wealth. In Africa, the objective has been primarily the reform of state-owned enterprises (SOEs); and liquidation or closure has occurred commonly since obsolete facilities, poor quality, and low productivity have meant that the enterprises were not attractive to private domestic or foreign investors.[4]

The gains from privatization are assumed to derive principally from competition, lower prices, improved availability and quality of public services, and higher productivity. There is evidence of some of these benefits occurring, although it would not be difficult to show improvements compared with the pre-privatization situation. Overall, there have been positive impacts in respect of increased capital investments, and inflows of technology and managerial expertise; as well as additional revenue generation and deficit reduction. Moreover, the multiplier effects of FDI associated with privatization have been significant. FIAS (1997) estimated that $1 brought in through privatization attracted another $0.88 in additional FDI inflows. For infrastructure privatizations, the equivalent figures were $1 and $2.4.

Privatization has posed certain important issues, especially with respect to regulatory measures required for privatized monopolies (such as telecommunications and other services, or in basic industries such as steel or petrochemicals), consequent on increased fees and charges, and absorption of surplus labour. This suggests that pricing of products and services will need to be regulated, and programmes for retraining and employment of redundant labour instituted.

For many developing countries there are still huge challenges concerning privatization and investment in infrastructure. One study indicated that power cuts cost the Indian economy between 1 and 3.5 per cent of GDP (Sanghvi, 1991). The demands are also enormous, with the World Bank (1997) estimating that infrastructure development in East Asia would cost $1.5 trillion by 2004, with half of this in China alone. Foreign investors are being sought again to provide the necessary capital and technology, although other possible sources of finance exist, including bond issues, bank lending and equity flotations.

From the perspective of the investor, infrastructure projects involve high risks. These include potential future expropriation, and also commercial risk from high fixed or sunk costs, long investment timescales and possible price controls and other regulations (OECD, 1998). In addition infrastructure projects have been beset by problems, including delays in programme start-ups, contract cancellations and legal disputes (Seder, 2000).

Policy reform

Empirical evidence confirms the benefits from liberalized trade and investment, although there is continuing debate over the effects of growth and FDI on poverty reduction (OECD, 1999).[5] Nevertheless, the experiences of individual developing countries are quite diverse. The majority of LDCs have begun to make efforts in the direction of trade and investment liberalization (even if they have not always taken 'ownership' of development strategies and programmes). In some ways these efforts could be viewed as moves in the direction of alliance capitalism since they are indicative of greater cooperation and positive relationships with foreign investors. However, among the least developed countries certainly, there is disappointment and frustration that market reform and liberalization have not been reflected in substantially increased FDI inflows. A continued FDI liberalization momentum requires that there are identifiable gains from market reforms at country level within a reasonable timescale. Developing countries perceive that they have implemented the economic and market reforms required of them by the multilateral institutions and the developed world, accepting the high costs associated with these reforms in respect of rationalization of former state-owned enterprises. But they have still to see the compensating benefits in terms, for example, of substantially higher FDI inflows.

In truth, liberalization and privatization *per se* are inadequate, and need to be part of a holistic and coherent set of policies and reforms (OECD, 1999).[6] Included within these are policies to ensure macroeconomic stability; strong financial systems; sound public and corporate governance; and environmental management. Moreover, there needs to be support for both multilateralism and regionalism. The former is necessary to aid the continued development of the global economy, and to provide security for investors and a barrier against protectionist pressures. Support for regional integration is also critical given that many LDC markets are too small to attract domestic-oriented FDI.

A second level of required policy intervention concerns industrial policies. In most developing countries, there are major market failures which act as constraints on the improvement of competitiveness and the sustained development of the market economy (UNIDO, 1995). These involve areas of industrial strategy, including technological capabilities (adaptation, upgrading and innovation); human resource development; network or cluster support (UNIDO, 2000); entrepreneurship and small- and medium-sized enterprise development; and rural industrial development. Allied to these are the necessary institutional support facilities, including financial institutions; training facilities for local entrepreneurs, etc.; facilities for the development of quality standards; institutions for investment promotion and technology inflow, absorption and adaptation; and institutions for information and research. The importance of the institutional framework is confirmed in the work of Brunetti et al. (1997; see also Pain, 2001) who found that security of property rights, reliability of the judiciary, and the extent of corruption and political stability, were positive determinants of the level of FDI inflows in a study of 20 transition economies in the 1990s.

These problem areas are mostly known – or at least external advice from donors has highlighted the issues – but they are not really seen in either a holistic or a collaborative way. And developing country governments and bureaucrats are at once antagonistic (because of the effects on their power bases and corruption income), bemused and lacking in both resources and capabilities to be able to respond.[7]

Governance

In the context of alliance capitalism, problems of public and corporate governance loom large, with institutional reform as an essential constituent of a wider process of transformation (Cohen and Boyd, 2000; Menard, 2000). Such governance challenges result *inter alia* in corruption, which is endemic in many developing and transition economies (in respect of the latter, see EBRD, 1999). For example, Habib and Zurawicki (2001) confirmed a negative relationship between corruption and FDI flows in a wide-ranging country study; although the degree of international openness and the political stability of the host market moderates the influence of corruption. Perspectives on corruption in the literature focus, on the one hand, on corrupt bureaucrats operating within a system where public sector salaries are low; and, on the other, on corruption as a consequence of the political system and crony capitalism which leads to patronage and extortion (Charap and Harm, 2000). Others (Hellman and Kaufman, 2001) question whether corruption (termed 'state capture') is a symptom of weak institutions or of powerful politicians and bureaucrats who have an interest in maintaining these weak institutions. By the latter perspective, crony capitalism and the creation of monopolistic firms is a rational strategy for maximizing expected income (Tanzi, 1998). Furthermore, changing legislation alone may be insufficient when powerful business families can influence both the content of the legislation and its implementation; such families may be directly involved in politics.

China represents a particularly challenging case in the context of the reform of its state-owned enterprises (SOEs) and their participation in joint ventures with Japanese and western companies. Accepting that the reform experiments have been genuinely creative, Broadman (2001) highlights major problems including asset stripping, tax evasion, decapitalization, wage manipulation, privatization of assets but socialization of liabilities, and corruption. Corporate governance incentives are conflicting since the state is both ultimate owner and regulator. Effective corporate governance is difficult to exercise when the financial information available is neither timely, accurate nor useful. In addition, SOE governance is still hampered by barriers to entry for new firms and a lack of competition.

In the context of FDI in Africa, corruption emanates from both political structures and tribalism as well as dishonest bureaucrats, and the system is characterized by weak or non-existent institutions. Moreover, opposition to reform within the executive branch means that corruption is not simply financial in nature but is also reflected in delays and obstructiveness. In the case of FDI specifically, there is, in addition, opposition to MNEs as neo-colonialists (including concerns about FDI by specific ethnic groups such as Asians and white South Africans in East and Central Africa).

Emery and Spence (1999) assessed the obstacles to FDI that derive from persistent 'second-tier administrative barriers', which lead to duplicative, complex, and non-transparent procedures and lengthy delays in investment approvals. The barriers also hinder trade in both its export and import forms through the effects on competitiveness of high transaction costs. These 'red tape' barriers derive from outdated procedures, inappropriate policies, poor implementation and a lack of institutional capacity in government agencies.

Foreign investors have a crucial role to play in the process of improving corporate governance through the restructuring of the state-owned sector as part of privatization. And MNEs can play a part in acting as lobbyists, activists and advisers to government. A number of LDCs have now established investment steering committees (chaired by the head of state) to deal with transactional barriers; and private sector development committees designed to promote private sector development and entrepreneurship. In both cases foreign investors may be represented on the committees concerned.

From the developing country side, better regulation in respect of taxation; land planning and allocation; labour laws; business licensing and registration; and import–export procedures, as well as commercial dispute resolution, is essential. An important prerequisite for stronger corporate governance is also stronger regulation of monopolistic private sector utilities (often foreign-owned). Many LDCs have competition policies, at least in name, but implementation is weak. The necessary establishment of clear and independent regulatory authorities for privatized industries such as telecommunications is problematic for LDCs too. Having been exhorted to liberalize, the notion of regulation (and the fact that the market is not a free good) is not well understood. This is particularly the case when regulation is designed both to protect customers (e.g. monitoring price levels), and to provide incentives to private investors to undertake major capital expansions. In addition, the capacities and capabilities in government to handle complex regulatory issues are lacking.

Overall, governments in LDCs face major challenges in undertaking the next level of deep reforms necessary to maintain the momentum of private sector reform, as well as providing a business climate which is attractive to MNEs in a highly competitive global environment. As yet there are questions as to whether the understanding, the capability or the will exists to undertake these reforms. Along with the host countries themselves, both MNEs and multilateral organizations have a role to play in facilitating what is, in effect, alliance capitalism. Unemployment and poverty associated, for example, with privatization and civil service reform, are a major challenge for all stakeholders.[8]

The Multilateral Policy Challenge

The unprecedented rise in living standards in the period since the end of World War II, associated with the freeing of international trade and payments and more recently FDI (along with improvements in science and technology) is well documented. Policy liberalization at all levels (national, regional and multilateral) has played its part; but the multilateral institutions have been particularly significant in providing a global framework for the expansion of trade, investment and payments. The importance of the World Trade Organization (WTO) *per se* is shown in the large expansion of membership to incorporate most developing as well as other nations, and its emergence as a global rulemaker on trade and investment-related issues. Its ongoing agenda which includes, for example, services liberalization and Chinese (and probably Russian) membership provides some momentum for continued liberalization. However, the 1990s may yet turn out to have been the high point of multilateralism (Brewer and Young, 2000).

The challenge to the multilaterals

Debates concerning rising inequality within and between countries, the potential exclusion of the poorest nations and peoples from increasing worldwide prosperity, and environmental degradation have been brought to the forefront of public attention by the non-governmental organizations (NGOs). In addition, the failure of the Multilateral Agreement on Investment (MAI) in 1998 and of the Seattle Ministerial Conference of the WTO a year later, revealed deep fault lines in the multilateral system.

Systemic problems of multilateral institutional governance are widely acknowledged. One major issue relates to the so-called 'Washington Consensus' (Williamson, 1994) which was regarded as the received wisdom on the achievement of stabilization and growth and on dealing with structural issues. The negative outcomes, especially in terms of unemployment and poverty, were heavily criticized by host countries on the receiving end of such structural adjustment policies. In the latter half of the 1990s, however, a new agenda was introduced focusing strongly on the requirements for institution building and the quality of government, as well as on wider policy objectives including equitable income distribution, environmental protection and the provision of public goods (Kolodko, 2000, Chapter 5; Stiglitz, 2000). Even so, this new thinking is still to work through into the practice of reform, especially in Africa. Hence the claims that organizations such as the WTO have done little to tackle the problems of poverty and global inequality.

Other criticisms of the multilateral institutions include anti-democratic behaviour, lack of transparency, and failure to address regulatory coordination. In respect of the WTO, many of such difficulties are deemed to stem from its governance structure. Authors such as May (2001) and Ostry (2001) see the resolution of the 'democratic deficit' problem in weighted voting (related to the volume of trade and number and population size of members) and to the establishment of a smaller executive committee with rotating country membership; and to other innovations such as creating an outside body to review the work of the organization on a regular basis, and holding hearings on important issues, thereby opening up the WTO system to outsiders such as the NGOs.[9]

Developing country perspectives

The previous section highlighted the multifaceted challenges facing the LDCs, in particular, in their efforts at market reform, and the implementation of outward-oriented development strategies. Many of these are internal problems, concerned both with public and corporate governance, as well as with macroeconomic and industrial policies which are necessary to improve the business climate and competitiveness.

However, as the OECD (1999) has highlighted, there are, in addition, a number of external factors which help explain the disappointing performance of the least developed countries (LDCs). These include the high concentration of exports in commodities, which are characterized by a declining share of world trade; weak prices related to unstable or declining terms of trade; tariff and non-tariff barriers facing LDC exports in areas of potential advantage, such as agriculture and textiles; and weak supply capabilities. An underlying concern which is widely held in developing countries is that they face pressures to liberalize imports (under IMF-World Bank conditionality and WTO rules), while being unable to benefit from increased exports.[10]

Broadening the discussion and looking forward to future negotiations within the WTO, a wide range of potential agenda issues have been discussed by the developing countries. These include the following (UNCTAD, 2000a):[11]

- The need to improve market access for the agricultural exports of developing countries: the tariffs of many agriculture items of interest to developing countries are prohibitively high, while domestic subsidies in OECD countries have risen. Agricultural negotiations need to be linked to agricultural productivity and competitiveness, while meeting non-trade concerns such as poverty reduction.
- In textiles, only a few items which developing countries export have been removed from the quota list, which throws doubts on the achievement of a quota-free textile system by the target date of 2005.
- The provisions of the TRIMs (Trade-related Investment Measures) agreement (Article 5.3), recognizing the trade, development, and financial needs of developing countries, need to be reaffirmed. Specifically it is being argued that developing countries should be given another opportunity to notify existing TRIMs; the transition period should be extended; and a number of measures should be exempted from TRIMs because of their significance in achieving development goals. Specifically, the latter include currently banned measures such as local content and foreign exchange balancing rules.
- The need for a review of the transitional periods in a number of agreements, particularly TRIPS (Trade-related Intellectual Property Rights) and TRIMs, since many countries were facing difficulties in adapting their national laws and regulations and in improving their institutions to meet their WTO obligations.
- Reviews of the Agreement on Subsidies and Countervailing Measures (Annex VII), and of the TRIPS agreement (Articles 7, 8 and 66.2 relating to technology transfer) were necessary to take account of the development needs of developing countries. There was also a need to maintain and develop technical and capacity building assistance activities through the Integrated Framework.
- There should be confirmation that no provision of the TRIPS agreement prohibits members from formulating laws to provide access to medicines at affordable prices and to promote public health and nutrition.
- The implementation of developed countries' obligations had not

been effective, in respect, for example, of special and differential (S&D) measures for developing countries.

Developing countries have not been able to reach a consensus on the proposals to establish rules on the so-called 'new issues', namely, investment, competition policy, trade facilitation, transparency in government procurement, environment and e-commerce. However, they are opposed to the inclusion of social and environmental standards in the WTO, because of fears that they will be used as a form of protectionism.

In the present context, the investment-related issues are particularly important. The developing country viewpoint is that the inclusion of investment on the WTO agenda is not aimed at enhancing inward FDI flows, but rather is designed to further protect the rights of foreign investors (although it was clear from the earlier discussion that investors still need protection, for example, in respect of FDI in huge infrastructure projects). Among the issues of potential concern to developing nations are the freedom of foreign investors to enter countries without conditions; the granting of national treatment and MFN (most favoured nation) status; and the prohibition of performance requirements and of restrictions on movements of funds. They are also opposed to strict standards of protection for investors' rights, in relation to expropriation of property. Underlying some of these concerns is the fact that many LDCs that provide for free entry and operation of investment have benefited little in terms of higher investment inflows.[12]

After the failure of the WTO Ministerial Meeting in Seattle, USA, in 1999 to reach agreement on a new round of trade negotiations, the deadlock was finally broken in November 2001 at the Ministerial Meeting in Doha, Qatar. Events post-1999 have made it clear that the multilateral institutions, developed countries and multinationals have to address a wider agenda, which includes greater recognition of the external problems of the LDCs. In theory at least, it appeared from the Doha meeting that many of the concerns of developing countries were taken into consideration in setting the negotiating agenda (*Financial Times*, 2001). The reality will, however, be apparent by 1 January 2005, when negotiations are due to be completed.

A NEW APPROACH TO THE CHALLENGE OF ALLIANCE CAPITALISM: BARGAINING POWER VERSUS ALLIANCE COMPACT MODELS

Bargaining models were initially proposed for understanding relations between MNEs and developing country governments in the era of the

1960s and 1970s when confrontation characterized relationships. Despite this, recent work still focuses on bargaining models, even if the process is now seen as two-tier, multi-party bargaining (Ramamurti, 2001). Traditional bargaining models assumed that MNEs' entry into developing nations involved direct, case-by-case negotiations, with the actual entry terms depending on the respective power of the parties. The two-tier model, by contrast, incorporates the possibility of host developing countries bargaining bilaterally with industrialized countries and/or with multilateral institutions on FDI-related matters. According to Ramamurti (2001), the collective impact has been to strengthen the bargaining power of MNEs and weaken that of developing nations. Multinationals have acquired more scope for leverage and for independent location choices as they have expanded their international production systems; and, with international concentration trends, the more successful MNEs are further advantaged in dealing with developing country partners and host governments (see Hobday, 1995; Brewer and Young, 2000; a different perspective is in Brothers and Bamossy, 1997).

The continuing emphasis on 'bargaining' is contradictory to the notion of JVs as strategic alliances. Inkpen and Beamish (1997) have suggested that at the time of formation, partners need to cooperate to ensure access to critical inputs and resources. Over time, however, the bargaining power of one partner may be enhanced as dependencies alter. This is in line with Hamel's (1991) notion that alliances represent a 'race to learn', with the partner learning fastest dominating the relationship, and win–lose outcomes emerging. (For an alternative cooperative view of MNE–host government relations, see Luo, 2001.)

Madhok (2000, p. 295) provides a helpful perspective by characterizing alliance collaboration as a 'mixed-motive game' involving both collaboration (for creation of the pie) and competition (for distribution of the pie). It is argued that: 'Some conflict is probably healthy since it leads to commitment of the partners. Successful resolution of differences not only further strengthens the relationship but . . . brings diverse capabilities together constructively.' This recognizes that even if fundamentally cooperative, relations between partners may involve elements of competition or bargaining.

The evidence of this chapter is that businesses and multilateral institutions need dialogue with developing countries and the vociferous and powerful global civil society. Indeed the continuance of a liberal trading and investment system depends on constructive alliances involving diverse groups and interests in all parts of the world. From the multinational and multilateral side, a number of initiatives have been instituted, including the following:

Multilateral level

- UN-sponsored *Global Compact*. Signed in July 2000 by 50 of the world's largest MNEs, this commits the companies to adhere to nine principles in the areas of human rights, labour and the environment.
- The Organisation for Economic Co-operation and Development's (OECD), *Guidelines for Multinational Enterprises* were first published in 1976 and have been regularly updated since then. The latest set of rules were agreed in June 2000, with strengthened sections on the environment, labour relations and business policies, and attempt to address more effectively the issue of implementation. Like the UN Global Compact, the Guidelines are non-binding and represent recommendations on responsible business conduct addressed by OECD governments to MNEs. A full review of measures addressing the 'social responsibility' of multinationals in international investment agreements is contained in UNCTAD (2001c).

Corporate level

- Corporate codes of conduct. There is evidence to indicate that the majority of large MNEs now have their own codes of business conduct (see, for example, *Financial Times*, 2000).[13] In respect of coverage, emphasis is on three issues; namely, fair business practices, environmental stewardship and fair employment.

Responses to these initiatives have not been encouraging. The UN and OECD proposals have been criticized by the NGOs because of their non-binding nature. In a survey by Kolk et al. (1999), relating to corporate codes, furthermore, it was shown that almost one-third of firms did not monitor compliance, while a further 58 per cent undertook the monitoring themselves. The NGOs have been equally sceptical of corporate codes, and are still seeking binding mechanisms to enforce corporate social responsibility; this is despite recent programmes to promote independent verification of codes of conduct (Brewer and Young, 2000, p. 284). The OECD Guidelines, moreover, have been discredited following the demise of the MAI within which they were to be incorporated.

In any event, these initiatives do not promote the reciprocity among players which alliance capitalism requires. There are a range of areas where MNEs and host governments do interact constructively. Examples include joint programmes to develop supplier linkages (see recent proposals in UNCTAD, 2001a);[14] sectoral training initiatives involving a number of MNEs and the host government; and MNE participation in private sector interest and advocacy groups. Many other illustrations could be presented, such as after-care programmes, where host governments may on occasions assist MNE affiliates in taking a case to the parent company for additional investment, new product mandates, etc. Similarly, MNE affiliates will often assist the Investment Promotion Agency when potential investors are visiting the country. However, these are not systematic or integrated.

As an alternative to the 'bargaining power' model, the 'alliance compact' model is presented in Figure 12.1. Its overall objective is to promote an alliance approach (involving MNEs and other stakeholders) to the development of a liberalized market economy and improvements in the business environment for private investors (foreign and indigenous); and to assist in poverty alleviation. It is designed to promote collaboration and mutual understanding and thereby secure win–win outcomes.

Focusing on MNEs *per se*, there has, of course, to be a reason for corporate involvement in the alliance compact. Since many MNEs now operate codes of conduct (albeit with limited or only internal monitoring), the alliance compact could be regarded as a mechanism for implementation, although the issue coverage may be different. In a general sense, the encouragement of the market economy and of liberalized trade and investment is both directly and indirectly beneficial to multinationals. Directly, improvements in the functioning of markets assist MNEs as, for instance, importers or exporters; similarly better public governance should reduce risks associated with corruption, administrative barriers, etc. Longer term, there will be gains in respect of higher economic growth and larger markets. In addition there should be benefits in respect of poverty reduction, within which extremism and associated violence can breed. This big picture perspective needs top executive commitment and support, since affiliate managers are, inevitably, bottom-line driven.

Securing MNE cooperation is undoubtedly the critical issue. Culpepper (2000) provides a helpful analysis of how governments can help private actors overcome public goods problems in the context of the labour market in France. The key challenge is how to get firms to cooperate despite the temptation to free-ride. Emphasis is placed on the requirement for an incremental approach to allow actors to build confidence in the cooperative behaviour of others. In this way, the company gradually gains information which permits it to improve its estimate of the returns from cooperation. Some association of MNEs would be required to facilitate implementation and perhaps to establish sanctioning mechanisms.

What would such a compact comprise? What is envisaged is a non-binding, semi-formal agreement between parties, updated annually. The MNE affiliate–host agreement would be prepared on an individual

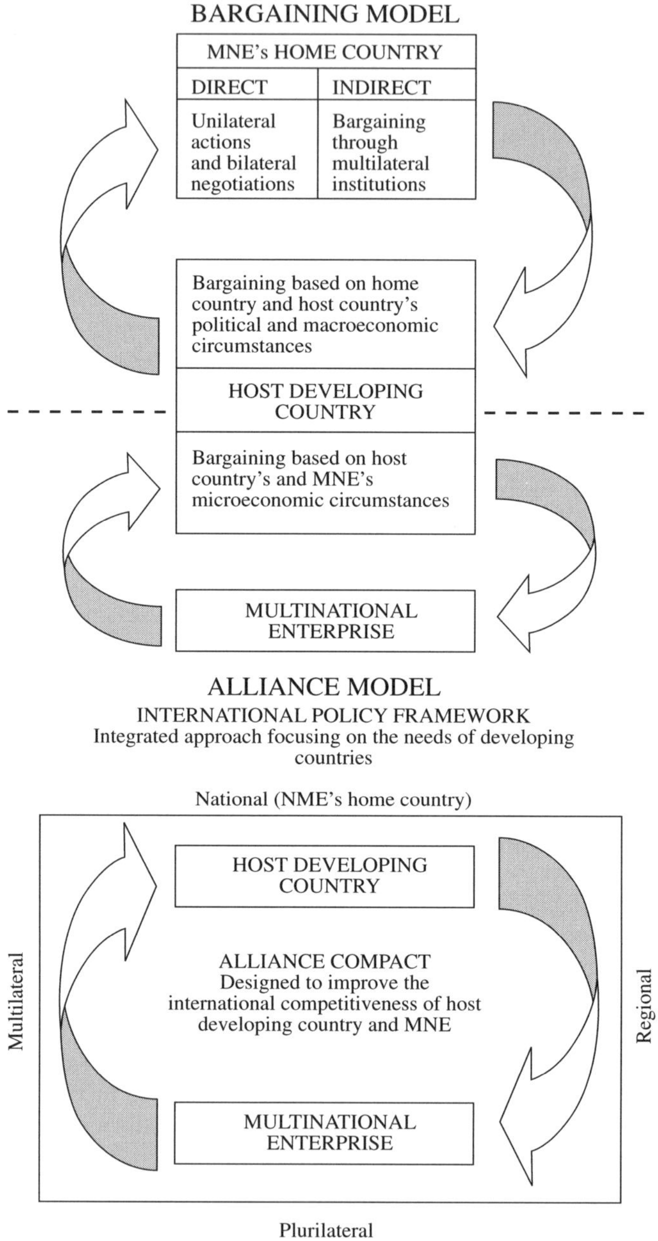

Figure 12.1 Alternative perspectives on MNE activities in host developing countries

company basis as an evolving partnership. At least in the first instance, this could only be operated with a group of the largest MNEs. The potential MNE contributions (without the direct business activities of the company) are highlighted in Table 12.1, distinguishing between areas where MNE managers may be able to offer comment or advice or direct participation. Large MNEs, experienced in operating in developing countries, are already involved in a number of these activities on an informal basis. The advantage of the semi-formal arrangement proposed is that the contributions would be recorded. In partnership discussions with host governments, agreement would be reached on the nature and extent of MNE participation within the policy areas listed; but the emphasis should be on focus and action-orientation.

Table 12.1 Potential issues for inclusion in alliance compact and MNE affiliate involvement

Policy area	MNE affiliates in host country
Macroeconomic policy	
Monetary, fiscal, exchange rates, demand	✔ (C)
Regionalization and globalization	✔ (A)
Macro-organization policy	
Market reform and privatization	✔ (C)
Trade and FDI (liberalization and removal of barriers)	✔ (A)
Transport and communications (infrastructure improvements)	✔ (A)
Competition and regulation (privatized monopolies)	✔ (C)
Education and training (school, vocational, university, firm & sector)	✔ (P)
Environmental management	✔ (C/A)
Regional policy	✔ (C)
Microeconomic policies and measures	
Investment promotion and after-care (including support for Investment Promotion Agency)	✔ (A/P)
Trade promotion and facilitation	✔ (A)
Entrepreneurship and SME development	✔ (A/P)
Innovation and technological development	✔ (A/P)
Supplier linkages and clusters	✔ (P)
Regulatory reform (removal of administrative barriers; institutional reform)	✔ (A)
Stakeholder participation (internal marketing, e.g. promoting benefits of FDI and of privatization; private sector advocacy)	✔ (A)

Note: C = comment; A = advice; P = participation.

The host nation side of the compact needs to be viewed within the framework of government goals for the particular year. For the compact with MNEs, emphasis will clearly be on macro-organizational and microeconomic issues, which pertain to FDI either directly (e.g. removal of trade barriers) or indirectly (e.g. market reforms). Depending on institutional structures, the most appropriate organization to handle coordination from the government side would probably be the planning authority in association with the investment promotion agency. Most of the commitments from the government side would be common to all compacts with MNEs, although there may be specific elements e.g. supplier initiatives (where the link with after-care programmes has to be clarified).

With respect to the compact with the multilateral and other donor institutions, coordination of initiatives and programmes – currently a fragmented patchwork at best in most host countries – is absolutely crucial. Similarly, the hierarchical donor–recipient nature of most aid programmes has to be replaced by collaborative relationships with government; this, in turn, requires a planning framework for prioritizing and directing donor resource allocations. Underlying everything, there has to be an effort by the multilateral institutions, in particular, to reach broad agreement on their own philosophy and goals, without which efforts at coordination are pointless. Finally, actions have to be taken to ensure that excessive demands are not placed on already over-stretched government bureaucracies.

CONCLUSIONS: A NEW BEGINNING

The purpose of this chapter has been to contribute to the debate on alliance capitalism in developing nations, with particular reference to the role of multinational enterprises. Even before the terrorist outrages of September 2001, the multilateral trade and investment system was facing major challenges, highlighting the urgent need for debate on cooperation across frontiers and among stakeholders, with particular reference to the needs of poor countries (Edwards, 1999). Since September 2001, there have been major negative effects on the drivers of globalization through tighter border controls; intensified surveillance of electronic communications; increased security measures at airports and in aircraft; and a slowdown in both business and tourism traffic internationally. Generally the costs and complexity for the international movement of people, goods, services and capital have increased, which at the very least represents a tax on international business. However, the costs of non-cooperation among peoples and societies have also risen sharply since late 2001. Tackling these will be the real benefit from promoting alliance capitalism in LDCs and other developing economies.

NOTES

Sincere thanks are due to Taffere Tesfachew for his assistance in a personal capacity during the research phase of this chapter, and to the editors for their helpful comments on the draft chapter.

1. Stopford also cites Julius (1993, p. 7) who has argued for long-term commitment by both sides:

   > Companies must commit . . . to develop distant markets. Governments must commit to continuing the politically difficult process of economic liberalisation . . . If such commitments can be made and kept, then together we can reap the growth potential from building an increasingly integrated world community.

2. *Joint ventures in China*. A significant body of literature has emerged on the subject of JVS in China. Issues studied include the choice of mode and of ownership stake (Pan, 1996; Pan and Tse, 2000); joint venture performance (Luo et al., 2001); multiple foreign partner factors (Pan and Tse, 1996); and future prospects (Child and Tse, 2001; Pan and Li, 1998).
3. This section draws on a number of the *Investment Policy Reviews* undertaken by UNCTAD, including those in which the author has been involved (see UNCTAD, 1999, 2000b, c, 2001b).
4. Successful privatization thus requires prior investment in rehabilitation or modernization, sale at nominal prices, and other policy measures. See Megyery and Sader (1997), and Haveylyshyn and McGettigan (1999).
5. Summarizing the evidence, the OECD (1999) concludes that open economies have grown significantly faster than closed economies over sustained periods of time; growth has also been associated with poverty reduction; the income levels of 'open' developing countries have been converging towards those of developed countries; there has been a positive association between sustained liberalization and improvements in core labour standards; and open economies have been able to take much greater advantage of skilled workforces than closed economies (given the association between outward-oriented policies and high literacy rates).
6. According to the OECD (1999), policy challenges identified as being necessary for developing countries to benefit from open trade and development are as follows:

   - Macroeconomic stability. Stable and sustainable macroeconomic policy is a precondition for taking advantage of the opportunities by globalization, as well as for successful structural reform.
   - Governance. Quality of governance and the level of trust among networks of economic actors are key. Main elements of governance are (i) an institutional and legal framework that supports the emergence of an enterprise-based economy and an efficient public sector; (ii) rising levels of participation in economic and political life as a basis for broadly based growth, social cohesion, and effective democratic institutions; (iii) development of a competitive environment that enhances the efficient functioning of markets; (iv) a good corporate governance framework providing for transparency of corporate structures and operations and the accountability of management; and (v) action to fight corruption and organized crime. There has been a general recognition that real economic benefits flow from improving the institutional and policy environment.
   - Financial and corporate sector strengthening. (i) This requires modernizing and strengthening financial systems and upgrading regulatory and supervisory frameworks to encourage rigorous risk assessment and market discipline through increased disclosure and transparency; and ensuring that regulators have the resources and support to do their job effectively; (ii) it also requires reforming systems of corporate governance, competition policy and taxation, and countering bribery.

- Human resource development.
- Managing adjustment. A system of social protection is a central ingredient of public action.

7. There are many other problems in the LDCs, specifically, for example, political instability; low levels of education and health; and poor infrastructure (including commercial and transport infrastructure capable of linking with global markets) – export competitiveness is undermined by high transport costs in regulated shipping and airline industries as well as, of course, by corruption.
8. A valuable overview of the challenges facing Africa is contained in the December 2001 issue of *Finance and Development* on the theme of 'Globalization and Africa' (see IMF, 2001).
9. The multilateral organizations are now trying direct dialogue with the non-governmental organizations. For an illustration relating to the WTO, see *Finance and Development*, March 2001, including Larsen (2001).
10. According to IMF (1999) estimates, although the developing countries have been liberalizing their trade and investment policies, their trade policies remain more restrictive than the rest of the world.
11. See also Khor (2001); and UNECA & OAU (2001).
12. For some authors (Roffe and Tesfachew, 2001, p. 402), there is still a vision of completing 'the *unfinished agenda* of the 1970s', although the mechanisms for doing this are quite different to those envisaged three decades ago.
13. Corporate codes are only one indication of company attempts to engage with the NGOs and developing countries. There is, for example, an extensive literature on corporate citizenship. See the special issue of *Business and Society Review* (2000) on the subject, including a paper by Mirvis (2000) on 'Transformation at Shell: 'Commerce and Citizenship'. The Royal Dutch/Shell group, of course, was a major target of protesters in its operations in different parts of the world in the late 1990s.
14. UNCTAD (2001a) suggest measures that may be taken by both MNEs and host governments to create and deepen linkages. Although a collaborative approach was not proposed *per se*, measures suggested for foreign affiliates concerned finding new local suppliers; transferring technology; providing training; sharing information; and providing financial support. For governments, proposals related to information and matchmaking; technology upgrading; training; and finance. Ways could be devised of developing an alliance approach model for promoting linkages by bringing the two sides together.

REFERENCES

Barkema, H.G., Bell, J.H.J. and Pennings, J.M. (1996), 'Foreign entry, cultural barriers and learning', *Strategic Management Journal*, **17**, 151–66.

Barkema, H.G., Shenkar, O., Vermeulen, F., and Bell, J.H.J (1997), 'Working abroad, working with others: how firms learn to operate international joint ventures', *Academy of Management Journal*, **40**, 426–42.

Barkema, H.G. and Vermeulen, F. (1997), 'What differences in the cultural backgrounds of partners are detrimental for international joint ventures?', *Journal of International Business Studies*, **28**(4), 845–64.

Beamish, P.W. (1988), *Multinational Joint Ventures in Developing Countries*, London and New York: Routledge.

Beamish, P.W. (ed.) (1998), *Strategic Alliances*, Cheltenham, UK and Northampton, MA: Edward Elgar.

Beamish, P.W. and Delios, A. (1997), 'Incidence and Propensity of Alliance

Formation', in P.W. Beamish and J.P. Killing (eds), *Cooperative Strategies: Asian Pacific Perspectives*, San Francisco: The New Lexington Press, 91–114.

Berglof, E. and von Thadden, E.-L. (2000), 'The Changing Corporate Governance Paradigm: Implications for Developing and Transition Economies', in S.S. Cohen and G. Boyd (eds), *Corporate Governance and Globalization*, Cheltenham, UK and Northampton, MA: Edward Elgar, 275–306.

Brewer, T.L. and Young, S. (2000), *The Multilateral Investment System and Multinational Enterprises*, Oxford: Oxford University Press.

Broadman, H.G. (2001), 'The business(es) of the Chinese state', *The World Economy*, **24**(7), 849–75.

Brothers, K.D. and Bamossy, G.J. (1997), The role of key stakeholders in international joint venture negotiations: case studies from Eastern Europe', *Journal of International Business Studies*, **27**(2), 285–308.

Brunetti, A., Kisunko, G. and Weber, B. (1997), 'Institutions in Transition: Reliability of Rules and Economic Performance in Former Socialist Countries', *World Bank Policy Research Working Paper No. 1809*, Washington, DC: The World Bank.

Charap, J. and Harm, C. (2000), 'Institutionalized Corruption and the Kleptocratic State', in C. Menard (ed.), *Institutions, Contracts and Organizations*, Cheltenham, UK and Northampton, MA: Edward Elgar, 188–208.

Child, J. and Tse, D.T. (2001), 'China's transition and its implications for international business', *Journal of International Business Studies*, **32**(1), 5–21.

Cohen, S.S. and Boyd, G. (eds) (2000), *Corporate Governance and Globalization*, Cheltenham, UK and Northampton, MA: Edward Elgar.

Culpepper, P.D. (2000), 'Can the state create co-operation?: Problems of reforming the labour supply in France', *Journal of Public Policy*, **20**(3), 223–45.

Dunning, J.H. (1997a), *Alliance Capitalism and Global Business*, London: Routledge.

Dunning, J.H. and Hamdani, K.A. (eds) (1997), *The New Globalism and Developing Countries*, Tokyo: United Nations University Press, 125–54.

Edwards, M. (1999), *Future Positive*, London: Earthscan Publishers.

Emery, J.J. and Spence, M.T. (1999), *Administrative Barriers to Investment in Africa: The Red Tape Analysis*, Washington, DC: Foreign Investment Advisory Service, World Bank, June.

European Bank for Reconstruction and Development (EBRD) (1999), *Transition Report 1999*, London: EBRD.

Financial Times (2000), 'Mastering Management', Part 7, London: *Financial Times*, 13 November.

Financial Times (2001), 'All Night Haggling Ends in Agreement', London: *Financial Times*, 15 November.

Foreign Investment Advisory Service (FIAS) (1997), *Foreign Direct Investment: Lessons of Experience*, Washington, DC: World Bank.

Habib, M. and Zurawicki, L. (2001), 'Country-level investments and the effect of corruption – some empirical evidence', *International Business Review*, **10**(6), 687–700.

Hamel, G. (1991), 'Competition for competence and inter-partner learning within international strategic alliances', *Strategic Management Journal*, **12**, 83–104.

Harrigan, K.R. (1988), 'Strategic Alliances and Partner Asymmetries', in F.J. Contractor and P. Lorange (eds), *Cooperative Strategies in International Business*, Lexington, MA: Lexington Books.

Haveylyshyn, O. and McGettigan, D. (1999), *Privatization in Transition Countries: A Sampling of the Literature*, IMF Working Paper WP/99/6, Washington DC: International Monetary Fund.

Hellman, J. and Kaufman, D. (2001), 'Confronting the challenge of state capture in transition economies', *Finance & Development*, **38**(3), 31–5.

Hitt, M.A., Dacin, M.T., Levitas, E., Arregle, J.-L. and Borza, A. (2000), 'Partner selection in emerging and developed market contexts: resource-based and organizational learning perspectives', *Academy of Management Journal*, **43**(3), 449–83.

Hobday, M. (1995), *Innovation in East Asia*, Cheltenham: Edward Elgar.

Hyder, A.S. (1999), 'Differences between developed and developing country joint ventures – a reality or a myth?', *International Business Review*, **8**, 441–61.

International Monetary Fund (IMF) (1999), *Integrating the Least Developed Countries Into the International Trading System*, presentation to the WTO High Level Symposium on Trade and Development, Washington, DC.

International Monetary Fund (IMF) (2001), 'Globalization and Africa', *Finance and Development*, **38**(4).

Inkpen, A.C. (2001), 'Strategic Alliances', in A.M. Rugman and T.L. Brewer (eds), *The Oxford Handbook of International Business*, Oxford: Oxford University Press, 402-27.

Inkpen, A.C. and Beamish, P.W. (1997), 'Knowledge, bargaining power, and the instability of international joint ventures', *Academy of Management Review*, **22**(1), 177–202.

Julius, DeAnne (1993), 'Liberalisation, Foreign Investment and Economic Growth', *Shell Selected Paper*, mimeo, March.

Khor, M. (2001), *Present Problems and Future Shape of the WTO and the Multilateral Trading System*, New York: Office of the Chairman of the Group of 77.

Kolk, A., Van Tulder, R. and Welters, C. (1999), 'International codes of conduct and corporate social responsibility: can transnational corporations regulate themselves?', *Transnational Corporations*, **8**(1), 143–80.

Kolodko, G.W. (2000), *From Shock to Therapy. The Political Economy of Postsocialist Transformation*, Oxford: Oxford University Press.

Lane, H.W. and Beamish, P.W. (1990), 'Cross-cultural cooperative behaviour in joint ventures in LDCs', *Management International Review*, **30**(Special Issue), 87–102.

Larsen, F. (2001), 'The IMF's dialogue with nongovernmental organizations', *Finance and Development* **38**(1), 54–6.

Li, J. and Guisinger, S.E. (1991), 'Comparative business failures of foreign-controlled firms in the United States', *Journal of International Business Studies*, **22**(2), 209–24.

Li, J., Lam, K. and Qian, G. (2001), 'Does culture affect behaviour and performance of firms? The case of joint ventures in China', *Journal of International Business Studies*, **32**(1), 41–58.

Luo, Y. (2001), 'Toward a cooperative view of MNC–host government relations: building blocks and performance implications', *Journal of International Business Studies*, **32**(3), 401–19.

Luo, Y., Shenkar, O. and Nyaw, M.-K. (2001), 'A dual parent perspective on control and performance in international joint ventures: lessons from a developing country', *Journal of International Business Studies*, **32**(1), 115–31.

Madhok, A. (2000), 'Inter-firm Collaboration: Contractual and Capabilities-based Perspectives', in N. Foss and V. Mahnke (eds), *Competence, Governance and Entrepreneurship*, Oxford: Oxford University Press, 276–303.
May, B. (2001), 'Globalisation, Democracy and Trade Policy', in K.G. Deutsch and B. Speyer (eds), *The World Trade Organization Millennium Round*, London: Routledge, 72–82.
Megyery, K. and Sader, F. (1997), *Facilitating Foreign Participation in Privatization*, FIAS Occasional Paper 8, Washington, DC: Foreign Investment Advisory Service, World Bank, January.
Menard, C. (2000), *Institutions, Contracts and Organizations*, Cheltenham, UK and Northampton, MA: Edward Elgar.
Miller, R., Glen, J., Jaspersen, F. and Karmokolias, Y. (1997), 'International joint ventures in developing countries', *Finance and Development*, March, 26–30.
Mirvis, P.H. (2000), 'Transformation at Shell: commerce and corporate citizenship', *Business and Society Review*, **105**(1), 63–84.
Narula, R. and Sadowski, B.M. (1998), 'Technological catch-up and strategic technology partnering in developing countries', *International Journal of Technology Management*, Summer.
Organisation for Economic Cooperation and Development (OECD) (1998), *Foreign Direct Investment and Economic Development: Lessons from Six Emerging Economies*, Paris: OECD.
Organisation for Economic Cooperation and Development (OECD) (1999), *Reaping The Full Benefits of Open Markets*, Paris: OECD.
Ostry, S. (2001), 'The WTO and International Governance', in K.G. Deutsch and G. Speyer (eds), *The World Trade Organization Millennium Round*, London: Routledge, 285–94.
Pain, N. (2001), 'Openness, Growth and Development: Trade and Investment Issues for Developing Economies', in A.M. Rugman and G. Boyd (eds), *The World Trade Organization in the New Global Economy*, Cheltenham: Edward Elgar, 216–56.
Pan, Y. (1996), 'Influences on foreign equity ownership level in joint ventures in China', *Journal of International Business Studies*, **27**(1), 1–26.
Pan, Y. and Li, X. (1998), 'Alliance of foreign firms in equity joint ventures in China', *International Business Review*, **7**, 329–50.
Pan, Y. and Tse, D.K. (1996), 'Cooperative strategies between foreign firms in a foreign country', *Journal of International Business Studies*, Special Issue, 929–46.
Pan, Y. and Tse, D.K. (2000), 'The hierarchical model of market entry modes', *Journal of International Business Studies*, **31**(4), 535–54.
Ramamurti, R. (2001), 'The obsolescing "bargaining model"? MNC–Host Developing Country Relations Revisited', *Journal of International Business Studies*, **32**(1), 23–39.
Roffe, P. and Tesfachew, T. (2001), 'The unfinished agenda', in S.J. Patel, R. Roffe and A. Yusuf (eds), *International Technology Transfer*, London: Kluwer Law International, 381–404.
Sader, F. (2000), *Attracting Foreign Direct Investment into Infrastructure: Why Is It So Difficult?*, FIAS Occasional Paper 12, Washington, DC: Foreign Investment Advisory Service, World Bank, January.
Sanghvi, A. (1991), 'Power sharing in developing countries', *Energy Policy*, June.
Saxton, T. (1997), 'The effects of partner and the relationship characteristics on alliance outcomes', *Academy of Management Journal*, **40**, 443–61.

Shenkar, O. and Zeira, Y. (1992), 'Role conflict and role ambiguity of chief executive officers in international joint ventures', *Journal of International Business Studies*, **23**(1), 55–75.

Stiglitz, J.E. (2000), 'Reflections on the Theory and Practice of Reform', in A.O. Krueger (ed.), *Economic Policy Reform. The Second Stage*, Chicago: The University of Chicago Press, 551–84.

Stopford, J.M. (1994), 'The growing interdependence between transnational corporations and governments', *Transnational Corporations*, **3**(10), 53–76.

Tanzi, V. (1998), *Corruption Around the World: Causes, Consequences, Scope and Cure*, IMF Working Paper WP/98/63, Washington, DC: International Monetary Fund.

Tatoglu, E. and Glaister, K.W. (1998), 'Performance of international joint ventures in Turkey: perspectives of Western firms and Turkish firms', *International Business Review*, **7**, 635–56.

UNCTAD (1999), *Investment Policy Review Egypt*, New York and Geneva: UN.

UNCTAD (2000a), *Positive Agenda and Future Trade Negotiations*, New York and Geneva: UN.

UNCTAD (2000b), *Investment Policy Review Uganda*, New York and Geneva: UN.

UNCTAD (2000c), *Investment Policy Review Peru*, New York and Geneva: UN.

UNCTAD (2001a), *World Investment Report 2001. Promoting Linkages*, New York and Geneva: UN.

UNCTAD (2001b), *Investment Policy Review Mauritius*, New York and Geneva: UN.

UNCTAD (2001c), *Social Responsibility*, New York and Geneva: UN.

United Nations Economic Commission for Africa and Organization for African Unity (UNECA & OAU) (2001), *Conclusions and Recommendations*, High-Level Brainstorming Meeting for African Trade Negotiators Preparatory to the Fourth WTO Ministerial Conference, Addis Ababa: UN Conference Centre.

UNIDO (1995), *Industrial Policy Reforms: The Changing Role of Governments and Private Sector Development*, Global Forum for Industry, New Delhi, 16–18 October.

UNIDO (2000), *Promoting Enterprise through Networked Regional Development*, Vienna, January.

Vonortas, N.S. and Safioleas, S.P. (1997), 'Strategic Alliances in Information Technology and Developing Country Firms', *PSD Occasional Paper No. 29*, Washington DC: Private Sector Development Department, The World Bank, February.

Williamson, J (ed.) (1994), *The Political Economy of Policy Reform*, Washington, DC: Institute for International Economics.

World Bank (1997), *Global Economic Prospects and Developing Countries*, Washington, DC: The World Bank.

13. Alliance capitalism and collective management

Gavin Boyd

As deepening integration continues in the world economy, with increases in foreign direct investment, and trade in goods and services, structural interdependencies between industrialized and industrializing states become more complex, and set more and more demanding requirements for wide ranging cooperation between governments, and between the firms whose international operations are linking production and marketing processes across borders. At the same time imperatives for collaboration between governments and firms become stronger. Many enterprises, however, manage their activities more and more independently as they extend their international operations in competition for world market shares, and this competition intensifies despite the evolution of forms of strategic cooperation. Major overall effects include continuities in global concentration trends.

The structural linking and market linking can be viewed with expectations of efficiencies, driven by competition, that enhance the productivity of successful enterprises, and that may enhance the structural competitiveness of individual countries. Domestically, competitive performance may be considered to require what has been perversely called a 'natural' level of unemployment, for inflation control and advances in productivity: in this perspective there are no concerns with social justice. Meanwhile, because of the efficiencies attributed to competition, gains from international commerce by one state may be considered to be losses for its trading partners.[1]

The maintenance of an appropriate level of unemployment, however, has been viewed as a government function in a relatively closed economy, to be performed through monetary management: it has not been regarded as a market function, and as a supposed government responsibility it presumably cannot be discharged without some mechanism that can be dominated by business interests. Discussion of this topic, however, now has to take into account the weakening of monetary policy that has resulted from the internationalization of financial markets. It has also been necessary to recognize that inflation can be held down through openness to low cost imports from developing countries, but also that inflation can be driven up by international firms that price to market while gaining prominence in global concentration trends.[2] Further, it has become important to understand that productivity in given sectors can decline as production processes are moved to foreign areas offering superior location advantages, and that, while unemployment will increase with the deindustrialization, inflation may also increase with inflows of portfolio investment attracted by speculative stock increases. Finally, in all the discussions of economic policy issues it has became imperative to understand that gains from international commerce are increasingly appropriated by transnational enterprises, and that estimates of national accounts have to be sensitive to major uncertainties because of very high volume trade in extremely risky opaque financial assets.[3]

At national policy levels, then, there are clear requirements for prudent macromanagement, to cope with what must be recognized as the internationalization of market efficiencies and failures that results from deepening integration, and in particular from concentration trends and from externalities associated with those trends. The weakening of monetary policy capabilities, however, due to cross-border financial flows, has been part of a larger weakening of economic sovereignty, and this has made corporate cooperation all the more important for the macromanagement tasks of governments. At the same time technocratic services to facilitate cooperation *between firms* have also become more important; that is, for productive achievements that would not otherwise be possible.

Prudent macromanagement, because of the rising levels and increasing complexities of structural interdependencies, has to be attempted with the cooperation of other governments, as well as firms: there are imperatives to develop systems of *collective* management, in regional contexts, as is being striven for in the European Union, and at the global level. There are challenges to undertake highly constructive and high principled initiatives, with emphasis on reducing the costs and increasing the benefits of deepening integration, and on expressing a new doctrine of broadly collaborative capitalism. Rivalries between states for shares in the gains from world commerce motivate efforts to increase structural competitiveness, as well as to exert leverage over questions of market access, but structural competitiveness changes with the expansion of complex structural interdependencies. Corporate competitiveness becomes, more and more, a cross-border process, while the firms gaining such competitiveness in different markets tend to lose their national identities and loyalties. Transnational enterprises increasing their international market strengths and assuming prominence in global concentration trends, moreover, can bargain more and more effectively with diverse host governments and with their original home administrations.[4]

The macromanagement activities of governments are becoming, of necessity, *interdependent*, although with continuing differences in performance and capacities to control market access and to enlist cooperation from firms that are still domestic and from transnational enterprises. This macromanagement interdependence is developing principally between the USA and the European Union, as Japan's economic difficulties remain very serious. Order and growth in the world economy depend very much on the closely linked American and European macromanagement processes, and on the ways in which these can provide leadership for, and contribute to, collaborative macromanagement in the rest of the world.

Corporate operations, combining various degrees of cooperation and competition, tend to become increasingly interdependent, subject to the effects of ongoing concentration trends, because of the multiplication of advanced technologies. The potential for individual entrepreneurial ventures, moreover, has to be identified with extensive information about the capabilities and orientations of numerous firms active in world markets. Prospects for coordination have to be explored on a vast scale, but there are practical requirements for close intensive managerial exchanges of tacit as well as codified knowledge.[5] Such exchanges are facilitated by industrial clustering but, especially with the proliferation of cross-border corporate linkages, the exploration of opportunities for complementary entrepreneurship can benefit from technocratic advice and information services.

Influential streams of economic advice, and the dynamics of policymaking, tend to activate strongly competitive macromanagement in major industrialized states. This tendency becomes stronger during phases of stress in the world economy. Interdependent growth with minimal strains, however, has to be made possible through integrative approaches to problems of corporate cooperation and policy level coordination. The necessary collaboration has to become *relational* (building trust and goodwill) rather than instrumental, with opportunist motivations and low trust. With the increasing internationalization of market efficiencies and failures, the logic of relational cooperation between firms and governments, and between governments, becomes stronger, in the common interest, to promote order and equity in all the asymmetries of globalization.

COMPETITION, COOPERATION, AND MACROMANAGEMENT

National patterns of corporate activity, while being penetrated increasingly by the operations of transnational enterprises, exhibit differing blends of competition and cooperation, with contrasts in motivations deriving from established cultures, and from the influence of technological factors and market trends. In a strongly individualistic culture, competition is more common than cooperation, and collaboration between firms tends to be managed with low levels of trust and goodwill, with limited sharing of knowledge, and with opportunism that can involve emphasis on precise agreements and on the exploration of opportunities for mergers and acquisitions. The dynamics of intercorporate interactions that are more competitive than cooperative tend to be associated with agency (market based) systems of corporate governance, in which managements are under pressure to serve the interests of portfolio switching shareholders by producing high short-term profits.[6] Technological advances obligate recognition of interdependencies in the development of production capabilities, and the large numbers of firms active in the integrating world markets necessitate collaborative solutions to information problems, but striving for competitive advantage tends to be the dominant motivation. Perceptions of the potential benefits of increased cooperation, moreover, tend to be influenced by awareness of general corporate instability, due to the frequencies of acquisitions.

Relational cooperation between firms, typically developing in communitarian cultures, is managed on the basis of diffuse, enduring informal obligations, with trust, and active sharing of knowledge and risks, and with spontaneous tendencies to widen the areas of collaboration while respecting each partner's autonomy. Stable corporate identities facilitate this cooperation, and it is also sustained by the operational logic of stakeholder systems of corporate governance. It can be argued, with reference to Germany, that relational intercorporate ties are conducive to incremental rather than rapid and radical innovations, but this line of reasoning is less persuasive with respect to the Japanese record, despite the problems that have developed in its financial sector.[7]

The potential for continuity in relational cooperation can be altered as firms extend their operations outside their home political economies, and macromanagement processes in those political economies can change with incoming direct investment by firms based in countries with individualistic cultures. The absence of shared values can result in less relational cooperation in the host political economies and at home. Meanwhile incentives to engage in technology based cooperation with diminished or nonexistent relational ties can become stronger, as has been evident in the strategies of Japanese firms operating in the USA.[8]

In deepening integration the dilution of a communitarian culture, then, is to be expected, because of the effects of nonaffinitive foreign environments on national firms moving into international operations, and because of the penetration of culturally different foreign enterprises. Meanwhile macromanagement can be affected by the dilution of the culture, as this reduces corporate cooperation with the policy level, and intercorporate collaboration. The fragmenting effects, however, can be reduced by vigorous solidarity-building leadership, although this possibility may seem remote because of the continuing dilution of the culture and the politically divisive effects of the costs of globalization – the employment losses and sectoral dislocations associated with deepening integration.

The contrasts with individualistic national political economies tend to be gradually less significant, notably when Germany is compared with the USA, but there are numerous complexities, the overall consequences of which draw attention to the costs of deepening integration when pervasive emphasis on individual autonomy hinders institutional development and consensus formation. Where firms relate distantly and distrustfully to their national administration, problems of governance which affect its performance can add to their motivations to advance their interests through international operations. In the financial sector, meanwhile, much energy and resources can be directed into speculation that raises stock prices to unsustainable levels, thus precipitating sharp declines. The real economy is then affected by losses of confidence, contractions of productive investment, and greater corporate emphasis on foreign production in quests for world market shares; this can entail increased deindustrialization in the home economy, with shifts in popular attitudes that aggravate problems of governance. Altogether, the costs of globalization can thus be greater, and more unequally shared, than in a communitarian political economy advantaged by relational cooperation between its firms, and between those firms and its administration.

The comparisons, however, have to be made with awareness of differences in national attributes that have further significance. A very large integrated internal market provides opportunities for growth enhancing specializations, thus attracting investment and entrepreneurial energies from countries whose growth potentials are limited by smaller size and relatively restricted access to external markets. The smaller countries may have communitarian cultures, but their collective potential may not be sufficiently functional because of political cleavages, collusive practices, and virtual limitations on the scope for entrepreneurship. Welfare burdens in these states moreover may be higher because of slow growth and population decline. These general observations relate especially to the contrasts between the USA and Germany, and those are undergoing further change as Germany becomes more immersed in and penetrated by the enlarging European Union.[9]

The principal macromanagement task, in deepening integration, is to promote balanced interdependent growth. This task, it must be reiterated, can be approached with hopes of securing superior gains from involvement in world commerce, but there are moral obligations to consider the international common good, and these obligations become more significant as structural linking through investment and trade continues. A basic concern has to be the provision of high quality infrastructure and administrative services, at reasonable cost, in a stable business environment, so that industrial clustering will result and exert strong attractions, drawing national and foreign investment. In the industrial clusters there can be rapid diffusions of advanced technology, with much information sharing that is conducive to entrepreneurial collaboration.[10] Location with these advantages, however, increases corporate capabilities to develop international production systems.

For US policymakers the appropriate calculations in the structural policy area have become highly complex, and this is all the more significant for the world economy because of the decline of Japan and the persistence of slow growth in Europe. There are urgent imperatives to work for balance in the current account by increasing the service of foreign markets through exports rather than international production, and increasing domestic output to meet internal demand. There are even more urgent imperatives to reduce, drastically, the dangerous speculation in financial assets, which overshadows the structural policy area, especially by making the home business environment less attractive, while drawing investment away from productive use.

The severe effects of the US post-bubble recession have altered perspectives on macromanagement processes in Europe, in effect giving more prominence to imperatives for financial sector stability in the service of real economies, and for reduced vulnerability to destabilization through investment and trade linkages with the USA. The need for broadly collaborative macromanagement has become greater in the European Union, but has become more difficult to meet, because the challenges of slower and less secure interdependent growth have tended to obligate greater reliance by member governments on their own structural policies: consensus for a common structural policy has become less attainable. In principle the Union is committed to a growth strategy relying on the anticipated efficiency effects of increased intraregional competition that is expected to result in the emergence of strong Union firms through intrazonal mergers and acquisitions, but the commitments of member governments to this are tacitly qualified by concerns with the structural competitiveness of their own economies.[11]

Macromanagement problems in the USA, because of its central significance in world production and finance, have to be of special concern in the European Union, not only because of its vulnerabilities in the

Atlantic system of interdependencies, but also because the Union is the only significant potential source of external policy advice, and relates to the USA in a context of mutual informal accountability. Europe, however, does not have a unified voice for the provision of knowledge intensive inputs into US decision processes, and in Atlantic interactions the USA's informal accountability is limited because the Union's internal cleavages and rivalries provide scope for divisive US diplomacy. Moreover the USA's tradition of independent management of its external relations limits openness to any European advice, and it must be stressed that Europe's status in the relationship is adversely affected by its prolonged economic stagnation as well as its problems of governance.[12]

CHANGING SYSTEMS

Capacities for interdependent macromanagement are changing in the USA and Europe, mainly because of strains over growth and distributional issues associated with deepening integration. These strains affect the performance of political institutions coping with demands for increased prosperity and security, in the context of diverse class and ideological cleavages. In Europe, economic policy orientations have reflected general emphasis on the efficiency effects of market forces, and therefore on reducing welfare costs and the costs of unionized labour, but popular pressures for the maintenance of welfare systems and the preservation of union roles have tended to increase, due to the persistence of slow growth and to the perceived negative effect of globalization. In the USA, policy emphasis on market driven efficiencies is greater, at elite levels, partly because of awareness of inefficiencies in governmental economic involvement in Europe, but popular concerns with the costs of globalization appear to be stronger, to the advantage of the Democratic Party's distributional image.

Structurally, the USA is more extensively linked with the rest of the world economy, and US structural links with Europe are more active than those of European economies with the USA, while financial flows from Europe to the USA are relatively passive compared with the entrepreneurial thrust of portfolio investment in Europe from the USA. As global trade in financial assets tends to be concentrated in the USA, providing very high volume credit for speculation that becomes destabilizing, moreover, change in the US political economy has vital international significance. Problems of advanced political development in the USA have become all the more serious because of propensities to tolerate the very high volume financial sector rent seeking, the wealth effects of which go mainly into consumption rather than productive investment.[13] In prospect are further booms, and declines in which recovery will be difficult because monetary loosening will provide financial enterprises with opportunities to make available low cost funds for higher yield speculative operations, exploiting volatility in equity and currency markets, rather than funding productive firms.

The balance between competitive and cooperative corporate activities in the USA is thus tilted in a way that entails an acute and complex form of market failure that is politically difficult to remedy through official intervention. The financial sector directs funds into rent seeking on a very dangerous scale, while subjecting productive enterprises to pressures for high short-term returns, at the expense of long-term investments in new technology and human capital – and with adverse consequences for intercorporate stability.[14] Further, capital flight from slower growing areas of the world is attracted, especially by the prospective rent seeking opportunities. An issue of advanced political development, then, is financial sector reform, in the interests of comprehensive funding for growth in the real economy, without the attraction of investment needed elsewhere.

For financial sector reform, and more generally for substantial increases in intercorporate trust and goodwill, profound changes are needed at fundamental levels of belief and motivation, especially to reverse a closely observed decline in US civic virtues, and a related decline in wellbeing which has also been evident in other industrialized states.[15] With diminished civic virtue, interests tend to be asserted more aggressively, generating sharper conflicts and thus further weakening political institutions, while necessitating the trading of favours on a wide scale to ensure the performance of executive and legislative functions. Hence, for the administration, pressing political exchange concerns tend to dominate the functional requirements of macromanagement.

The increasing costs of globalization – employment losses and sectoral disruptions – and the costs of the post-bubble recession, are tending to make the USA's problems of governance more serious. Imperatives to promote more production at home for export, for a more appropriate ratio to foreign production, and imperatives to reform the financial sector, are becoming more difficult to meet. The problems of governance are acute because of the evolution of a political culture of *permanent campaigning*, in which policymaking is oriented toward continuous contests for office, with an emphasis on competition with superficial value-free media framing and treatment of sensational issues, in sequences that change frequently because of public appetites for news.[16] Administration as an agency task on behalf of aggregated interests has become randomly subjected to the shifting dynamics of media interactions, on a short-term basis. Public understanding of substantive questions of economic policy is confused, and there is a lack of confidence in the integrity and competence of legislators and the administration. Numerous social groups and enterprises are affected by the combined costs of globalization and recession, but there is no representative structure with a capacity to promote concerted entrepreneurship for restoration of balance in the current account, and reduction of the risky speculative propensities in the financial sector. The representation of business interests remains fragmented, and the intense individualism of the campaigning political culture prevents institutional development in the major political parties.[17]

The USA's macromanagement problems are challenges for the European Union: its system of collective management has to become much more functional, especially to increase internally based growth and reduce capital flight to the USA, as well as to manage Atlantic structural interdependencies more productively. The European Union's enlargement, with the admission of East European members, increases functional imperatives for deepening integration, but threatens to intensify the difficulties of pluralistic decision making in a system in which developmental issues set requirements for further institutional development. Resolution of these issues, and institutional progress, depend very much on the evolution of Germany's role as the central, most highly industrialized, and most integrated political economy in the Union.

The German political economy is a form of alliance capitalism, distinguished by relational corporate cooperation, a stakeholder type of corporate governance, and a consensual policy style, guided by independent research intensive advice. There are disruptive pressures, however, as exposure to intensifying competition in the world economy tends to make industrial relations conflicted, in a context in which organized labour and bank financing have been considered responsible for technological lags, through restraints on entrepreneurship.[18] Germany is the principal European exporter of manufactures to the USA and, while coping with the trade effects of that country's downturn, it has been obliged to respond to the expansion of the highly competitive US corporate presence in Europe. Strong attachments to the distinctive communitarian culture of the national political economy have restrained corporate interest in production at foreign locations, but this interest has tended to increase, because of cost factors, particularly in Eastern Europe. Within the Union the integrated intercorporate system resists penetration through mergers and acquisitions, but is being extended, apparently with some gradual weakening, through direct investment in other member states. Because of cultural differences, these states are not open to absorption of the German system of integrated capitalism, but their business systems do not generate comparable efficiencies.

Germany's involvement in European collective management necessitates emphasis on cooperation with France, the terms of which are gradually changing as the central German role in the Union is strengthened through relatively superior structural competitiveness. The strongly individualistic French culture, in which there are deep ideological cleavages, does not sustain a system of alliance capitalism, and its pattern of industrial relations is quite conflicted.[19] Italy tends to be aligned with Germany, and this German advantage is being strengthened by the development of German direct investment and trade links with East European states in line for membership of the Union. Britain, with its status as a reluctant supporter of European integration, has been on the periphery of the Union system of collective management and its system of capitalism has affinities with that in the USA.

The European mix of political economies is evolving, it must be stressed, with internal structural policy rivalries that have divisive effects. These prevent both the formation of a consensus for a common structural policy *and* the rationalization of corporate capabilities through competitive pressures to which member governments are committed in principle. The functional logic of alliance capitalism is expressed mainly in the German system, and is not spreading in the Union. The complexities of Union decision processes, moreover, which are forms of conflicted rather than integrative bargaining, tend to absorb political energies and attention, thus perpetuating parochial and inward looking orientations. These are reflected in the multiplicity of political groups represented in the European Parliament, which remain distinctly national, despite conventions based on ideological affinities that can facilitate cross-border collaboration between such groups.[20] Issue-based coalitions can form between the affinitive groups, but their domestic ties are tending to become stronger as differences between member governments increase over problems of adjustment to deepening integration and enlargement, in conditions of slow growth and high unemployment.

Resolution of the problems of advanced political development affecting the European system of collective management, and the integration of its economies, is becoming more and more necessary for the evolution of comprehensive Atlantic cooperation. Reciprocal policy learning and accountability, sustained politically and structurally by wide ranging intercorporate collaboration, will have to be promoted in Atlantic relations through European and American initiatives. This has become imperative to cope with the internationalization of problems of market failure and government failure in the world economy's main area of deepening integration. It has also become imperative for growth, order, and equity in the global pattern of production and finance, in which a key requirement has become the restoration of a dynamic economy in Japan.

INSTITUTIONALIZING COMPREHENSIVE ATLANTIC COOPERATION

Comprehensive Atlantic cooperation, especially to overcome the costs of insufficiently coordinated deepening integration – the results of market and government failures – will have to be based on full development of the logic of alliance capitalism as an international public good. Market failures are basically failures in entrepreneurial cooperation – cooperation that is insufficiently integrative for the common interest, specifically with respect to the restraint of competition to prevent abuses of oligopoly power, the disruption of sectoral interdependencies through relocations of production, and the neglect of opportunities for productive complementary specializations. Entrepreneurial cooperation to achieve efficiencies compatible with social justice has to develop with high principled spontaneity, but with encouragement from the policy levels, where for the common good authority has to be exercised as well through regulatory functions. Government failures that assume cross-border dimensions, contributing to and tolerating the internationalization of market failures, evidence the effects of dysfunctional inputs into policy, including assertions of interests by groups profiting from market failures.

A philosophy of macromanagement in deepening integration, engaging constructively with issues of policy interdependence and structural interdependence, while relating to firms operating in numerous jurisdictions, has to be given expression in a process of advanced international political development. In Europe, at the Union level, a fundamental problem is that functional advances in elite driven integration are insufficiently supported by progress in regional community formation: civic loyalties and virtues based on beliefs of European identities are weak. Political processes in member states tend to perpetuate national attachments and loyalties, and the economies of these states are seen to be in competition, within a regional setting in which collective management has a liberal orientation, focused on the efficiency effects of strong corporate rivalries. This is not tending to build a regional solidarity system, because of general awareness of sharp contrasts between the rival states and between the competing enterprises.[21] Firm public commitments by member governments to a doctrine of entrepreneurial collaboration across the Union, and the practical implementation of such a doctrine by numerous major firms, could have the strong integrating effects that would be needed for community formation. For such a major advance in the development of the regional political economy, very intense policy learning by European political elites would clearly be required. A very demanding challenge, then, can be seen for European policy research institutes.

The European context is distinguished by a large highly competitive American corporate presence. This contributes to general awareness of ongoing struggles for shares of the integrating single market, and of resultant imbalances in gains, within and between member countries. A doctrine of entrepreneurial collaboration accordingly would have to promise effective participation by US enterprises on terms of equal partnership in the development of a solidarity based system of regional capitalism. The credibility of the partnering, and the dynamic results that could be anticipated, would depend on the change to a system of collegial capitalism in the USA. Such a change has become necessary, it must be stressed, because of the negative effects of the strong orientation toward competitive rather than cooperative activity in US corporations.

In the USA the systemic requirement for transformation into a system of collegial capitalism is urgent for stability, and for more functional involvement in deepening integration. The problem of destabilizing speculation has to be overcome, and deindustrialization has to be avoided while transnational production becomes more extensive. High volume speculative trading in shares exerts pressures on managements to demonstrate short-term profitability at levels that will appreciate stock values, and this happens selectively because of the manipulative strategies of institutional investors – with consequences for overall productivity and stability that indicate serious deficiencies in capital markets. Changes to stakeholder systems of corporate governance, and to substantial reliance on bank financing, especially of a kind that becomes significantly relational, could promise greater and more continuous efficiencies in the implementation of long-term plans.[22] The potential for developing complementary entrepreneurial ventures would then be enhanced, while motivation to initiate such ventures would be encouraged by recognition of their benefits and, hopefully, by a spirit of collegiality. That at could draw inspiration from Aristotelian concepts of civic friendship as a basis for collaborative production – concepts that have been enriched in theological writings on the social aspects of freedom for economic initiative and, implicitly, in the functional analysis of linkages between issues of social justice and economic efficiency.

Deindustrialization, as one of the major costs of globalization, is a challenge for managerial reorientation toward collegial ventures in transnational production, with active concerns for human capital development and the promotion of harmonious intersectoral and intrasectoral interdependencies in the home economy, and in host economies. The incentives for US firms to move aggressively into foreign production projects individually and in instrumental alliances, managed with opportunism, are strong, as has been evidenced by the size of outward direct investment flows. The higher profitability, the spreading of risks, the lower tax exposure, and the weaker competitiveness of European and Japanese rivals assume greater prominence in managerial calculations than the externalities to be reckoned with by communities and other industries in the USA. Civic virtues, then, clearly have to become more active.[23]

The promotion of solidarity based capitalism in Europe and the USA would help to make possible comprehensive relational Atlantic cooperation, at governmental and corporate levels. This would replace a conflicted and increasingly imbalanced pattern of structural and policy interdependencies that is vulnerable to destabilization. Imperatives for wide ranging integrative coordination in the management of those interdependencies are becoming more urgent, and there is a clear danger that in a crisis individual corporate and government responses will be severely dysfunctional.

The necessary Atlantic relational cooperation, if promoted through vigorous advocacy, will have to be institutionalized. The commitments of managements and policymakers will have to be given repeated affirmation in structured arrangements, designed for the development of entrepreneurial complementarities through consultations aided by American and European technocratic services, based on assessments of emerging trends in frontier technology and in structural interdependencies. The consultations could be hosted by an independent Atlantic commission of experts in international management and applied technology.

Widening exploration of interdependencies in evolving corporate production capabilities, in the light of progress in advanced research, would provide the basis for the entrepreneurial consultations.[24] These, it would have to be recognized, could be exploited for oligopolistic collusion, but that would have to be dealt with by US and European competition authorities. The spirit of collegial cooperation that would be generated in the consultations, especially through technocratic contributions guided by concerns with public goods, would be a restraint on oligopolistic collusion, but surveillance by competition authorities would remain necessary. International corporate alliances and networks are evolving in contexts that are being changed by global concentration trends which challenge US and European competition authorities,[25] and these authorities would have to have some involvement in the work of the independent Atlantic commission of experts.

The development of the commission's functions could be aided by contributions to its assessments and forecasts by the European Commission, the US Department of Commerce, and the International Monetary Fund. With such involvement the managements taking part in the consultations would benefit from a wider knowledge intensive environment, in which they would experience more extensive informal accountability. The US and European technocrats in the commission would also be informally challenged to demonstrate objectivity and impartiality in the common interest, while learning in the area of comparative entrepreneurship through interactions with managements.

A transregional pattern of dynamic corporate linkages could be in prospect. The likely alternative future is conflicted policy level exchanges, especially over issues of market access, in which the objectives are hard and precise agreements suited for future litigation. From a European perspective the USA could assume the image of a relentlessly competitive form of capitalism, increasing the costs of globalization at home and in the rest of the world, while drawing global investment during booms and then exporting recessions in which its own firms will be advantaged relative to weaker competitors. From a US perspective Europe could be seen only as a region of slow growth under poor governance that can benefit from American direct investment and exports if opportunities for these are increased through leverage.

PACIFIC COOPERATION

Solidarity based Atlantic economic cooperation could inspire and support Pacific collaboration to overcome the severe effects of East Asia's financial crises. Comparative perspectives on these crises have had to be expanded to bring into view speculative trends leading to recession in the USA, as its experience of destabilizing asset appreciation has had same similarity with Japan's. The most important theme in constructive Pacific engagement that can be proposed for US and European decision makers, however, is that a doctrine of relational entrepreneurial cooperation has to be spread transnationally and at the policy levels. This would acknowledge the highly functional effects of the Japanese system of alliance capitalism before these were disrupted by dangerous speculation.[26]

The Atlantic system's most substantial and most dynamic external linkages are with Japan, the centre of what has been an integrated East Asian production pattern. The disruption of financial sectors in that pattern has made Japan more heavily dependent on service of the US and European markets through exports and transnational production. Structural and policy interdependencies in these relationships have to be managed with weakened bargaining strength, and with the disadvantages of relative political isolation, due principally to unique cultural factors. In the immediate environment difficult choices have to be made about economic links with the Chinese communist regime, which, because of the size of its market, can bargain advantageously with the USA and the European Union on trade and investment issues.

Alliance capitalism in Japan has had an intensely nationalist quality, based on a communitarian culture and on awareness of acute resource deficiencies. The collegial capitalism which can be advocated for the USA, and for Atlantic structural partnering, would have a highly significant functional logic for the building of Atlantic relational cooperation with Japan. This, moreover, would have a vital security dimension, related especially to Japanese and US defence interests.

Atlantic solidarity capitalism could become active in East Asia through the sponsorship of conferences on the potential for entrepreneurial complementarities. There could be marked asymmetries in the interactions because US and European representatives could be relating to Japanese managements that are linked in cohesive industry groups and have their own systems of information sharing and entrepreneurial collaboration.[27] The industry group bonds, however, could be expected to become gradually more open, while relational ties between US firms and between European enterprises, as well as in the Atlantic pattern, would be tending to increase. Evolution of the conferencing would depend on numerous managerial and official contributions to the development of trust and goodwill, and on the results of efforts to institutionalize the exploration of prospective complementarities.

A Euro-Pacific commission, sponsored by the USA, the European Union, and Japan, could be set up to host the conferences on Pacific entrepreneurship. This commission would stand apart from the Asia Pacific Economic Cooperation (APEC) forum, which is likely to remain a loose association working mainly for the reduction of regional trade barriers, under constraints resulting especially from failures in community formation within the Association of Southeast Asian Nations (ASEAN). The primary objectives of the conferencing would be the promotion of alliances and networks for complementary ventures by US, European and Japanese enterprises. As in the proposed Atlantic commission, this activity could be aided by the International Monetary Fund. Association with the main complementary ventures would have to be made possible for South Korean, Taiwanese, Hong Kong and Malaysian firms, through participation in the conferences as industrializing open economies. Participation by mainland Chinese firms would become feasible as the transition of their economy to a system under informal central control continues.

The development of solidarity based Euro-Pacific capitalism could have very beneficial effects on economic growth in East Asia, and in particular on economic and political change in mainland China. Thus far that regime's elites have had opportunities for interaction with mainly competitive rather than cooperative forms of capitalism, and have had to recognize the dangers of financial liberalization that would open the way for large movements of funds in speculative operations. They have been made well aware that they have to be able to defend their currency against speculative attacks by predatory western financial institutions, that capital flight to foreign bubble economies has to be prevented, and that informal controls of their financial sector, supplementing firm explicit regulations, have become all the more important as their economy becomes more open.[28]

Japan's failures in financial sector regulation and surveillance, which have had very severe effects, and have hindered economic recovery by facilitating capital flight, mainly to the USA, could be gradually overcome through the growth made possible in an expanding pattern of Euro-Pacific solidarity based capitalism. Low interest rates in Japan, intended to assist recovery, have facilitated borrowing for investment in higher yield foreign markets, notably during the boom phase of the US business cycle. This capital flight restrained the currency appreciation that tends to result from large trade surpluses, but at the cost of reduced funding for domestically based growth, and increased financial sector reliance on returns from foreign investment. Solidarity has been weakening in Japan's prolonged crisis, but reversal of this trend, with the support of regional alliance capitalism, would provide a comprehensive solution.

Relational development of complementary production specializations in the proposed Euro-Pacific pattern would ensure the restoration of high and more stable growth in industrializing East Asian states that have had very active trade and investment links with Japan. Those links, moreover, would be able to develop with more balance and diversification, due partly to US and European corporate involvement. Meanwhile the Chinese regime's participation in the regional pattern, and acceptance of its spirit of solidarity, would add to its dynamism. Regional trade and investment liberalization, in line with objectives endorsed by the APEC forum, would become more feasible, in a way that could facilitate the development of an East Asia economic community. Such a community could became the basic component of a Pacific Monetary System that would work in cooperation with the European Monetary Union and the USA for global monetary cooperation, and the reform of world financial markets.[29]

COOPERATION IN THE AMERICAS

The prospect of a Free Trade Area of the Americas has strong attraction for Latin American countries, especially because of the failures of several regional cooperation projects in their area, the opportunities for increased access to the US market and, it seems, tacit expectations that US involvement in the Free Trade Area would contribute to reductions of rivalries and conflicts that have hindered commerce within and between regional groups, including Mercosur. There are widely shared concerns about the possible costs of penetration by highly competitive US enterprises, and about the difficulties of securing wider entry to the US economy, but there is some basis for hope that increased collaboration between Latin American governments would make possible more equal bargaining with the USA. There are also grounds for optimism that the growth prospects of regional trade liberalization would draw more European investment.

The development of collegial capitalism in the USA, especially if in a larger context of collaborative Euro-Pacific capitalism, would offer Latin America possibilities for higher and more equal growth through expanding forms of complementary entrepreneurship. The spreading transnational commercial linkages, moreover, expressing a new culture of trust, goodwill, and cooperative innovation, would assist the development of cross-border aggregations of interests to which national administrations would tend to became more responsive. Such responsiveness is needed to overcome failures in fiscal, monetary, and structural policies that have contributed to crises and severe downturns in Mexico, Brazil, Argentina, and neighbouring states over the past decade.[30]

The record of instability in Latin America indicates that a regional structure with responsibilities for fiscal and monetary discipline, and effective regulation of the financial sectors, will have to be established. Negotiations for the formation of a Free Trade Area of the Americas, if sufficiently related to fundamentals critical for regional development, could be managed in ways that would make evident the imperative for such a structure, and the advantages of basing it on a broadly inclusive stability pact. Recognition of this requirement by Latin American elites would be aided by the forms of entrepreneurial cooperation that would spread with the expansion of collegial capitalism from the USA. Under the regional macroeconomic discipline, meanwhile, member governments would be challenged to focus on the structural tasks of facilitating the development of complementary corporate specializations, at home and across the region. Increased scope would thus be provided for the formation of cross-border aggregations of interests, to sustain the operations of the regional macroeconomic structure.

Without the development of collegial capitalism in its own political economy the USA would be at a disadvantage if endeavouring to build support for the formation of a Latin American macroeconomic authority. This problem would have a to be foreseen because the history of US involvement in Latin America has bred fears of US economic penetration. These persist despite the prospective benefits of closer economic association with the USA. As part of a Euro-Pacific pattern of alliance capitalism the relational cooperation promoted in the USA would have a status that could be especially helpful for constructive engagement in Latin America. If European alliance capitalism was also active in the sponsorship of entrepreneurial collaboration in Latin America, the establishment of the regional macroeconomic authority could become more feasible. European advocacy, based on the European Union's experience in deepening integration, could be especially effective.

A US–Latin American commission to sponsor conferences on corporate cooperation, could be formed after appropriate initiatives by US, European, and Latin American authorities and industry associations. This would have to stand apart from the regional macroeconomic authority, so as to function in an atmosphere of complete freedom for information sharing and the exploration of potentials for parallel production ventures. The development of a regional culture of integrative managerial cooperation would have to be a clear objective, kept in view through continual affirmations of collegiality.

In negotiations for a Free Trade Area of the Americas the Latin American participants may well have to reckon with US efforts to secure hard and precise agreements, in line with precedents set by the interactions that led to the Uruguay Agreement.[31] The bargaining is likely to be difficult, because of pressures on the US administration from farming and textiles lobbies to maintain restraints on imports from Latin America, and the efforts of US negotiators to secure increased access to Latin American markets for manufactured products. Perceived inequalities in bargaining leverage, and selective uses of that leverage, could make the interactions lengthy and bitter.

Initiatives to promote parallel entrepreneurial ventures in a spirit of alliance capitalism could provide a more favourable environment for the trade negotiations. It could then be possible to give the bargaining an integrative orientation, with adequate recognition of Latin American interests in expanding exports of agricultural products and low technology manufactures in order to finance industrialization up to levels required for relative equality in structural interdependence with the USA. For Latin American negotiators the desirable shifts in bargaining orientations could be made more feasible if there were concurrent exchanges with the European Union for separate trade liberalization arrangements. Such exchanges could also benefit from an atmosphere of goodwill generated through progress toward the development of solidarity based capitalism in Europe, and European association with such a trend in the USA.

PRIORITIES IN COLLECTIVE MANAGEMENT

The spirit of alliance capitalism could alter priorities in foreign economic policies, through effects on corporate inputs into governmental decision making, and through corporate reshaping of the structural interdependencies that such policies are intended to manage. The established priorities in the USA, Europe, and Japan are the maintenance of restrictions on imports to meet the demands of politically prominent domestic producers, and the use of market opening leverage against major trading partners. Foreign trade management is the most politicized area of economic policy in the large industrialized states, and pressures from domestic producers have tended to counter governmental efforts to enhance growth through reciprocal reductions of trade barriers: policy level understandings of the overall benefits of liberalization have had to recognize the political strength of protectionist groups, which has generally been more significant than that of producers seeking wider access to foreign markets.

During recessions the protectionist and market opening demands of domestic producers increase, especially if there are much publicized trade deficits, as in the USA, and favourable policy level responses can seem all the more appropriate because of public concerns about the general effects of globalization. The credibility of official declarations about the growth effects of international trade declines, especially because of failures in the market for policy relevant information, due to sensationalism in the media.

The priorities accorded to trade policy in the USA, Europe, and Japan are made evident in competitive and even adversarial contexts, and tend to reinforce understandings that agreements for liberalization have to be negotiated aggressively. Advocacy of solidarity building through the sponsorship of alliance capitalism can thus seem utopian. There is little public awareness in the industrialized states of the degrees to which technology advances are increasing interdependencies in the development of corporate production capabilities, and of the extent to which overall growth can be enhanced through complementary entrepreneurial specializations that have to develop with sustained integrative collaboration. The USA is the most active promoter of international trade liberalization, and its legislators and members of its administration are especially responsive to constituency interests affected by foreign penetration of the domestic market, as well as by European and Japanese trade barriers.[32] The European Union's trade policy, managed through interactions between the member governments and the European Commission, has reflected increasing assertiveness by the former, under pressure from domestic groups.[33] Japanese trade policy, advantaged by pervasive informal protection of the internal market, is expressed in relatively soft market opening diplomacy, sensitive to irritations, notably in the USA, caused by large trade surpluses.

Policy literature on world trade tends to focus on the dynamics of bargaining between the USA and the European Union, because of their dominance of the world trading system, and rather neglects discussions of fundamentals. Issues concerning the structural foundations of international commerce can thus receive little attention. These foundations, however, are being changed continually as transnational enterprises expand their international production systems through direct investment, while drawing home and foreign enterprises into alliances and networks, and displacing rivals, including companies that have been mainly producing at home for export. An overall effect is that trade barriers – duties, quotas, and standards – become less and less significant for the transnational enterprises, compared with firms producing at home for export, while the volumes of transnational production become very much larger than those of arm's length trade. Increasing proportions of the commerce associated with the transnational production are intrafirm, intranetwork, or intra-alliance shipments at different stages of processing which can be rerouted to take advantage of changes in trade and foreign direct investment policies.

Managements of transnational enterprises operate with diminishing country attachments and loyalties, and with generally increasing capacities to deal instrumentally rather than relationally with governments. Incentives to engage in complementary entrepreneurial endeavours, moreover, change in the course of global concentration trends as well as with shifts in interactions with governments. Altogether, the structural foundations of international commerce are being altered through transnational production in ways that tend to diminish the significance of trade barriers, while the cross-border linking of production processes results in an increasing internationalization of market efficiencies and failures.

A spirit of alliance capitalism, especially if developing in the USA, as the principal base of multinational operations, could moderate trade policy conflicts and introduce more equity and order into the expanding pattern of transnational production: the internationalized market efficiencies would increase. This might not seem probable in view of the widening scope for independent operations that transnational enterprises acquire with prominence in global concentration trends, but a culture of relational entrepreneurial cooperation could be cultivated through intensive conferencing under technocratic sponsorship. Associated with that sponsorship, moreover, there could be collaborative structural policy initiatives, principally in Atlantic relations, in conjunction with competition policy measures, to increase the sensitivities of multinational managements to internationalized public goods problems, and other issues in globalizing markets. Multinational freedoms for entrepreneurship, becoming more socially responsible, and more respectful of the interests of other firms, would thus take more profoundly innovative orientations, avoiding predatory and rent seeking ventures.

Expanding international production operations, and resultant increases in global market shares, enable transnational enterprises to explore opportunities for complementary entrepreneurship more extensively, with firms of similar or inferior status, but also to acquire or compete more actively against such firms. Calculations of long-term benefits may be seen to justify collaborative choices – recognizing the potential for innovation in the other firms – but shareholder pressures for higher profits can have strong effects on managerial motivations; institutional investors, moreover, can mobilize shareholder support for changes in management. Managerial vulnerabilities to shareholder pressures can be reduced by accumulating internal resources for expansion, buying back shares, increasing reliance on bank financing, and opening up opportunities to secure private or official funding abroad. Yet the increased range of managerial discretion may be used with greater emphasis on acquisitions.[34]

Fundamentals, therefore, make the promotion of a spirit of alliance capitalism – oriented toward real cooperation for complementary ventures – all the more important in the business cultures of the industrialized states. This has to be asserted in a public goods perspective focused on trade policy conflicts – the perspective in which such conflicts assume prominence in economic policymaking. The rationale for promoting alliance capitalism, however, has wider application: there are macroeconomic imperatives.

Fiscal policy tasks, the financing of regulatory functions, infrastructure development, and distributional activities, phased to smooth business cycles, can be made extremely difficult by failures in entrepreneurial coordination as deepening integration continues: the internationalization of market failures, skewing the effects of internationalized market efficiencies, can seriously hinder fiscal management. The costs of promoting adjustment, moreover, can increase with rises in unemployment and sectoral dislocations, while revenue may decline with the outward movement of production operations.

A culture of alliance capitalism, inspiring relational intercorporate collaboration in complementary ventures, and relational corporate cooperation with structural authorities, could assist fiscal management. The growth effects of the complementarities would reduce the distributional demands and costs of adjustment associated with increases in foreign production. At the same time the relational cooperation would be a source of diffuse restraints on political competition that could lead to fiscal expansion, with accumulations of governmental burdens that would slow growth and perpetuate high taxes. This may be doubted, in the light of Japan's very serious failures to achieve fiscal discipline in the 1990s: Japanese alliance capitalism had little effect on the growth of large budget deficits. The recent history of German fiscal discipline, however, despite the high costs of rehabilitating the formerly communist Eastern area, has illustrated that relational intercorporate cooperation can certainly restrain government spending – in a communitarian system that allows more scope than Japan for strong leadership, and that sustains a policy style open to independent research intensive advice.[35]

In the USA, promotion of a spirit of alliance capitalism could generate pervasive restraints on federal spending, and could make these restraints more functional by contributing to the development of strong peak economic associations. The longstanding fragmentation of business associations, due to intense individualism, would then no longer leave the way open for the unrestrained competition between constituency interests that has driven federal debt to high levels. Over the past two decades failures to maintain fiscal discipline in the public interest have contributed to the growth of internal demand in excess of output, while there has been substantial expansion of production abroad; moreover internal demand has also been increased by very high speculative valuations of stocks, financing mainly consumption rather than productive investment.[36]

Monetary policy functions in industrialized states would also benefit from cultures of alliance capitalism. Monetary management for price stability and exchange rate stability has been made very difficult for US, European, and Japanese authorities because of vast increases in the international trading of financial assets. The availability of financing from these markets limits the degrees to which any monetary tightening can reduce inflation, and shifts in the strategies of major institutional investors can have destabilizing effects on prices, production, and exchange rates. Monetary loosening, to increase consumption and production during economic declines, can instead facilitate low cost borrowing for investment in higher yield speculative operations in global financial markets. The erosion of monetary sovereignty through high volume growth in those markets has became a very challenging problem for the USA: its economy has attracted large investment flows from Europe and Japan, but with considerable volumes being directed by US financial enterprises into global speculative activities, while nevertheless contributing to dollar appreciation and generating pressures for stock appreciations.[37]

During the USA's speculative boom in the 1990s, stock appreciations, although clearly unsustainable, were ignored in official estimates of inflation, which were low because of imports of cheap consumer items that held down basic living costs. The wealth effects of the stock appreciations, however, it must be stressed, were evident mainly in rising consumption. When recognition of the need to dampen the speculative stock appreciations was increasing, at policy levels, due partly to warnings from the International Monetary Fund (during the 2000 election campaign), large losses of investor confidence were already evident. Monetary loosening to promote economic recovery during 2001 did not significantly increase production and consumption but was followed by large increases in the international speculative trading of financial assets by US institutional investors.[38]

To orient financial sectors toward productive service of the real economies while increasing monetary sovereignty, in the context of deepening integration, a spirit of alliance capitalism could be a potent force for reform. The urgent public goods requirement is to reduce the very high volume investment in rent seeking manipulation of international markets for financial assets which draws vast sums away from productive use, particularly toward areas where stock and property appreciations are pushed to extraordinary levels by collusive speculation. Internationalized failures in financial markets, invalidating claims that these markets move funds to most productive use, are extremely difficult to overcome through regulatory measures. The solution, in the public interest, has to be the development of relational financing for genuinely productive purposes. Investment in trade in financial assets offers higher and faster returns than investment in manufacturing, with less tax exposure. Taxation of the trade in financial assets is generally considered to be impractical, due to the complexities of the investors' craft, and the opaque character of its instruments. High risk speculation by financial enterprises, moreover, can threaten severe disruptions, as was evident in the failure of the New York firm Long Term Capital Management, which virtually obligated a rescue by the Federal Reserve.[39]

For monetary management tasks, financial market reform is even more urgent than it is for the public interest tasks of fiscal policies. The requirements for wide ranging and highly constructive policy level and corporate cooperation are very demanding. The danger of a deep and prolonged global recession has become very serious since the sharp declines in US stock prices in 2001, and it must be stressed that monetary loosening to increase the funding of production and consumption, and to revive general confidence, has diminishing significance because of the opportunities it provides for low cost financing of speculation in world financial markets, including operations taking advantage of the low credit ratings of distressed firms. Such speculation can be seen to offer higher returns than those to be anticipated from the funding of productive ventures in a recession. The potential benefits of relational funding of numerous forms of complementary entrepreneurship, to enhance growth in real economies, become more evident in economic declines which persist while diversions of investment into rent seeking continue.

PROMOTING POLICY LEVEL AND CORPORATE COOPERATION

The USA and the European Union have the most substantial capacities to overcome internationalized market failures and to work for greater efficiencies and greater social justice in the world economy. There are adequate American and European research capabilities to support Atlantic policy learning focused on the management of fundamentals in deepening integration, and especially on imperatives to promote extensive intercorporate cooperation for entrepreneurial complementarities. Motivations to activate more intensive learning at policy levels and in corporate managements can draw inspiration from western theological literature that has built on Aristotelian concepts of civic friendship and related them to problems of coordination in industrialized states. Study of this literature is being challenged to undergo further development in response to the extraordinary dimensions of potentially destabilizing rent seeking by major international investors operating with high degrees of independence from governmental authorities.

Intensive learning in US and European policy communities will have to be promoted through frequent consultative exchanges. These could develop under the auspices of an Atlantic Council of Economic Advisers, appointed for fixed terms by the US administration and the Council of the European Union. The Advisers would sponsor macroeconomic and microeconamic policy conferences aimed at forming an Atlantic pattern of macromanagement, with reciprocal restraints on fiscal expansion, concerted efforts to orient financial markets toward stable and comprehensive service of the real economies, and prudent use of the monetary sovereignty that would increase with reform of the international financial system. Key figures at the macroeconomic conferences would be high ranking representatives from the US Federal Reserve and the European Central Bank, and it would be advisable to have in attendance a delegation of staff members from the International Monetary Fund. The microeconomic policy conferences, dealing especially with trade, foreign direct investment, and competition issues, could draw representation from the European Commission, the US Department of Commerce, and US antitrust authorities.

The Atlantic Council of Economic Advisers could provide leadership for the establishment of the independent Atlantic Commission of technocrats and international management experts which has been suggested as the institution to sponsor corporate exchanges on opportunities for complementary entrepreneurship. Under Council surveillance the Commission would provide technology and market forecasts while facilitating intercorporate exchanges of information as well as technocratic briefings on public goods problems and other developmental issues in Atlantic structural interdependencies. The Commission's work, benefiting from increases in expertise through continuous interactions with corporate managements, would enable it to make critical contributions to the activities of the Atlantic Council of Economic Advisers, and indeed could help to make their surveillance more functional.

The conferences for policy communities sponsored by the Council of Economic Advisers would activate challenging accountabilities as well as learning experiences for officials who would otherwise remain absorbed in relations with domestic interests. This is not to deny that there could be trading of favours in the conferences, but detection and criticism of these would be a Council responsibility; it would also be, in practice, a Commission function, in so far as much relevant information would inevitably reach members of the Commission. It could be argued that the sponsorship of conferences for policy communities by the Council would lack democratic accountability, since the discussions would have to be confidential for the intended policy learning, but it would have to be made clear that the Council's prime tasks would be exercises of dedicated expertise, and would not be defined on the basis of agency type principles of government.

In the activities of the Atlantic Commission the technocratic contributions and the exchanges between corporate representatives would have to develop with autonomy undisturbed by outside observers and the media, although with the involvement of reputable consulting firms.This would be desirable for maintenance of an atmosphere of trust and confidentiality suited for intensive interactive learning. It would also be helpful, directly, for the development of an Atlantic business culture in which the spirit of alliance capitalism would reorient financial sectors more toward the funding of growth in real economies. Problems in investor psychology and the use of risk calculation methods that are conducive to unwarranted optimism could be gradually overcome through the influence of managements focused on productive activity and attentive to the benefits of relational financing.[40]

A charter document from the Atlantic Council of Economic Advisers could set out the rationale for the Commission's conferences by emphasizing the significance of information asymmetries that affect entrepreneurial potential. Information asymmetries have been studied thus far mainly in market contexts, where they are especially significant because of their effects on gains from trade. Entrepreneurial potential however is affected by failure to exchange mainly tacit knowledge that develops as it is shared in the exploration of possibilities for complementary specialization.[41] This failure, and failure to recognize complementarities between existing and evolving corporate capabilities, account for the information asymmetries that the Commission's conferences would be intended to overcome.

A fundamental purpose of deliberations within the Atlantic Council of Economic Advisers would be the development of its own self-sustaining culture of dedicated counselling on the management of Atlantic structural and policy interdependencies. This would be more than the sponsorship of transfers of economic knowledge detached from governmental and corporate responsibilities in the context of cross-border market failures as well as efficiencies. A professional culture averse to engagement with policy issues would have to be excluded. For highly constructive judgemental advising directed at European and American policymakers, moreover, the ambiguities of considerable volumes of economic analysis would have to be avoided. These ambiguities typically result from awareness of uncertainties about the rationality of corporate managements and policymakers in scenarios projected from observable trends.[42] Such uncertainties cannot be eliminated, but the Council's mission would be to reduce them through diffusion of a pervasive spirit of relational cooperation, at governmental and corporate levels: rationality in the service of public goods would be increased.

The expansion of Atlantic alliance capitalism into the Pacific and into Latin America would be possible through demonstration effects and affirmations of the moral and functional imperatives for multilevel and multinational integrative cooperation. The demonstration effects could in particular offer guidance for a recovery of alliance capitalism on a sound basis in Japan, with a transformation of its financial sector. The Chinese endeavour to build a dynamic solidarity system under strong administrative control could be reoriented, with more respect for individual freedoms. In Latin America collectively more self-reliant and more substantial growth, with more equal hemispheric structural interdependencies, would become feasible.

ALLIANCE CAPITALISM AND THE WORLD ECONOMY

The logic of building relational intercorporate cooperation, and relational systems of interdependent macromanagement, if given substantial expression in the Atlantic context, and then extending it into the Pacific and Latin America, would have highly significant consequences for governance of the world economy. The industrialized states dominating the International Monetary Fund would be challenged to extend their collaboration for a major institutional advance: the Fund would be given enhanced capabilities and greater authority for the task which has demanded its attention since the formation of the European Monetary Union. World growth and stability now depend very much on Atlantic monetary cooperation under Fund surveillance. The contributions of an Atlantic pattern of alliance capitalism to such cooperation will have to be supplemented by an institutionally more developed Fund. This involvement, to be comprehensively constructive, would have to be accompanied by Fund initiatives in support of Atlantic efforts to promote reform in international financial markets.

There is a well recognized danger that Atlantic monetary relations will not be managed with the enlightened cooperation that is demanded by the magnitude of the structural interdependencies which they vitally affect. Inward looking policy processes on each side may allow destabilizing swings in exchange rates that will be all the more serious because of manipulation in financial markets that are still inadequately regulated. The interests of international investors in euro holdings will be influenced by trends in the US current account, fiscal management, and business cycle, as well as related phases of monetary loosening or tightening.[43] Atlantic monetary policy interdependence will tend to force mutual responsiveness, but with sufficient pressure only in crises. An institutionally stronger IMF, therefore, has become necessary, but will be difficult to establish if severe volatility has already developed in euro–dollar exchange rates.

The urgent international public goods requirement is an IMF that can be a potent source of pressure for firm regulation of international financial markets through the imposition of realistic capital adequacy standards, the taxing of trade in financial assets, the encouragement of shifts to stakeholder systems of corporate governance, and the use of tax measures to increase industrial use of bank financing. All this would complement efforts at national levels to introduce the spirit of alliance capitalism into financial sectors. Vigorous European support would be especially helpful for a strengthening of the IMF that would enable it to take on the necessary financial market reform functions. European motivations could develop with more acute awareness that European growth is adversely affected by large scale capital flight to the USA, and that US institutional investors are better placed than those in Europe to exploit volatility in Atlantic exchange rates, with consequences that can increase the funding of US corporate expansion in Europe. The European interest, it must be stressed, is in the development of more balanced Atlantic structural interdependencies.

Initiatives by a strengthened IMF for financial market reform would assist its necessarily more results oriented surveillance of Atlantic macroeconomic interactions. This surveillance could support forceful advocacy of an Atlantic Stability Pact, in which the fiscal discipline of the European

Monetary Union would in effect be extended, in conjunction with its inflation targets. Political will for this very active cooperation with a more potent IMF role could be sustained through the interlinking effects of increasingly relational European and American intercorporate cooperation.

Japanese collaboration for the formation of a greater IMF role in governance of the world economy could be encouraged by the prospect of Atlantic monetary stability and international financial market reform. Japan is more exposed than the European Union to the adverse effects of business cycle changes in the USA and volatility in euro–dollar exchange rates, and also has to cope with capital flight to the USA. While the IMF could be a stronger forge for financial sector stabilization in Japan, Japanese motivations to support the development of a more effective global governance role for the IMF could be activated by an understanding that such a rode would enable the Fund to assist the development of an East Asian monetary system in which Japan would be a key member.

A further extension of the Fund's greater role would be to advise and support the strengthening of Latin American financial sectors, supplementing the work of a regional governance authority that might be established with the spread of a culture of alliance capitalism. Drains on the Fund's resources to cope with Latin American financial crises could thus be substantially reduced. Unified representation for the European Monetary Union in the IMF would help the development of increased accountability in Latin American relations with the Fund, which thus far have been overshadowed by the USA's very strong influence in Fund decisions. US decision makers could welcome the European Monetary Union as an equal partner in the Fund not only because of its potential for constructive involvement in the Atlantic context, but also because its more active presence in Latin America would be beneficial for hemispheric growth.

All the enhanced collaboration for institutional development of the IMF, together with the wider spread of the logic of alliance capitalism, would help to prepare international assent to principles for institutional development of the World Trade Organization. US and European dominance, based on market size, has tended to perpetuate this institution's status as a bargaining forum, while tacitly preventing its acquisition of substantial independent research and surveillance capabilities: it is a member driven structure without a significantly representative system of decision making, and has little capacity to assume responsibilities in international competition policy enforcement. A culture of adversarial bargaining has evolved, with emphasis on the negotiation of hard and precise agreements, bargained unequally because of great disparities in capacities for leverage.[44] Many developing countries, having to contend with marked asymmetries in interactions with industrialized states, have been alienated by the persistent efforts of the latter to exclude them from an inner circle that has sought to function in a steering capacity for the preparation and conduct of multilateral negotiations.[45]

The European Union's enlargement, and the expansion of its preferential trade agreements with nearby countries, together with the prospective formation of a Free Trade Area of the Americas, are altering the significance of the World Trade Organization as a forum for multilateral trade liberalization. European and US interest in the institution may decline while large volumes of commerce increase within and between the major regional systems, and while authorities in these systems see ways of negotiating favourably unequal trade arrangements with diverse developing countries that are not members of viable coalitions or trade groups. The international public goods function that could be served by an institutionally developed World Trade Organization, however, demands general recognition. For this, diffusion of a spirit of alliance capitalism can be seen to be imperative: there is a clear social justice requirement that should not be obscured by rhetoric about the developmental benefits of free trade on terms that are known to be asymmetric.

There is a long history of discrimination by industrialized states against the exports of Third World countries, particularly their low technology manufactures. This discrimination has contributed to the dependence of developing states on foreign private investment and assistance from industrialized nations as well as the World Bank, mainly for infrastructure development. The foreign investment has exploited investment rivalries between host governments and has been managed with limitations on technology transfers. The official assistance, while significant, has generally not been sufficient to support domestically based growth that would offset the problems of trade discrimination by advanced countries. Considerable proportions of this assistance, moreover, have been diverted from public use by corrupt officials.[46] Private sector groups that would become larger through expanded exports to industrialized states could exert pressures for reform of their corrupt bureaucracies.

The generally inferior production capabilities of Third World firms limit their potential for developing complementarities with enterprises based in the industrialized states, but a culture of relational cooperation could generate much dynamism in parallel ventures. At the same time this culture, spreading from the Third World firms absorbing it, could evoke the development of technocratic capabilities in reforming national administrations: conferences for the sponsorship of entrepreneurial complementarities could then be very productive. Structural policy activism of this kind, emphasizing interactive consultative learning, has received little attention in literature on Third World development.

Concentration on infrastructure development in its client states would become more feasible and more productive for the World Bank if the integrative spirit of complementary entrepreneurship could become pervasive in advanced country firms active in Third World areas, and in the national enterprises of those areas. This can be asserted with reference to the larger context of recurring financial crises in industrializing countries that have necessitated adjustment assistance by the IMF. Research on these crises has identified serious problems in financial sectors, but these have been assessed mostly without regard for the importance of widely concerted entrepreneurship for recovery, and for the prevention of further crises.[47]

PROSPECTS

The concept of alliance capitalism has come into literature that has been oriented toward study of the efficiency effects of competition – between firms, between economic groups seeking to influence or control policy, and between governments acting as rivals to attract productive ventures and financial enterprises. Yet some of the lessons of recent history are that financial sector competition, driving speculative booms, can be severely destabilizing; that competition generates market failures as well as efficiencies, in sequences through which concentration trends increase; and that the disruption of real economies by financial crises can make governance more conflicted and less functional. All these lessons have to be put into the context of deepening integration, in which market efficiencies and failures assume increasing cross-border dimensions, in conjunction with government efficiencies and failures – the latter tending to become more serious when strains in the linked economies intensify. Complex coordination tasks can thus be seen, and attention can focus on the functional significance of differences in the quality of coordinating ventures.

The main contemporary trend in deepening integration is intensifying corporate competition for world market shares – competition between firms that are acting very independently in quests for such shares, while driving weaker enterprises into decline, but are also entering into alliances with rivals, suppliers, and distributors. Shareholder pressures on managements tend to drive the competition in ways that, overall, increase concentration in the world economy. International competition policy issues are thus likely to continue to assume more prominence, notably in Atlantic relations, and particularly because of European concerns about increases in mergers and acquisitions in the USA that have regional and global implications. European interest in giving the World Trade Organization a competition policy responsibility must be expected to remain active, but for the

USA this represents an endeavour to seek allies in competition policy disputes that have resulted from European Commission objections to projected concentrations of the market strengths of US firms.

A further trend in deepening integration is more active rivalry between governments to enhance the structural competitiveness of their economies, while seeking greater access to external markets for their national firms. This trend is more evident in Europe than in the USA, and, driven by concerns about lagging competitiveness, is likely to continue, with further strains in Atlantic relations because of US opposition to European industrial subsidies. While the European Union enlarges it will undoubtedly have more scope than the USA to extend its system of preferential trade agreements: domestic opposition has become a serious constraint on the negotiation of such agreements by the USA.

Promotion of a culture of intercorporate cooperation, however, will be feasible in Atlantic relations if efforts are made to build on the occasional consultations between European and American enterprises in the Transatlantic Business Dialogue. Such consultations could be expanded and given more scope to moderate frictions over trade and competition policy issues: there are opportunities for highly constructive political entrepreneurship aimed at the development of complementarities. These opportunities are far more significant than those for the promotion of a spirit of cooperation for international financial market reform. That will remain very difficult because of the scale of international financial market integration and the independence with which major investment firms can undertake very high volume speculative operations without effective regulation: national policymakers compete to provide favourable environments for this activity.

Capacities to take initiatives for the promotion of entrepreneurial complementarities will probably be more significant at policy levels in Atlantic relations than in business associations and corporate networks. The fragmentation of business associations and the strength of the individualistic business culture in the USA tend to hinder spontaneous development of collaborative endeavours – in conjunction with the restraints of antitrust policy. Administrative sponsorship of a collaborative revival of the US semiconductor industry, however, has been successful, and has contributed to the development of international consortia in this sector. In Europe, and especially in Germany, management orientations are more open to rationales for intercorporate cooperation and for corporate–government collaboration, but because of the mix of national cultures the capacity of the European Commission to draw regional corporate cooperation has special significance.

Policy level initiatives, with corporate support, could be given serious consideration in the European Union high level meetings on deepening regional integration as the European Monetary Union becomes established. The logic of deepening regional integration has become stronger since the onset of the 2001 recession in the USA: higher regionally based growth, with reduced vulnerability to adverse trends in the US economy, has become all the more necessary, while imperatives for harmonious management of structural interdependencies with the USA have become more compelling. Building consensus in Europe for deepening integration, however, is likely to remain difficult, especially because the pattern of national political parties is fragmented, offering few possibilities for transnational coalition building and for the emergence of Union level leadership roles.

The USA's differing policy level capabilities and orientations offer greater potential for leadership, depending on executive personality factors, but in a context dominated by a tradition of government aloofness from industry – a tradition that continues to limit the scope for structural policy endeavours, despite the success in the semiconductor sector. Potentials for policy level perseverance with any structural policy project, moreover, seem to be weaker than in Europe, where there is substantial continuity in the institutionalized functions of the European Commission.

Consideration of structural policy options in the USA and Europe must be expected to be influenced by political and security perspectives. These have had mixed effects on each side of the Atlantic, motivating European efforts to assert more independence and show less deference to the USA as a global power, but increasing unilateral tendencies in US external policy, especially in response to European decisional problems. Affirmations of the differing perspectives in national and Atlantic policy communities are affected by what may be called the political counterpart of the bounded rationality discussed in literature on economic behaviour. Bounded political rationality, affecting economic policy choices influenced by personal and group interests, limits possibilities for the recognition of public goods, and the development of commitments to work for such goods. If a spirit of alliance capitalism can spread in European and American corporations, through new thinking on the social responsibilities and complementary potentials of managements, there may well be scope for reciprocal learning between the private sectors and the policy levels. A public goods responsibility of great significance can be seen for all the institutions of learning that shape political and corporate cultures through communicating beliefs and values. The context of primary concern is Atlantic, but as deepening integration becomes more global, alliance capitalism will have to become more multicultural, yet with more dynamic fundamentals, demonstrated humanistically, and with magnanimity.

NOTES

1. See Ralph E. Gomory and William J. Baumol *Global Trade and Conflicting National Interests*, Cambridge, MIT Press, 2000
2. On pricing to market by US international firms see Subramanian Rangan and Robert Z. Lawrence *A Prism on Globalization*, Washington DC, Brookings Institution, 1999.
3. See David Folkerts-Landau and Peter M. Garber 'Derivative Markets and Financial System Soundness', in Charles Enoch and John H. Green (eds) *Banking Soundness and Monetary Policy*, Washington DC, International Monetary Fund, 1997, 290–304, and *International Capital Markets*, International Monetary Fund, August 2001, ch 6.
4. See symposium 'The multinationals: the Janus face of globalization' in *Journal of International Business Studies*, 32, 3, Third Quarter, 2001, and Thomas A. Gresik 'The Taxing Task of Taxing Transnationals', *Journal of Economic Literature*, XXXIX, 3, September 2001, 800–38.
5. See Nicolai Foss and Volker Mahnke (eds) *Competence, Governance, and Entrepreneurship*, Oxford, Oxford University Press, 2000; Sheila C. Dow and Peter E. Earl (eds) *Contingency, Complexity and the Theory of the Firm*, Cheltenham, Edward Elgar, 1999; and Birgitte Andersen, Jeremy Howells, Richard Hull, Ian Miles and Joanne Roberts (eds) *Knowledge and Innovation in the New Service Economy*, Cheltenham, Edward Elgar, 2000.
6. See Mary O'Sullivan *Contests for Corporate Control*, Oxford, Oxford University Press, 2000.
7. See Thomas S. Arrison, C. Fred Bergsten, Edward M. Graham, and Martha Caldwell Harris (eds) *Japan's Growing Technological Capability*, Washington, National Academy Press, 1992.
8. See Helene Blanc and Christopher Sierra 'The internationalization of R&D by multinationals: a trade off between external and internal proximity', *Cambridge Journal of Economics*, 23, 2, March 1999, and Glenn R. Fong 'Follower at the Frontier: International Competition and Japanese Industrial Policy', *International Studies Quarterly*, 42, 2, June 1998, 339–66.
9. See O'Sullivan, cited, and Kathleen Thelen 'Why German Employers Cannot Bring Themselves to Dismantle the German Model', in Torben Iversen, Jonas Pontusson and David Soskice (eds) *Unions, Employers and Central Banks*, Cambridge, Cambridge University Press, 2000, 138–72.
10. See references to exchanges of tacit knowledge in Foss and Mahoke, cited. See also Pari Patel and Keith Pavitt 'The Wide (and Increasing) Spread of Technological Competencies in the World's Largest Firms: A Challenge to Conventional Wisdom', in Alfred D. Chandler Jr, Peter Hagstrom and Orjan Solvell (eds) *The Dynamic Firm*, Oxford, Oxford University Press, 1998, 192–213.
11. See references to industrial policies in Thomas L. Brewer, Paul A. Brenton and Gavin Boyd (eds) *Globalizing Europe*, Cheltenham, Edward Elgar, 2002.
12. See references to US policy in the same volume.
13. See Annamaria Lusardi, Jonathan Skinner and Steven Venti 'Savings puzzles and saving policies in the United States', *Oxford Review of Economic Policy*, 17, 1, Spring 2001, 95–115.
14. See O'Sullivan, cited.
15. See Robert D. Putman 'Civic Disengagement in Contemporary America', *Government and Opposition*, 36, 2, Spring 2001, 135–56, and Robert E. Lane *The Loss of Happiness in Market Democracies*, New Haven, Yale University Press, 2000.
16. See Norman J. Ornstein and Thomas E. Mann (eds) *The Permanent Campaign and its Future*, Washington DC, American Enterprise Institute and Brookings Institution, 2000.
17. See references to business groups in William D. Coleman, *Financial Services, Globalization and Domestic Policy Change*, London, Macmillan, 1996.
18. See O'Sullivan, cited, and Thelen, cited.

19. See *West European Politics*, 22, 4 October 1999, symposium on The Changing French Political System.
20. See Svein S. Anderson and Kjell A. Eliassen (eds) *Making Policy in Europe* London, Sage, 1993.
21. See *Globalizing Europe*, cited.
22. On the rationale for changes to stakeholder systems see Margaret M. Blair and Mark J. Roe (eds) *Employees and Corporate Governance*, Washington DC, Brookings Institution, 1999.
23. See Putnam, cited, and Gresik, cited.
24. This observation is based on work by Patel and Pavitt, cited.
25. See *World Investment Report 2000*, United Nations Conference on Trade and Development, New York and Geneva.
26. See Shumpei Kumon and Henry Rosovsky (eds) *The Political Economy of Japan*, vol 3, Stanford, Stanford University Press, 1992.
27. *Ibid.*
28. See Reuven Glick, Ramon Moreno and Mark M. Spiegel (eds) *Financial Crises in Emerging Markets*, New York, Cambridge University Press, 2001.
29. The weaknesses of ASEAN present serious problems: see Tamim Bayoumi and Paolo Mauro 'The suitability of ASEAN for a regional currency arrangement', *The World Economy* 24, 7 July 2001, 933–54.
30. For a review of these problems see Jeffrey J. Schott, *Prospects for Free Trade in the Americas*, Washington DC, Institute for International Economics, 2001.
31. See symposium on legalization in *International Organization* 54, 3, Summer 2000.
32. Alan V. Deardorff and Robert M. Stern (eds) *Constituent Interests and US Trade Policies*, Ann Arbor, University of Michigan Press, 1998.
33. See references to trade policy in *Globalizing Europe*, cited.
34. See material on acquisitions in *World Investment Report 2000*, cited.
35. See references to Germany in *Globalizing Europe*, cited.
36. Lusardi, Skinner and Venti, cited.
37. See *International Capital Markets*, cited.
38. See Robert Clow 'Demand for Hedge Funds of Funds Looks Set to Increase', *Financial Times*, 11 October 2001.
39. See Wendy Dobson and Gary Clyde Hufbauer *World Capital Markets*, Washington DC, Institute for International Economics, 2001, and *International Capital Markets*, cited.
40. On problems in investor psychology see Andrei Shleifer *Inefficient Markets: An Introduction to Behavioural Finance*, Oxford, Oxford University Press, 2000, and on investor calculations see Barry Riley 'The Troubles with Technical Trends', *Financial Times*, 5 October 2001. See also Brent Keltner 'Relationship banking and competitive advantage', *California Management Review*, 37, 4, Summer 1995, 45–72.
41. See Richard N. Langlois and Nicolai J. Foss 'Capabilities and Governance: The Rebirth of Production in the Theory of Economic Organization', *Kyklos*, 52, 2, 1999, 201–18, and Peter Maskell and Anders Malmberg 'Localised learning and industrial competitiveness', *Cambridge Journal of Economics*, 23, 2, March 1999, 167–85.
42. See for example the uncertainties discussed in *International Capital Markets*, cited.
43. See Robert Mundell and Armand Clesse (eds) *The EURO as a Stabilizer in the International Economic System*, Boston, Kluwer, 2000 and C. Randall Henning and Pier Carlo Padoan *Transatlantic Perspectives on the EURO*, Washington DC, Brookings Institution, 2000.
44. See *International Organization*, cited.
45. See Richard Blackhurst 'Reforming WTO Decision Making: Lessons from Singapore and Seattle', in Klaus Gunter Deutsch and Bernhard Speyer (eds) *The World Trade Organization Millennium Round*, London, Routledge, 2001, 295–310.
46. See Christopher L. Gilbert and David Vines (eds) *The World Bank*, Cambridge, Cambridge University Press, 2000.
47. See references to emerging markets in *International Capital Markets*, cited.

Index